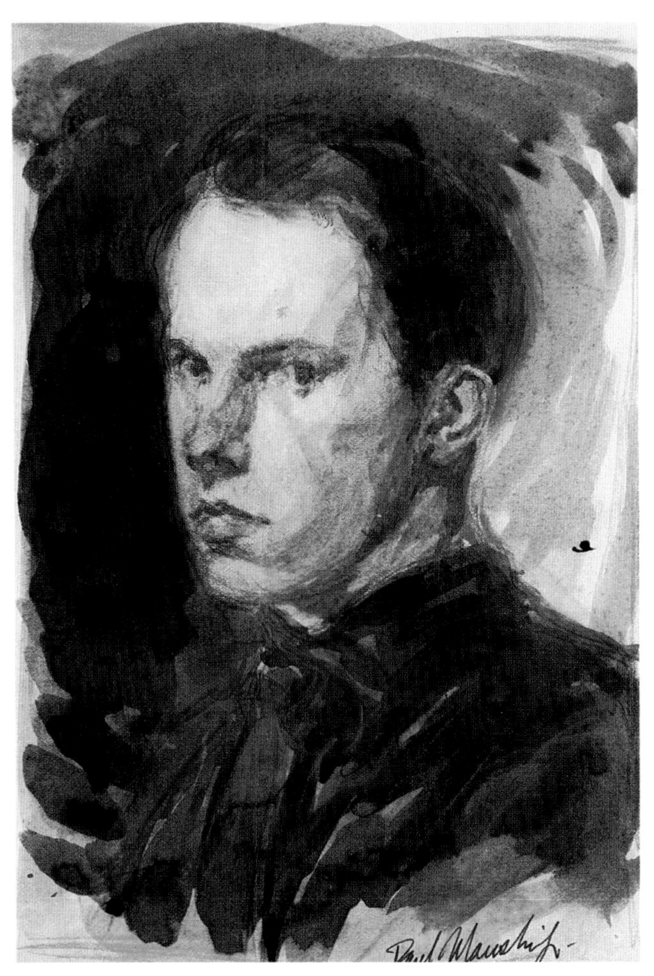

PAUL MANSHIP

HARRY RAND

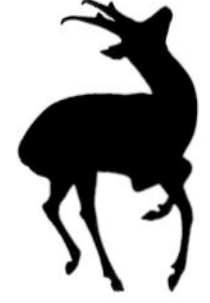

Published for the National Museum of American Art
by the Smithsonian Institution Press
Washington and London

To the memory of
Nikhil Banerjee and Peter Colaclides

Published for the exhibition
The Art of Paul Manship

National Museum of American Art,
Smithsonian Institution, Washington, D.C.
17 February–4 July 1989

Columbus Museum of Art, Columbus, Ohio
10 December 1989–4 February 1990

Archer M. Huntington Art Gallery, Austin, Texas
16 March–29 April 1990

Fort Wayne Museum of Art, Fort Wayne, Indiana
2 June–29 July 1990

Tampa Museum of Art, Tampa, Florida
8 September–4 November 1990

Memphis Brooks Museum of Art, Memphis, Tennessee
1 December 1990–3 February 1991

Milwaukee Art Museum, Milwaukee, Wisconsin
7 March–5 May 1991

The Metropolitan Museum of Art, New York, New York
11 June–1 September 1991

Unless otherwise noted, all works illustrated in this book are by Paul Manship and are from the collection of the National Museum of American Art.

Front cover: *Diana* (see fig. 64)
Frontispiece: *Self Portrait* (see fig. 1)

The paper used in this publication meets the minimum requirements of the American National Standard for Permanence of Paper for Printed Library Materials Z39.48–1984.

Library of Congress Cataloging-in-Publication Data

Rand, Harry.
Paul Manship / Harry Rand.
p. cm.
—T.p. verso.
Bibliography: p.
Includes index.
ISBN 0-87474-834-8 (alk. paper), ISBN 0-87474-807-0 (pbk. : alk. paper)
1. Manship, Paul, 1885–1966—Exhibitions. 2. National Museum of American Art (U.S.)—Exhibitions. I. Manship, Paul, 1885–1966. II. National Museum of American Art (U.S.) III. Title.
NB237.M3A4 1989
730′.92′4—dc19

ISBN 0–87474–834–8 (cloth)
ISBN 0–87474–807–0 (pbk)

Contents

Foreword

The appropriate metaphor for Paul Manship's art might be a bridge, for his work provides passage between opposing shores with a formal elegance and sleek efficiency. On one side lies a *terra historica* well populated with the gods and goddesses of the humanist tradition; on the other, the frontier of modernism, largely unexplored in Manship's day but already generating its own mythologies based on the pace and possibilities of life in an industrial age. Manship elides past and future with such grace that the transition seems painless, even joyful. There is an irrepressible energy in his art that sweeps us along almost effortlessly into a brave new world.

The dramatic rise and fall of Manship's career, however, show that his art does not span normal generational change, but a deep fault line separating two worlds and competing concepts of art. As Harry Rand explains in this book, Manship invented a personal, original response to the conditions that propelled modernism. He evolved his synthesis so completely, however, and conditioned it so thoroughly on the taste of his age, that there was little room left for further development and little sympathy for his solution once the fashions had changed. His art will probably continue to gain and lose popularity as certain attitudes about the relationship of art and life fade in and out of favor. The current Manship 'revival' coincides with the rediscovery of the Art Deco aesthetic he helped foster, which in turn reflects our failing faith in the purist modernism of the International Style. The Manship revival goes along with the belief in a social function for art and a love of ornament, formal wit, and sophistication.

Harry Rand explores all the implications of an art firmly linked to taste, but he also sifts for us Manship's highly inventive approach to sculptural form, showing that there is something more satisfying than fashion in this work. Almost with a touch of irony, Rand uses the instrument of formal analysis—the tool by which Abstract Expressionism and the International Style triumphed over historical tradition, and so over Manship's own conceptions—to reveal the artist's most original contributions.

Along with Manship's belief in historical tradition went a deep commitment to institutions. One of several that he served devotedly was the National Museum of American Art. As a member of its Board of Commissioners from 1931 to 1966, and as chairman from 1944 to 1964, he wisely counseled the museum on the direction a national collection should take. The growth of the museum during his tenure on the commission is in part due to his efforts. Fortunately, his fellow commissioners persuaded Manship that his own work was a national treasure, so that at his death in 1966, his artistic estate was divided between this Smithsonian museum and the Minnesota Museum of Art in his native city, St. Paul.

In 1984, the National Museum of American Art presented a group of forty sculptures and drawings from our extensive holdings of over 350 works by Paul Manship, and the response to this modest installation showed that we had only whetted the public's appetite. The following year, the Minnesota Museum of Art mounted a touring centennial exhibition and gathered together essays by several scholars, greatly increasing both the audience for Manship's art and our understanding of it. The book that we are now publishing, which accompanies a large exhibition drawn from our holdings that will be seen throughout the country, is the first complete overview of Manship's life and art. It is complemented by a new full-length biography written by the artist's son, John Manship. The wheel of fortune has come full circle, but we believe the decade of the 1980s has so clearly established this wonderful artist as a significant figure in American culture that even its continuing revolutions cannot obscure his contributions a second time.

Elizabeth Broun
Acting Director

Acknowledgments

The number of people who, during the development of this work, have proven essential to its further progress inculcates in the author a deeper humility than is his usual demeanor; at the same time, it is refreshing to recall with what good will and zeal a host of professionals contributed their talents and energy to seeing that Paul Manship's art passed from twilight to dawn. In particular, my editor, Mary Kay Zuravleff, directed my path from the precipice of chaos to the still waters of grammatical sense, and she served as the first sampler and commentator on this work, a surrogate for you, the reader.

You are seeing the works of Paul Manship through the eyes of some extraordinary photographers who have brought the range of scale and textures, colors and masses to our eyes—no easy task, and one that is, when most successful, invisible in the shadow of the artist's accomplishment; Edward Owen, Michael Fischer, and Margaret Harman are to be saluted for their work.

The conservators who have revived works long dormant should be recognized by the reader for a difficult task beautifully done: Fern Bleckner, Catherine Maynor, Eileen Werner-Blankenbaker, and Stefano Scafetta. Valuable advice, on the text and on the contents of the accompanying exhibition, was offered by Charles C. Eldredge, former director of the museum, and by acting director Elizabeth Broun, as well as by Dr. Jennifer Gibson and Professor Joseph Connors. Kathleen Howe was an able assistant during the earliest stages of the work, and, nearing its completion, the artist's son, John Manship, helped—unstintingly despite his own labors on a biography of his father. Finally, to all the sculptors whose voices murmured comments throughout the composition, and especially to the late Seymour Lipton and my teacher, Benjamin R. Rowland, Jr., my thanks for borrowing your muse.

H.R.

Boyhood and Family Background

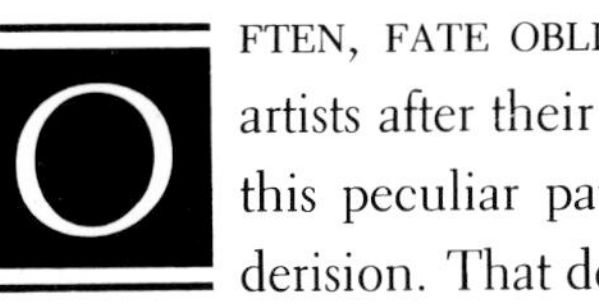

OFTEN, FATE OBLITERATES the reputations of America's prominent artists after their own generation. Following a lifetime of celebrity this peculiar pattern dictates a total eclipse into the shadow of derision. That descending arc has no more poignant example than Paul Manship. His renown was so great while he lived and his ignominy so complete during the next generation, that his fame and obscurity express reciprocal orders of magnitude.

If Manship's stature was indisputable during most of his lifetime, his artistic influence was narrow. Undefended, with few disciples, he became a natural target for the avant-garde. The power he wielded and the effect of his art were almost entirely associated with the man in his time. With distance from that moment of Manship's greatest achievement we can attempt some reevaluation.

Paul Howard Manship's ancestors arrived in America before the Revolutionary War. His grandfather, Charles, had been trained to do ornamental painting; he did stencil work and wood graining in Maryland. When Mississippi was admitted to the Union, he moved to Jackson. There Charles Manship became a prominent figure. He established an interior design business and worked on the Governor's Mansion and the State Capitol and served as mayor of Jackson during the Civil War. Following the war, Charles Manship built a Gothic Revival-style house for his family; the house has been designated a National Landmark.

Paul Manship's father fought in the Confederate army and was married to Mary Etta Friend, whose family had come from Maryland. The family moved to Minnesota after the Civil War as there were few opportunities in the ravaged South. Born on Christmas Eve 1885 in St. Paul, Minnesota, Paul was the seventh of their children. The grandfather's talents and interests passed down in the family; Luther, one of Paul's brothers, was an academic impressionist painter who taught art in the public schools, while his brother Albert was a poet.

At Mechanical Arts High School, Nathaniel Pousette-Dart, who eventually became a well-known painter himself, was one of Paul Manship's friends. Manship's asthma made it impossible for him to spend much time in the countryside; nevertheless, he participated in the youthful activities of a robust boyhood in the North, including hunting and fishing. At the St. Paul Institute, Manship studied art, at first painting—a realm foreclosed to him when Manship discovered he was color-blind. He then switched to modeling in clay. Just as remarkable as this rich childhood environment was Manship's subsequent dismissal of it: "I was born and raised in St. Paul Minnesota in a family that was not any different from other mid-western families. Art was not a tradition in our family either."[1]

By the time he was fifteen Manship decided to be a sculptor, and he began by making masks of his family members. At the age of sixteen, when he was in high school, he took a course in modeling. He disregarded his school work and devoted more and more time to modeling in clay, which, he recalled, "was so fascinating that I neglected my studies until I was finally given the choice of making up my academic work or else."[2] Once Manship decided on his future course as an artist it was hard to concentrate on other matters. He left high school at seventeen rather than be ejected for failing grades, and he opened his own design business—"Paul H. Manship, Illustrator and Designer, 368 ½ Robert St., St. Paul." For a year he did sign painting and lettering (an interest he carried into his later work, particularly his medals).

With the help of his older brother Luther, a commercial artist, he worked for a time at the Bureau of Engraving in Minneapolis. Then, Manship chose to become a designer in an advertising firm; he was sufficiently successful to put aside the money to come to New York. "I realized at the age of nineteen that I must make more of my life and be something other than a commercial designer."[3]

In early 1905, with the assistance of his oldest brother and the support of their grandfather, Manship entered the Art Students League of New York as a pupil of George Bridgman, who was a specialist in artistic anatomy. As a nineteen-year-old at the League, Manship was taught how to make a sculpture's armature by Jo Davidson, the famous portrait sculptor. After a few months of formal study, Manship began to serve as an assistant to Solon Borglum. Although this job only lasted from 1905 until 1907, the relationship Manship established with Borglum was cherished years after the apprenticeship. Manship always kept Borglum's photograph on the wall of his New York studio.

Borglum's specialty was animal sculpture and instilling his work with a thorough sense of reliable structure (his posthumously published book was titled *Sound Constructions*, 1923). Manship stayed with the Borglum family, working with Solon and studying French with Borglum's wife. At the end of

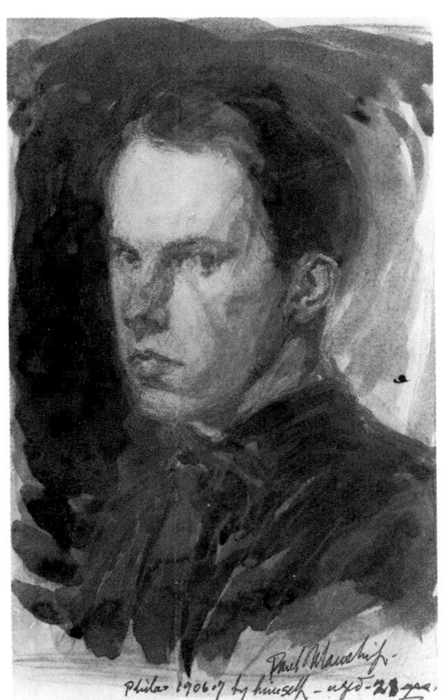
Fig. 1. *Self Portrait*, 1906–07; pencil, watercolor, ink, and sanguine chalk on paper; 8 x 5½ in.

the workday he would begin studies of drawing and anatomy that often kept him late at the studio. Solon inculcated in Manship a further knowledge of anatomy—at morgues and through the dissection of dogs and horses at the veterinarians—contributing vastly to his store of useful knowledge. There exists a plaster cast he made during the dissection of a dog. More important, Borglum employed Manship as an assistant on two monuments on which Borglum was then at work. One, the *Rough-Rider* Monument, instilled in Manship a lifelong, and never realized, desired to execute an equestrian monument.

This sound, if conservative, training was enhanced during 1907–08 when Manship studied at the Pennsylvania Academy of the Fine Arts in Philadelphia with Charles Grafly—a drawing student of Thomas Eakins.

On his *Self Portrait* (fig. 1), Manship overwrote his inscribed date as if he were correcting a recollection—which suggests that this watercolor was inscribed sometime after the twenty-three-year-old Manship painted it for Grafly's class. The near monochromatism of the warmly colored washes reflects Manship's color blindness or, perhaps, indicates his interest in recording masses and form in light and shadow without relying on hue; color played an insignificant role in his mature works. Grafly was a portrait specialist, but although Manship was enrolled, he defiantly refused to attend Grafly's portrait classes. Instead he studied in the life class, which Grafly also taught.

Strolling among the wharves of North River in the summer of 1907 with Hunt Diederich (later to be distinguished as a designer in iron), Manship decided that he wished to go to Spain. Starting out with forty dollars and a bottle of whiskey, Manship and Diederich left for Spain the next morning. For a month they walked in Andalusia, sleeping on beaches and roadsides. Almost incidentally, Manship confronted the traditions of the Mediterranean world, but the effect was electrifying. Manship sketched and molded animal figures in clay.

Among Manship's very few remaining sculptures of this period, Auguste Rodin's influence, along with that of all the French late nineteenth century, is strong. The clay animal figures Manship modeled in Spain, now lost, probably reflected the sculptural traditions generally accepted in America around the turn of the century, when Rodin was the dominant influence. Rodin's freely modeled forms attracted popular and critical approval, and art students around the world tried to emulate him. Dramatic gestures, with an emphasis upon strongly illusionistic light and shadow, typified such works.

Although the *Wrestlers* (figs. 2, 3)—a 1908 sketch in green patinated bronze that is a unique cast—hardly seems to depict a mythic situation, it might refer to the quintessential wrestling match of antiquity, that between Antaeus and Hercules. Manship produced numerous drawings and sculptures of Hercules, so it is not far-fetched to think that he was attracted to this theme

Figs. 2 and 3. *Wrestlers,* 1908; bronze; $12\frac{7}{8}$ in. high.

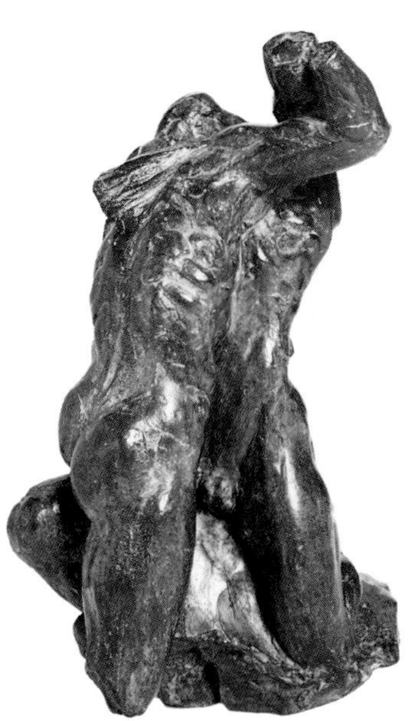

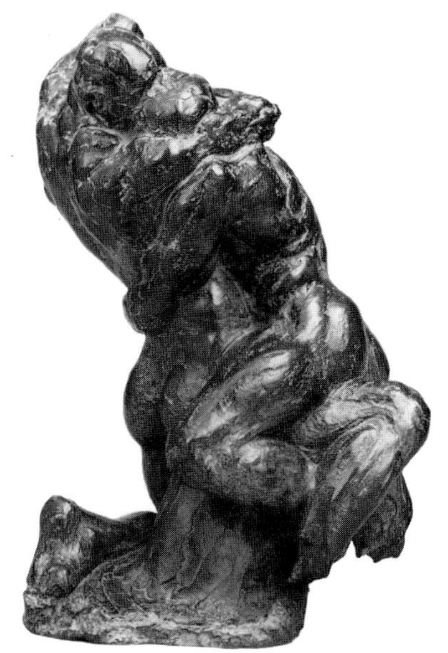

early in his career. The son of Poseidon (god of the sea) and Gaea (goddess of the earth), Antaeus was a giant who lived in Libya. When travelers chanced to pass nearby, he challenged them to wrestle with him. Contact with his mother, the earth, gave Antaeus renewed strength and made him practically invincible. After he killed his opponents, he used their skulls to roof his father's temple. Hercules (in Latin; Heracles, in Greek) was the son of Zeus and Alcmene. His name, which means "Hera's glory," was related to his association with Argos, where Hera was worshiped. When Hercules journeyed through Antaeus's country, Antaeus issued his usual challenge. By lifting him off the ground to deprive him of his mother's earth-given strength, Hercules squeezed Antaeus to death.

The formal qualities of this work are enormously compelling as well. Later in his career, Manship rarely truncated the arms and legs of his sculptures as he did in *Wrestlers,* but the procedure was put to good use here. In this dense multifigure composition, Manship produced a tight mass with two "backs" and an invisible interior, which recalls Medardo Rosso's penchant for gathering sculptural incidents *inside* his works. The sculptures of Rosso, the late nineteenth-century sculptor who worked mostly in Florence, often have their most compelling and important gestures occurring within the form. As a lost profile in painting may place a figure's features beyond our sight, so Rosso placed embraces and crucial interactions within his sculptures and out of our sight—a highly effective device. The limbless figures occupy a columnar form, forecasting Manship's much later work in which combined bodies make thick, tubular forms, opaque and impenetrable as the *Wrestlers.* Later, when this theme reappeared in his work, Manship opened a space between the figures

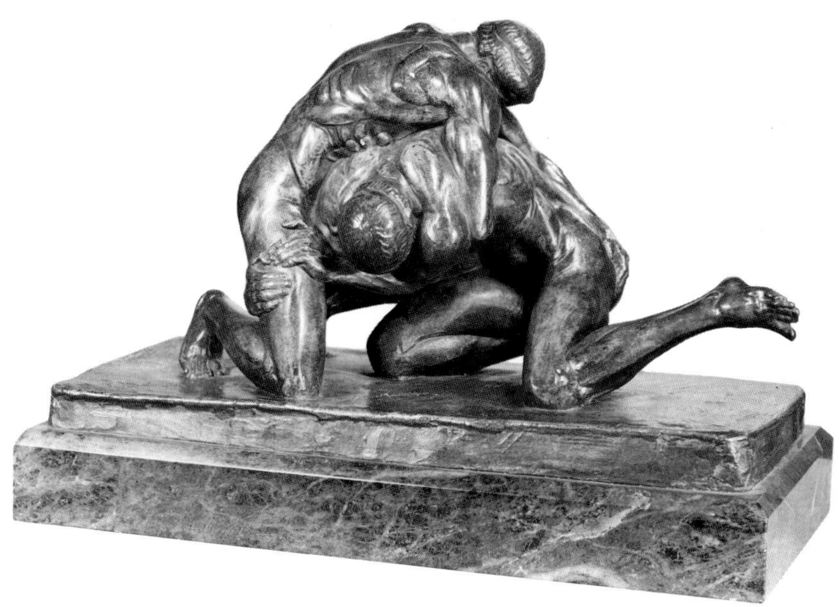

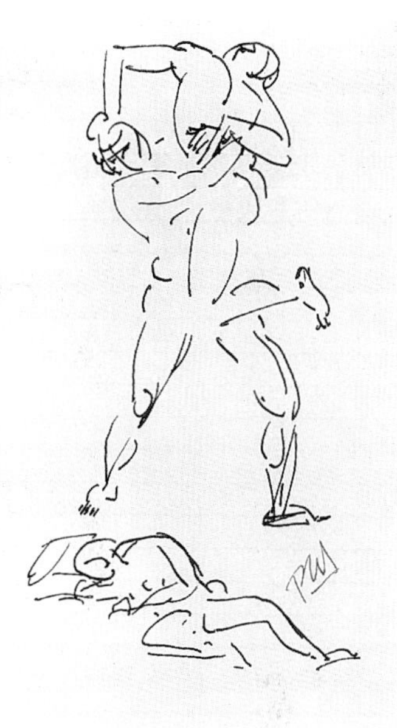

Fig. 4. *Wrestlers*, 1915; bronze, in an edition of six copies; $11\frac{1}{4}$ in. high. The Metropolitan Museum of Art, Gift of Edward D. Adams, 1927.

Fig. 5. *Sketch of Wrestler* (Hercules and Antaeus); pen on looseleaf notebook page; 6 x $3\frac{1}{2}$ in.

(figs. 4, 5). To dwell on wrestling was to forcefully propel bodies together—a genteel surrogate for sex or explicit intimacy.

Although his depiction of wrestling was not limited to Hercules, the most popular of all Greek heroes, Manship reinvestigated the subject of wrestling and the personality of Hercules often in his career. In one drawing Hercules struggles with Hippolyte, Queen of the Amazons, who possessed a magnificent girdle as a mark of her sovereignty (fig. 6). Fetching the belt of Hippolyte was one of Hercules' twelve tasks. When Hercules reached the Amazons, Hippolyte agreed to give him the girdle, but Hera was enraged by this and spread the false rumor that Hercules planned to abduct the queen. The Amazons attacked, and believing that they had betrayed him, Hercules slaughtered the Amazons and their queen and took the girdle. This was the only wrestling drawing in which Manship included a woman.

At first, Manship's works were indebted to the brothers Solon and Gutzon Borglum. Throughout his life Manship named Solon Borglum as one of his crucial influences. Solon affected Manship's working methods and the essential character of his sculpture (fig. 7). Both Borglums served as renowned models of serious professionalism, while their studious home lives and marital stability were an example to the young man. Gutzon—certainly the more famous of the brothers—represented a model of achievement. In 1906 Gutzon Borglum sold his *Mares of Diomedes* (1904) for $25,000 (an enormous sum for the time) to a benefactor who gave it to the Metropolitan Museum of Art—the first work by an American sculptor acquired by the Metropolitan. Clearly, Gutzon Borglum's *Mares of Diomedes* (fig. 8) served as a precedent for Manship's *Horses in a Storm*, 1906 (fig. 9).[4] The works are obviously of the same "school,"

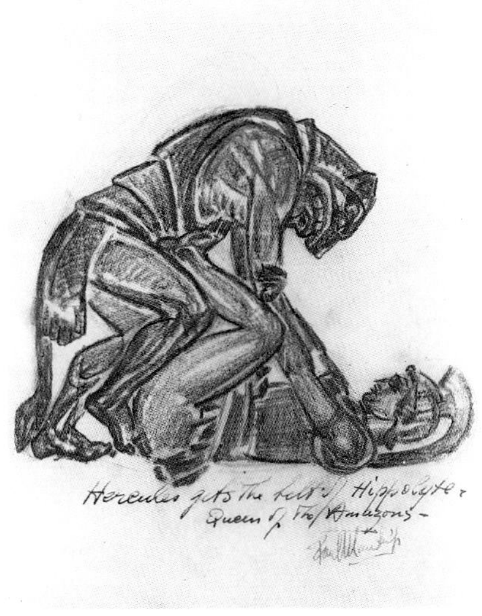

Fig. 6. *Hercules Gets the Belt of Hippolyte, Queen of the Amazons*; pencil and crayon on tracing paper; $10\frac{5}{8}$ x $8\frac{7}{16}$ in.

Fig. 7. *St. Paul Pioneer Press*, 1906, with an illustration of *Pulling*, 1906; plaster; destroyed by the artist.

Creditable Sculpture by a St. Paul Youth. 1906

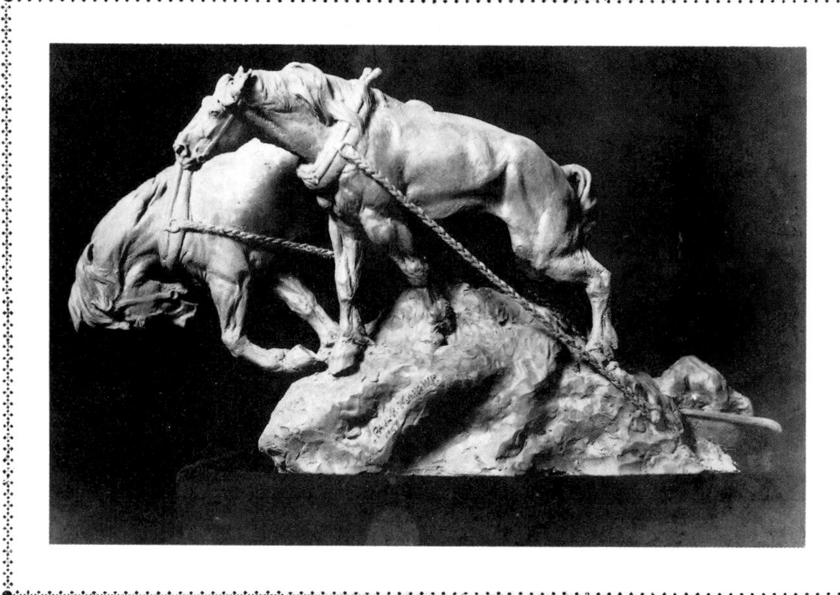

The above model, "Pulling," is the work of a St. Paul boy, Paul H. Manship, a student of the Mechanic Arts high school, and the St. Paul School of Fine Arts. About a year ago he went to New York to study, and became a pupil of one of America's greatest animal sculptors, Solon H. Borglum, with whom he now lives, and assists in all his great work. He has just passed 21 years of age and all his work, so far, shows unusual merit for one so young. His home in St. Paul is with his parents, Mr. and Mrs. C. H. Manship, Nelson avenue.

and so close in conception and treatment as to suggest one atelier. More important, *Horses in a Storm* began Manship's evolution from the relative security of relief sculpture to explorations of freestanding figures.

In 1908–09 Manship chose his next master. For two years he assisted and grew close to Isidore Konti, who taught him the techniques of modeling. It was Konti who pursuaded Manship to compete for entry to the American Academy in Rome—an honor akin to a Rome prize awarded to Konti himself as a student in Vienna. (Konti had studied with Karl Bitter, whose esteem for classical and archaic antiquity Konti transmitted to Manship.) Manship won the prize with his relief *Rest After Toil*.

The Prix de Rome was offered to aspiring sculptors by the Rinehart Fund of the Peabody Institute in Baltimore. The Maryland sculptor William Henry Rinehart left a significant estate, and—after a generation passed and his invested funds increased dramatically—a committee decided to create scholarships to send worthy applicants to Rome or Paris. The Rinehart committee chose Richard Morris Hunt (who was succeeded by John Quincy Adams Ward), Daniel Chester French, Charles F. McKim, E. H. Blashfield, and Augustus Saint-Gaudens as advisors. One scholarship was to be offered for study in Rome and one in Paris; each was tenable for four years: "Finding that two thousand dollars (to which the annual stipend grew at one time) for four years was rather more than could be advantageously used by young sculptors, the

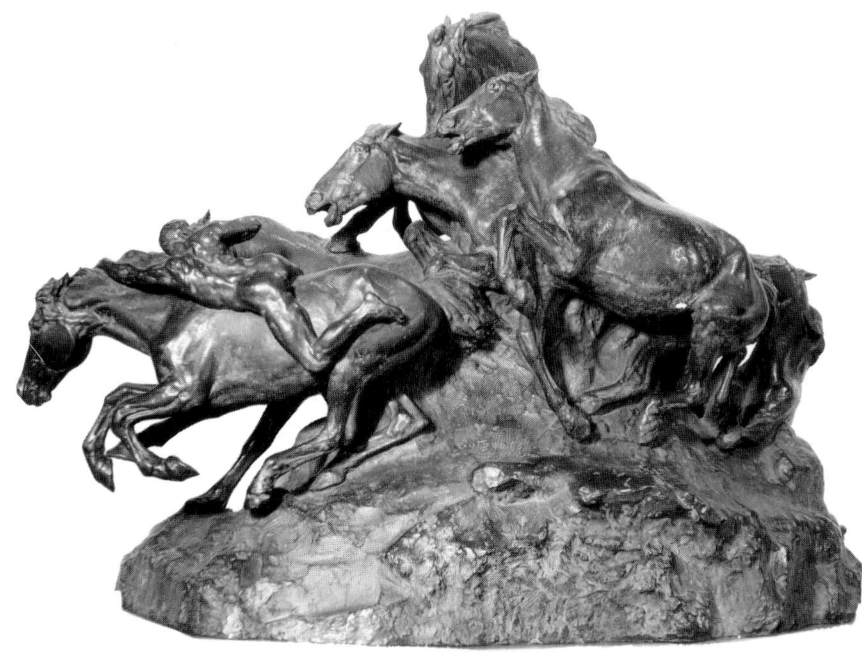

Fig. 8. (John) Gutzon (de la Mothe) Borglum, *Mares of Diomedes*, 1904; bronze; 62 in. high. The Metropolitan Museum of Art, Gift of James Stillman, 1906.

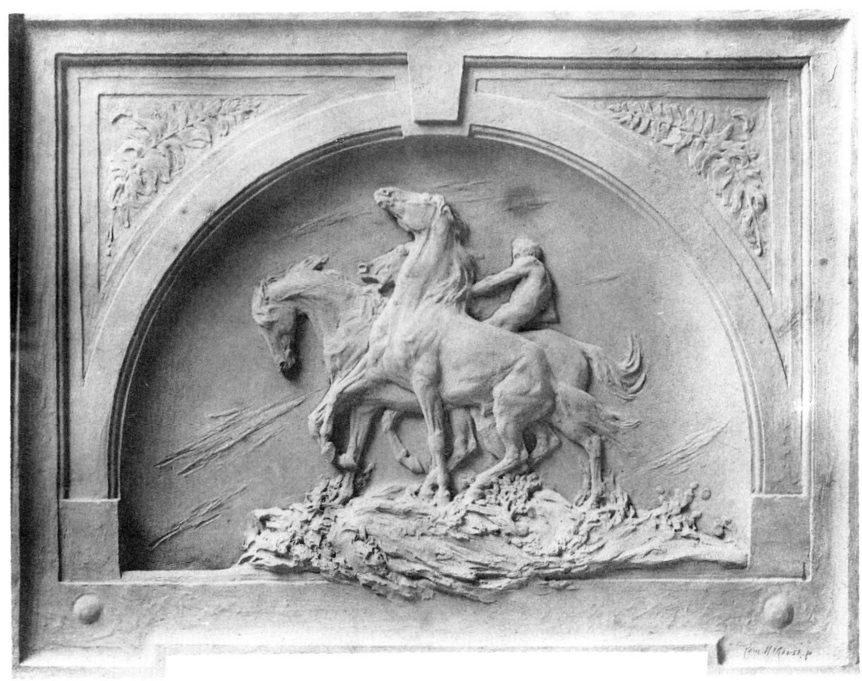

Fig. 9. *Horses in a Storm*, 1906; plaster; present whereabouts unknown.

trustees decided to give the scholarships in the form of fellowships to the American Academy in Rome."[5]

The Rinehart Fund's Prix de Rome reflected the values of an earlier generation. During the heyday of Neoclassicism in the nineteenth century, Italy—Rome but especially Florence—possessed an allure for American sculptors. Horatio Greenough, Hiram Powers, and Edmonia Lewis all held forth from Italy, but by the turn of the century, Italy was eclipsed as an art center. In spite of the academy's award, Manship had never harbored a desire to go to Rome, which was then an artistic irrelevance. Later, confessing his initial lack of attraction to Rome, Manship admitted that Paris had already become the polestar of art.

The directors of the academy had several goals: the academy was to have no staff or instructor, nor would it teach technique, for the course of study was to consist of observation and research amid Rome's libraries and the ample remains of classical sculpture everywhere at hand. The academy aimed "to form a correct taste and to impress upon the mind, by daily contact with great examples, those fundamental principles that are essential to enduring quality in art."[6] However unforeseen, the Roman experience was the single greatest formative influence Manship's art was to know. The great transformation starts to appear in work created soon after his arrival.

While in New York Manship had corresponded with his family in Minnesota; in Rome he continued writing to relatives who enjoyed his special trust or affection. In particular, Manship mailed a postcard photograph to his favorite cousin, Sevilla Stees, showing the interior of his workspace, the earnest young artist himself, and the contents of his studio (figs. 10, 11). The message reads

> Hello Sevilla, Rome is a great place. Each day I find new places of interest. The winter is one continual May. I am having the time of my young life. Love to both you & Aunt Virginia, yours Paul.[7]

On the lower shelf we see tools for working clay, and behind these are four framed pictures. Manship must have arranged these so they would be visible to the recipients of the card, but, unfortunately, the image at the far right is too murky to be legible. On the left, a woman's head is crowned by a fashionable hat; next is a small, framed image of a seated nude—though seen from the back, she is posed in a studio whose corner has a large mirror that shows us the front of the figure; the third picture is a landscape. As a constellation of images—and we must presume that Manship was their author—they cover the range of expected student subjects. The upper shelf is more telling.

Manship rests his left arm near a clay or plaster study of a centaur approaching a woman (a nymph perhaps), who flees to the left. We witness the first dawning of Manship's classicism in this work. In subject, composition,

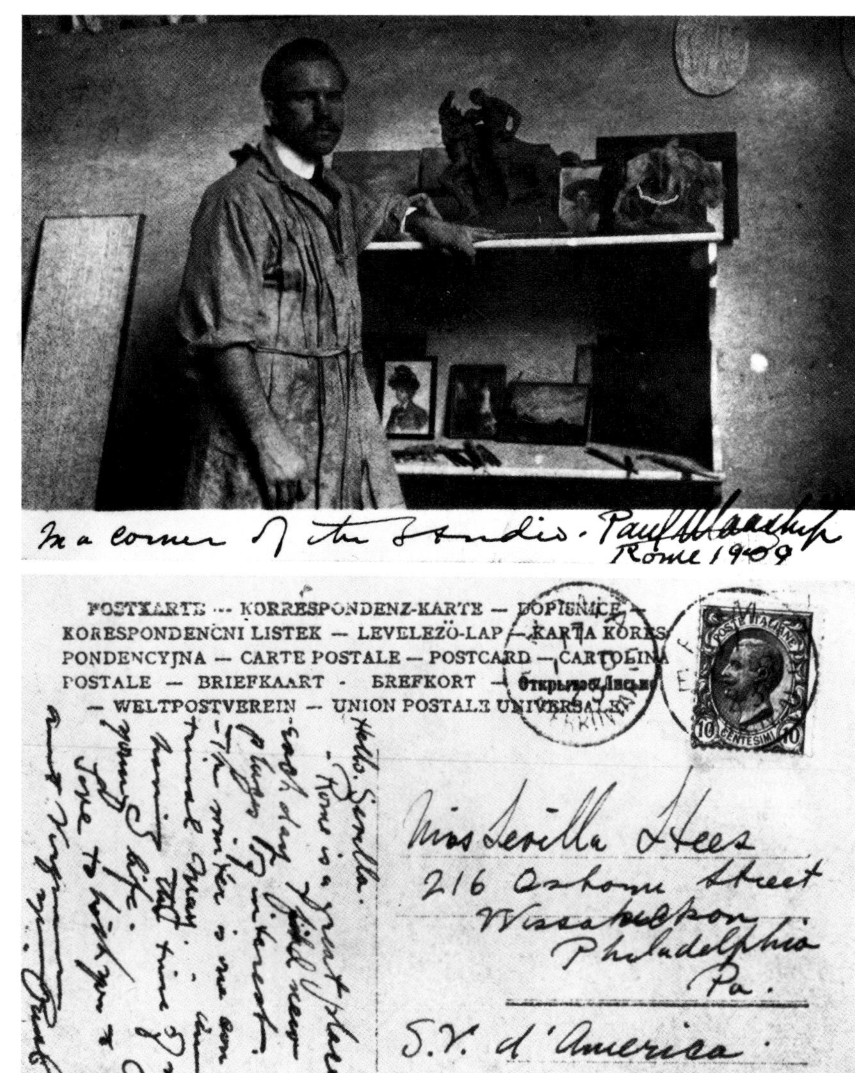

Figs. 10 and 11. Postcard, front and back; "In a corner of the studio/ Rome 1909/ Paul Manship." Paul Manship Papers, Archives of American Art, Smithsonian Institution.

and treatment the piece anticipates his 1913–14 *Centaur and Dryad.* This predecessor is so close to the later sculpture that the two may form a continuum of prototype and final work. Manship chose to place this work near him as a signal of his growing affections and new viewpoint animated by his Roman experience.

At the other end of the shelf rests another study—in some ways as remarkable as the mythological work that pointed the way to the future. This piece, long thought to be lost, can now be identified as *End of Day* (fig. 12). Comparing this early work with Manship's subsequent pieces, we can begin to chart the path of his evolution. The title *End of Day* elucidates its subject, a labor-wearied man who leans against one of two equally tired horses. This sculpture shows the effect of Manship's Roman sojourn; while it recalls Solon

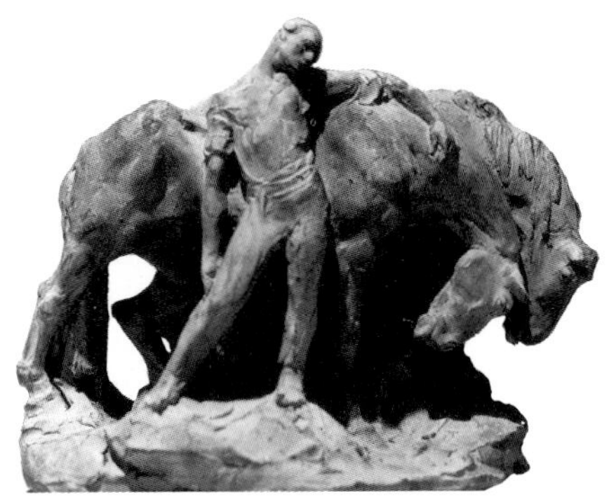

Fig. 12. *End of Day,* 1909; terra cotta; $8\frac{13}{16}$ in. high.

Borglum's work, *End of Day* evidences the waning moments of Manship's artistic adolescence.

Manship's cataloguer, Edwin Murtha (also Manship's son-in-law), lists the piece as a bronze, adding to the confusion surrounding the work's whereabouts. Murtha claimed this piece was made in a single bronze cast, but the Smithsonian's National Museum of American Art holds the sculpture in terra cotta. Perhaps this work is an advanced version of *Rest After Toil,* the relief sculpture with which Manship won the Prix de Rome. *Rest After Toil* does not appear in Murtha, which is an odd omission since it is upon this piece that the sculptor's subsequent career rests. It seems unlikely that Manship would forget to mention so important a work to Murtha. *End of Day* may never have been made in bronze, having been misremembered by Manship, or the piece may not have been made in Rome. It could have been taken to Rome by Manship as a souvenir and inspiration of the Borglums. It is possible that Manship did have it cast once to make some money, before his fortunes improved dramatically upon his presentation in America. Then, he did not have to sell old work, as his new pieces supported him grandly.

Several hypotheses can account for the appearance of the *End of Day* in the postcard, its odd catalogue entry, and its survival at the National Museum of American Art thanks directly to Manship's care in preserving it for his bequest to the Smithsonian. Without additional evidence, no single hypothesis can be preferred exclusively.

Throughout Manship's stay at the American Academy, he systematically collected information and experiences. Manship's approach was not based on a theoretical aesthetic that balanced one set of ideas against another in a dialogue about the past and its possible meaning and value. Instead, his private pedagogy empirically weighed the merits of one sculpture against others. His taste was formed by an immersion in the heady Roman environment. Objects in Rome's museums and sculpture on its buildings and fountains supplied art of many periods. Manship borrowed concrete citations from the past rather than abstract concepts, and this practical approach thrived when he was surrounded by sculpture representing a more or less unbroken tradition of some twenty-five hundred years of decorative and monumental commissions. Fountains, applied sculptural ornament, and freestanding statues met his gaze wherever he turned. Being in Rome also distanced Manship from the towering figure of Rodin. For example, with the notable exception of his early *Wrestlers,* Manship rarely employed the fragmentary figure (as Rodin did routinely).

Balanced against the pressing reality of modern art was a reservoir of precedent on which to draw, and Manship tapped this trove with unparalleled seriousness and invention. In Italy Manship studied the work of Michelangelo and Donatello; his fellowship's requirement that he travel to Greece, where he saw the most recent archaeological discoveries, also influenced his rudimentary classicism.

During Manship's three-year internship at the American Academy in Rome, he fell under the spell of an unmediated classicism that invigorated his work thereafter. The antique approach elevated conception above perception. Thought was preferable to mere sensation, and the excesses of unpredictable and idiosyncratic invention were discarded.

Pompeian frescoes inspired Manship by their mysterious and graceful maidens and haunting architectural remains. On vase paintings, decorative ornament, a sense of surface design, and deftly drawn figures covered objects whose utility and proximity to the lives of their owners were beguiling to Manship. (This aspect of the classical world foretold a thoroughly designed visual environment that became the guiding principle of both Art Deco and the Bauhaus.) Roman bronze statuettes and bowls offered the model for elevating the implements of daily life to an important level of craftsmanship; Manship saw that these same utensils could inject into daily life a classic beauty, an elegance irrespective of size.

He found the mechanical regularity of the modern world a threat to human character, and Manship wrote that it seemed

> unnatural for the artist to find his inspiration in a country where machinery is standardized and quantity production is the rule; where handicraft has not expressed itself in producing the divine beauty of nature, the human form, but rather has chosen to produce the machine which exploits and commercializes the tireless energy of natural forces. No, America is not the place for the sculptor to find the finest examples of his art. The masterpieces of all periods have been gathered together in Italy.[8]

Archaic Greek figurative sculpture, which is so much more abstract than Hellenistic or Roman work, particularly impressed Manship. As a term, "archaic" art derives from a time before cultural relativism held sway; not all of the past was equally valuable or venerated. The archaic (from the Greek *arke* "to begin") means specifically the earliest part of civilization, before the Mediterranean cultures arose upon which the classical world was founded. Western art's authoritative values derive from the classical period, which successively informed the Roman world, the Renaissance, and subsequent revivals of the style. Accordingly, "primitive" art had nothing but a pejorative connotation, and the archaic was viewed as akin to the primitive. Archaic art refers to objects made in those periods before the establishment of the classical heritage (especially, the mature products of Greek and Roman society); it is a stage shared by many civilizations and characterized by a simplicity of forms, specifically distinct from the classical, which was seen as the early phases of art.

Manship traveled to the eastern Mediterranean in pursuit of this art, and the balance that he observed of decorative stylizations, especially evident in

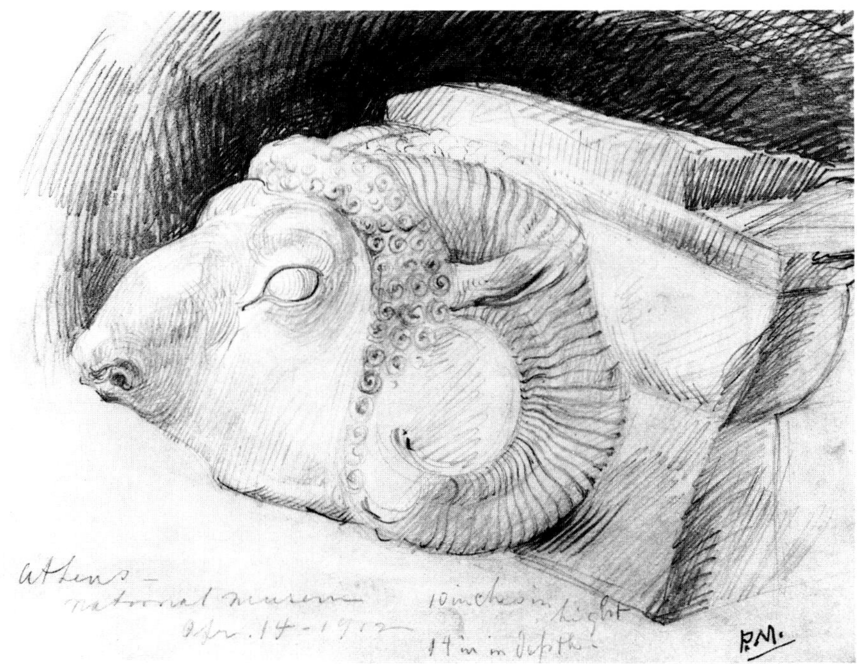

Fig. 13. *Ram's Head from the Athens Museum,* 1912; pencil on paper; 6 x 8¼ in. Minnesota Museum of Art, St. Paul, Gift of Dr. and Mrs. John E. Larkin, Jr.

hair and drapery, ornamenting simple masses redirected his thinking about sculpture. Manship's interest in these contrasts of decoration and plain surfaces, of rhythm and rest, appeared early in his work.

In *Ram's Head,* 1912 (fig. 13), Manship captured the smoothly worked surfaces as well as the insistent cadence of the striated horn and the stylized curls of the ram's wool. The darkly hatched background makes the glowing foreground of the *Ram's Head* stand out, as in the glare of a Mediterranean noon. To preserve a gauge of scale Manship recorded the dimensions of the carving. This magnificent drawing demonstrates how he saw and gathered evidence. In his travels through Italy and Greece, he was building a visual vocabulary of forms. These forms derived from work that had long been ignored or that had just been brought to light with the trowel of modern archaeology. Manship was the first American sculptor to exalt archaic principles over the classical art of Phidias and Polykleitos. Egypt provided another form of antiquity, and eventually he absorbed influences from the Minoan and Assyrian cultures, as well as from Gandharan and Kushan Greco-Indian sculpture. From his sketches, notebook jottings, daybooks, lecture notes, and drawings, we can determine some of the specific pieces that impressed him.

In Rome, during May 1912, Manship read a paper called "The Decorative Value of Greek Sculpture" at the American Academy. His statement reveals his thinking about archaic sculpture at the time. Discussing two such statues, Manship noted: "We feel the power of design, the feeling for structure in line, the harmony in the division of spaces and masses—the simplicity of the flesh admirably contrasted by rich drapery, every line of which is drawn with precision. It is the decorative value of the line that is considered first."[9] Manship stressed the linear, the silhouette, and the sharp edge—not softly modeled transitions from light to shadows. He had arrived at an anti-Rodin position that was also being pursued, although to different ends, by modernist sculptors as different from him as Matisse or the Cubists. Manship continued his lecture by suggesting that when a sculptor carries out such a sculptural program

> Nature is formalized to conform with the artist's idea of Beauty. Just as the sculptor in modelling foliated forms to be used in architectural decoration reduced nature to its decorative essence and considered the relationship of lines and masses rather than reality, so in these statues the artist has subordinated everything to his formal composition. The entire statue can be considered as a decorative form upon which all the detail is drawn rather than modelled.[10]

Manship's works announced not only the revival of *antique* sculptural qualities and subject matter but also the resuscitation of certain *archaic* Greek conventions, for example, the forms of garments folded flat with swallowtail hems. Manship was the first significant American sculptor to mine an earlier, less evolved art in order to realize anew the properties of his medium. His turn to the archaic resulted in more than superficial borrowings.

Not until the early twentieth century did artists consider it acceptable to repair to the archaic, as opposed to classically derived art. "Archaism," then, appealed to a broad front—architects, sculptors, and painters—who tapped archaic art to exploit its clean forms. Manship's infatuation with the archaic paralleled modernism's interests in archaism. The early modernists—Matisse, Picasso, and Lipchitz among them—sought art's primordial roots to simplify their work and return it to the origins of the artistic enterprise. What to our eyes clearly separates primitivism from archaism was not so easily distinguished by them.

Manship's search was not limited by geography or period; he pursued archaic clarity wherever he found it. The distinct qualities of archaic culture appeared outside Greece as well and far afield of the Mediterranean basin. Egyptian sculpture—probably the artistic ancestor of the Greek—was carved into the block from four sides, resulting in sculptures that were more formally rigorous and less animated than those of classical Greek art. The classical work of Greek antiquity, more evolved and more florid, was preferred to this archaic sculpture, thereby demoting Egyptian and archaic Greek art. A change in artistic direction drew its impetus from the appearance in England of the early classical Elgin Marbles of the Parthenon.[11] Also, "the discovery of the Aegina pediments in 1811, a series of spectacular finds [that] were made at such sites as Selinus (Sicily), Delos, Olympia, Athens, and Delphi"[12] accented the primitive works that appeared in various world's fairs throughout the nineteenth century.

All these discoveries introduced large audiences to the possibility of artistic quality issuing from societies that were neither scientifically nor technologically advanced. As classicism had risen in the wake of the discoveries at Pompeii, archaism was nourished by more recent archaeology of less modern cultures. Today we might say that as a historical term, archaism "is reserved to characterize the streamlined figurative mode popularized by academic sculptors of the early twentieth century."[13] Manship was among its most distinguished practitioners.

Conceptually, archaism imbues current art with a simplicity that is meant to recall or derive from earlier moments of art. As a period style it extracted the historically essential kernels of art. Springing from entirely different urges and needs, primitivism embodies characteristics alien and antithetical to Western heritage; for this reason, both Manship and political propagandists rejected primitivism. Unfortunately, propagandists of the following decades saw the potential for usurping archaic art to spread their doctrines. The salutary rejuvenation of art that archaism produced was eventually perverted to serve Mussolini's agenda of denatured and blandly overpowering monumental art. Archaic art can be cherished as, rightly or wrongly, the symbolic source of a people's identity; the childhood of civilization was enslaved to allegorize the "youth" of Fascism. Hitler's dogma profitted from the dual nature of archaism to simultaneously simplify forms and to recall primal societies and cultural roots. Archaism was exploited by Fascist propagandists at the expense of other modern art; hence, the very notion of archaic art proved distasteful for a generation after World War II.

Manship's appreciation of his Roman stay remained genuine throughout his life. He recalled the special community and his discovery of antique utilitarian objects: "Today, the young sculptor goes to Rome, not only to model and to study sculpture, but also to study the other arts and their connection with his own."[14] To his Rome studio Manship brought the observation gathered from his research and trips; there, he consciously amalgamated selected moments from the history of sculpture into a personal statement. In 1912 he returned to the United States with works that declared the elements of this new style.

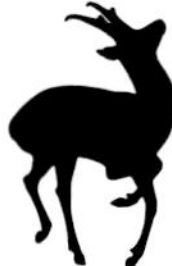

Overnight Success

MANSHIP RETURNED TO AMERICA in the fall of 1912, bringing with him the carefully wrought sculptures he had executed in Rome. The shape and force of his career appeared suddenly, shining from an exhibition that the Architectural League held in New York at year's end. The results were legendary. All ninety-six bronzes in the show sold. The critics and public unanimously acclaimed him a major new talent. Manship's first reviews were marvelous, as they were to remain for three decades. On the basis of his enthusiastic reception, offers for works poured in faster than Manship alone could fulfill. The young sculptor had launched a successful career that would last fifty years.

He moved into a comfortable studio in Washington Mews in Greenwich Village. On a little green door that separated Manship from the busy world, the exotic workmanship of an astonishing iron doorknocker displayed the technique of a great artisan. Although he was open to mirth and whimsy, Manship did not present a fanciful character:

> There is nothing about Manship that savors of the denizen of the Latin Quarter. He possesses the attributes of a man of affairs. He might easily be mistaken for a broker, or a prosperous operator in real estate. But his studio is literally full of examples of that extraordinary craftsmanship which has made him the envy of half the sculptors in America and the despair of a host of would-be imitators.[1]

In 1912 Manship was approached by a destitute Gaston Lachaise. At first Manship rejected Lachaise's request for work, but after a second meeting he hired Lachaise as an assistant. Lachaise regularly put in twelve hours at Manship's side before returning to his nearby Greenwich Village studio to pursue his own sculpture (sometimes during unpaid vacations).

Three years Manship's senior, Lachaise had trained at the Académie des Beaux-Arts, worked with the renowned jeweler René Lalique in Paris, and assisted the American sculptor Henry Hudson Kitson. Lachaise's training proved invaluable in helping to execute Manship's Neoclassical carvings, which required considerable skill and technical prowess. Manship's finely detailed ornaments of foliage on bases and pedestals were among Lachaise's assigned tasks. Ever generous and thoughtful, Manship introduced Lachaise as a distinguished fellow-sculptor to some of his own patrons; Lachaise was invited to accompany Manship to prestigious dinners where the fashionable and wealthy—potential clients—were present.

On New Year's Day 1913 Manship wed Isabel McIlwaine (whom he had met seven years earlier at Solon Borglum's house), and they remained happily married for fifty-three years. That new year proved additionally fateful; the National Academy of Design showed ten works by Manship, who was hailed as a prodigy. It is difficult to reconstruct the effect these works had on their first spectators. Now, we recall Walker Hancock's admonition that "it may not be easy, in the context of today's sculpture, to think of Paul Manship's early work as revolutionary. But he so regarded it." Hancock further declared (and we have to heed his pronouncement to truly grasp Manship's accomplishment) that "the array of bronzes the young man brought back from the American Academy in Rome in 1912 surprised connoisseurs from New York to San Francisco by a use of the medium that was new in this country."[2]

Recollections of the classical world have been the mainspring of occidental art—we happen to live in the first moment that has shaken off antiquity's hold—and even now, post-modernism attempts to mine the classical past. The medieval world aspired to re-create the clarity and serene masterfulness of the Mediterranean cultures. Gothic art strove to surpass the achievements of Roman architecture, whose ruins sprouted from the European landscape, taunting the puny accomplishments of artists and builders. And the Renaissance—whose artists loom as titanic figures—was itself an attempt to revive the classical world. For generations, the high classical *Apollo Belvedere*, which seems today so wanly effeminate, epitomized good taste, the ideal of sculpture and art. Only the arrival of the Elgin Marbles in the British Museum opened a new vista—the *early* classical Mediterranean—for the Western world. Inherited ideals had been challenged and seemingly bested.

Classicism, as espoused by Ingres for example, collided with the living experience of the Mediterranean world that Delacroix encountered in his excursion to North Africa. Thereafter, classicism—as taught from plaster casts and replicas of antiquity—became disreputable. Manship, a young, energetic, and not inherently reactionary artist, began to make his most vigorous and successful works in what had become a despised form of expression. He was driven by an attempt to escape the overarching and ubiquitous presence of Rodin.

At the start of this century, Rodin was lionized; he commanded attention to a degree that is hardly comprehensible now. Manship's flight from Rodin fostered a special view of the past. At the time, Manship's quest was recognized by the public and critics alike. Reviewing an exhibition at the galleries of the American Fine Arts Society, which displayed work from the American Academy in Rome, the eminent critic Kenyon Cox noted, in particular, a group of some ten pieces of sculpture by Manship, who had just returned to America after his three years' study at the Roman school:

> There is no rarer or more delightful sensation than the recognition of a new and genuine talent. This sensation I have experienced at the present exhibition. . . . The [works] . . . give one some clear notion of a personality still in the making but already full of originality and charm. . . . The only thing that distinguishes this production from that of almost any other clever young sculptor is the entire absence of the influence of Rodin—an influence found nearly everywhere today.[3]

Driven by his discomfort with modernism's severity and Expressionism's arbitrary distortions, Manship fashioned a synthesis. Neither cerebral purity nor emotional chaos were acceptable foundations for his art.

His exhibition at the National Academy of Design was an instant success; Herbert Adams, president of the National Sculpture Society, wrote to Oliver La Farge, then secretary of the American Academy in Rome:

> It seems to me that here is a man who, if given a chance to work out his natural bent, may do American art an incalculable good. I do not refer to the archaic or archaistic spell to be noted in some of his work, but rather to his ability and skill in design and execution.

And Adams cautioned

> Don't let the architects ruin him by giving him a lot of big work which must be hastily executed. . . . It is not impossible that this man alone may be worth to American art all the effort the American Academy in Rome has cost![4]

Adams was prescient about both points. Even today, more than seventy-five years after his Prix de Rome, Manship remains the most celebrated alumnus of the American Academy, and Adams's warning proved all too accurate. In later years, Manship's talent was taxed by huge architectural commissions executed under the most pressing constraints of time—with a concomitant falling off of quality of which Manship was well aware. But at this brilliant dawn of his career, not even the faintest hint of gloom threatened.

His growing fame soon commanded attention outside New York. In 1914 Manship exhibited at the Pennsylvania Academy, where he received the Widener gold medal for *Duck Girl*, a lighthearted piece the City of Philadelphia purchased. One of the qualities that Manship's contemporaries found especially appealing (and which seems only distantly accessible at the end of the twentieth century) was the note of gaiety in his work. Following the "brown decades," his carefree subjects' vitality was welcomed after a long absence from American sculpture. Manship's exhibition at New York's Architectural League especially delighted architects, who sensed a relief from a diet of ponderous, moralizing statues; they had been waiting for such an artist. The collection of works sold out. Next, a commercial gallery show also sold out.

Manship had mastered a vivacious revival style of Roman bronze-work by 1911. A convincing, sometimes playful, and always animated approach, his pieces never copied antiquity exactly. Manship interpreted his classical inheritance. His works combined the ductile quality of molten metal with its liquid gestural potential. For Manship, classicism offered the opportunity for detail expressed as ornament; his meticulously chased metal surfaces are a sensuous component independent of the sculpture's subject.

Each of the elements of Manship's *Lyric Muse* (fig. 14) harks back to some artistic precedent. Yet, the sculpture is so skillfully synthesized that antiquity is sensed throughout without any major component recalling a specific reference to a unique work. While *Lyric Muse* does have a frontal view, the piece is modeled in the round, as opposed to a series of reliefs projected onto a cubic volume. The *Muse*'s body is independent of, and does not resolve into, a pattern projected upon a single plane. In addition, the bronze's textural mimicry of smooth skin convincingly serves anatomical truth, which Manship studied and reproduced in his apprenticeships and schooling. The singer's open mouth amplifies antique sculpture's slightly parted lips.[5]

The Muses, all of whom were women, are among the most lovely and beneficent creations of mythology. They inculcated wisdom, brought purifying music, and personified the most exalted intellectual achievement. (These goddesses were the daughters of Zeus and the Titaness Mnemosyne, whose name means memory.) Hesiod, an eighth-century B.C. Greek poet, named the Muses and fixed their number at nine; the Romans assigned their individual specialties. They inspired poetry, presided over the fine arts, music, literature, and in later mythology, a wider range of intellectual pursuits such as history, philosophy, and astronomy. The Muses were popular with poets, who attributed their inspiration to them and invoked their aid.[6] Manship's *Lyric Muse* can be identified as "Erato" (which means *lovely*), the Muse of lyric poetry or hymns. Both her pose and her principal attribute, the lyre, place her in an unbroken tradition that extends from dim antiquity. Even in medieval sculptures the figure of Erato presided over scholars and poets.

Horace composed poetry that might have been in the mouth of Manship's figure as she, rising, sounds her lyre:

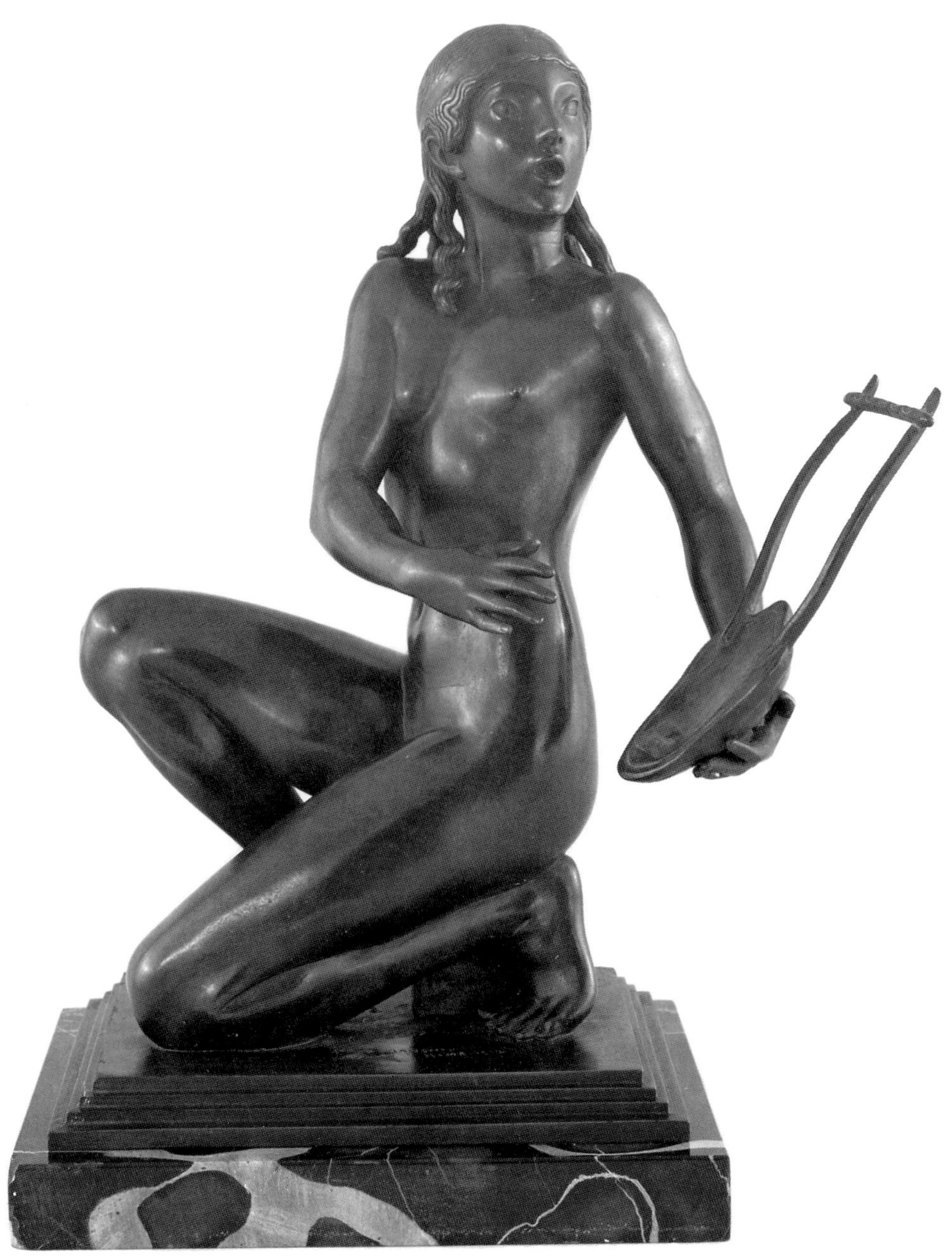

Fig. 14. *Lyric Muse*, 1912; bronze on marble base; $6\frac{7}{16}$ in. high.

But if you give me a place among the bards of the lyre,
I shall lift up my head till it strikes the stars.

Sappho's lines are also appropriate:

I took my lyre and said:

Come now heavenly
tortoise shell: become
a speaking instrument

Or one may think of Sappho's boast:

To me the muses brought honor,
They gave me the secret of their craft

Manship taught himself French and Italian with the help of Solon Borglum's wife, and though he lacked certification by schools, he hoped his spectators would recognize and savor the classical references in his works. With references both straightforward and esoteric, Manship illustrated passages of classical literature, both common and obscure. An autodidact in things literary or academic, Manship did not wish to be thought casual or ignorant on these points. Such scrupulousness earned what diplomas might have bestowed—legitimate access to the past that archaeology discovered and scholarship invigorated.

Manship carefully read history and art history. Among his contemporaries, he maintained contacts with Bernard Berenson, Archibald MacLeish, Thomas Craven, Etienne Gilson, and Stanley Casson; and the critic Martin Birnbaum was an intimate acquaintance. Not only did he study Vasari's *Lives of the Artists*, but he also read Robert Graves on Greek mythology and Aristophanes' *The Frogs* and *Clouds*. In addition, he studied the canonical texts of the north: the *Prose Edda* of Snorri Sturluson, and the *Saga of the Volsungs*. Manship's familiarity with classical literature was his passport to an esoteric realm, and he always kept his passport visible to maintain his spectators' confidence. When Manship was attacked for flaunting mannered atavisms, Kenyon Cox defended his works as the "experiments of a young man in search of his manner," an emerging artist unwilling

> to submit himself to the dominating influence of his own time. And if the mixed style he has employed in them should harden into a premature mannerism, as I do not believe it will, it would, at least, have the merit of being his own mannerism, not that weak reflection of the mannerism of Rodin which seems to be the stock in trade of most of our younger sculptors.[7]

Manship never translated a graphic idea into three dimensions. Instead, he accounted volumes and surfaces separately and always gave precedent to sculptural conception. He applied ornament to surfaces that were the sheaths of form, and the figure of the *Lyric Muse* is highlighted by areas of archaistic pattern limited to the hair. Manship graphically balanced accents of geometric ornament with the smooth planes of each piece's single formal unit. Rising in one powerful spiral, the *Lyric Muse* relies on an elemental sculptural form. Mastered early and used thereafter, the strong helix or spiral form became a basic part of Manship's vocabulary.

Formal conception served mythology. Manship's first statuettes were deemed charming, but more important, the subjects were seen as essentially modern, direct observations of life that were archaistically treated. They were not considered merely revivals, blank recitations of sources. Luckily for Manship, contemporary critics immediately grasped this aspect of the originality of his work:

> To see this archaistic manner applied to figures with a quite unarchaic freedom of movement, doing things that no archaic sculptor would have thought of making them do, is oddly exhilarating. Perhaps the best of them all is the *Playfulness;* the slim young mother with the wide-open archaic eye, slightly uptilted at the corners, gayly playing at ride-a-cock-horse with the baby.[8]

To our eyes such innovation feels minimal, almost unnoticeable, but in its time Manship's invigoration of antique forms was refreshing. More important, his work offered promise to those who resisted modernism's utter radicality. Through the first decades of this century, Manship's subjects possessed the power to please and shock.

In its time, Manship's 1913 work *Centaur and Dryad* (fig. 15), a half man, half horse pursuing a fleeing woman (which won the National Academy's Helen Foster Barnett Prize), caused some controversy; in 1914 the postmaster of New York charged the work with displaying bestiality and prohibited a magazine that illustrated the sculpture to go through the mails. The relief on the base of *Centaur and Dryad* depicts satyrs chasing maenads, a subject that is also inherently lusty. Maenads in Greek means "frenzied women," and in mythology maenads are those who followed Dionysus (also called Bacchus) and—dressed in the skins of fawns or panthers and carrying oak leaves, snakes, or grapes—celebrated his rites of ecstatic, frenzied songs amid the mountains. These women were inspired to great physical strength; together with the satyrs, who are half man, half goat, the maenads (called bacchantes, "women of Bacchus") made up the retinue of the god of wine. Manship's sculpture group celebrating the god's cult procession was conceived in Rome (see fig. 10), but the base was finished in New York, to which circumstance we owe the lucky survival of a wonderful drawing, *Satyr Chasing Maenad* (fig. 16).

This drawing on tracing paper reverses the design found on the back of the pedestal of *Centaur and Dryad;* however, the drawing does not copy exactly the existing sculpture, from which we can infer that the augmented tracing

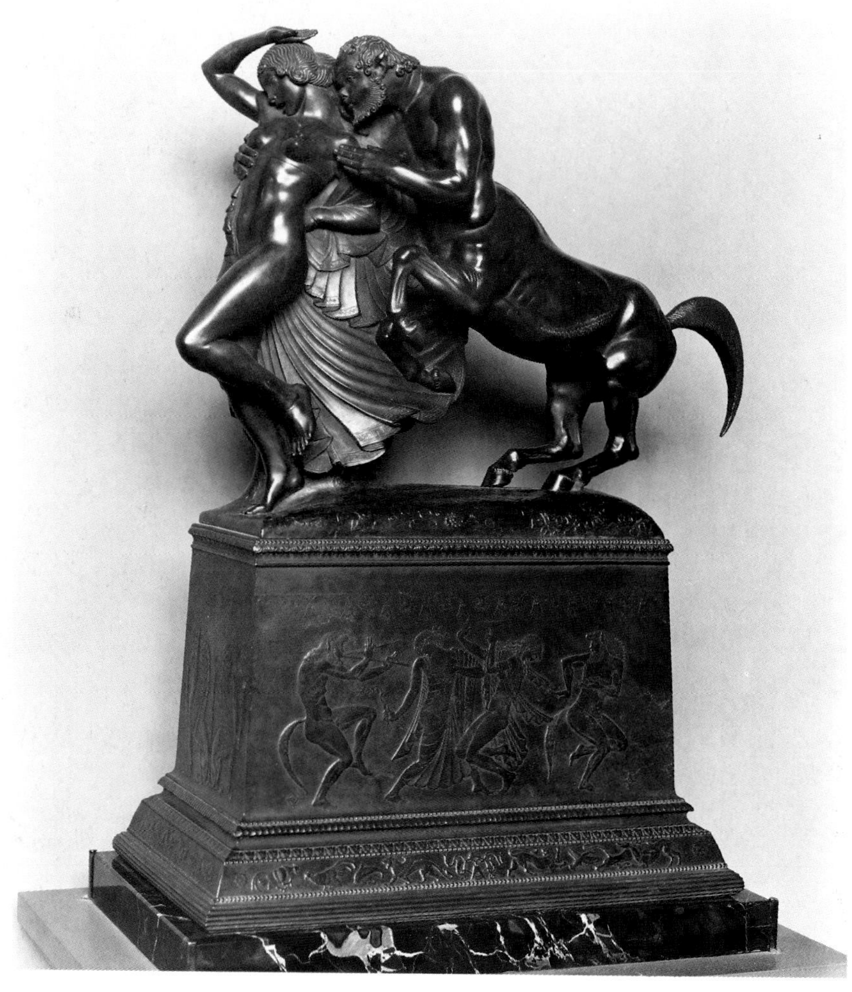

Fig. 15. *Centaur and Dryad*, 1913; bronze; 28 in. high. The Metropolitan Museum of Art, Amelia B. Lazarus Fund, 1914.

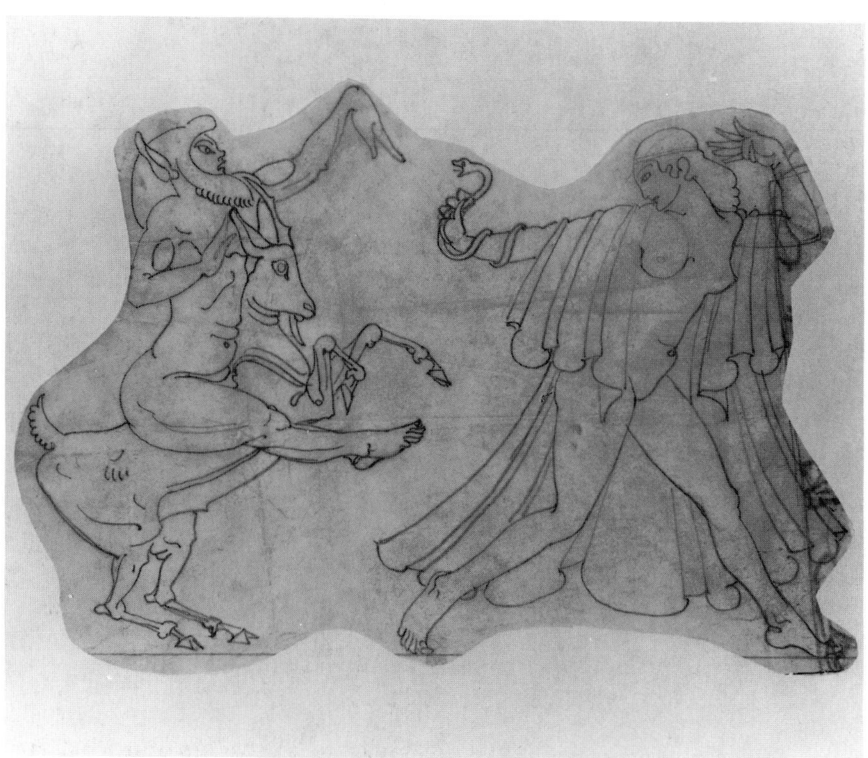

Fig. 16. *Satyr Chasing Maenad*, ca. 1913; pencil on paper; $5\frac{3}{4}$ x $8\frac{5}{8}$ in.

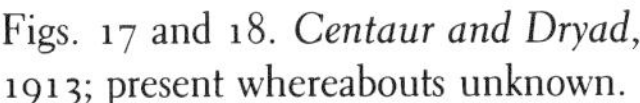

Figs. 17 and 18. *Centaur and Dryad*, 1913; present whereabouts unknown.

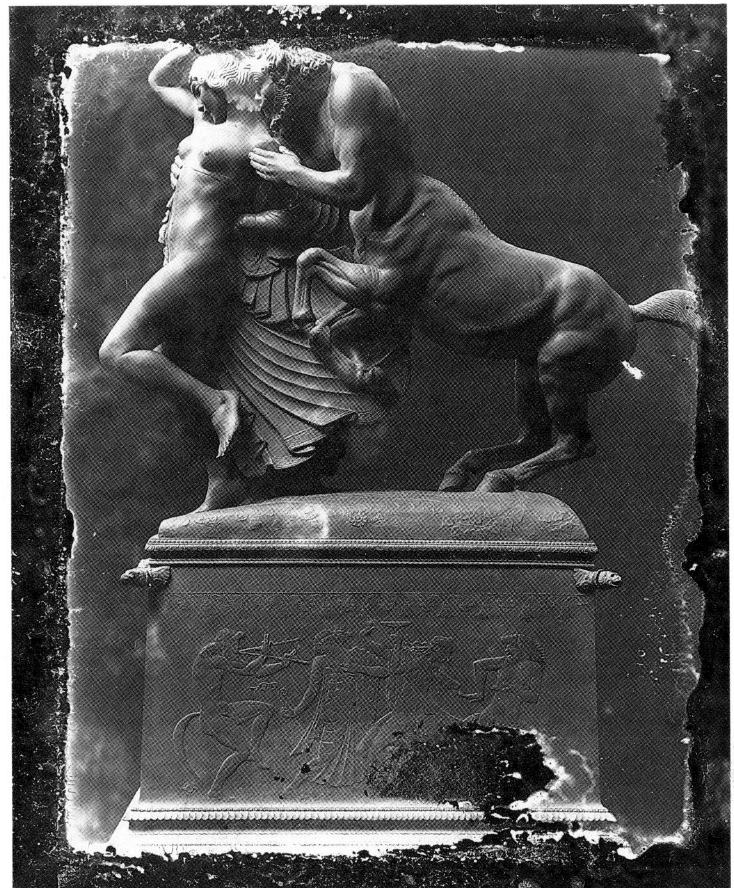

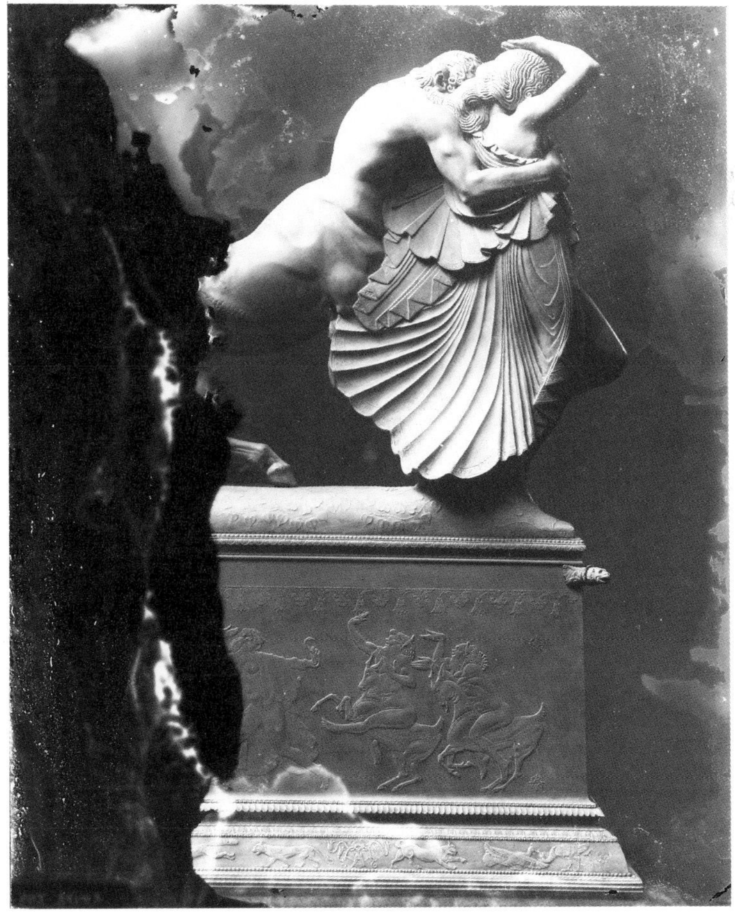

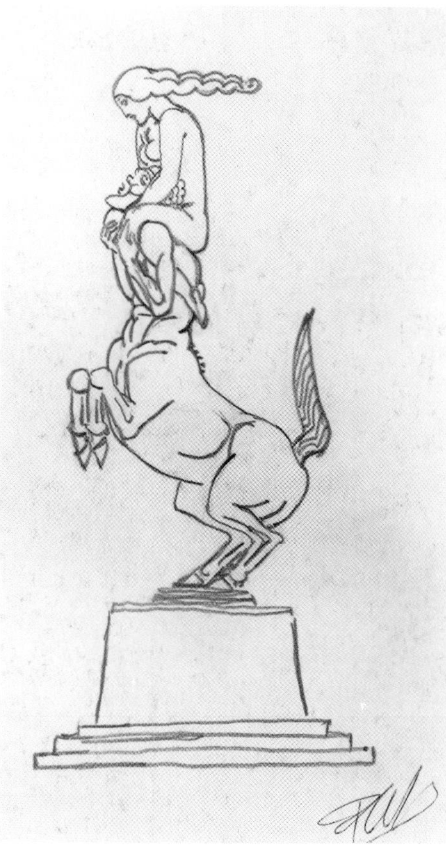

Fig. 19. *Centaur and Nymph*; pencil and pen and ink on paper; 8¼ x 5⅝ in.

preserves another version of the nearly finished design. Indeed, documentary photographs of the evolving work (probably a nearly completed version in clay, photographed as a reference for the artist) show the differences between the sculpture that we know and Manship's deliberations among a variety of possibilities—even at this late stage of work (figs. 17, 18). Most prominent, rhyton-shaped terminals at the four upper corners of the sculpture's plinth were eventually removed, as Manship may have felt that such a horizontal movement robbed the piece of its concentrated lascivious writhing. These animated figures and their poses of lusty abandon represent the most sensual work Manship ever did (fig. 19). Perhaps the controversy that the sculpture aroused caused him to retreat from the vivacity of such work, or perhaps his own reticence won out. Whatever the cause, he never again executed such humanly sympathetic images, although he could present human appetites only in mythological shapes. Increasingly, Manship dwelled on an ideal of sculpture that conversed with past sculpture and not with present mortality.

In *Playfulness* (fig. 20), a work of the same era, Manship contrasts naturalism—in the conception of a young woman playing with a baby—with the conventionalized treatment of form emphasized by patterned drapery and hair. In works like *Lyric Muse*, *Playfulness*, and *Little Brother* (figs. 21–23), originality dominated eclecticism. The slightly almond-eyed figures recall Egyptian or early Greek work—in their vacant facial expressions and their handling. At the dawn of carving and art itself, perhaps sculptors were less capable than now of recording shades of expression, or perhaps, before likeness and portraiture evolved, the mere representation of the figure was sufficiently daunting. Egyptian and early Greek sculpture rarely shows personality; however, the pose—the whole disposition of the body and the accompanying attributes—carries the freight of expression.

In the 1920s, the general public was caught up in a new interest in the archaic. The startling finds from "King Tut's" tomb in the Valley of the Kings, as well as the Berlin Museum's acquisition of the head of Nefertiti and the great sixth century B.C. Greek kouros, alerted the general public to a new aesthetic. This archaistic revival was part of the cluster of values subsumed under Art Deco, but Manship was ahead of his time.

Two years after his triumphal return to the United States, Manship designed the *Infant Hercules Fountain* and gave it to the American Academy in Rome in appreciation of his three years of study there. In the courtyard of the academy complex on Janiculum Hill, the fountain/statue presides. Ten years later, Manship asserted the value of his Rome training and its place in the modern world:

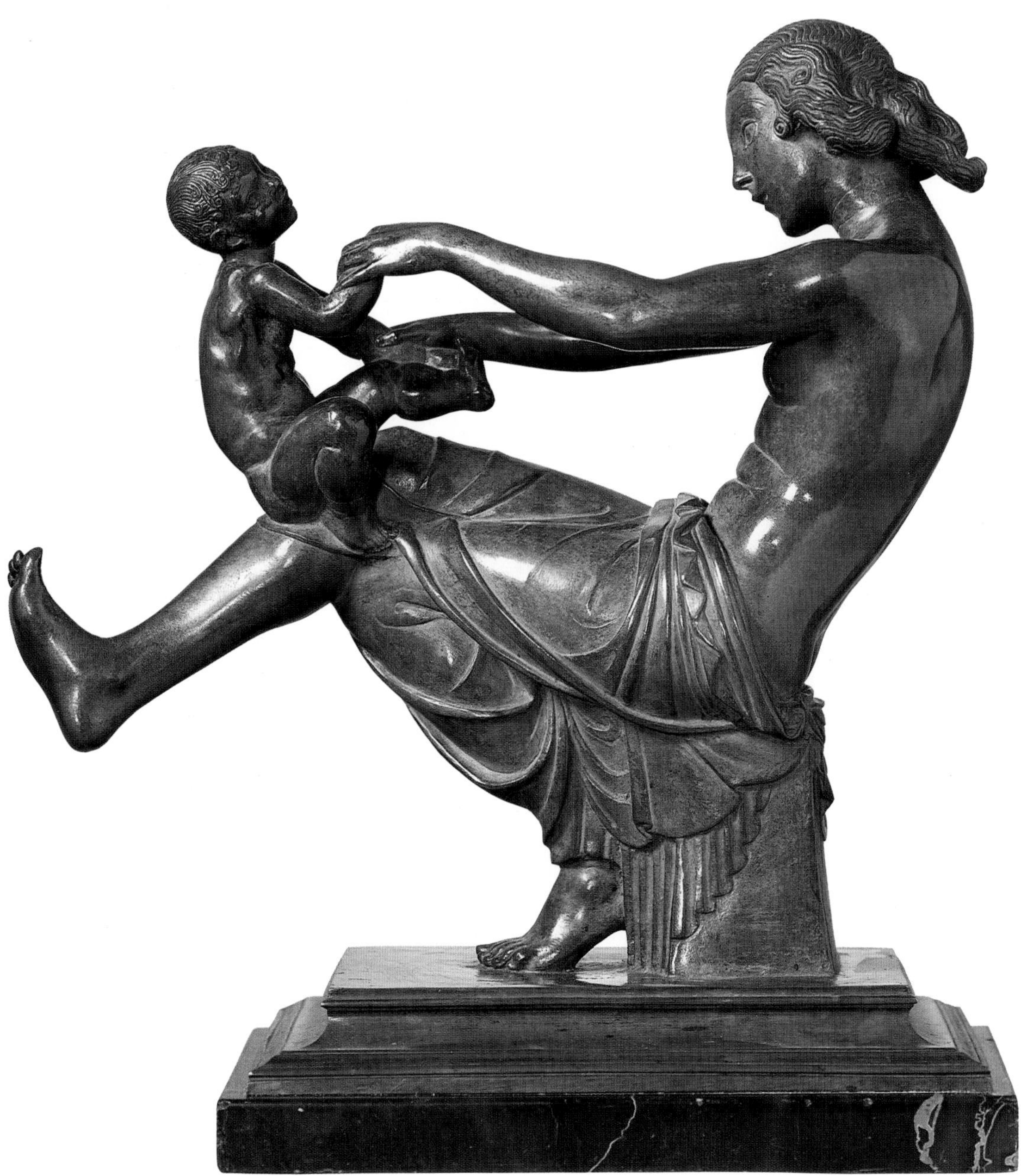

Fig. 20. *Playfulness*, 1912–14; bronze on marble base; 13⅜ in. high.

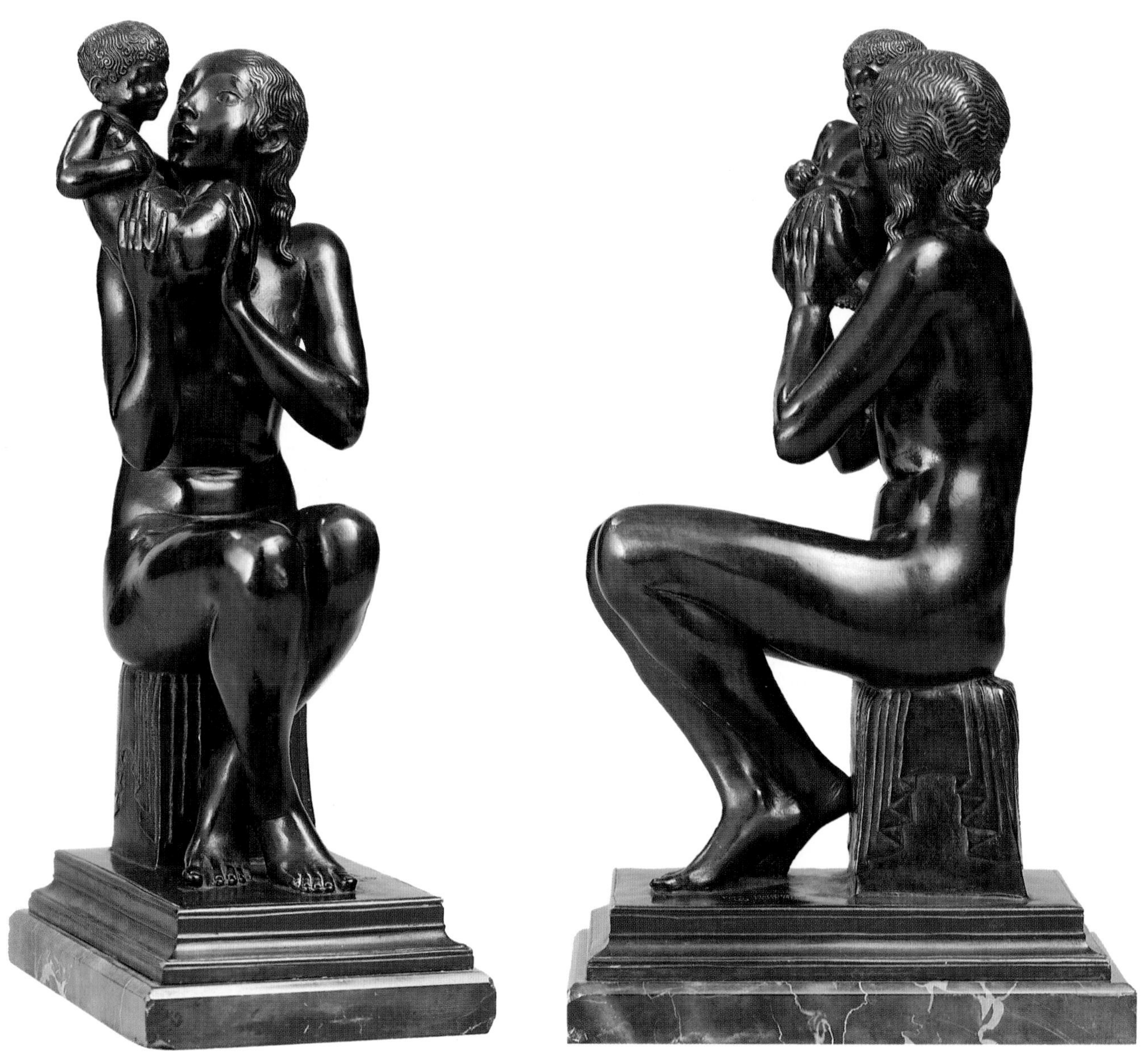

Figs. 21 and 22. *Little Brother*, 1912–14; bronze on marble base; $13\frac{1}{2}$ in. high.

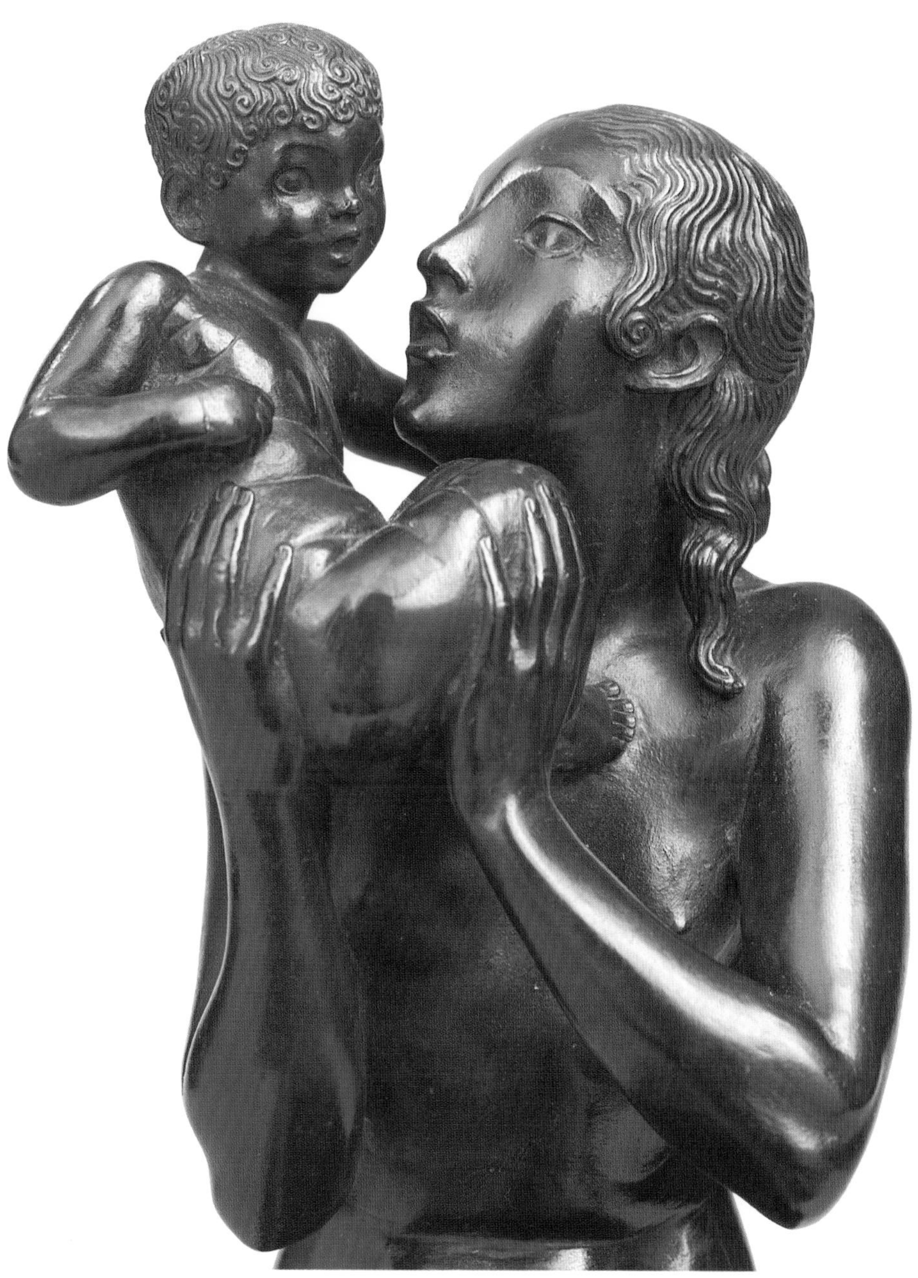

Fig. 23. Detail, *Little Brother*.

> We need today more team-work and less diverse individual effort. It is in that direction that the American Academy in Rome will exercise a practical and valuable influence upon the future of American art. . . . It will prepare the artist who is to furnish the much-needed decoration of our public buildings, raise the taste in mural painting from its present banal and commonplace level, set a new standard for sculpture in the many directions where that art is applied to public buildings, monuments, gardens and decorative purposes, and create an higher ideal in portraiture.[9]

Public enchantment with the archaic was amplified by major archaeological finds, but Manship's interest in the past had been growing since his Prix de Rome trip. When he fashioned the *Infant Hercules Fountain*, he imbued every element with rich antique references (fig. 24). Even the six waterspouts for this fountain, small *Grotesque Figures* or *Gnomes* (fig. 25), combined satyrs' heads (which in the classical Mediterranean world served as waterspouts) with the compact body of atlantes (formed in the style of medieval Indian Gupta sculptures); each *Grotesque Figure* sits perched on a pattern of solar disks derived from Indian art. The bodies of these gnomes are covered with a swirling tattoolike pattern, and this surface ornament contributes a fine level of detail to the stocky forms of the compact sculptures. Manship had them individually cast forty years after they were originally fashioned. The *Grotesque Figures* show us how Manship excelled at manipulating dense volumes and space as well.

In pendant pieces *Indian Hunter* and *Pronghorn Antelope* (figs. 26, 27), Manship activated the empty air between the Indian and his prey. The separation of the two sculptures serves as a kind of "spark gap"—the imagined flight of the arrow as it lands in the side of the rearing antelope carries the viewer's eye over this space. The antelope's backward curve returns the spectator's gaze to the Indian, completing the circuit. Manship's archer composes the centrifugal shape of a swastika; moreover, the *Indian Hunter* is formalized as to location, a place from which the arrow springs. The pair, the kneeling bowman and the staggering surprised animal, share bases of the same size, but Manship varied the depicted terrain on those bases to indicate the distance between them. The two pieces might also relate to the zodiacal sequence of Saggitarius and Capricorn, giving this old-world astronomical relationship a new-world flavor. Engaged in the resuscitation of antiquity, Manship was often the inventor of images that recalled his boyhood in midwestern America. In that sense, he also invokes the new world with the old.

At the time *Indian Hunter* and *Pronghorn Antelope* were first shown, reviewers particularly noted Manship's precise modeling, which resulted in a carefully deliberated work that "presents a complete design, quite the antithesis of the modern impressionistic sketch."[10]

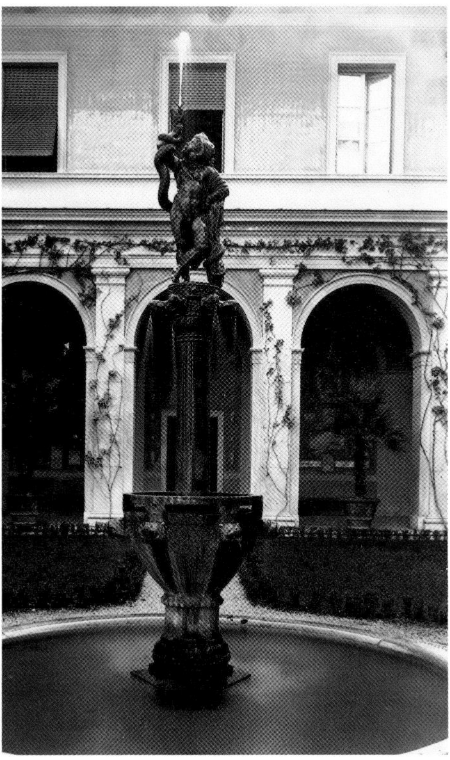

Fig. 24. *Infant Hercules Fountain*, 1914, bronze. American Academy in Rome Fellows Work Collection.

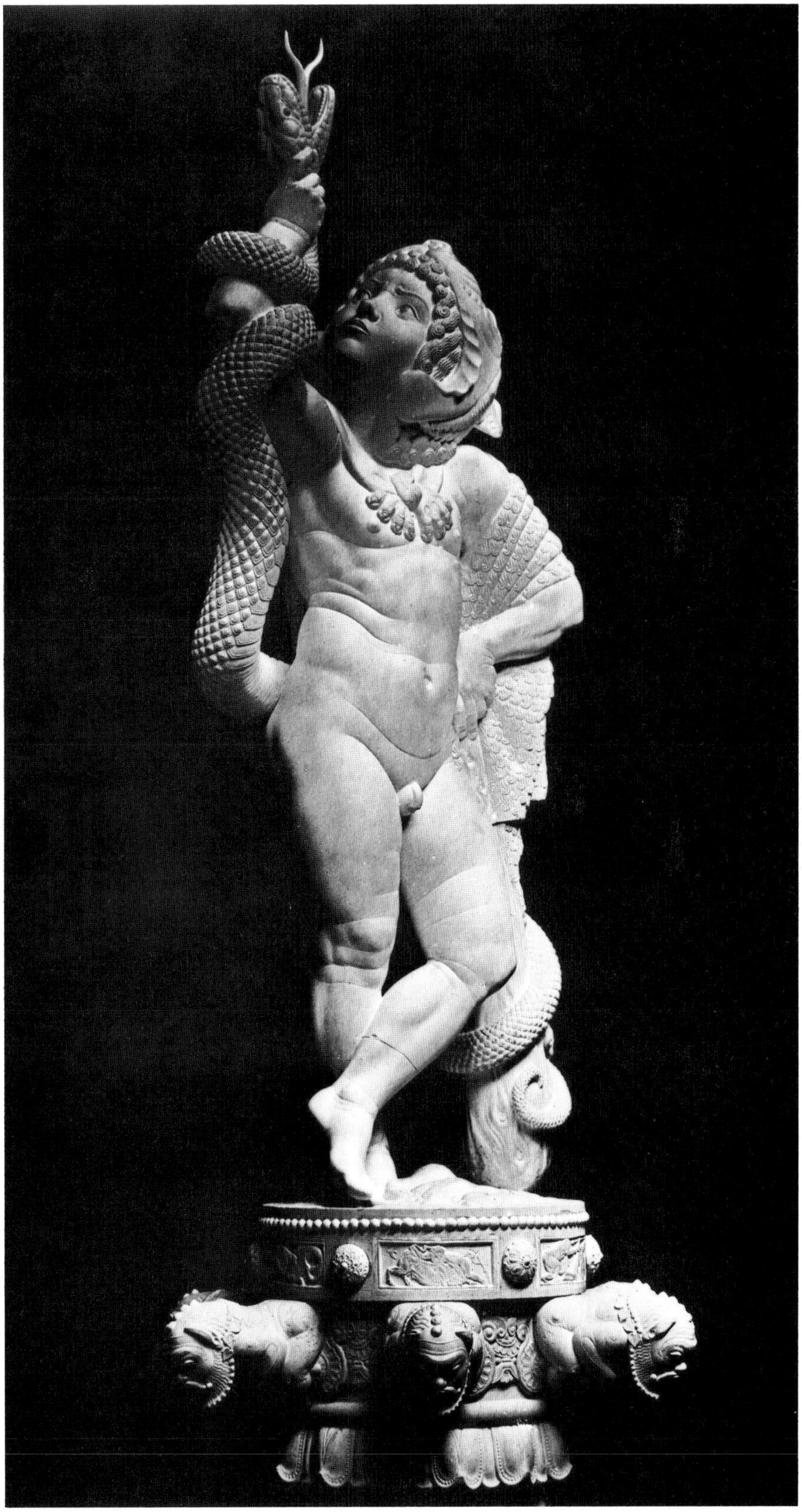

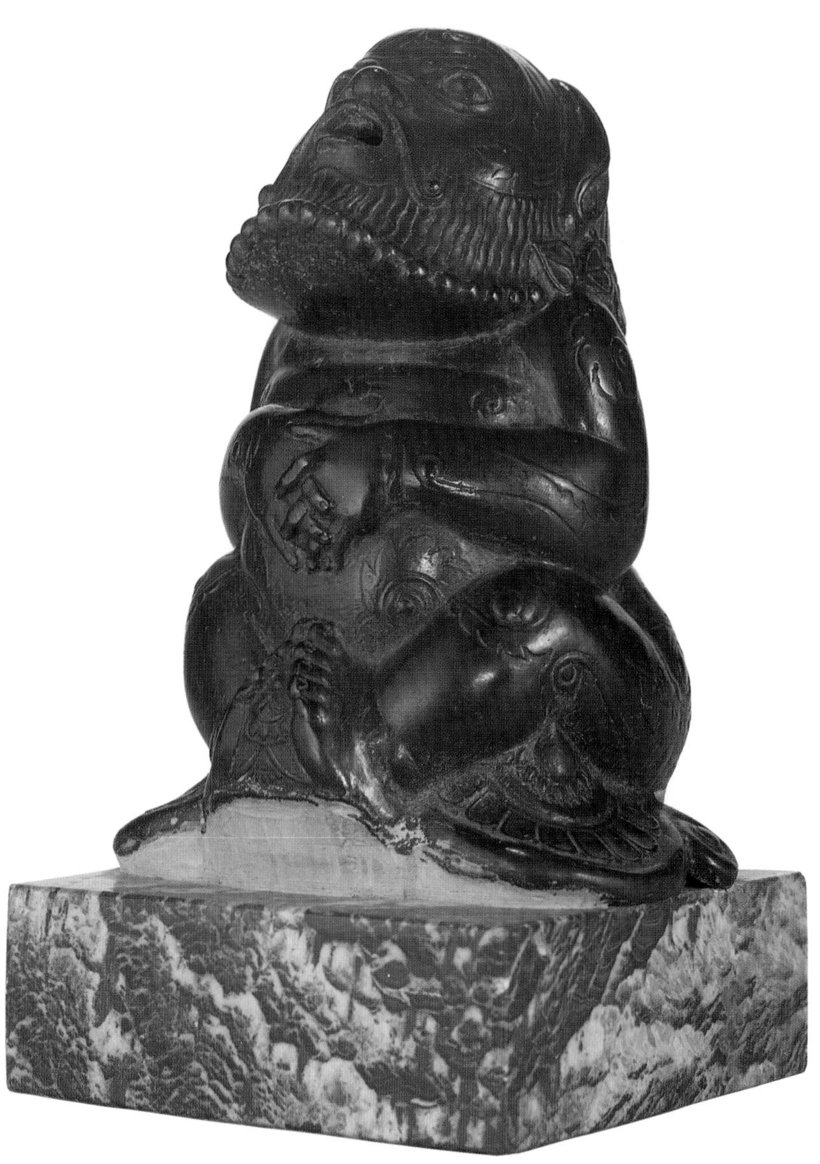

Fig. 25. *Grotesque Figure* ("Gnome"), modeled 1914, cast 1955; waterspout for the *Infant Hercules Fountain*; bronze; 8$\frac{11}{16}$ in. high.

Manship's instant fame brought him more commissions than he could execute. One day, buying a newspaper in Greenwich Village from an impoverished immigrant, he discovered that the boy happened to be a young sculptor of whom Manship had heard good reports. The paper boy, Beniamino Bufano, had previously served as an assistant to Herbert Adams, the founder of the National Sculpture Society. Bufano had also worked with James Earle Fraser, whose *Buffalo Nickel* (modeled in his Greenwich Village studio, which later became the site of the Jumble Shop, a meeting place for the next generation) and *End of the Trail* approximate Manship's taste. Manship offered the young man a part-time job; Bufano turned the street corner over to his brother and reported to Manship's studio the next morning. Assisting in the installation of Manship's work at the 1915 San Francisco Panama-Pacific International Exposition, Bufano began a long association with the Bay Area, eventually becoming its unofficial artist laureate.

The gospels of Matthew (14:1–12) and Mark (6:14–29) relate the story of Salome—retold countless times, notably by Oscar Wilde and in Richard Strauss's opera based on Wilde's drama. Salome, who lived in the first century A.D., was the daughter of Herodias and stepdaughter of Herod Antipas, ruler of Galilee. Herod had imprisoned John the Baptist for condemning his marriage to Herodias, his dead brother's wife, yet Herod was afraid to execute John. At a festival dinner, Salome danced lasciviously for the king, who, surrounded by his nobles, promised to give her whatever she wanted in exchange for this favor. In Wilde's version, Salome's unrequited lust for John resulted in a humiliating rejection, and prompted by Herodias, the girl demanded of Herod her reward: the head of John the Baptist on a platter.

Contemporary critics were taken by Manship's treatment of *Salome* (fig. 28). She disports herself in an attitude dictated by sweeping design; her composed draperies were arranged for the mere love of line. Rather than biblical solemnity, Manship—ever invigorating the past—injected a charming line and a verve seldom encountered in representations of this gruesome and barbaric subject. Previously, he had sympathized with Greek and Roman stories, perceiving mortal emotions in the gods' gambols, and now Manship resurrected the human dimension of canonized New Testament narrative.

Perhaps the greatest spontaneous acclaim Manship ever knew greeted his *Dancer and Gazelles* (fig. 29), a consummate synthesis of both formal and intellectual sources. Manship's complex, if gracefully executed, agenda for *Dancer and Gazelles* won over all viewers. Although the work is dated 1916, favorable reviews were already pouring in by February of that year. In particular, critics took notice of the *Dancer and Gazelle*'s floating draperies, which extended the formal possibilities contributed by *Salome*'s dress. These draperies lend "a movement as enticing as it is noble, . . . the lovely folds of the skirt rippling about the ankles with the rhythm of waves breaking on the shore."[11]

In the autumn of that year, A. E. Gallatin (writing in the *Bulletin of the Metropolitan Museum of Art*) had singled out "the lessons the artist has learned from Indian art, particularly from Hindu and Buddhist sculpture." Gallatin's admiration for the grace of *Dancer and Gazelles* was based on "the significance that the Indian artist attaches to gesture, as well as the symbolism of hands. [Manship's] gazelles and his antelopes possess a smoothness and vitality one very rarely finds outside of Indian art." Commenting on Manship's grace of

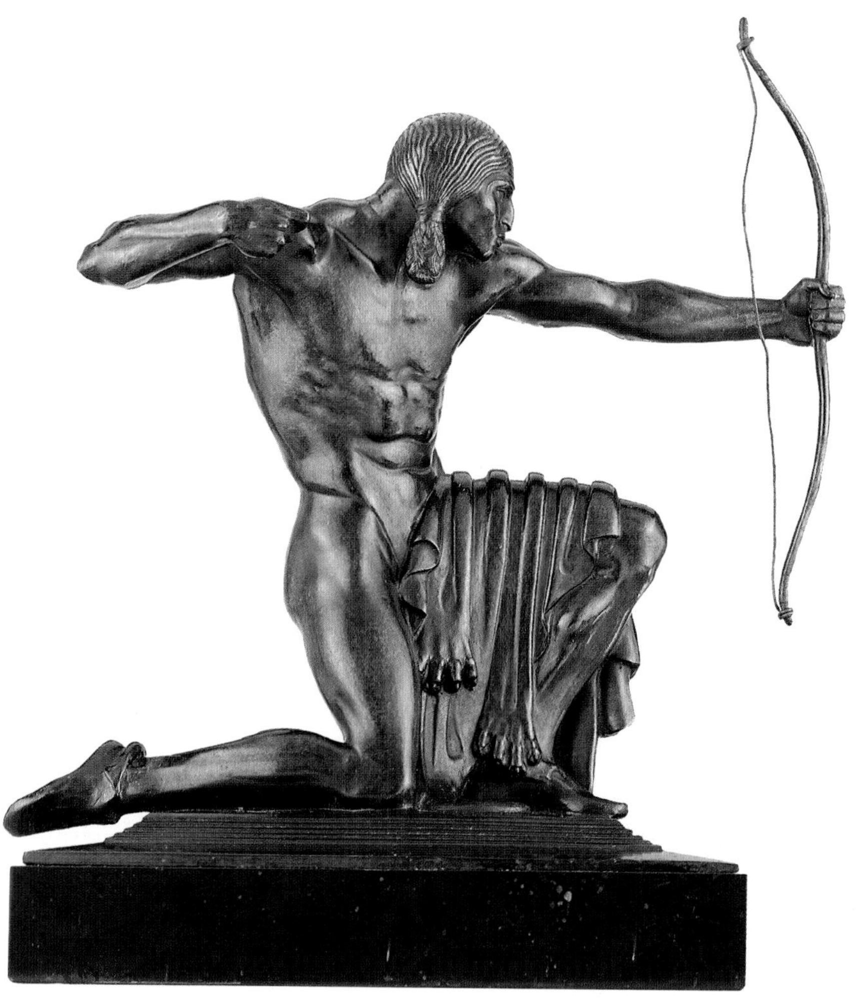

Fig. 26. *Indian Hunter*, 1914; bronze; 14½ in. high.

line and suggestion of movement, the *Bulletin of the Detroit Museum of Art* ended 1916 with a note of triumph for this work, which had already established itself a classic: "*Dancer and Gazelles* is one of the most important of Paul Manship's sculptures. . . . In it the sculptor has attained a decorative effect almost incredible in a work of three dimensions."[12]

The exhilaration of Manship's critics was partly due to the novelty of the sources he had tapped. Observations of Manship's Indic sources proved a dominant motif in analyses of *Dancer and Gazelles*. One has only to examine a *ragmala* painting—a painting that illustrates an Indic musical composition—to understand the degree of Manship's homage to this art (fig. 30). In the female composition (Indian musical compositions and paintings of them possess gender) to be performed in the early morning, *Todi Ragini*, a woman in a flaring skirt wanders through the woods carrying a vina (a stick-zither), an

Fig. 27. *Pronghorn Antelope*, 1914; bronze on marble base; 13 9/16 in. high.

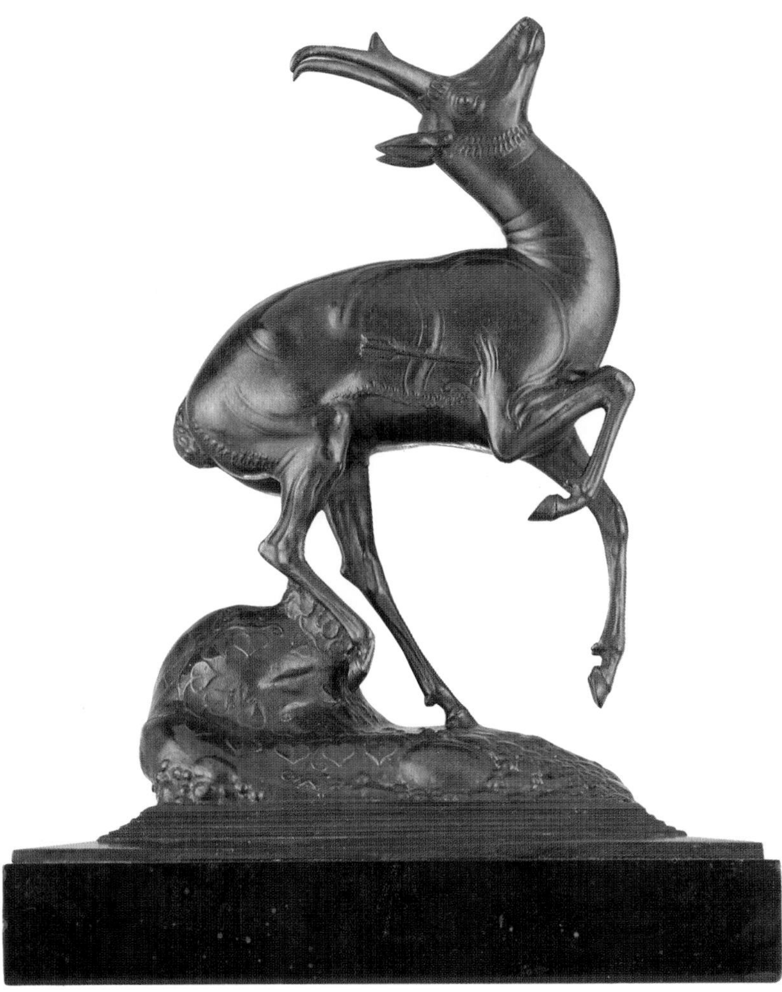

ancestor of the lute family. The alert gazelles respond to her as attentively as Manship's gazelles react to his dancer's gestures. While it is certain that Manship looked at innumerable works of Indian art—*ragmala* paintings like this, as well as sculptures—his sources were never limited to one culture and one time. He attempted to merge the best features of pre-modern art into an amalgam that was vigorous, direct, and consciously beautiful. He could have amplified a source like the Indian woman's delicate pose in conjunction with a powerful figure, such as a Romanesque "Christ in Judgment" (fig. 31). Manship almost certainly consulted a work like the tympanum of the Church of Ste-Foy in Conques, France.

This Romanesque church dates from the middle of the eleventh century, and its tympanum—an enormous composition that can be dated between 1130 and 1140—features 124 figures that, indicating the growing concern for

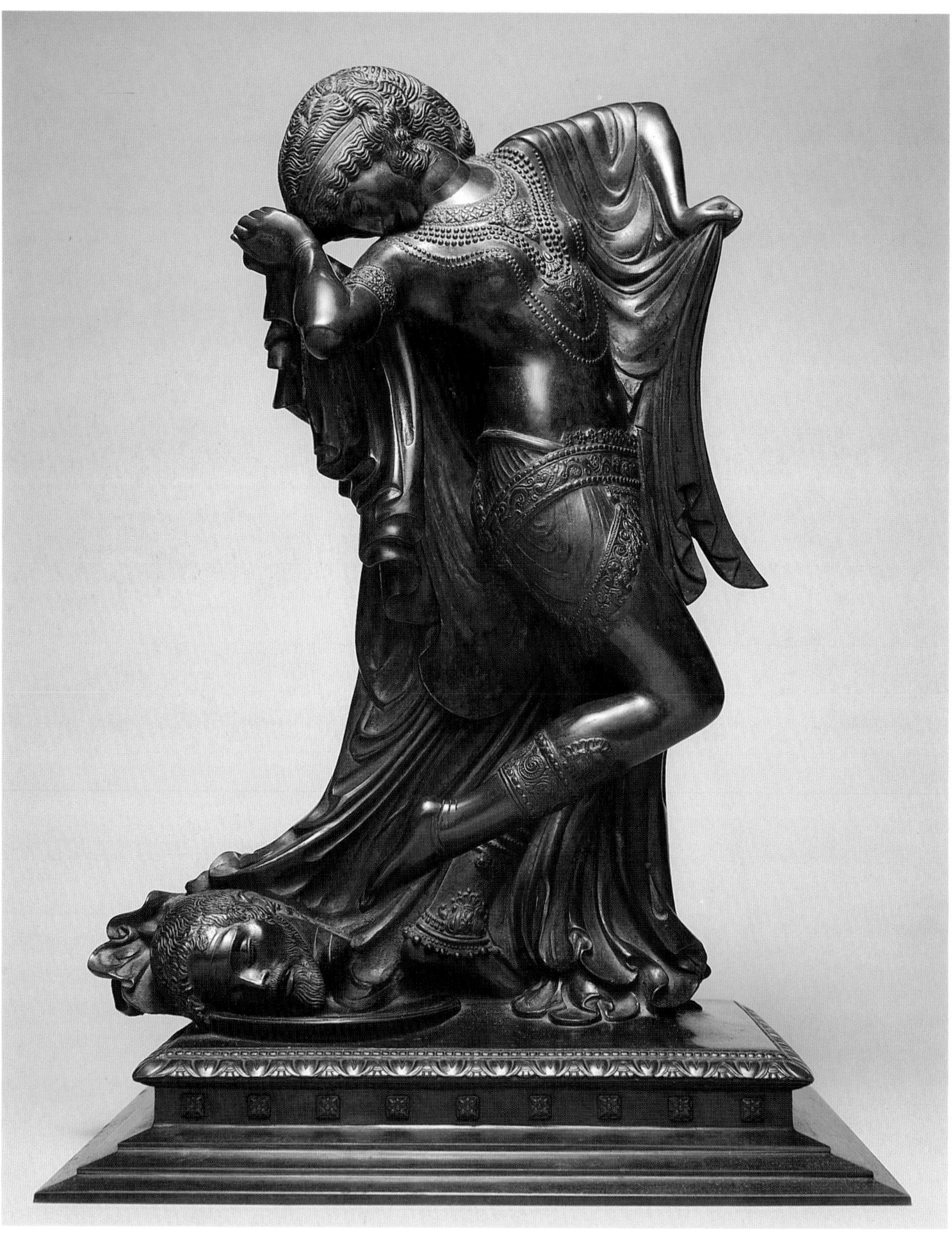

Fig. 28. *Salome*, 1915; bronze; 19 in. high.

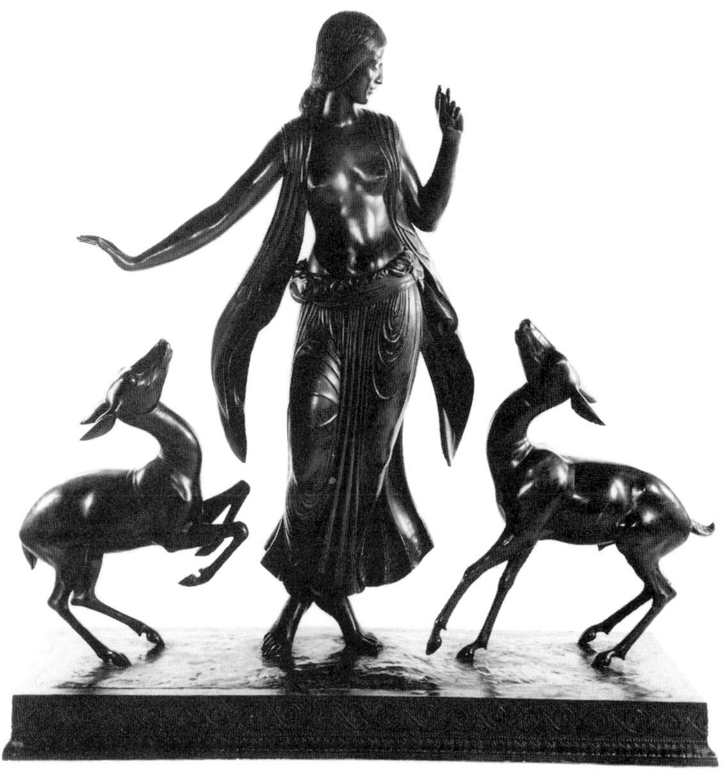

Fig. 29. *Dancer and Gazelles*, 1916; bronze, in an edition of two copies; 67 in. high. The Corcoran Gallery of Art, Washington, D.C., Museum purchase, 1920.

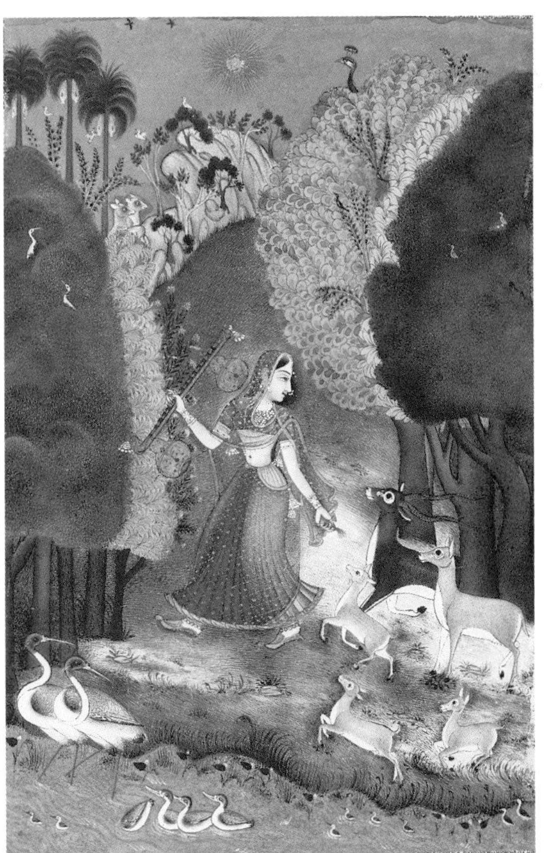

Fig. 30. Rajasthan Bundi, *Todi Ragini*, ca. 1725; painting on paper; $7\frac{1}{8}$ x $4\frac{3}{4}$ in. Museum of Fine Arts, Boston, Gift of John Goelet.

Fig. 31. Romanesque; West Portal Tympanum. Church of Ste-Foy, Conques, France.

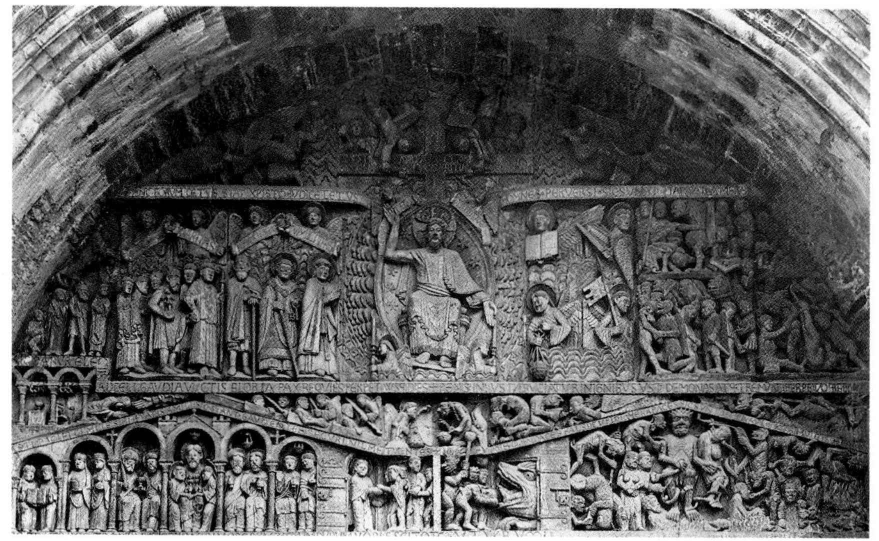

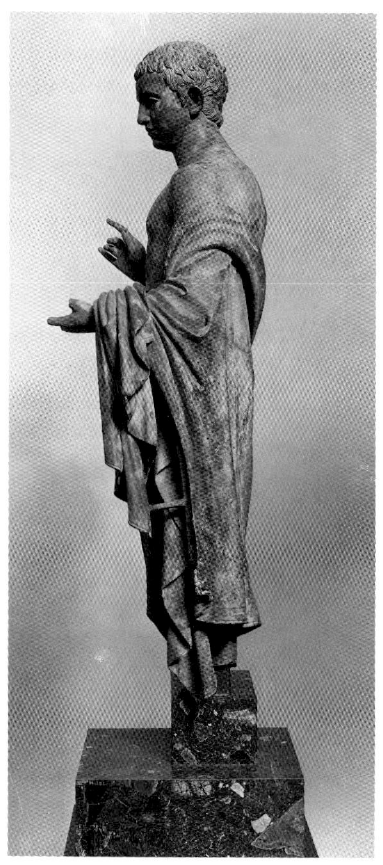

Fig. 32. Roman, Augustan Period; *Statue of a Youth*; 48½ in. high. The Metropolitan Museum of Art, Rogers Fund, 1914.

naturalism in late Romanesque art, are proportioned normally and appear relatively "realistic." The huge ensemble, accompanied by inscriptions, illustrates a Christ in judgment, surrounded by stars and clouds, presiding over heaven and hell. With one hand, Jesus welcomes the saved to paradise, while by a sign of his other hand, he condemns the damned to hell. Manship's *Dancer and Gazelles* similarly distinguishes between the animal on the left, whose prancing is calmed by the woman's gesture, and the animal on the right, whom she faces and who attends to her uplifted arm and visage. To the attentive animal, the dancer offers encouragement; the other overeager gazelle is cautioned. Two natures are accounted, the energetic and impulsive and the carefully stable. (The gazelles' bounding energy had its precedent in Manship's own *Pronghorn Antelope*, whose animated curving outline expressed pain and startled bewilderment.)

The rhythmic outer line of *Dancer and Gazelles* was not so much borrowed from Indian paintings, like *Todi Ragini*, as absorbed. Manship incorporated such paraphrases into his art as the highest form of salute to cultures and artists. He fashioned the flaring hem from more than one cultural source. The stolelike draping of the *Dancer*'s garment recalls a classical toga, and we find the swallowtail folds in antique statuary (fig. 32) as well as in oriental art. The inner back-and-forth movement of the *Dancer*'s stole also contributes a minor, but immensely pleasing, cadence to the sculpture, a detail spectators favorably noted.

Almost two-thirds of the 150 pieces in Manship's 1916 solo exhibition at the Berlin Photographic Gallery in New York were sold. *Dancer and Gazelles* was the star of the show, distinguished by a breathtaking refinement of design that contrasted mass and linear ornament in a wholly novel manner which captured his audience. Clearly, Manship had shrugged off Rodin's titanic presence in early twentieth-century art. In Manship's magnificently finished craftsmanship, early spectators savored an alternative to the expressive, if unsystematic sculpture of Rodin. Rodin's art represented the gigantic outpouring of an enormous personality at a time when art searched for a conceptual foundation for its further progress. Rodin's unpredictable sculpture offered not only heroic possibilities but also the liability of bathos, which is evident in his lesser works.

Cubism was the most obvious response to modern art's search for a rigorous method to replace the often haphazard expressiveness of the late nineteenth century. Some artists (who were later to become prominent Cubists) sought their own way out of the dilemma, even as Manship was moving from late nineteenth-century standards. For example, in his 1911–12 bronze *Femmes et Gazelles* (fig. 33), Jacques Lipchitz essayed the possibilities of stripped-down forms in a multifigure composition. His solution, the radical simplification of the figure, was so eloquent and so obviously "right" (although less directly the forerunner of his great cubist pieces) that *Femmes et Gazelles* undoubtedly served as a precedent for *Dancer and Gazelles*, although Manship discounted it as an influence.

Manship fulfilled the expectations of his early supporters and established a standard of technical proficiency to which American sculpture of a certain quarter would thereafter strive. Manship's beautiful execution—his conscious pursuit of beauty in both the naturalistic appearance of his work and the abstract relationships—revealed a new path for sculpture, another alternative for modern art, remote from Rodin's instruction. Manship became a legitimate, if unexpected, heir to nineteenth-century romantic exoticism as he rallied diverse sources from antiquity and the Orient; he convened the disparate

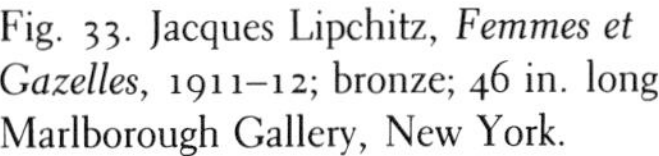

Fig. 33. Jacques Lipchitz, *Femmes et Gazelles*, 1911–12; bronze; 46 in. long. Marlborough Gallery, New York.

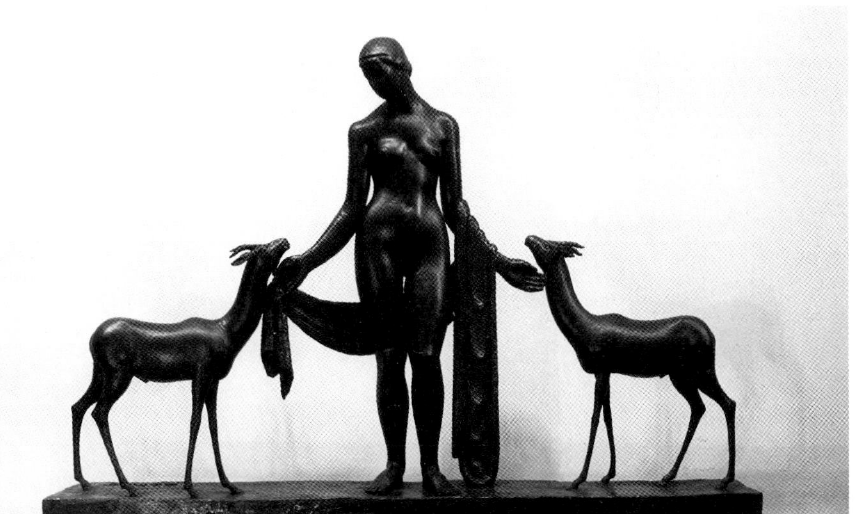

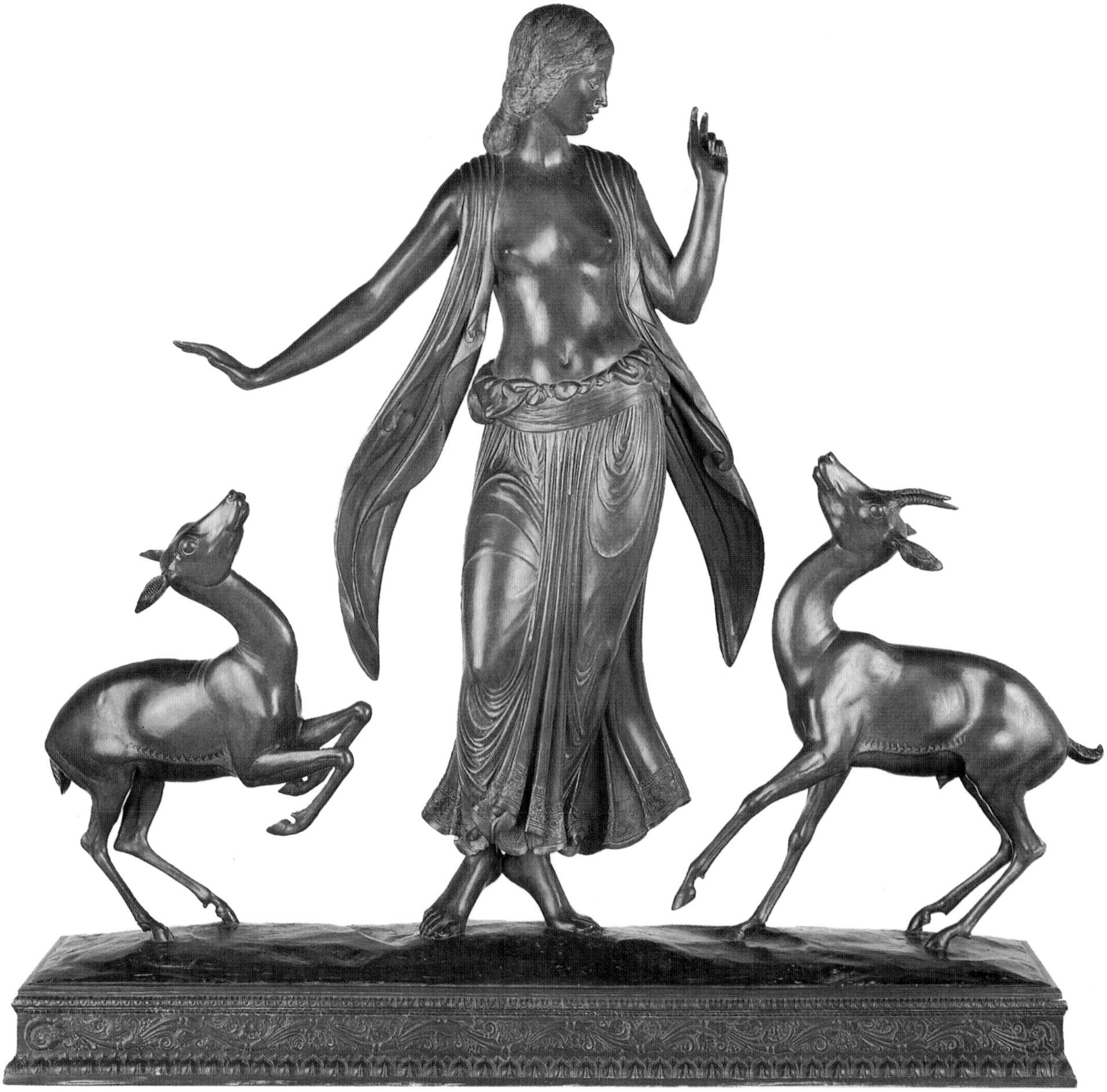

Fig. 34. *Dancer and Gazelles*, 1916; bronze; 32½ in. high.

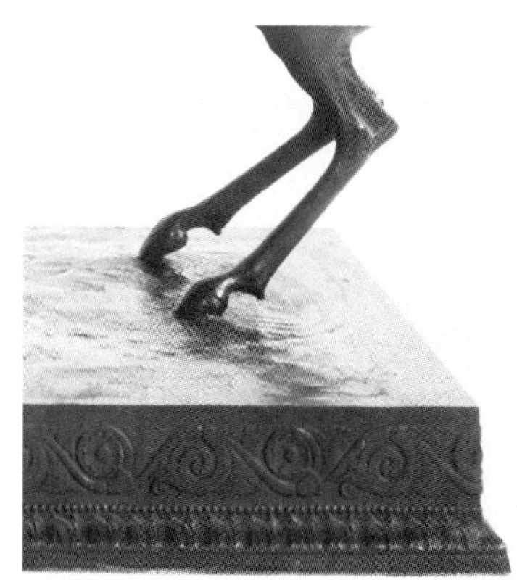

Fig. 35. Detail, *Dancer and Gazelles*, 1916; bronze. The Corcoran Gallery of Art, Washington, D.C., Museum purchase, 1920.

elegance of past formal achievements in a meeting of styles that was never debased into a medley. Instead, at his best, he succeeded in merging his sources into a new amalgam with a recognizable personality and style. His detractors have found the seeds of kitsch in his art's inherited assumptions—order, beauty, craft, lack of spontaneity—but regardless of how his audience and his critics received his work, Manship treated his sources with the highest respect and the collegial affection of one craftsman reaching out across the ages in sympathy with other craftsmen.

Manship passed on to his own assistants a cluster of beliefs, notions he formed from his decisive Roman experience, from his own successes, and as a student of the previous generation's major sculptors. Impressed with Reuben Nakian's red chalk drawings, Manship hired the fledgling sculptor. Nakian, who had studied with Robert Henri and Homer Boss, had tried unsuccessfully to be admitted to the studios of many accomplished artists. Nakian worked with Manship and his principal assistant, Lachaise, learning the techniques of stone cutting, plaster casting, and the patination of bronze. Nakian also learned the interactive role of the sculptor as a collaborator with architects, planners, and clients who offered commissions. In Manship's employ, Nakian became a fast friend of Lachaise's, but he also absorbed a great deal of Manship's salutary attitudes about formal clarity, or at least those consistent with Nakian's own developing modernism.

Manship's original sixty-seven-inch version of *Dancer and Gazelles* exists in two life-size bronze copies (the Corcoran Gallery, Washington, D.C., and the Toledo Museum, Ohio); also in 1916, Manship cast a dozen reductions that were immediately sold—one to the French government. In the smaller version (fig. 34) the gazelle at the right sports a set of horns. Refinements of gesture, silhouette, and ornament render this reduction a superior work. The rinceau motif on the reduction's base is softer (fig. 35), losing all trace of mechanical hardness, while the silhouette of the plinth became less geometrized, its upper edge curling softly in a manner recalling South Indian architecture. Manship apparently planned for another, even smaller, version to be released, but this venture exists only in an eighteen-inch-tall plaster. In 1917 the *Dancer and Gazelles* won the National Academy's Helen Foster Barnett Prize for the best work by a sculptor under thirty-five, the same award he had won four years earlier for *Centaur and Dryad*. While many critical observers associated this sculpture with the art of India, which to our eyes seems altogether reasonable, at the time Indian art and the gigantic achievements of Hindu and Greco-Indian Buddhist sculpture were barely known in America.[13]

In 1917 Ananda K. Coomaraswamy became curator of America's first museum department of Indian art, at the Museum of Fine Arts in Boston. His enormously learned and magnetic presence, acute acquisitions, and eloquent writing had already greatly enhanced the study of Indian art in this country and brought that work to general attention. His presence is witnessed in pieces such as *Dancer and Gazelles*. Manship's sympathy for Indian sculpture advanced the taste of his countrymen and his own artistic enterprise.

Manship recognized 1916 as the year of his artistic maturity. His experiments with Indian art led him to emphasize balletic movement in space and to sharply silhouette his subjects to heighten a clearly defined outline; confined areas of decoration animate the sculptures' surfaces. Some critics admired suggestions of the same surface quality that distinguishes early Chinese bronzes; others noted the treatment of hair and the orderly arrangements of drapery indicative of the archaic Greek. Manship seemed to express modern ideas in terms of the primitive.

By the autumn of 1916 critics noted, perhaps for the first time, a dominant theme of Manship's career: he was able to reconcile the warring antipodes of modern art. From the beginning, Manship's first exhibition of sculpture in New York "created a veritable sensation. The extreme modernists and the academicians united in paying a tribute to his genius: his success was complete."[14] Sheer technical mastery confuted academics, who were pleased to discover a revivified version of their beloved ancients. At the same time, contemporaries recognized that Manship's work negotiated the treacherous passage between romanticism and an astringent modernism. The obvious simplicity of Manship's forms—their clarity and direct address—indisputably appealed to, and was an expression of, the modern spirit. His critics were silenced by his overwhelming learning and the force of his work, while the young man's sculpture satisfied reactionaries waiting for a return to old values.

EARLY REVIEWS

In June 1917 Gaston Lachaise, who was still working as Manship's assistant, was married in a civil ceremony; the Manships hosted the wedding supper. Social endorsement had its artistic counterpart, and the next few years mark the closest convergence of Manship's and Lachaise's ideas. Manship borrowed liberally from his assistant and Lachaise, while not generally considered his disciple, was decisively affected by Manship's massing of forms. What ultimately separated them as artists was the Gallic passion that propelled Lachaise to ever greater expressionist distortions of the figure. Manship strove for a broadly inclusive blending, and he was quite satisfied by sedate eloquence.

Whatever suppositions Manship had for his own art, his sculpture appeared to mirror prevalent, which is to say fashionable, taste, and his knowledgeable recycling of antiquity did not convince all viewers that he was more than a master craftsman. Still, official approbation continued to descend upon him. The central characteristic of his art had already been noted by 1916: "It is an unusual thing for an artist to be claimed by opposing camps and hailed as one by each of them. Paul Manship, whose sculptures have been an artistic sensation of the winter in New York, has had this strange experience." Those of modernist sympathies took pleasure in the simplicity of his forms; academics thought him one of their number and proudly singled out his superb technique. A contemporary noted that considering "ninety of his works were sold from his exhibition, [with] private buyers and public galleries competing for possession . . . he stands outside the easy and formal classifications."[15] Manship's work was adopted by distinct factions as an expression of their best hopes.

There was a rising tide of enthusiasm for Manship's graceful work; however, criticism of his self-imposed restraint was beginning to surface. As early as 1916, grumbling was heard amid the general acclaim. Manship's rather limited expressive range was found objectionable: "Mr. Manship, like Sorolla, is a capable, an extremely capable, and even a sincere craftsman. But that is the most that may be said safely of either of them and I am afraid that it is not much. Art requires more than craftsmanship . . . it requires a soul." The synthesis Manship wrought, which most viewers thought was a triumph of orchestration, had its objectors. Necessarily, Manship's recitation of sculpture's historical possibilities precluded other kinds of expression. He was accused of being "without emotional power" and having to "build form solely through intellectual processes"; the same critic believed that since "his intellectual processes are interrupted by emotional vagaries, at their greatest height, always inexplicable, he arrives at the coldest, the most detestable of virtues in art, perfection—if, indeed, perfection may be called a virtue."[16] In the midst of discussing Lachaise, e.e. cummings entered the fray with a witty, if stinging, critique of Manship:

> Paul Manship—a "sound" man, of course, but no slave to the Rodin tradition, nor the Saint Gaudens tradition, nor whatever [Bela Pratt] may have produced those fattish girls helplessly seated on either hand as you enter the Boston Public Library. . . . In his sculpture [Manship] is always chez les americains, besides having in everything a bon truc, a certain cleverness, a something "fakey." One wonders whether his winning the Prix de Rome accounts for the fact that in the last analysis Manship is neither a sincere alternative to thinking, nor an appeal to the pure intelligence, but a very ingenious titillation of that well-known element, the highly sophisticated unintelligence. At any rate, he was formerly popular, just as Nadelman. . . is at present supremely popular. . . . His work is, of course, superior to the masterpeices of such people as French, Barnard, Bartlett, the Borglums, and Bela Pratt—in so far as something which is thoroughly dead is superior to something which has never been alive.[17]

Manship's youthful stamina was undimmed by rejection, and his market was insatiable. His output for 1917 was prolific. It was in the midst of this rocketing career and the promise of a continuous stream of works eagerly received that global politics injected itself. Manship's patriotism was aroused, and in the fall of 1918 he served in World War I as a Red Cross volunteer in Italy. Luck always with him, he returned unharmed. To commemorate the

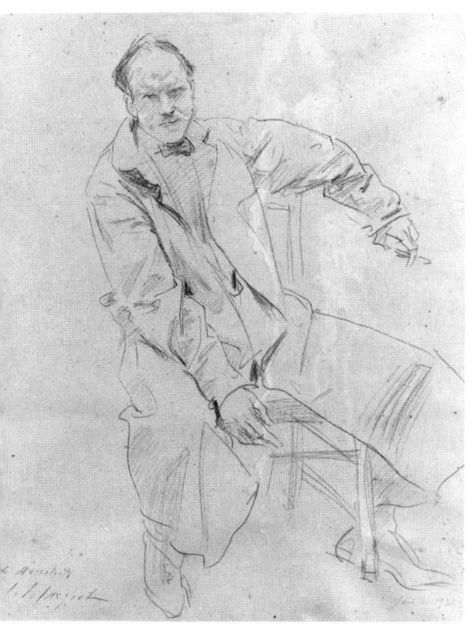

Fig. 36. John Singer Sargent, *Paul Manship*, 1921; pencil on brown paper; $21\frac{1}{4}$ x $16\frac{7}{16}$ in. The Metropolitan Museum of Art, Bequest of Paul H. Manship, 1966.

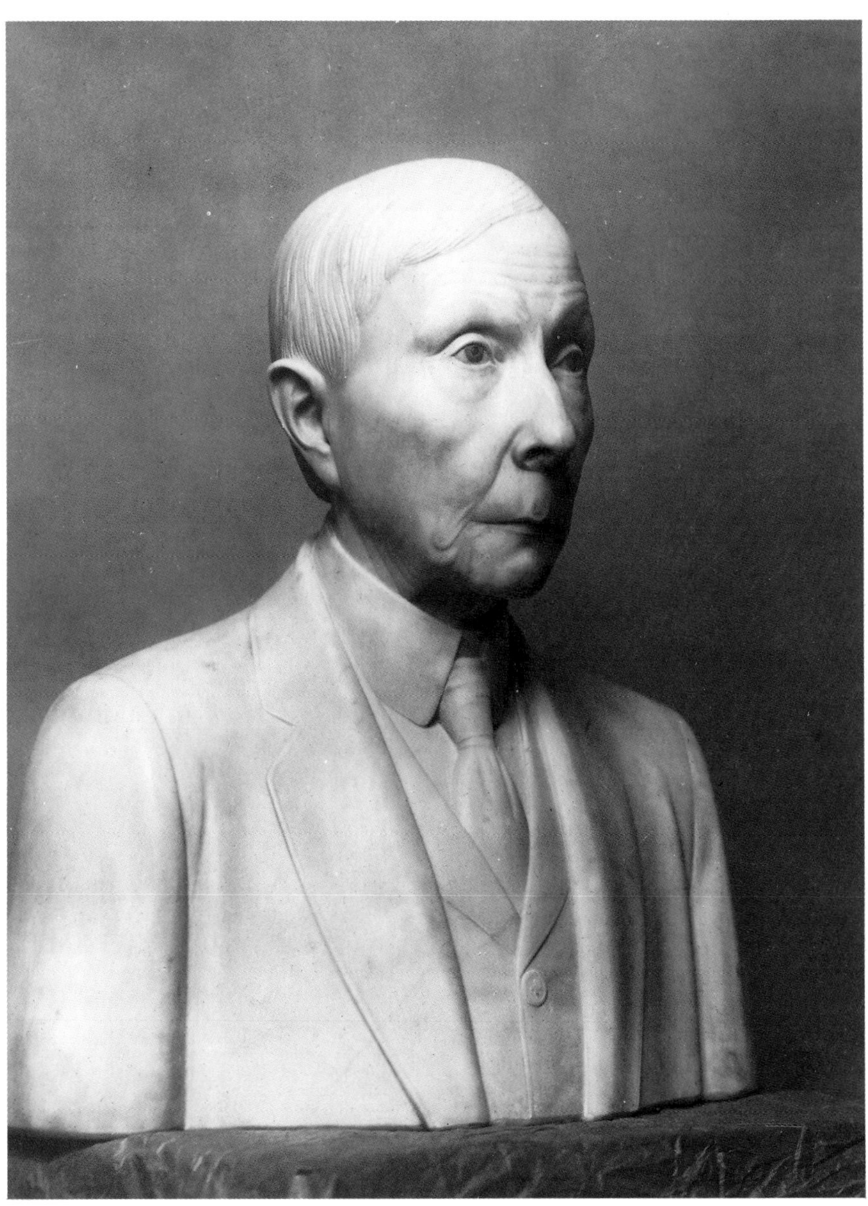

Fig. 37. *John D. Rockefeller*, 1918; marble bust with tinted eyes; 21½ in. high. Rockefeller Archive Center, North Tarrytown, New York.

war, Manship produced a souvenir bronze *Victory Pin* honoring the Allied triumph; it was sold for one dollar and all proceeds went to the Art War Relief. Patriotism and moral indignation moved the sculptor to issue a work for mass production and mass circulation as a fund raiser. Meanwhile, Manship continued to secure the most august private patrons.

In 1918 John Singer Sargent obtained a commission for Manship from John D. Rockefeller, and the result was a highly realistic portrait bust. Manship and Sargent were close friends (fig. 36). When Manship came to London in the 1920s, he stayed with Sargent, who helped procure eminent portrait commissions. Later, the Manship family moved to Paris, where two of their

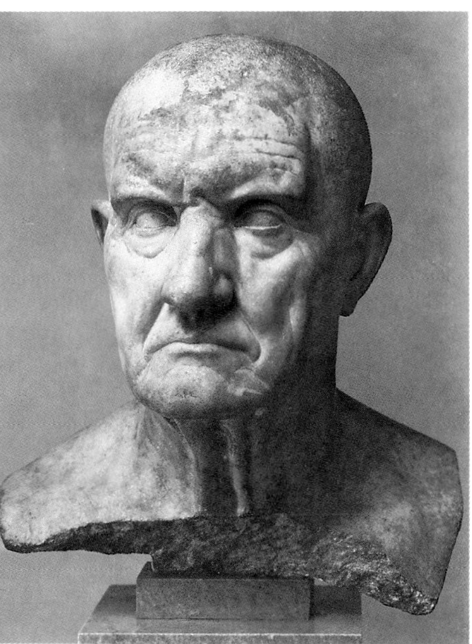

Fig. 38. Roman, ca. 100 B.C.; *Bust of a Roman*; marble; 14⅜ in. high. The Metropolitan Museum of Art, Rogers Fund, 1912.

four children were born—their only son, John, was named for Sargent—and where they stayed until 1937, when the impending war convinced them to abandon their home.

Manship's early preference for portraiture, expressed in Grafly's classes at the Pennsylvania Academy, bodied forth in the *John D. Rockefeller* bust (fig. 37), a celebrated work of the period. The world had come to admire Manship's decorative pieces, and in returning to portraiture to render so famous a subject, Manship put his reputation for competence at risk. Rockefeller's countenance was so widely known that success or failure could have been judged even by those unacquainted with the art of sculpture. Even Manship's most ardent admirers must have wondered if he could forsake the style that had made him famous, but Manship took on the challenge and won handily. When one reporter asked Manship if he would treat a portrait as he had his other works' details; he replied, "Why not?" Manship aimed to master not only decorative sculpture but every realm of the art. A reviewer of the *Rockefeller* bust declared, "The sculptor has now proved himself to be one of the very greatest portrait artists of all time. We declare this without fear of contradiction." Manship's cataloguer, his son-in-law Edwin Murtha, noted that, "Few saw it simply as a sculpture: for some it was sinister and forbidding; for others it had a religious expression."[18]

Owing to Lachaise's technical experience and training, Manship gave him the task of transferring the portrait's surface qualities of skin texture and hair to the finished stone. In friendly collaboration, Lachaise's contribution to the piece helped produce a work that neither he nor Manship could have sculpted by themselves. It was widely agreed that the bust was a masterpiece, although some critics regarded it more as a social document than a work of art. The *John D. Rockefeller* portrait marble showed once again how Manship had studied the ancients to good effect and how his knowledge had "enabled him to confront a purely modern problem with such authority of style and such technical mastery. . . . Whatever point of view we choose the line seems more interesting, the workmanship purer, the planes more surely and delicately defined, the psychology more penetrating. It is a great sculpture, as cruel as science and as pathetic as life."[19]

The immense sense of world-weariness that struck so many viewers was prompted by the hard, uncompromising vision of Rockefeller. In his treatment of the surface, capturing every line and fold of the skin, however unflattering, Manship strove to emulate the rigor of Roman republican portraits (fig. 38). The "objectivity" so typical of American colonial art (and American art thereafter) recalled its Roman forebears and confirmed the idea that to truly learn about America one ought to look at Rome. The ideal of the self-made man, the love of engineering, the republican virtues—all are shared in and expressed by Manship's conception. Even Rockefeller's marble eyes were tinted, emulating the now lost polychromy of Roman models. The likeness of the eighty-six-year-old struck most viewers by its breathtaking honesty, the vision of

> a most realistic portrait of an old man, a very old man. We have never before seen such a convincing picture of senility as this portrait of the Oil King. . . . The artist has departed from present day practise and like the ancients, he has tinted the iris of the eye blue, like that of the subject. Truly this portrait of Rockefeller is the most realistic likeness of modern times. No other American sculptor has dared to create such a work.[20]

Even as his first resoundingly successful decade as an artist was ending, dark, critical clouds began to gather; aggressively antipathetic voices began to be heard. To some, his archaistic conventions seemed mere adaptations of antique originals, and it was feared that the young man was already assuming mannerisms. No one knew if he possessed the patience and seriousness necessary to make a great artist. In 1919 the situation was summarized by Manship's friend, the critic Martin Birnbaum:

> From the very start he invariably produced something original, and when he returned to America with his early works . . . they were indiscriminately enjoyed and created an exhilarating sensation. . . . After the first flush of pleasure was over, however, his enthusiastic admirers became more sober, seized upon obvious debt to primitive sculpture, and the critical pendulum began to swing in the opposite direction. They began to have doubts about this remarkable facility and versatility.[21]

On the occasion of an exhibition of Manship's sculpture held in the summer of 1921 at the Leicester Galleries in London, A. E. Gallatin awarded Manship a favorable decision, citing august company in his remarks:

> His mind has acted as a crucible, and he is an excellent example of Sir Joshua [Reynold]'s dictum that the more familiar an artist be "with the works of those who have excelled, the more extensive will be your power of invention." . . . The creations of Manship showing this influence possess a spark of life and a vigour that one never finds in the lifeless and frigid imitations of Greek sculpture which were produced by Canova, Thorvaldsen and Flaxman. In these works, as in others, Manship's treatment of the hair is distinctly archaic, but at the same time it is peculiarly his own.[22]

Especially Manship's English critics admired his indebtedness to the Greeks—both the archaic and high classical—and the unimpeded facility with which he recalled these styles. The ease and charm with which Manship employed classical art did not repel the English; rather, they felt he was creating original sculpture with a rich lineage. The lack of spontaneity in Manship's sculpture was considered a positive virtue. In appropriately evolved forms premeditation and an obvious reliance on sources conferred a balance and timelessness that embodied truth's perdurable vivacity.

In a slowly growing litany, the American critics began to diverge from their European counterparts' evaluation. Amid continual praise in Europe of

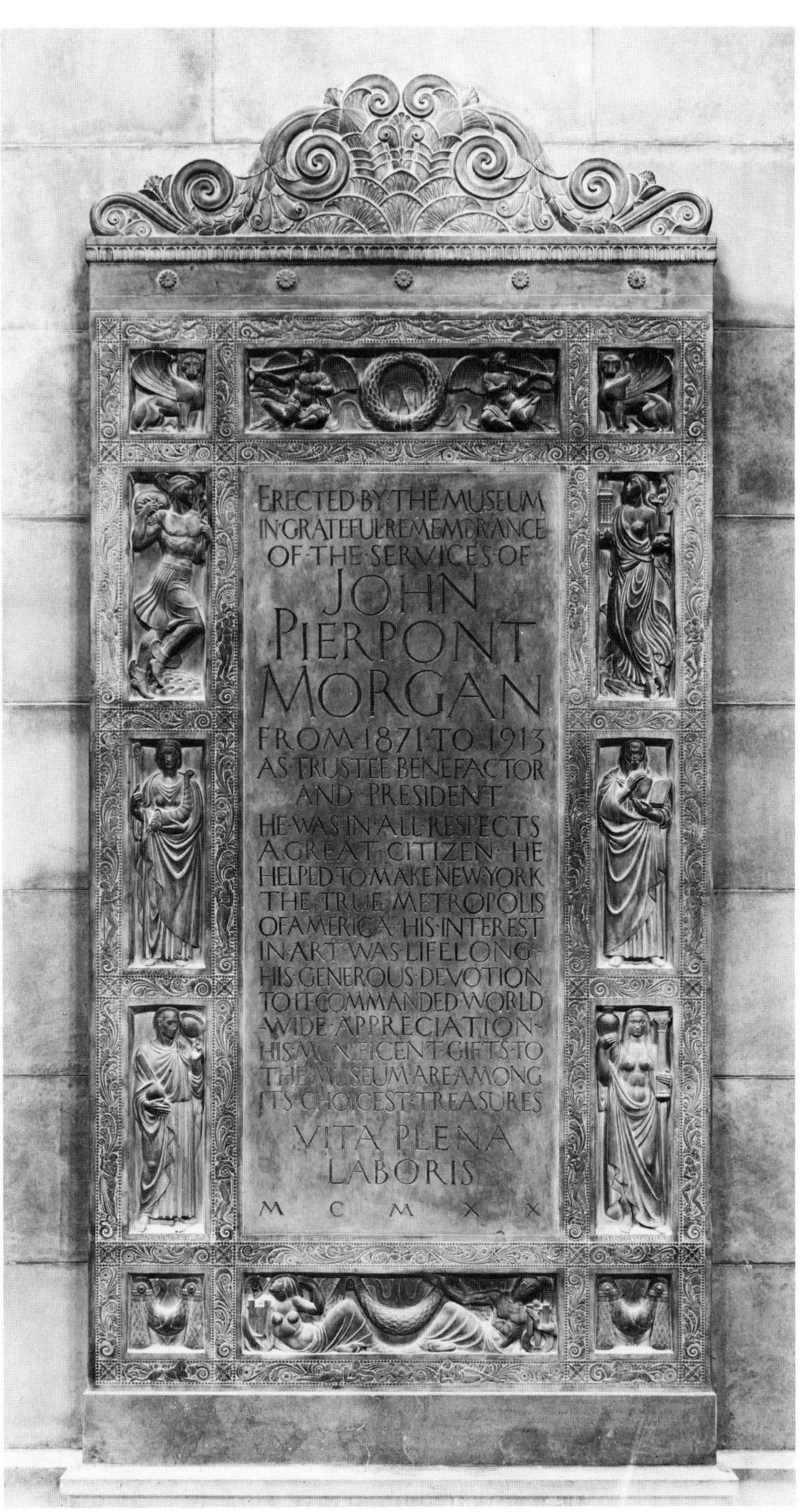

Fig. 39. *John Pierpont Morgan Memorial*, 1915–20; carved limestone tablet; 134 x 64 x 6½ in. The Metropolitan Museum of Art.

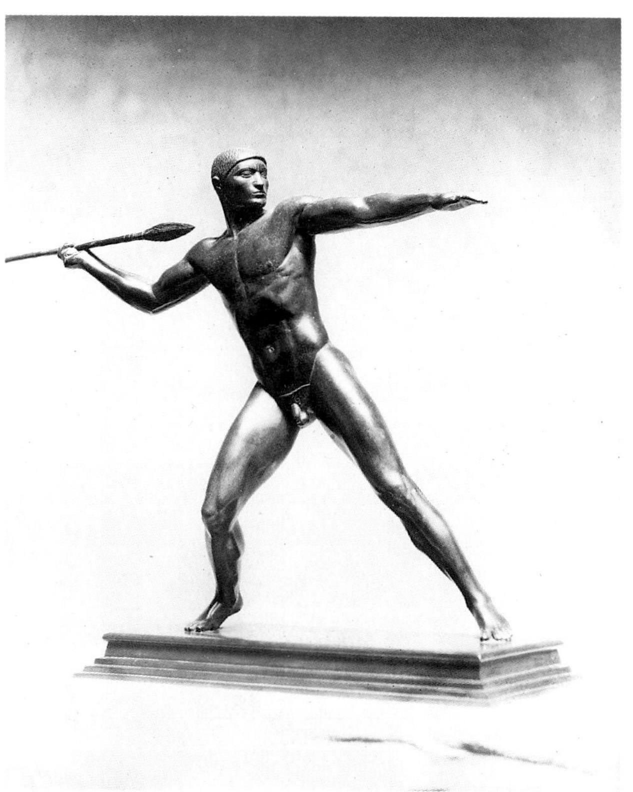

Fig. 40. Photo of *Spear Thrower* (cast 1921; bronze; 18 in. high).

Manship's restraint and tastefulness, American critics believed he was coyly avoiding root human nature as the origin of art. Manship may have been somewhat mystified by such remarks, as he sought neither to circumvent emotion nor to shock. His own aims were far narrower, more concerned with form than feeling. A. E. Gallatin stated it bluntly: "One would like to see more passion expressed in Mr. Manship's work and more emphasis upon sex."[23]

In 1914 Manship was commissioned by the Metropolitan Museum of Art to sculpt a tablet in memory of John Pierpont Morgan (fig 39); he spent six and a half years on its execution. The stone plaque was erected against the northwest pier (which supports the central dome of the main Fifth Avenue hall) of the museum, to which Morgan had been a major benefactor. Gaston Lachaise and an Italian stonecarver did most of the carving on the memorial. Despite Manship's repeated invitations to sign the work with him, Lachaise steadfastly refused to promote himself as Manship's collaborator—which would have certainly added luster to the unknown sculptor's reputation. Until 1920, when Manship closed his New York studio to live in Europe, Lachaise and Nakian continued as his assistants; thereafter, they both shared a studio until 1923.

After the Rockefeller portrait, Manship's admiration for Mediterranean antiquity took an unexpected turn when he began to consider the less

Fig. 41. Greek, ca. 460 B.C.; *Poseidon* (or *Zeus*); bronze; 82 in. high. National Archaeological Museum, Athens.

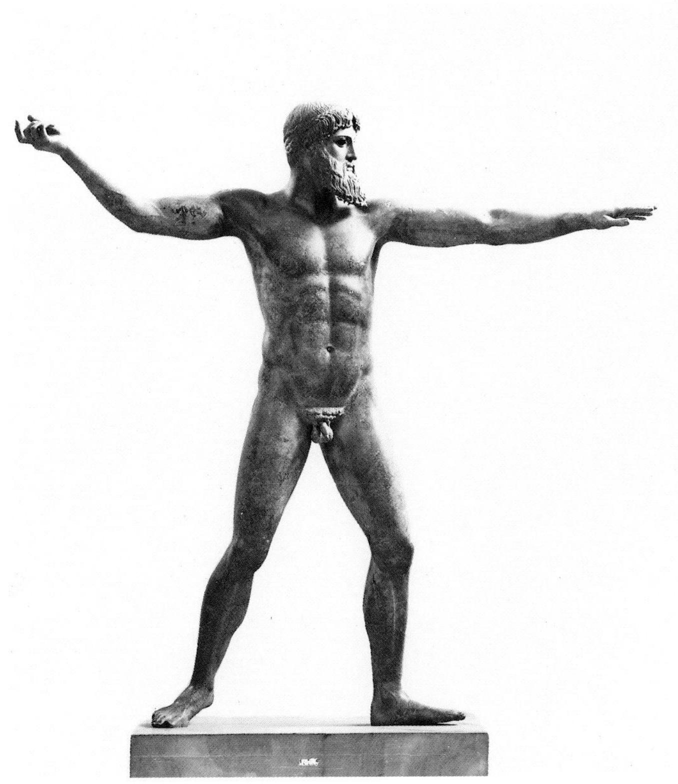

ornamented, more severe forms of classical sculpture. His work lost some of the balance between fine detail and overall formal conception and began to seem "stripped down." The first of his works to hint at this development was the *Spear Thrower* of 1921 (fig. 40), which is closely based on antique examples of Greek athletic figures typical of sculpture from the middle fifth century B.C.

The lean cylindrical rendition of a god was a familiar icon of the classical world. The most famous of these works—which were executed in every size from votive miniatures to large public statues—is actually an early classic figure, not an archaic work of the kind Manship was usually so fond. *Poseidon* (sometimes thought to be *Zeus*) is a magnificent life-size bronze circa 460 B.C. that now resides in the Athens National Museum (fig. 41). One of the best-known images from the past, it created a sensation in the late 1920s when off Cape Artemision, stunned fishermen unexpectedly caught it in their net. Presumably the bronze had once been part of a shipment of sculptures bound for an eastern port.

Poseidon is poised, body tensed in concentrated effort, with his right arm raised (to hurl the trident) in a traditional posture. (A thunderbolt would have identified the figure as Zeus.) Manship borrowed the striding pose wholesale; he tilted the figure's body back on the right leg, which added a note of naturalism but destroyed the godly power of the original. Manship's attempt to portray mortal strength (and thereby invigorate the past) diminished the majesty found in the original model.

In Manship's *Spear Thrower*, the figure's left hand extends straight out, reaching as far as the foot below it; this pose creates a vertical forward plane—an imaginary line about to be shattered by the spear thrust. The sculpture is finely proportioned to the standing figure, and carrying the athlete's weight slightly to the back of the work makes the base represent the very ground of the athletic field.

The *Poseidon*'s spare, easily legible forms and its enormous gesture counterpoise overall tubular shapes against detail (particularly in the hair and beard); this formula represented the ideals against which Manship measured his own best work. Producing a modern variation on this antique theme, Manship challenged his own heroes. His ideal remained unsurpassed. In the *Spear Thrower* we espy a stiffness that appeared when—prompted to grandiloquence by some personal program or public commission—Manship lost the isometry of form and ornament. But in some of his forays into the classical past, he *was* capable of balancing erudite references to mythology, lean forms that possessed clear tubular orientation in space, surface ornament, and gestural animation. One of his next works rebounded resiliently from the rickety *Spear Thrower*.

A fleet-footed virgin huntress, Atalanta decided she would only marry a man who could defeat her in a foot race, a contest in which she bested many suitors. Finally, when Meilanion (or Hippomenes) raced with her, he dropped three golden apples, one after another, which Atalanta stooped to pick up. This delay caused her to lose the race, and she was forced to take the winner as her husband. Little of the story survives in Manship's *Atalanta* (figs. 42, 43). Certainly none of the contest's urgency or its sexual tension is obvious in a nearly naked woman running unself-consciously. Formal lyricism triumphed over narrative in *Atalanta*—the story merely sanctioned the pose and flowing garments. Manship cared only for the obvious beauty of his model and the work's sculptural attractions. (We infer that Manship would have felt unseemly dwelling on the attractiveness of *her*—the actual model's—particular beauty.) His interest in the development and play of forms produced in this work the most daring exposition on the open circular composition until David Smith's *Circle* sculptures, forty years later.

After winning numerous awards in the United States and establishing his American reputation beyond serious challenge, Manship moved his family to Paris in 1921. He set up his studio in the building where the French decorative painter Jean Dupas worked. French sculptors such as Marcel Bouraine began

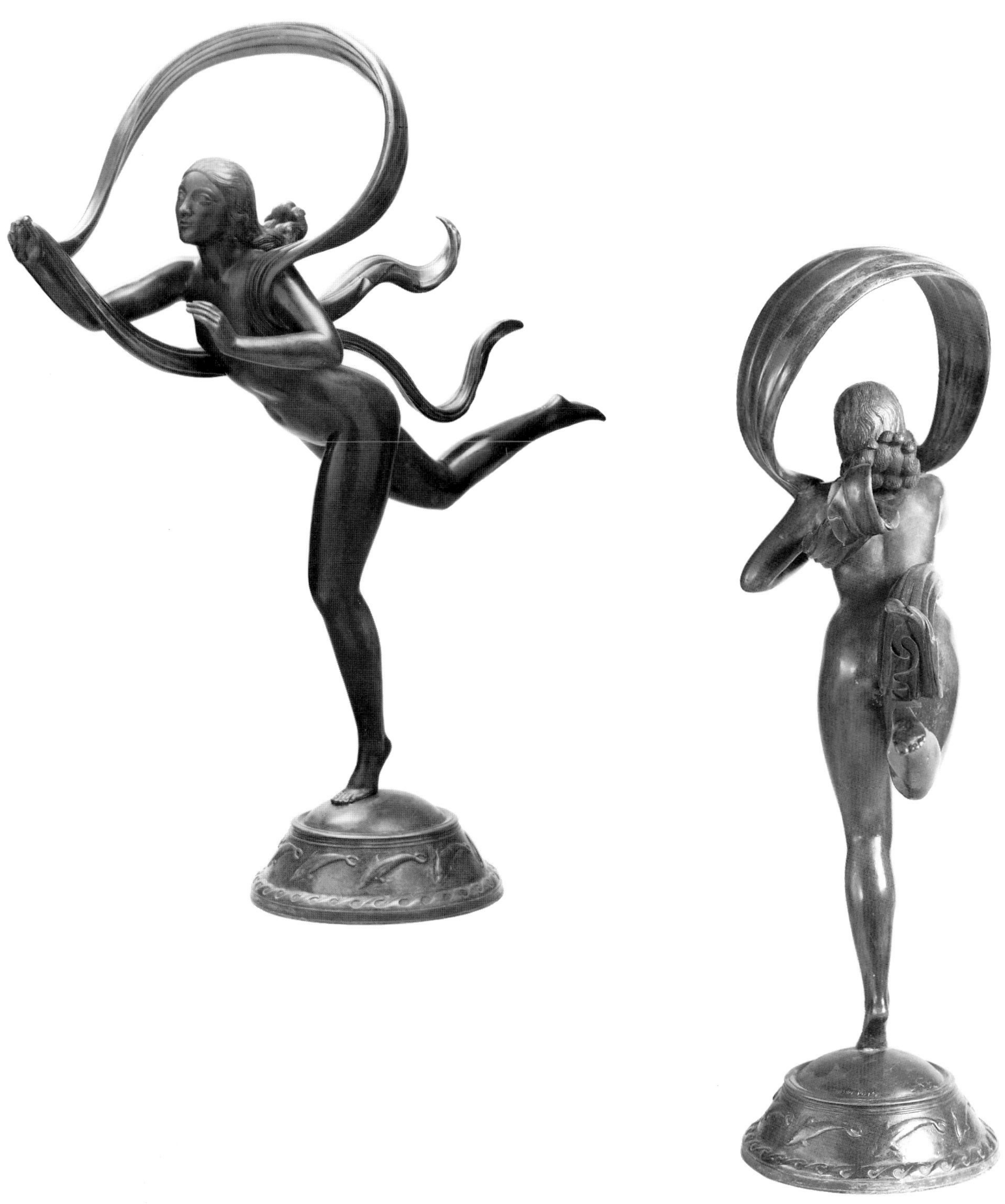

Figs. 42 and 43. *Atalanta*, 1921; bronze; 28$\frac{3}{4}$ in. high.

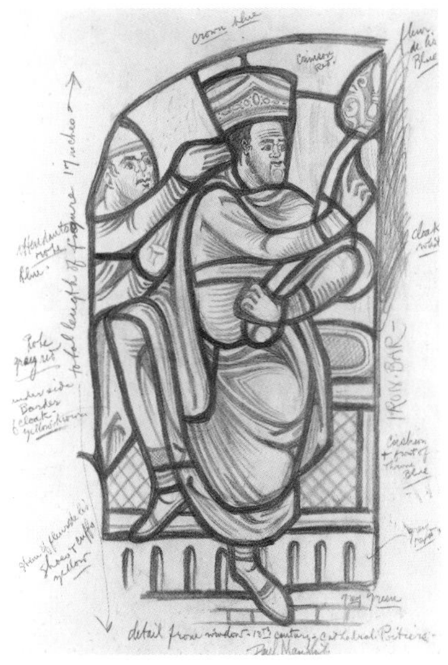

Fig. 44. *Detail from Stained Glass Window, Poitiers*, ca. 1922; pencil on paper; 14 x $9\frac{11}{16}$ in.

to think of Manship as worth emulating, and his influence was also apparent in the work of American sculptors of the 1920s and 1930s—especially Harriet W. Frishmuth. Undoubtedly, he made the acquaintance of other French artists, and he started to absorb something of Parisian decorative effects. A noticeable softening of his sculptural forms characterized Manship's Parisian works, unlike the Roman influence that refreshed his art with the firmness of the classical tradition.

Decidedly un-bohemian, Manship traveled in France in the 1920s. He closely observed the high arts in their historical setting, and he sought out masterpieces from which he could borrow. In addition, the best of the decorative arts surrounded him as part of the integrated design of a culture.

At the great cathedral of Poitiers he made careful drawings of stained glass, jotting down dimensions and colors, as well as the shape and placement of the functional iron supports (fig. 44). Uncharacteristic of a color-blind artist whose drawings and sculptures are almost entirely monochromatic, Manship made detailed notations of the colors in the window.

At the Romanesque Abbey church of Moissac, Manship sketched the famous figures on the trumeau (a central pillar supporting the tympanum or lintel) (figs. 45, 46). His sculptor's eye for detail ceaselessly at work, Manship recorded the particulars of the site, marveling at the dimensions his earlier colleague had been allowed: "figure over six feet tall" he inscribed with envy. Manship must have been especially attracted to the "plate folds" flatly layering the saint's

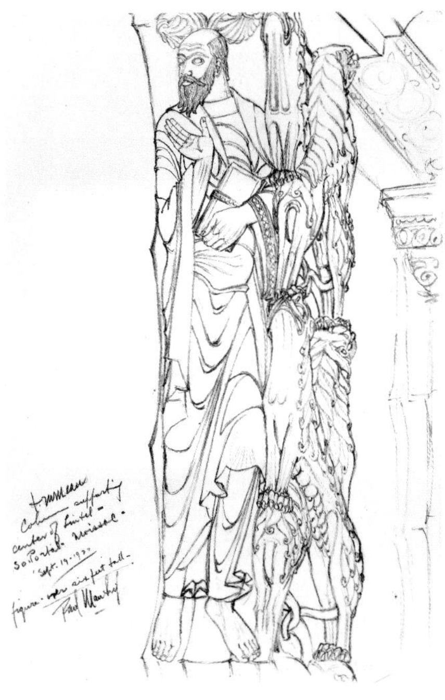

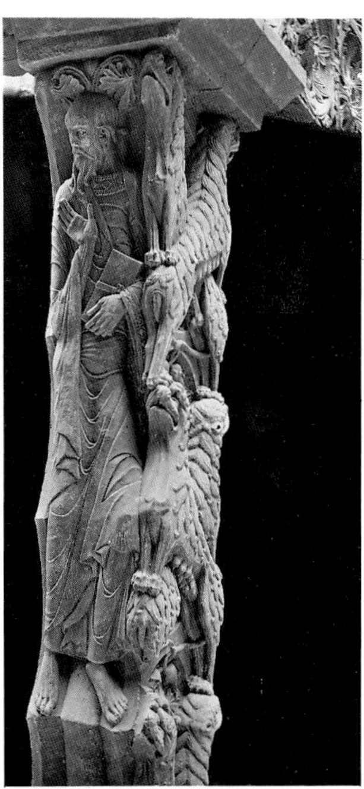

Fig. 45. *Saint Paul with Lions, Trumeau, Moissac*, 1922; pencil on paper; 14 x $9\frac{3}{8}$ in. Minnesota Museum of Art, St. Paul, Bequest of the Estate of Paul Howard Manship.

Fig. 46. Romanesque; South Portal Trumeau (detail). Church of St-Pierre, Moissac, France.

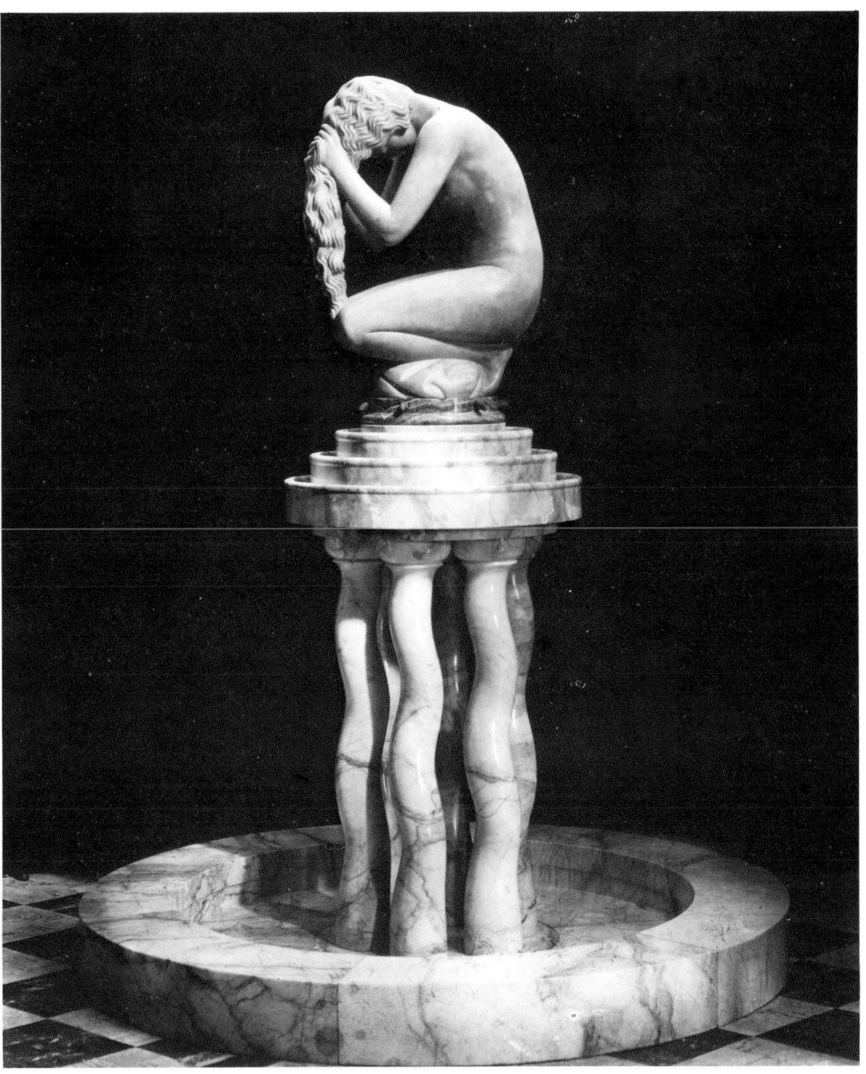

Fig. 47. *Venus Anadyomene Fountain*, 1924; marble. Phillips Academy, Andover, Massachusetts.

garments. He had frequently employed plate folds in his works, and in this drawing we can observe him studying his sources.

While in Paris, Manship participated in an important exhibition of American art presented by the Association Franco-Americaine. To Europeans, Manship was viewed not only as a quintessential American artist but also as one of our best. In addition to twenty sculptures by Manship, the exhibition featured sixty-three pieces by Dodge MacKnight, fifty watercolors by Winslow Homer, and seventy-five paintings by John Singer Sargent. In this exalted company Manship's works held their own. The French public was taken by his pieces' graceful lines and rhythmic movement.

In 1924 the Phillips Academy in Massachusetts commissioned Manship to create a fountain. For this work Manship carved a small statue of *Venus Anadyomene* from white Italian marble and a basin of veined marble (fig. 47).

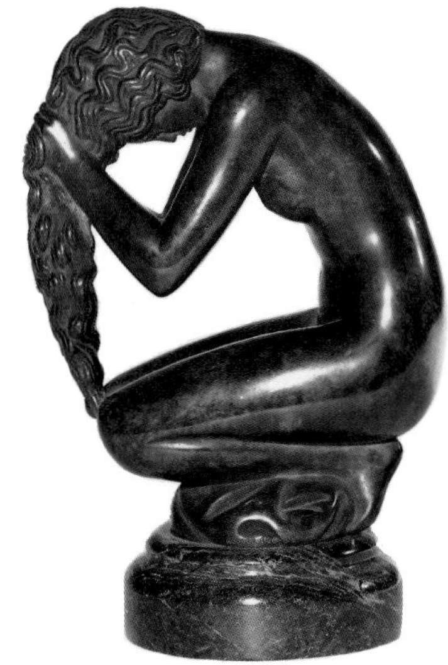

Fig. 48. *Venus Anadyomene (#1)*, 1924; bronze on marble base; 9 in. high.

The goddess of love, beauty, grace, and fertility in Roman religion, Venus was the daughter of either Jupiter and Dione or of Uranus, whose severed genitals mingled with the sea and produced Venus from the foam. Manship selected an exquisite instant in the myth of Venus; he depicted that first moment when, coming from the surf and washing the ocean from her hair, *Venus Anadyomene* (*anadyomene* is "born of water" in Greek) first touches land. The sculptor treated his subject with a rigor that belies its apparent grace.

The *Venus Anadyomene* fountain figure was mounted on spiral pillars surrounded by concentric basins. The goddess's body is a variation on the cylindrical curve, where Manship employed the form of a densely massed column to wonderful advantage. Essentially, the *Venus Anadyomene* is a pierced column that nowhere extends beyond the limits of a simple tube. Though he also cast a bronze version of *Venus Anadyomene* (fig. 48), he conceived the shape as an exercise in pure carving, as if he were whittling spaces from a solid cylinder. The sense of palpable volumes removed (and of polishing the remaining substance) took Manship from the additive mentality of a casting sculptor (who builds forms from clay) and brought him closer to the sensibilities of a carver than anything he had done.

The work's conception seems to have developed slowly and in a small pencil sketch (probably dating from the early 1920s), *Two Women, One Washes*

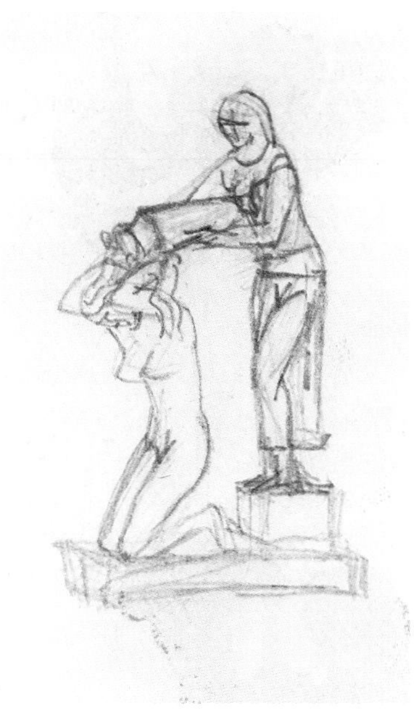

Fig. 49. *Two Women, One Washes the Other's Hair*, ca. 1922; pencil on paper; $2\frac{3}{4}$ x $1\frac{7}{8}$ in.

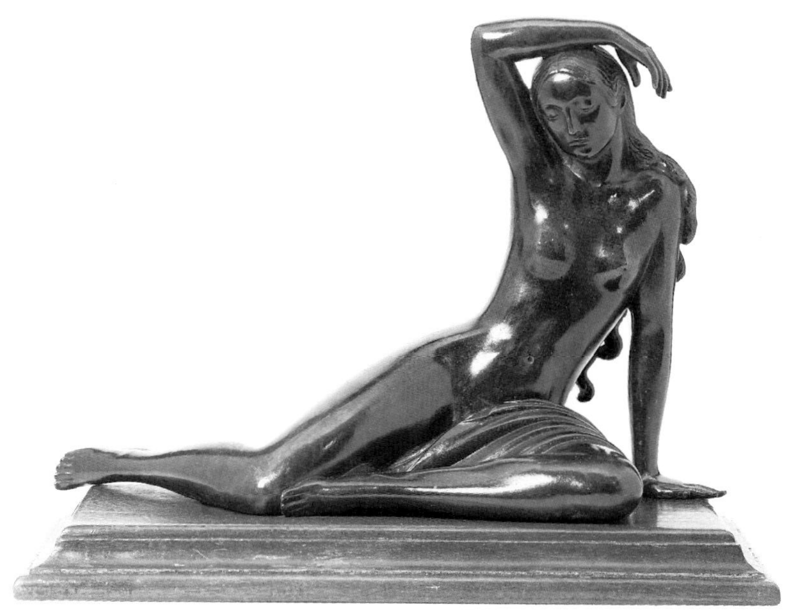

Fig. 50. *Danae*, 1921; bronze on wood base; $11\frac{1}{2}$ in. high.

the Other's Hair (fig. 49), we observe Manship deriving ideas from the common events of daily life. From such observations he rejuvenated ancient myths.

Manship's sculpture was not avant-garde; it did not engage in a critical reevaluation of the social order that supports artistic production. He wished to enhance the humanist tradition at its core. As time went on, such a position was misunderstood and often willfully misconstrued so as to back Manship into a corner. Not a polished rhetorician, he felt no need to retaliate when a newer generation of artists repudiated him.

Manship lavished attention on a small bronze figure, *Danae* (fig. 50)—evidenced in its attractively finished surface, a base carved especially for it (although he supplied different bases with different casts), and a rich, warm patina. Signed on the back of the drape "Paul Manship 1921," the *Danae* has long hair that tumbles behind her as she sits with both legs bent to the left. She transfers all the weight of her torso to the ground through the straight support of her left arm. She lifts her right elbow over her head, framing her face beneath her raised arm. With this gesture, Manship ornaments the uncomplicated, almost architectural, structure. Although Manship conceived *Danae* as a relief with a single strong viewpoint, such frontality had its detractors.[24]

Danae might best be considered a transitional piece. The National Museum of American Art's 1921 *Danae* is probably a variant or study for Europa's stance in Manship's *Europa and the Bull.* Manship recorded this pose in a series of sketches (fig. 51). In a beautiful back view, *Female Nude (Roxanne Berggren)* (fig. 52), Manship observed the model's placement of limbs—how legs bend outward, how shoulders react to carrying weight, and where the hips touch the ground as they tilt to accommodate the pose. He considered the figure from all sides, not just as a relief.

Manship recorded the body's volumes and gestures in a style very much wedded to his time. He made frequent broad passes with the pencil's edge and transcribed the masses as terse blocks, using a style also practiced by Rockwell Kent, George Bellows, and any number of artists on both sides of the Atlantic. A typical Manship trait, he left a thin line of white (the paper) uncolored around the figure; this halo sets off the figure from the background. Manship did not long maintain the figure's posture as part of his repertoire. Both the *Female Nude* sketch and the *Danae* statuette were apparently experiments toward a greater theme: *Europa and the Bull.*

Zeus, king of the gods, saw Europa, a princess of Phoenicia, playing with her maidens by the sea, and he fell in love with her. Zeus instructed Hermes to drive Europa's father's cattle to the seashore near where Europa was gathering flowers; there, Zeus took the form of a handsome white bull. At

Fig. 51. *Seated Female Nude*; pencil on paper; 6 x $5\frac{5}{8}$ in.

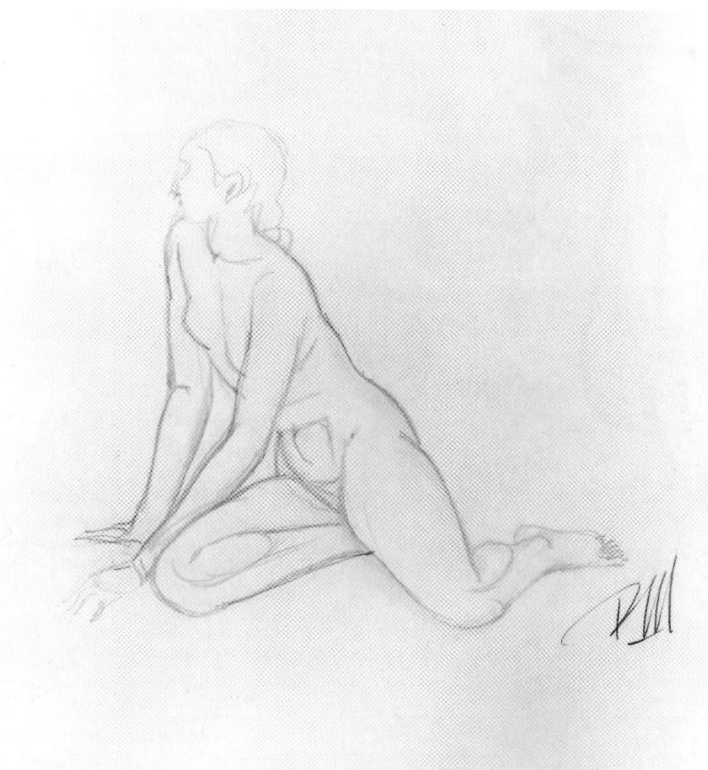

Fig. 52. *Female Nude (Roxanne Berggren)*; pencil on paper; $12\frac{1}{16}$ x $17\frac{15}{16}$ in.

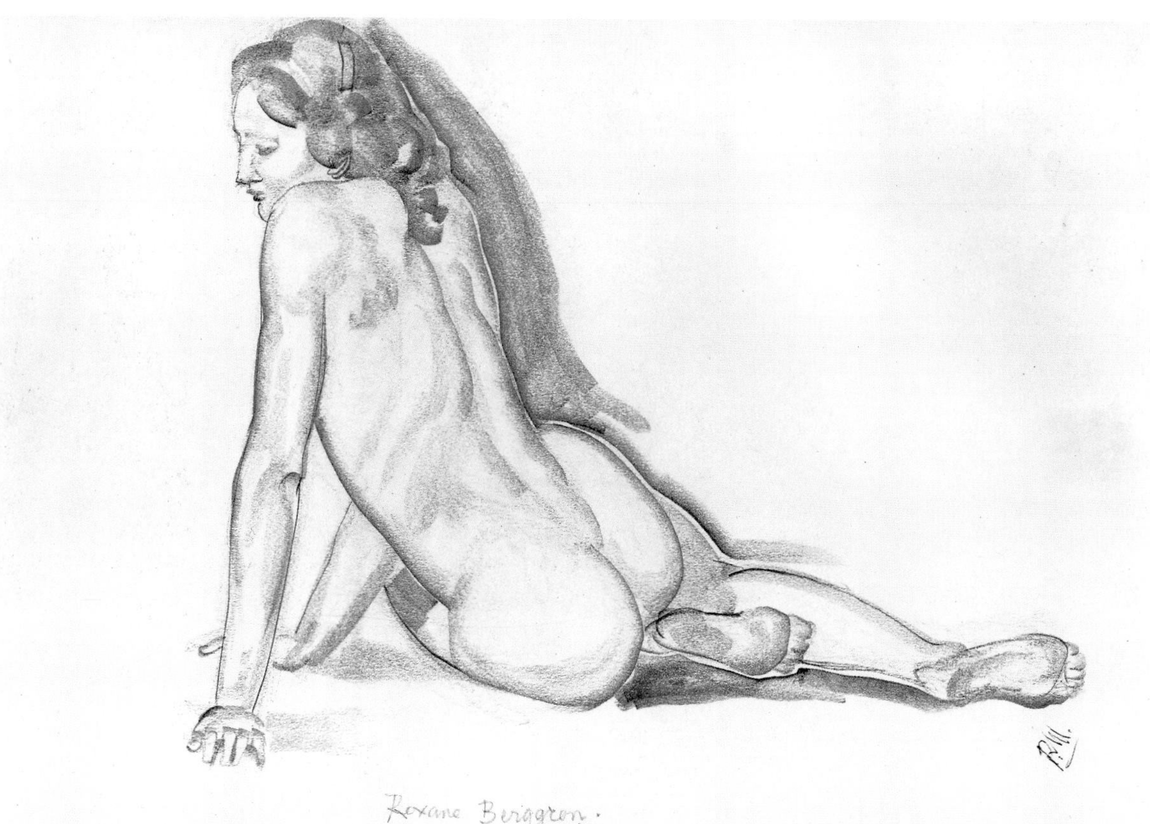

Roxane Berggren.
Ch3.9678.

first he frightened the girl, but soon she lost her fear and played with the great animal, garlanding his huge horns. When Europa climbed on the animal's back, Zeus slowly made his way into the surf and swam off. He carried Europa across the sea to Crete, where he shed his disguise and they made love. Europa bore Zeus three sons (Minos, Rhadamanthys, and Sarpedon) and in return he gave her three presents: an unerring spear, the inexorable hound Laelaps, and Talos, the bronze man who walked everyday around Crete and drove off strangers.

The reclining figure in *Europa and the Bull* (figs. 53, 54) tremendously improves on the *Danae*. The Europa figure is wrapped by the bull to form a tightly concentric composition, a more fully three-dimensional design than *Danae*'s linearity. *Europa and the Bull* imparts mass even more than volume; nowhere are its forms pierced to open an interior lightness. (Manship was recapitulating the interiorized conception of form that we first saw in the 1908 *Wrestlers* [see fig. 2].) The compacted composition based on the crouching bull has precedents in the great South Indian sculptures of Nandi, mount of the god Shiva (fig. 55). These figures of bulls rise, mountainlike, as opaque masses; in essence, their forms are shallowly tilted cones. Manship, expressing the contrast between the girl's limber figure and the hugeness of the bull, tucked the girl's legs beneath the animal so as to eliminate any spindly distractions.

Europa's weight passes backward into the mass of the animal. She no longer must place her hands flat on the ground to support herself (as in the *Female Nude*, drawn from life, or *Danae*), and the meaningless, though balletically pure, gesture of *Danae*'s right hand was replaced by *Europa*'s caress. In retrospect, it becomes clear that the upturned arm of the *Danae* must have been prepared to receive the bull's head. As the theme evolved, clear, if synthetic, meaning displaced vapid posturing.

Manship seems to have modeled this partly draped figure in 1922 as a bronze sketch in an unnumbered edition. By the next year the little figure was illustrated in *Vanity Fair*, captioned "The American Artist Sends Back His Work From Abroad" (which implied such statuettes were rakishly sophisticated and *continental*).[25] But the National Museum of American Art's example is inscribed in the cast, "To Marca with love from PM 1925," and other casts exist inscribed with other names, from which we can deduce that this sketch was kept in its working state and periodically cast by Manship as a souvenir for special friends. Indeed, the next version of the theme was far more formal (fig. 56). Cast in twenty copies and twice as large as the previous version, this work replaced the sketch's green patina in favor of a restrained but opulent brown. More important, the figure was radically formalized. Europa's girlish carelessness—legs wide and only partially covered—was clothed by regularly

Figs. 53 and 54. *Europa and the Bull* (#2), modeled 1922, cast 1925; bronze; $4\frac{3}{16}$ in. high; inscribed: "To Marca with love from PM 1925."

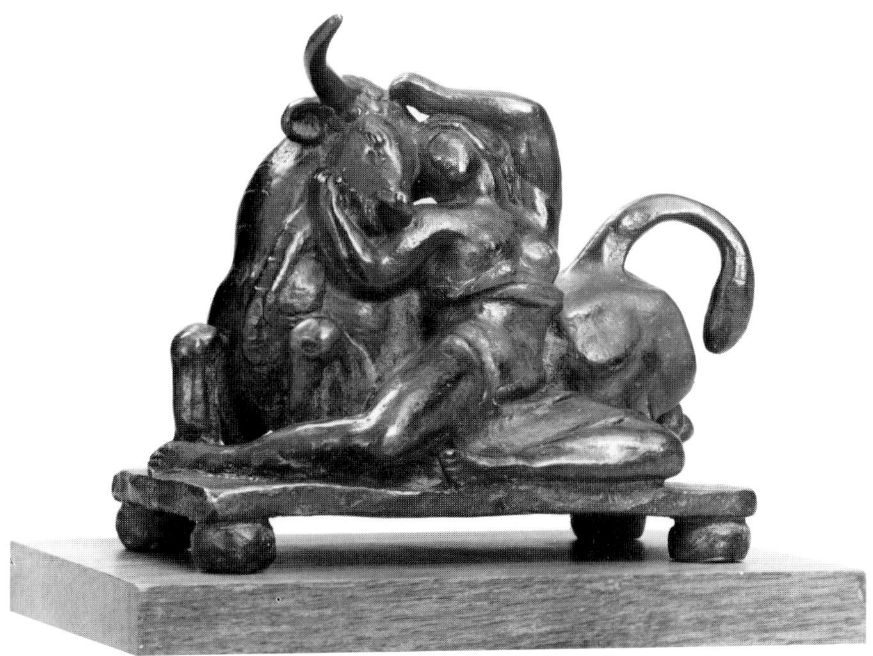

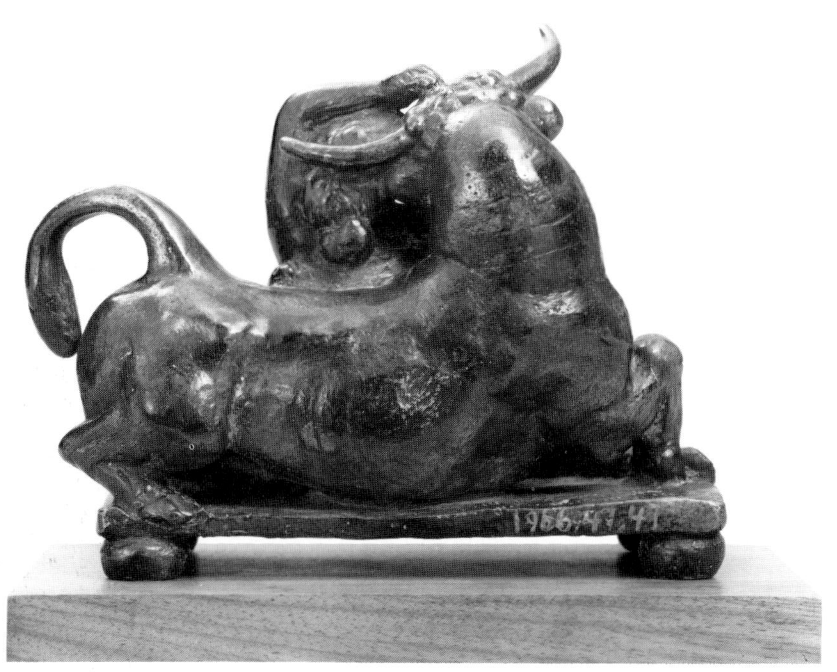

folded drapery. Geometrizing the theme, Manship closed the circle of the bull's raised tail; no longer an open gesture, the tail returns to the ensemble's mass. In the later version, Manship plugged the space between Europa's cheek and the bull with a passage of cascading hair that does not exploit the subject's frank erotic potential.

Presaging his late mythological miniatures, which are masterpieces of direct execution, the 1922 version was intended for limited circulation among his intimates. The more adjusted and refined 1924 statuette of *Europa and the Bull* introduced a wide public to Manship's magisterial command of sculpture's conceptual range.

As we have seen, Manship's use of the spiral was quite sophisticated. In *Lyric Muse* and other such works, the spiral extended into space as a spinning form within a column. Occasionally, Manship contracted the helix, concealing it as a component of his work. The compressed spiral lies at the heart of *Europa and the Bull* (a theme on which he worked from the early 1920s through the mid 1930s). Here, the outer form of the bull circulates around the spindle formed by Europa's torso. This formulation of volumes recalls Gaston Lachaise's 1924 *Reclining Woman with Arm Upraised* and his even denser *The*

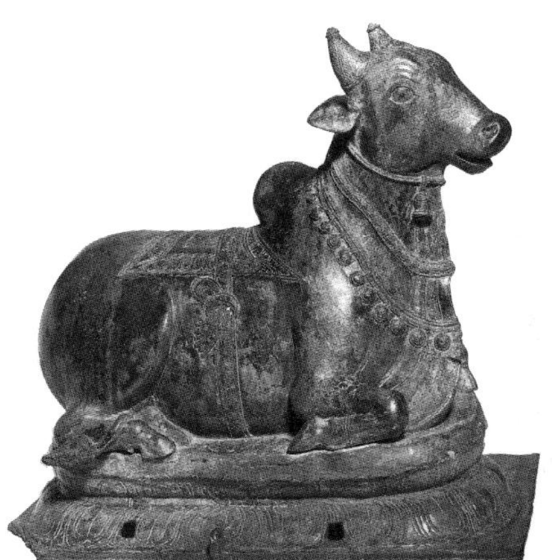

Fig. 55. Vijayanagar, 15th century; *Nandi*; bronze; 22 in. high. Freer Gallery of Art, Smithsonian Institution.

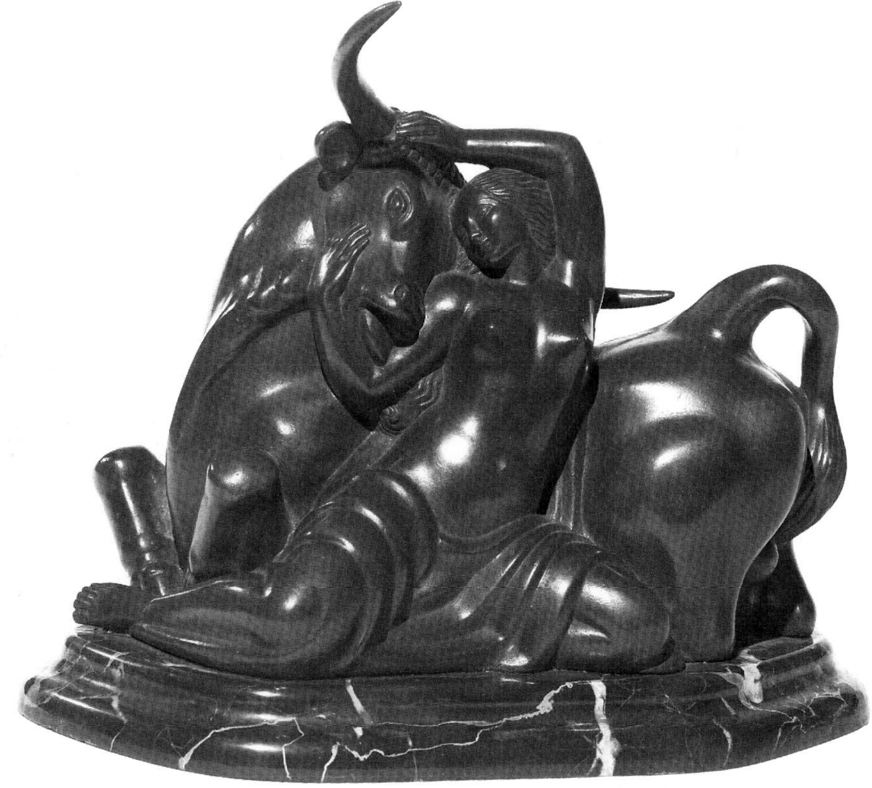

Fig. 56. *Europa and the Bull (#1)*, 1924; bronze on marble base; 10¼ in. high.

Mountain (figs. 57, 58), which appeared in versions between circa 1913 and 1934.[26] Unusual for its spatial opacity, this interpretation of the compressed helical form manifests Manship's understanding of its expressive potential.

Manship also pulled all the major figurative elements to the front of *Europa and the Bull*. Thus, though the work is conceived fully in the round, the major pictorial incidents are clustered in a fairly narrow wedge that represents the "front." This dialogue of sculpture in the round and a relief, which presents itself to us fully from one view, adds to a sense of intimacy, of a private space created amid the out of doors. Within this lovers' precinct, the seated Europa reaches up and behind her to caress the animal's massive head. Her pose—uncomfortable if actually struck—presents all the gestures frontally and brings the eye, in a narrowing gyre, from the ground inward to the very small area in which the two faces meet and Zeus-as-bull lightly licks Europa's inner arm. The theme's tender sensuality could not have been more magically

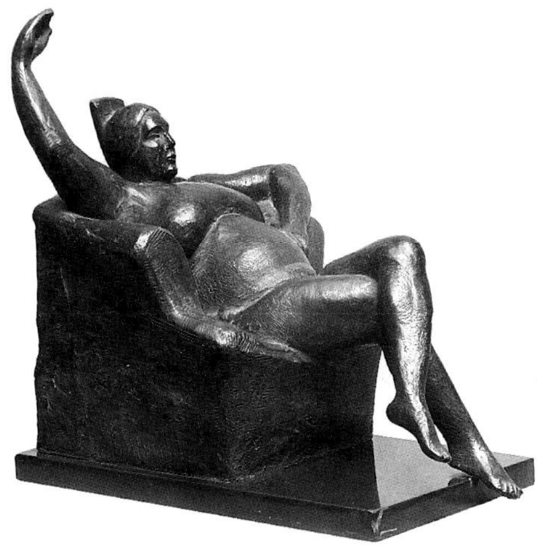

Fig. 57. Gaston Lachaise, *Reclining Woman with Arm Upraised*, ca. 1924; bronze; 13¾ in. high. Hirshhorn Museum and Sculpture Garden, Smithsonian Institution.

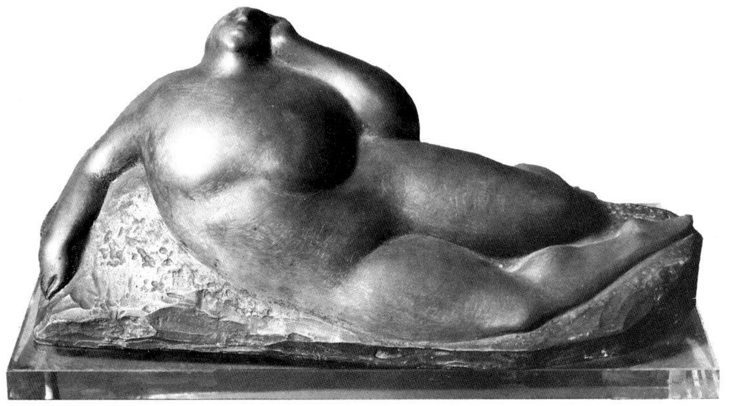

Fig. 58. Gaston Lachaise, *The Mountain*, ca. 1924; bronze with glass base; 7¾ in. high. The Metropolitan Museum of Art, The Alfred Stieglitz Collection, 1949.

expressed or given a better formal exposition. Mass (an aspect of the subject) contrasts with litheness; the smallest details discretely tell the fable of sex and surrender.

Manship soon returned to this myth; in 1925 he made twenty copies of *Flight of Europa* (fig. 59). At forty years of age (on the brink of what we would today call a "mid-life crisis"), Manship found appealing the story of the young girl who would elope with the bulky animal, a camouflaged god. Perhaps this theme equates with Picasso's suite of etchings, *The Sculptor's Studio*, in which the muscular sculptor nuzzles an "ingenue," both model and lover. Yet, unlike Picasso's, Manship's life proceeded placidly as ever, and no obvious autobiographical reference entered his work.

For the *Flight of Europa* Manship employed stylistic sources specific to the Cretan setting of the story, producing an elegantly economical set of internal references. Minoan bulls on the famous gold cups from Vaphio and the painted bull-leapers at the palace at Knossos (which had been discovered in the last twenty-five years) seem to have inspired the *Flight of Europa*. The bull's agile power and the long-waisted maiden's heroic ease bespeak protohistoric legend. But Manship was not tyrannized by his ancient sources. Shortly after *Flight of Europa* was shown, Stanley Casson recognized its innovative design: "The triangular shape of the whole composition brings with it great subtleties of balance in weight and in line."[27] Scattering patterned accents over the sculpture, Manship precisely balanced decorative details. He distributed sparkling elements of concentrated pattern, so the smooth simple forms do not culminate in a single climax, and no point on the work is far from another strong motif.

It might be said that the *Flight of Europa* consists of two strong views, front and back, but Manship's program for the piece was so careful that it is no longer possible to assign priority to the "front," as the details of the "back" recruit our attentions. Thus, we circulate in pleasant contemplation of the work.

In addition to his historical research, a more immediate source for the playful supporting dolphins is undoubtedly found in his assistant's *Dolphin Fountain* (fig. 60). A year before, Lachaise's fountain piece proposed a sportive pod of playing dolphins, some half-leaping from, and others half-submerged in, the base. Manship, whose sensitivity to materials and surfaces was unmatched, solicited a lovely metaphor from the grain of *Flight of Europa*'s marble base. Manship's dolphins plunge into the wavy stone as into water (and such references reappeared in his art some three decades later when purple quartz recalled clouds). A delightful play on materials, the relationship of the base to the massive sculpture was crucial to Manship's exposition.

Gilding levitates the bull's solid mass, an opaque volume that carries the prim Phoenician princess. The *Flight of Europa*'s gilding reflects light rather

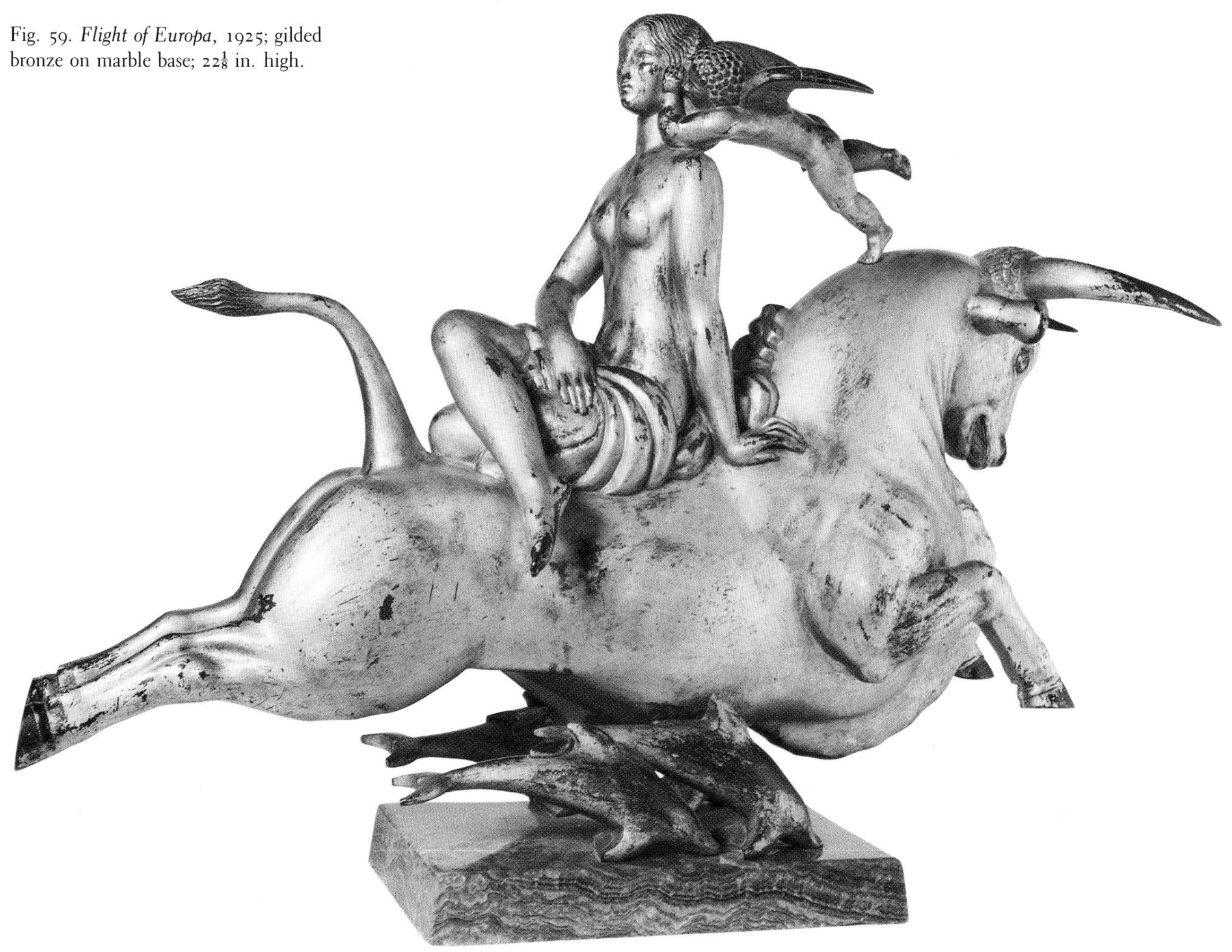

Fig. 59. *Flight of Europa*, 1925; gilded bronze on marble base; $22\frac{1}{8}$ in. high.

than absorbing it, which produces an indeterminate surface depth. And so shining gold both brightens the volumes and diminishes the sense of weight. (An insightful treatment of the Europa theme, gilding reappeared in Manship's most famous floating figure, *Prometheus*.) Charging westward, accompanied by leaping dolphins, Europa listens to a cherub's whispers, and intoxicated by the situation, she sits, gazing toward the distant horizon of the ocean. Europa hears her fate, to be the eponymous mother of nations; overwhelmed, she gives herself to visions amid the brisk ocean air.

The *Flight of Europa* was part of a thematic cluster, which was "distinguished by a marked simplification of style and by his choice of subjects—usually a group to which some fleet-footed animal imparts a feeling of strong and graceful action."[28] Many of Manship's contemporaries experimented with the expressive capacity of the Europa myth, which seems to have enjoyed something of a heyday. Carl Milles, who had worked in Rodin's studio,

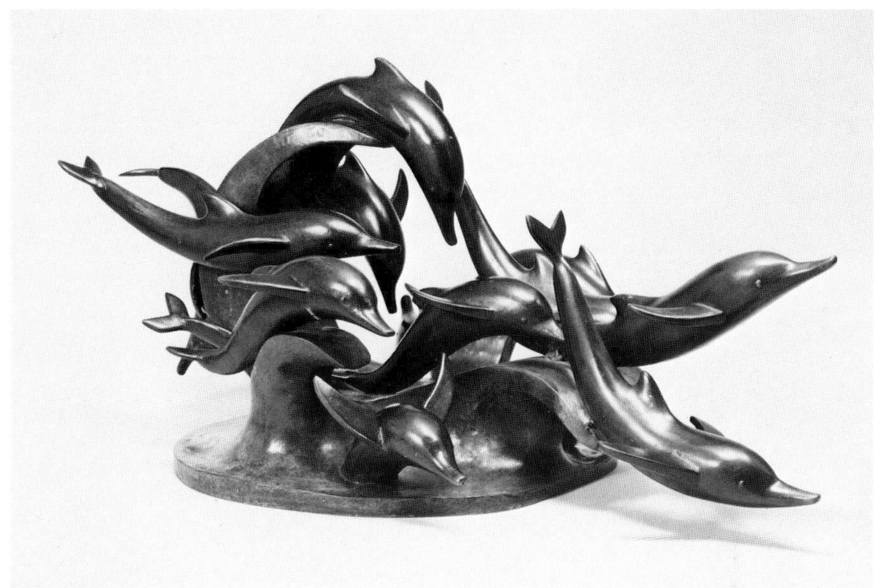

Fig. 60. Gaston Lachaise, *Dolphin Fountain*, 1924; bronze; 17 in. high. Whitney Museum of American Art, New York.

executed Europa in bronze with far less happy results. Milles folded the bull's legs beneath the animal, producing a solid, thick mass merged with the ground; the bull arches back his head and neck in a single great gesture—which curves toward the outstretched figure of Europa—and licks her hand. Compared with this blunt attempt at eroticism, Manship's adult sensuality swells the revelation of female triumph. Between 1937 and 1938 Waylande Gregory used the theme for a stoneware sculpture. Reuben Nakian modeled a version of the subject between 1938 and 1942; like Manship, his predecessor in many ways, Nakian elevated the mythic idyll to an enduring position in his art. In such works, *beauty* in its pre-modern sense more or less survives avant-garde assumptions and is still distant from kitsch. David Smith conjectured on the product of Zeus's elopment with Europa in his *Europa and Calf*, which foreshadows the planar arrangement of *Becca*, a work named for his daughter Rebecca. The Europa theme has had an underground survival in modern art. This compelling story attracted some of our most vigorous artists, and the best of their efforts did not go unrecognized; in January 1929, the National Arts Club announced its sculpture prize of $500 to Paul Manship for his *Flight of Europa*.

While obviously reliant on mythology, Manship never strayed into a personal fantasy world. His work was always sanctioned by tradition or the laws of nature; he could subscribe to either, but would never jettison both. His figures obeyed the laws of gravity unless they were buoyed by a scriptural or classical reference—Lucifer or Zeus, for example. Nor did Manship engage in phantasmagoria, although in his Parisian studio he worked at the epicenter of the surrealist revolution. Manship never exploited the idiosyncrasy bequeathed to the modern world by psychoanalysis; modern science, philosophy, and psychiatry might never have existed from the evidence supplied by Manship's sculpture. Nor do his images offer testimony about the form and direction of his life; no autobiographical clues issue from his works. Manship's subjects are conventional, they have names that can be found in books (usually those on classical mythology), and these themes sufficed for his exposition of human relationships.

Perhaps early popularity dissuaded Manship from soul-searching; there seemed no reason to tinker with success. Manship never delved into this frame of mind—its sources or motivations. His workmanlike approach precluded frivolity, experiments with controlled accidents, spontaneous eruptions of passion, or unpremeditated self-expression. In his art we find nothing confessional.

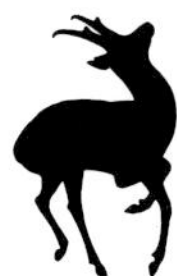

Art Deco

The credo of the artist must be the result of his education and environment. He cannot depart from his age, and its spiritual and material influences.[1]

MANSHIP'S PERFECT TECHNIQUE popularized the themes and the ornamental treatment of older civilizations. Thereafter, a generation of students at the American Academy in Rome adopted Manship's approach until the archaistic style came to be associated with the American Academy. Additionally, Manship's rendition of archaism was so powerful that it affected sculptors trained by the classicist Augustus Saint-Gaudens as well as those who had studied with the French Impressionists. Especially sculptors employed by architects fell into line. All found that the virtues of simplified forms responded to certain problems being raised by modernism. Moreover, for architectural commissions, the building style of the times favored precisely organized patterns that could treat either the repetitive imagery of machines or the semi-naturalistic flow of bodies, whose patterning mixed ancient and modern references. Accordingly, Manship found himself beatified as a patron saint of Art Deco, the style that, quintessentially, combined the force of machines with the sensuality of organic shapes.

Art Deco was sustained by an artistic vocabulary that Manship helped to create but whose decorative program he never endorsed. He did not call himself an Art Deco sculptor. Between the wars and before the term came into general use, Manship unknowingly participated in the formation of our era's most popular and enduring style of art and decoration. Indeed, Art Deco may well be the style that characterizes our century to future generations, and we cannot really assay Manship's career without reference to it.

Art Deco arose without a manifesto and gained an almost universal popularity. The uncodified Art Deco agenda included distinctive social features. Practitioners subscribed to the idea of progress, and the teleology of a clean, technological, and visibly mechanized society that mixed high density urbanism with a neopastoral of regulated farmland upon which the city or metropolis depended. Manship himself believed in a social context for his work: "Art at its best is the expression of common cultural ideals and aspirations and it finds its being in the temperament of the racial group as influenced by environment."[2]

He felt that art performed a humanizing and social function within a culture. His personal program accorded well with the public's notion of art, for gentility has long propounded the "fine" aspect of art.[3] Unwittingly absorbed into the movement, Manship saw the artist's function in a society not so much in terms of style but in terms of the integration of a healthy society following his vision of antiquity:

> Has anyone ever heard of a modest art critic, a blushing shrinking violet of an art critic, hesitating to take a positive stand on public guidance in matters of aesthetics or taste? Of course I have good friends in these professions of whose wisdom and judgment I have much respect. NO! Art should be understood by all, as it was in its days of past glory—then, there was but a single standard for judgment of excellence.[4]

Reconciling art and industry, Art Deco was heir of both art nouveau and Jugendstil. (And, as a force to integrate society, Art Deco offered "a single standard for judgment of excellence.") Its forms were modernist-inspired, although it relied on a vocabulary of academic formalism. Like some past academicisms, Art Deco was rife with literary references that could buttress flimsy thinking. This literary quality definitively opposed the self-referential character of modernism, which increasingly rejected gestures to anything beyond the work of art (such as literature, history, or myth). Modernist painting was about the conditions of painting; modernist sculpture about sculpture, etc. Accordingly, modernists saw these literary aspects in Art Deco as the survival of the most pernicious aspects of the academicism they tried to shrug off, if not bury. To modernists, Art Deco resembled kitsch in that it emulated the products (and effects) rather than the processes of art; modernists saw art in dynamic (if not dialectical) terms.

Stylistically, Art Deco absorbed citations from antiquity and exotic locales—the Aztecs and Mayans, the arts of India, China, Japan, and Oceania—all merged in the last gasp of an exoticism that had enthralled the nineteenth century. But as a purely twentieth-century quality, Art Deco reveled in a rakish love of speed that typified the modern era. (This sensibility was not limited to Art Deco; Futurism, the spawn of Cubism, relished pure velocity as an aesthetic.) The love of streamlined machine forms might have grown up in the modern period, independent of any form of modernism. A tautology of "speed = modernity" imposed streamlining on products that sitting still could thereby claim to partake of the cult of progress. This taste engulfed Manship's program—the simplification of forms and balance of large, easily legible, masses against small, decorative passages—although his assumptions preceded the widespread style.

Art Deco engaged the whole built/designed visual environment, and it was revolutionary because it succeeded where other campaigns for a planned and organized environment had failed (the Bauhaus, for example). Without either a coterie or haranguing theoreticians, Art Deco arose with popular support. Its style and philosophy addressed the complete surroundings and habitat as a unified field of design, including fabrics, buildings, parks, automobiles, ships, airplanes, monuments, graphics, and typography. The whole social fabric could be uniformly planned, and Manship, whose art and work carried a strong social component, both anticipated and benefited from this wave.

Planning on such a scale required access to the powerful and wealthy. The patronage of governments and persons of high station was sought; the ever genial Manship endeared himself to patrons and municipal planners. His art was politically neutral, his subjects conservative. His workmanlike sense of a job (and, for him, his large sculptures were *jobs*) put Manship in good stead with architects, who could count on him to come in on schedule, on budget, without fuss or bohemian tantrums. He was a known quantity. (Unfortunately, because his well-to-do clientele's expectations were based on his early works, the maturation of his style, or its evolution, was hampered. Manship never did develop a late twilight style. Many great artists—Beethoven in his Late Quartets, Pound in his last Cantos, Goya in his "black paintings"—achieved that secure, magisterial, and eloquent "old-age style" denied to Manship when he relied on commissions.) Finally, Manship's inadvertent association with Art Deco helped doom him for a generation when that style went out of favor, and the reconsideration of Art Deco in recent years has raised Manship's reputation on a tide of sympathetic reevaluation.

Lingering over his pieces' every detail, Manship produced work that displayed perfect craftsmanship. But craftsmen do not invent their forms, and Manship, a true academic, accepted inherited canons that governed proportion and detail (fig. 61). Like ancient Greek artists who strove to best their rivals by a personal interpretation of the canonic types, Manship created a distinctly personal style. Nevertheless, Manship was on the verge of rehabilitating the notion of the academic, which was beginning to fall into that ill repute in which it now seems irredeemably mired.

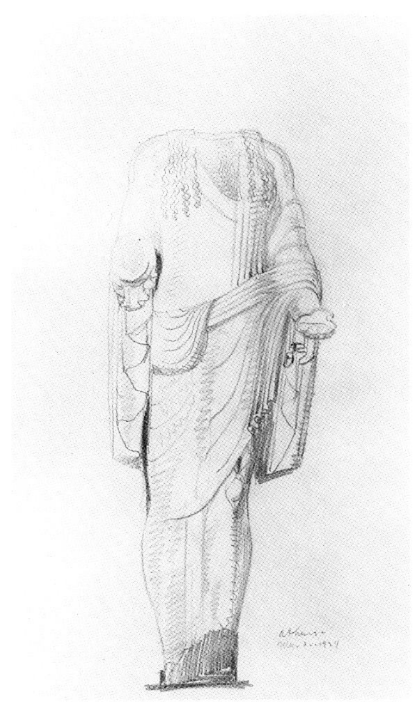

Fig. 61. *Standing Headless Kora Figure*, 1924; pencil on paper; 13$\frac{3}{8}$ x 10$\frac{3}{16}$ in.

Manship contemplated the story of Diana and Actaeon as early as 1915, while living in Cornish, New Hampshire; he began to sketch this theme, which engaged him for a decade thereafter. (Choosing the Diana theme, Manship challenged the monumental 1892 version that Saint-Gaudens had produced in hammered copper for the pinnacle of Madison Square Garden.) Following several experimental studies, the subject took form in two heroic groups. These monumental pieces were the center of attention at a 1925 exhibition of Manship's work in New York. *Diana* and *Actaeon* announced Manship's stylistic maturity.

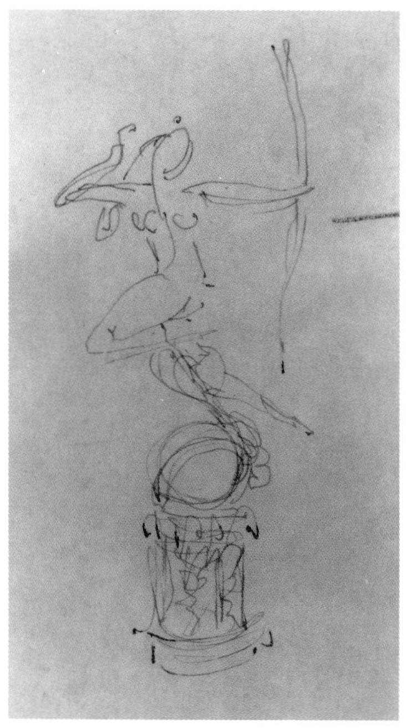

Fig. 62. *Nude (Diana)*; pen and ink on tracing paper; 5 x $2\frac{13}{16}$ in.

Diana (identified with the Greek goddess Artemis) is the ancient Italian woodland goddess of hunting and archery, and the defense of all wild animals, children, and weak things. In classical Greek literature she was characterized by a deliberately chosen and forcibly maintained virginity; she punished those who would violate this state.

Actaeon was trained as a hunter by his father. While hunting on Mt. Citheron, he came upon Diana at her bath and offended her by seeing her naked. To prevent Actaeon's boasting of this exploit, Diana turned him into a stag, which his own hounds—trained to hunt and not recognizing him—devoured; in some versions of the tale Diana threw a deerskin over Actaeon with the same result. The hounds were saddened by their master's disappearance, and so the centaur Chiron made a lifelike statue of Actaeon to appease them. This myth plays upon the origins of the horned cuckold (Actaeon became synonymous with "to cuckold") and incidentally salutes the sculptor's role in revivifying likeness. In this story we may glimpse Manship's possible identification with the centaurs that appear in his work.

One diminutive figure sketch of a nude, probably *Diana* (fig. 62), though slight as a work of art, indicates how Manship at first conceived of *Diana* as a statue, a running figure on a pedestal. As a document of his thinking, this sketch records the distance Manship traversed before arriving at the finished work. Like Lachaise's characteristic drawings of female figures, an easy, but not a glib, looseness bespeaks Manship's lively draftsmanship and human vitality.

The role of Diana's hunting dogs was refined as the theme developed (fig. 63). At last—as a single muscular animal leaping horizontally—the dog contributed powerfully to the ensemble (fig. 64). Almost incidentally attached to the central supportive frond, the dog floats free of the base, all four legs off the ground and head turned back to look up at his mistress. The dog's head is

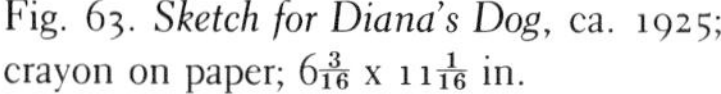

Fig. 63. *Sketch for Diana's Dog*, ca. 1925; crayon on paper; $6\frac{3}{16}$ x $11\frac{1}{16}$ in.

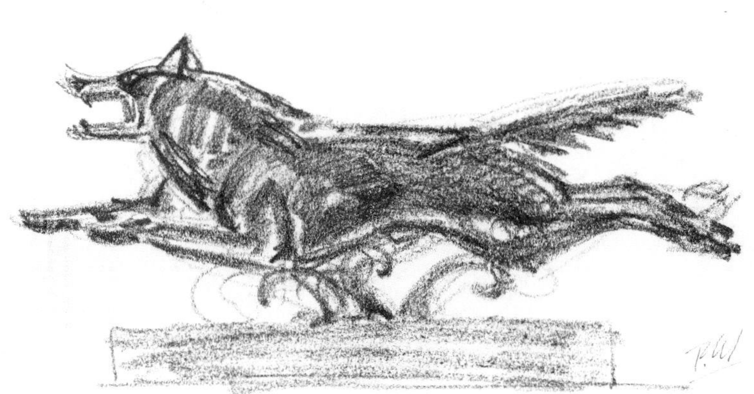

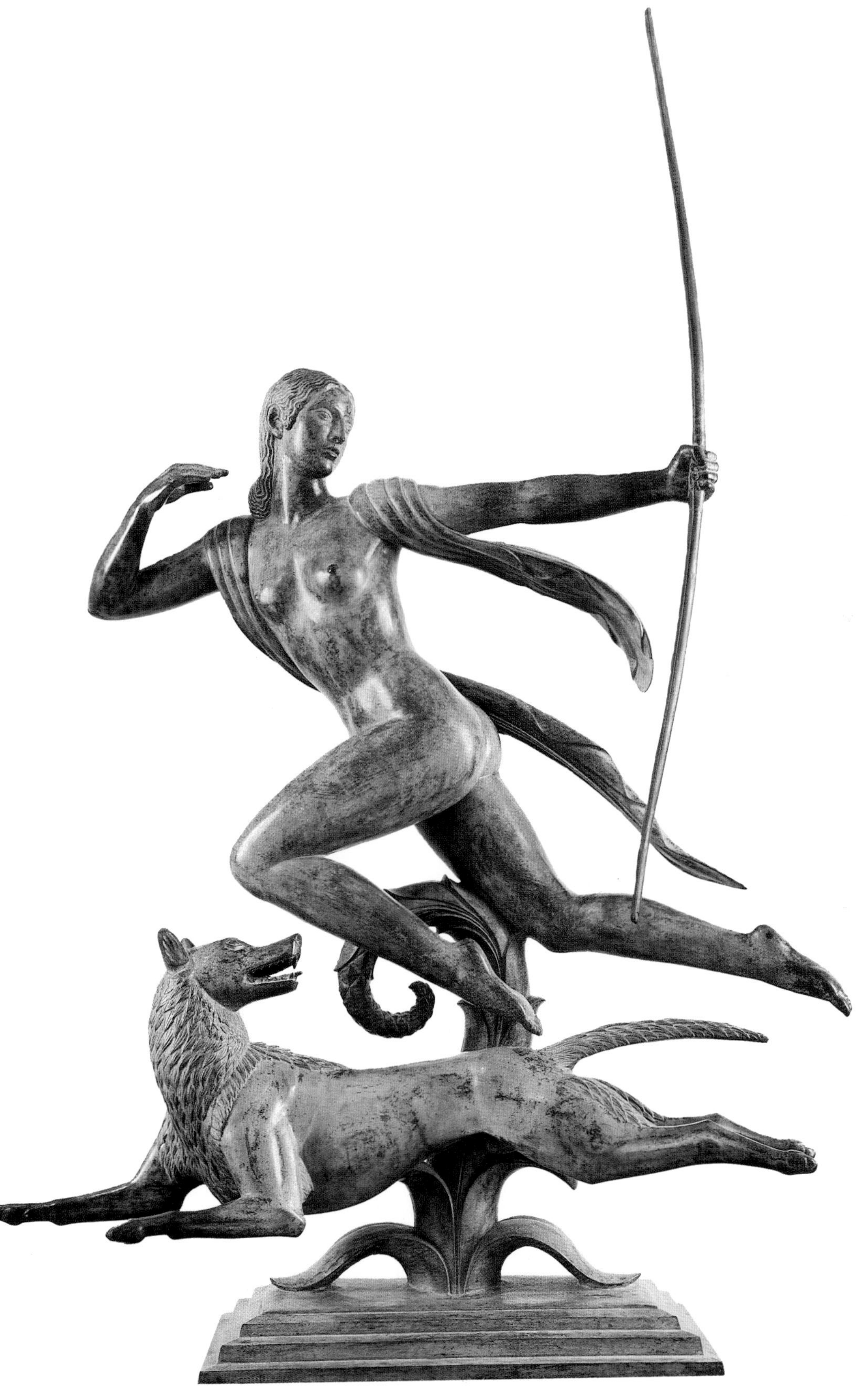

Fig. 64. *Diana,* 1925; bronze; 49 in. high.

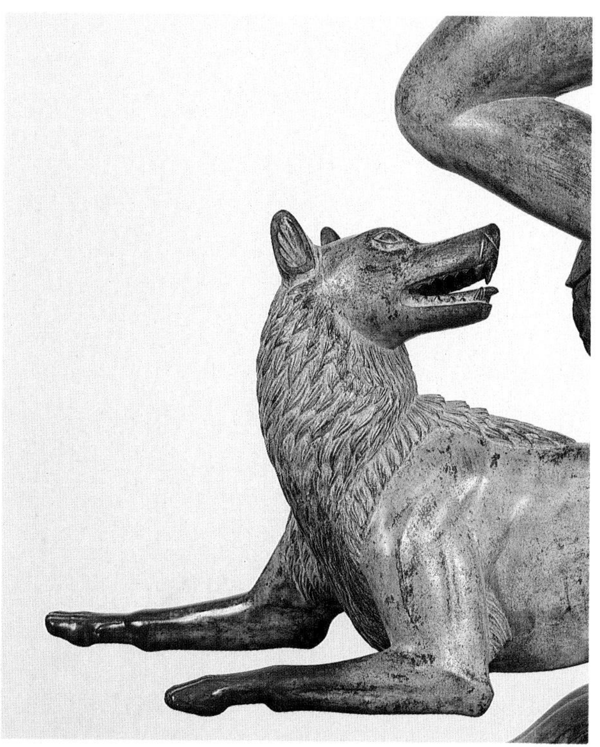

Fig. 65. Detail, *Diana*.

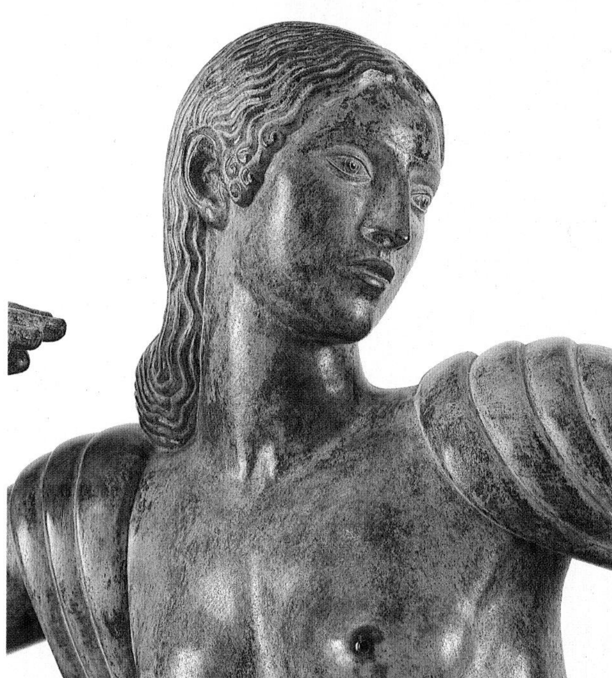

Fig. 66. Detail, *Diana*.

a strong compositional element; it points to the hand and the bow, while the dog's eyes and expression are focused on the goddess's face, as if to sense her mood and do her further bidding (fig. 65). A line connecting the furry, patterned areas of the dog's ruff and tail establish the base of a decorative triangle (capped by *Diana*'s rhythmically wavy hair), which circumscribes the areas of finest detail (fig. 66).

After arriving at the final composition, Manship executed three slightly varied versions in different sizes. As often proved the case for his work, the middle size most congenially balanced monumentality and decorative detail. Extreme magnifications rarely served Manship well; forms tended to become bloated rather than grandly simplified when enlarged. The heroic, over life-size *Diana* was finished at Rome in 1924; *Actaeon*, in progress at the same time, was completed in Paris. Manship conceived this largest version of the *Diana* and *Actaeon* group (in gilded bronze with eyes of blue and white enamel) as a heroic version (seven-and-a-quarter-feet high), which he cast twice—in 1924 and again in 1939. Yet the smaller life-size version is, in many ways, the triumph of his career. *Diana* embodied the best of Manship's art, the highest aspirations of archaism and contemporary academicism, the promise for a legitimate and potent alternative to modernism, and an unsurpassable performance in bronzework. The piece left Walker Hancock, among others, dazzled by what was "possibly the supreme example of the fluidity of line which Manship was able to achieve. . . . Its lightness takes every advantage of

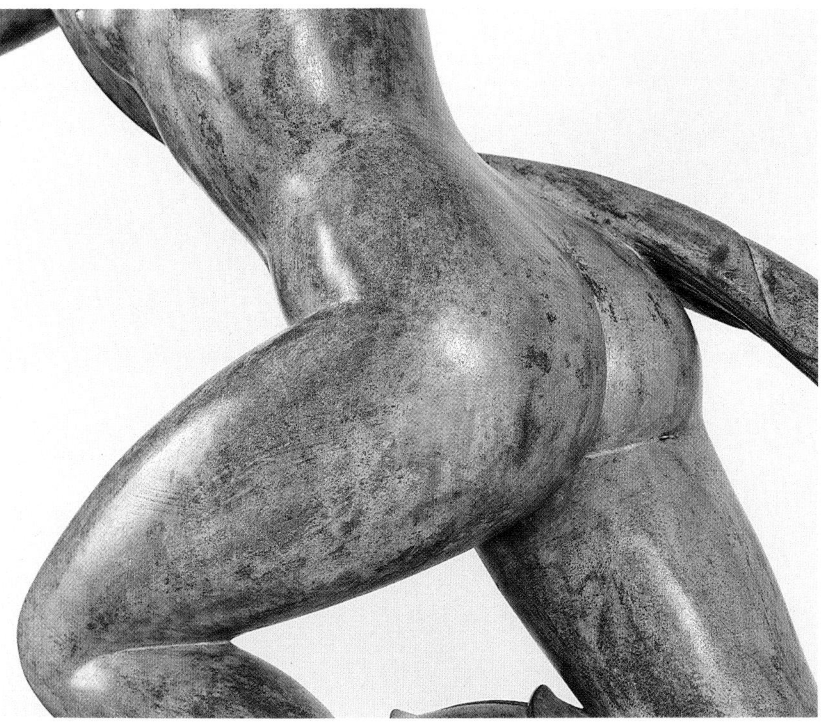

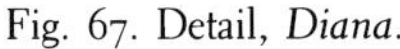

Fig. 67. Detail, *Diana*.

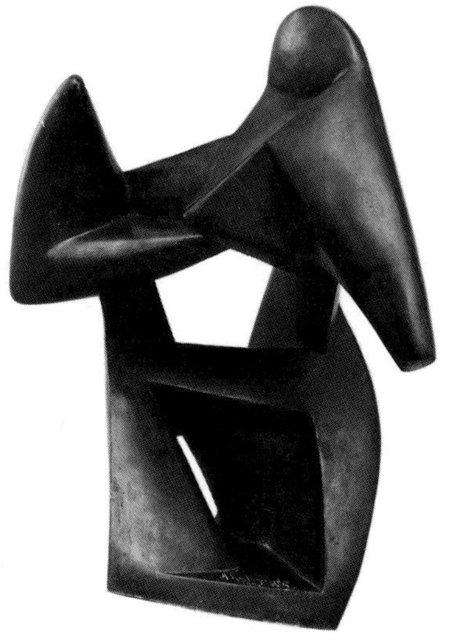

Fig. 68. Alexander Archipenko, *Struggle*, 1914; painted plaster; 23$\frac{3}{4}$ in. high. Solomon R. Guggenheim Museum, New York.

bronze as a medium in contrast to many later works in which the emphasis is on solidity and volume."[5]

Diana, though narrowly confined within two planes, is not a relief sculpture. A great triumph of linear conception—its silhouette swirls and leaps around the work's exterior—the piece's fundamental structural form is a great open spiral in three dimensions. Beginning at the floral base and, expanding in an ever-widening gyre, the spiral contains the bow and the bent right arm. The hunting dog establishes the sculpture's frontal plane. The implied surface glides at right angles to the spectator's initial field of view. Behind that plane, all is in motion. Belying its supportive function, the frond bends earthward above the dog; *Diana*'s body has been so twisted that almost all of her lower back has been rotated to the sculpture's front. The resulting sculptural passage is as beautifully abstract as anything attempted by vaunted practitioners of abstract sculpture. In counter-rotation to the direction of her hips, *Diana*'s shoulders twist until parallel to the plane established by the dog.

Diana hardly seems formally revolutionary, especially when compared with avant-garde sculpture—whose whole justification is a nonprogrammatic expression through form. Yet, Manship's tremendous accomplishment can be savored in favorable comparison with most of the avant-garde's nonobjective works. An arrangement remarkably similar to Manship's *Diana* governs Alexander Archipenko's 1914 work *Struggle*, although these sculptors shared little else (figs. 67, 68). *Diana* and *Struggle* share compositions of smoothly

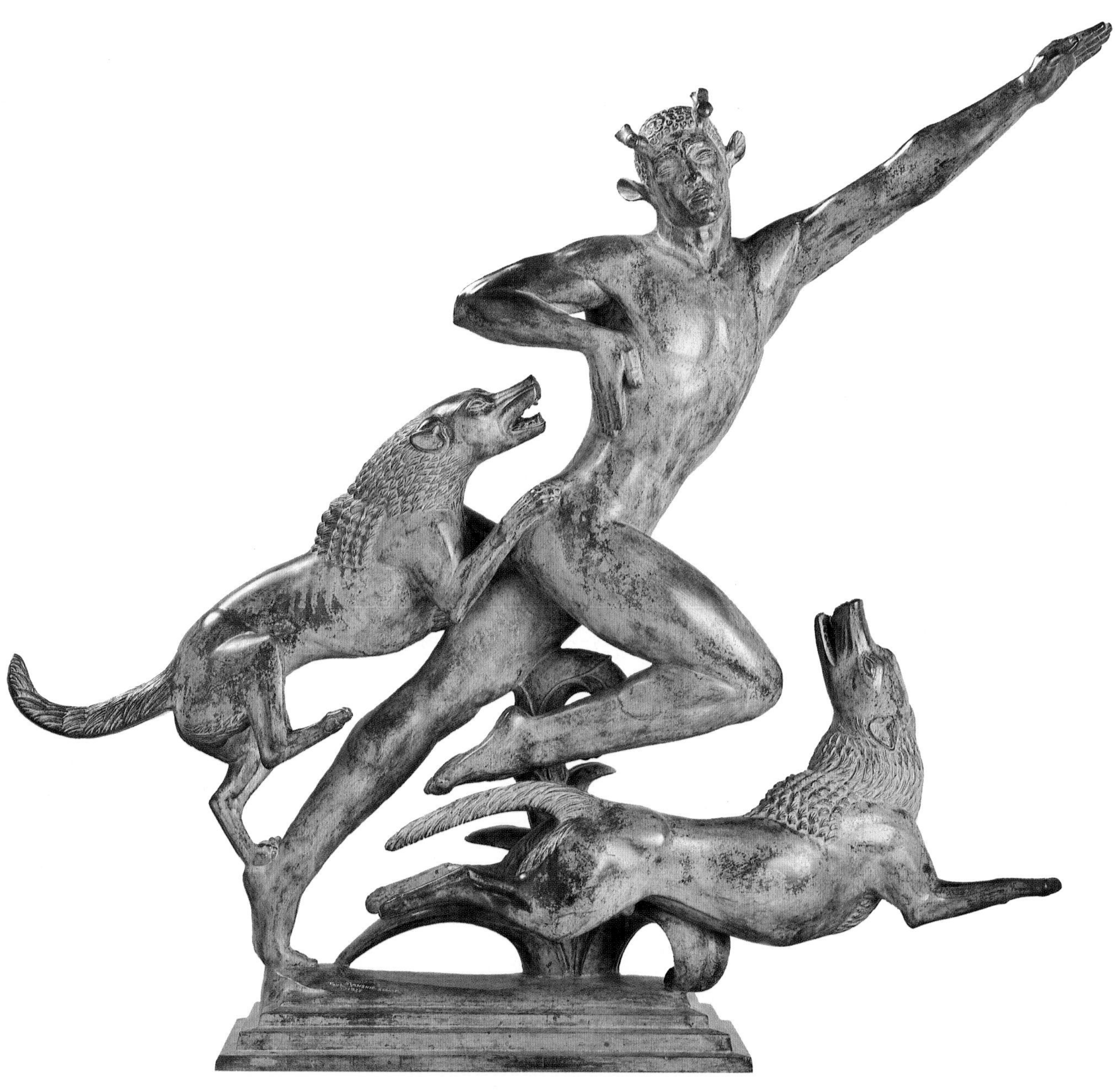

Fig. 69. *Actaeon (#1)*, 1925; bronze; 48 in. high.

turbulent forms in motion around a spiral center. If Archipenko's work epitomizes a certain uncompromising and blunt modernism, Manship's accomplishments, measured by the same scale of values, still succeed. Despite dissimilar ambitions, both Manship and Archipenko strove to bring sculpture into the modern world.

In addition to the wonderful massing of forms in *Diana*, surface rhythms unify the piece. Exquisite detail successfully weighed against strong silhouette and gestural massing. As Manship himself wrote: "I like to express movement in my figures. It's a fascinating problem which I'm always trying to solve." The work was an immediate hit—at its first appearance A. E. Gallatin lauded Manship's "astonishing command of rhythm . . . shown to advantage in his recent statue of *Diana* and her hound."[6]

The companion piece, *Actaeon* (fig. 69), depicts the moment when the goddess changes the unfortunate hunter into a fleeing stag about to be killed

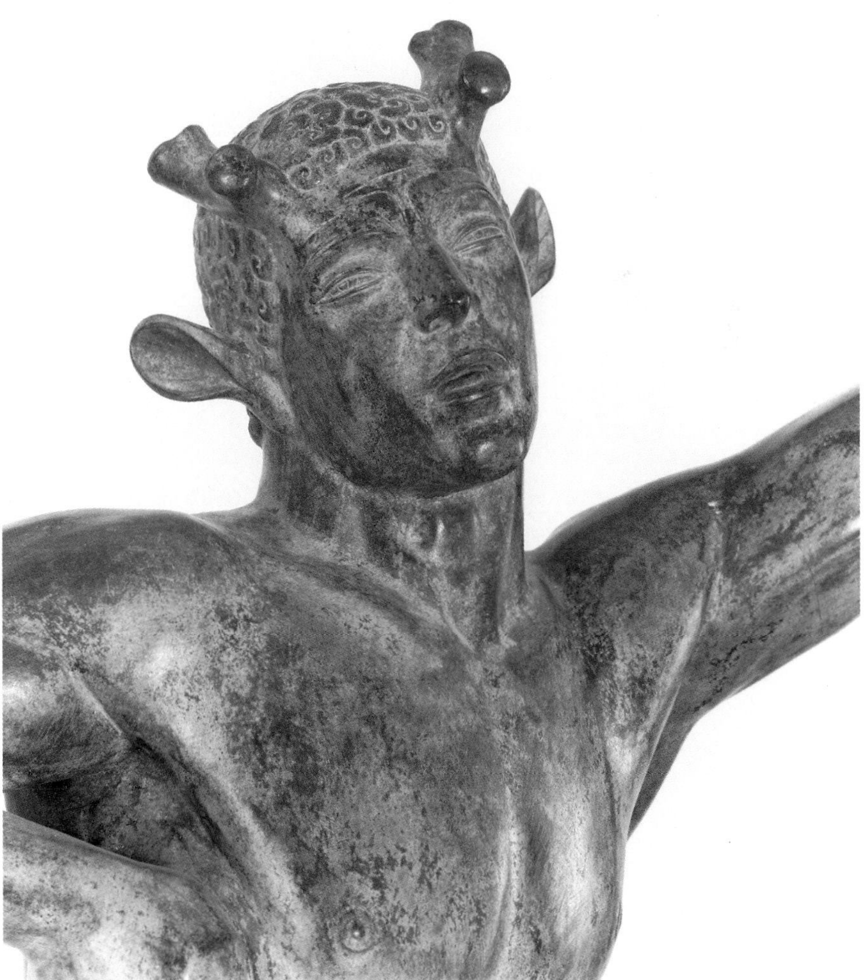

Fig. 70. Detail, *Actaeon (#1)*.

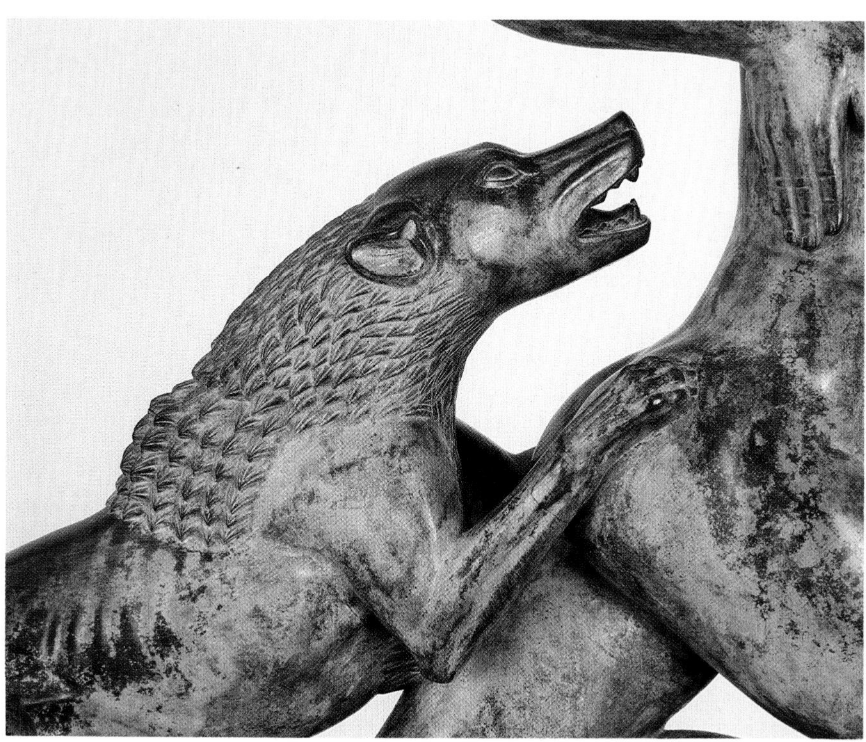

Fig. 71. Detail, *Actaeon (#1)*.

by his own hounds. Using the same device he employed in 1914 to connect the *Indian Hunter* to his prey, the *Pronghorn Antelope*, Manship activated and unified the gap between *Diana* and *Actaeon* with the imagined flight of an arrow. Having just released her bow, the vengeful Diana glowers at the escaping Actaeon, who clutches his wounded side.

Actaeon's hunting dogs relentlessly pursue the stag he is becoming (fig. 70). One dog leaps on him from behind (fig. 71); at his feet the other snarls. Unlike *Diana*'s, *Actaeon*'s strong diagonal composition—which begins at the heel of the left foot and continues unbroken to the statue's outstretched left hand—does not expand the piece s shallow space into three dimensions. The accusation of being merely decorative, with an excessive reliance on linear outline, found a target here. Although superficially the forms of the two sculptures are symmetrically blocked out, in fact, a host of sculptural devices does project *Diana* into three dimensions; still, the magnificent *Actaeon* perfectly counterbalances the active, twisting *Diana*. This opposition of effect springs from the sculptor's continuing dialogue with the past. *Actaeon*'s pose was a recitation of classical precedent. Manship certainly knew the most important antique example that *Actaeon*'s two-dimensional design echoes.

Seeking a model for the classical story of a man devoured by a beast, Manship could have relied on the tale of Laocoon, a priest of Troy who opposed moving the large Greek horse into the city. To silence his dire warnings, the gods sent an enormous serpent to strangle him and his sons. The most famous illustration of the story is undoubtedly the *Laocoon* ensemble, which has been attributed to a group of three sculptors from Rhodes who worked in the middle of the first century B.C. The spectacular marble group was discovered in the Bath of Titus in 1506, and after initial reconstruction of the parts, the ensemble was put on display to immediate acclaim. Michelangelo, among the artists of his generation, readily acknowledged the masterpiece status of the *Laocoon* group and freely drew inspiration from it. The fragments of the group were repeatedly restored as critics reconsidered the work's age and its creators' intent. The son's arms, for example, were removed before 1796, when Napoleon ordered the piece transported to Paris. There, plaster limbs were again added, and the group was returned to Rome in 1815. So matters basically stood until the middle of the present century. Such repeated attention was warranted as the work became a benchmark for taste in the seventeenth and eighteenth centuries.

When Manship saw the huge group in the Vatican Museum, Laocoon's right arm was reaching straight out (fig. 72) in a gesture that has since been understood to be an incorrect Baroque restoration. In 1954, a critical study of the work caused a basic revision of the figures' poses. In 1960, corresponding to archaeological finds of other works thought to be by the same Hellenistic sculptors, *Laocoon*'s right arm was reset into a bent position (fig. 73). A comparison with the pre-restoration *Laocoon* reveals the profound debt of Manship's *Actaeon*. Not only is the theme (the gods' retribution, executed by animals) shared, but also the basic composition is the same. *Actaeon*'s lunge echoes the strong diagonal that races through *Laocoon*'s body, and in a minor but important passage common to both works, the other arm rejoins the central mass. (The difference here is that *Actaeon*'s outstretched arm does not bend forward as *Laocoon*'s does, nor did Manship supply another motion that would three-dimensionally animate the space around *Actaeon*. In aggregate, such refinements separate the helical *Diana* from the flat *Actaeon*.)

Actaeon had to relate to *Diana*, in many ways a more powerfully appealing figure. A leaping hound, which corresponds to *Diana*'s faithful animal, declares the forward plane of *Actaeon*. Looking backward to observe the strange transformation overtaking its master, the dog seems denatured and overly abstracted; a sketch of 1922 is far more animated than the 1925 version. (Manship invoked archaic Greece in the sculptures' inset eyes and the dogs' stylized manes, particulary *Actaeon*'s dogs.) In the large bronze, the head of *Actaeon*'s dog was brought to the sculpture's front plane—wrenched into the spectator's field of view as *Diana*'s torso had been, but to less satisfactory effect. Little interest remains at the back of *Actaeon*; also, Manship failed to levitate *Actaeon* as successfully as he had *Diana*. When this contrast appeared, critics

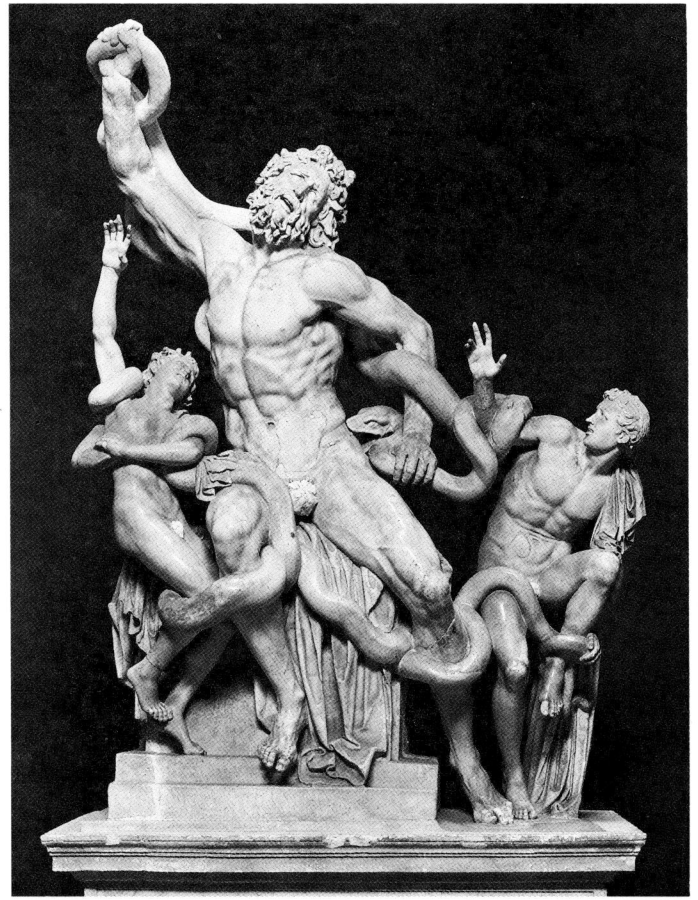

Fig. 72. Hellenistic, ca. 100 B.C.; *Laocoon* (before modern restoration); Rhodian marble; 7 ft. $11\frac{1}{4}$ in. high. Vatican Museum, Rome.

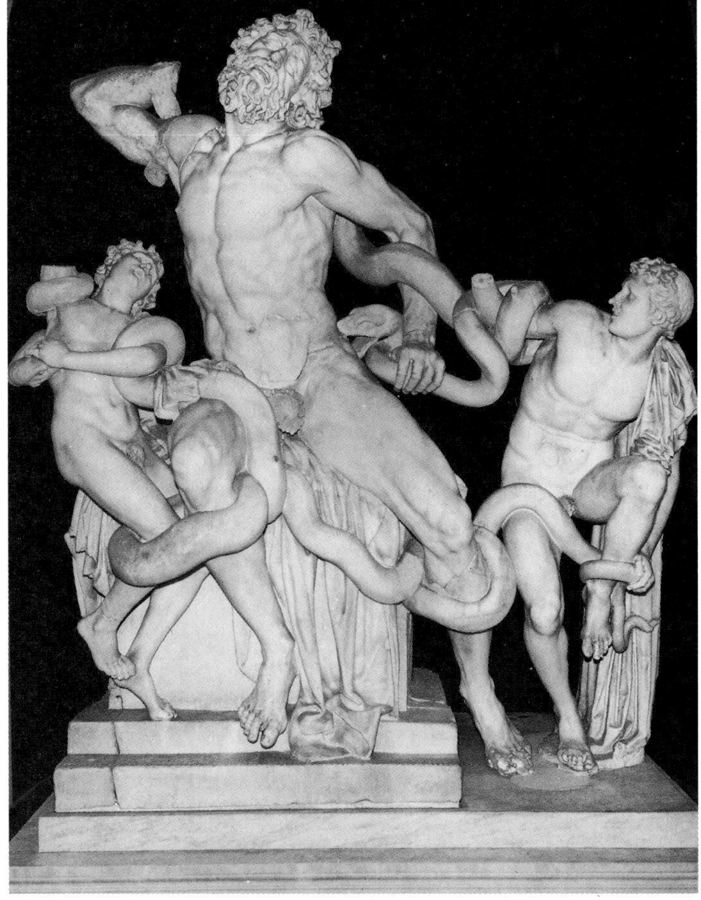

Fig. 73. *Laocoon* (after modern restoration).

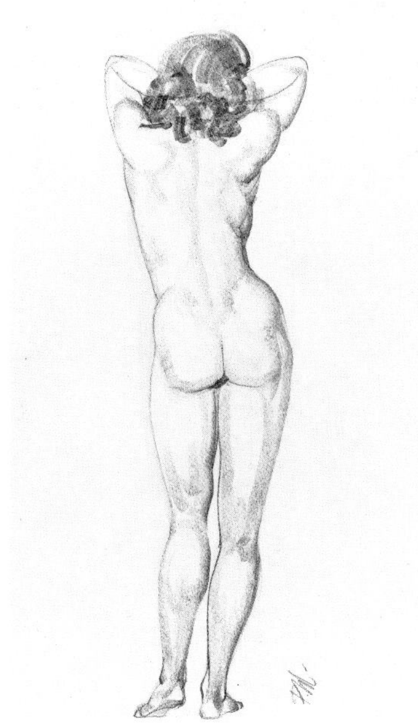

Fig. 74. *Standing Female Nude—Back*, ca. 1922; pencil on paper; $17\frac{15}{16}$ x $12\frac{1}{16}$ in.

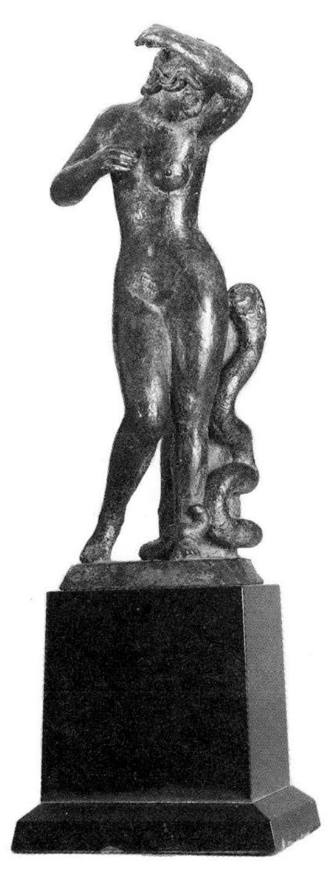

Fig. 75. *Eve (#2)*, 1922; bronze on marble base; $11\frac{5}{16}$ in. high.

noted that, "*Actaeon*, as he should be. . . is heavier. . . . These two figures balance one another in their big forms and emphasize contrast . . . swift on one side and slower on another."[7] Both works are limited to two views, front and back, but *Actaeon*'s silhouette is more powerfully decorative, deriving its appeal from the flow of lines and arabesque curves.

Manship's compression of forms in shallow space mirrored a psychological simplicity. In Manship's art there is no evidence that Freud ever lived. His female poses are healthy and titillating, but ultimately innocent; they lack that mystery of archaic Mediterranean sculpture that so hauntingly evokes the primordial discovery of gender. His well-muscled males possess none of the quivering tautness of antique sculpture.

Manship himself lived a normal, healthy life amid wife, children, and the quiet opulence he enjoyed thanks to his success in catering to wealthy clients. His family appears intermittently in his works, which seem strictly personal and occasional (but these are among his least successful pieces). As mythological avatars, the figures of *Diana* and *Actaeon* hardly testify to the fundamental isometry of male and female. Yet, compared to his genuinely academic contemporaries, even Manship's limited engagement of intuitive human need and nature stands clearly distinguished.

The two sculptural groups are eloquent as pure form—and are underrated, being some of the best formal sculpture of this century. Compared with what most contemporary sculptors were doing at the time, the purely sculptural quality of Manship's conception of *Diana* is staggering for its total command of spatial organization. Manship's clientele would have been displeased to encourage public salutes to sex. Any unbridled passion—except perhaps patriotism—would have thrown his professional status into question. Yet Manship, a careful observer of the body, was no prude. He did not blink when transcribing erotic beauty. He noted: "I'm not especially interested in anatomy, though naturally I've studied it. And although I approve generally of normally correct proportions, what matters is the spirit which the artist puts into his creation—the vitality, the rhythm, the emotional effect."[8]

Innumerable sketching sessions with the model yielded that solid knowledge of the figure already inculcated by early academic training. From studies such as *Standing Female Nude—Back* (fig. 74), Manship began to model small, experimental figures and explore new themes, such as *Eve* (fig. 75). He continued to rework this 1922 bronze sketch into the 1930s. Later, knowledge of the back's anatomy, its musculature and bones, served Manship well in *Standing Nude #1*. Static and unmoving from the front, *Standing Nude #1* reveals from the back that the introduction of slight asymmetries economically animates the whole (figs. 76, 77). These refinements distinguish Manship from obvious academic associates (who were incapable of vivacious subtlety) and

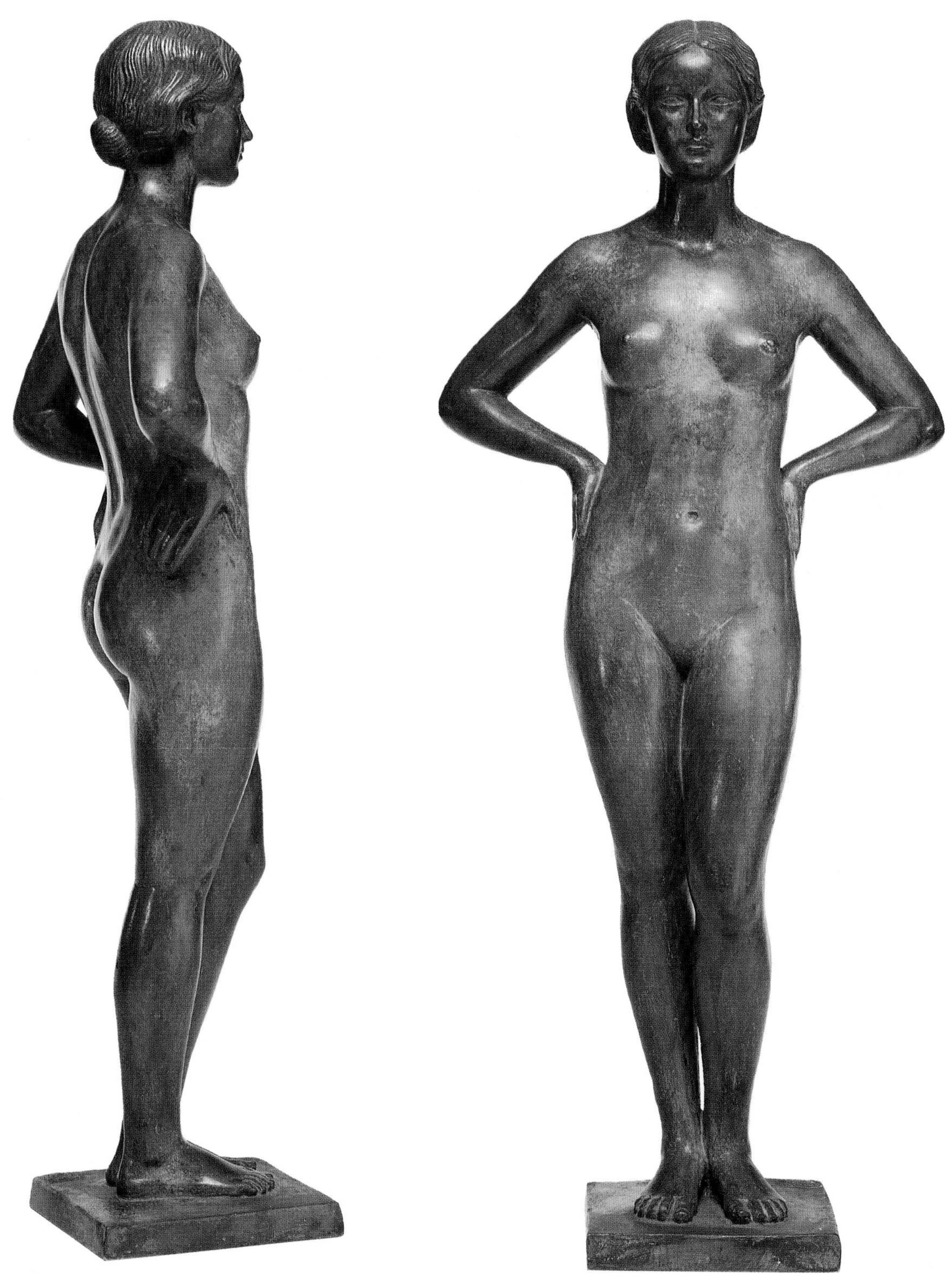

Figs. 76 and 77. *Standing Nude (#1)*, 1927; bronze; 17½ in. high.

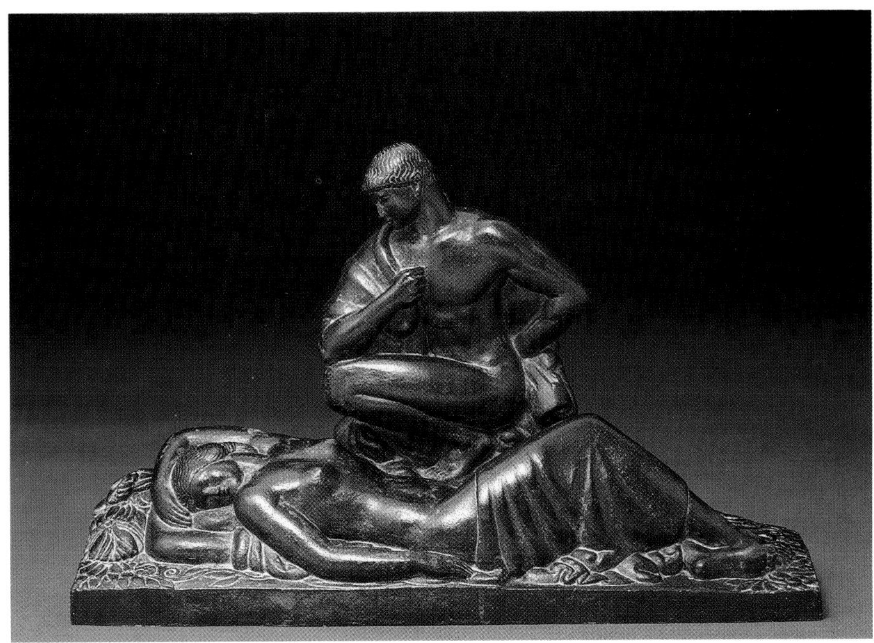

Fig. 78. *Theseus and Ariadne*, 1928; bronze; $7\frac{13}{16}$ in. high.

youthful modernists (whose radicalism eliminated all possibility and occasion for these notations).

Manship's powers of observation and his knowledge of sculptural balance advanced an idea of human nature that could serve classical myth, as in his 1928 bronze *Theseus and Ariadne* (fig. 78). The Athenian hero Theseus sailed to Crete to save fourteen Athenian children from an annual sacrifice to the Minotaur in his labyrinth. This sacrifice avenged the death of King Minos's son, who was killed by Athenians. Minos's daughter, Ariadne, fell in love with Theseus when he reached Crete. After extracting a promise of marriage from Theseus, Ariadne instructed him to escape from the labyrinth's complexity by following back a string that was tied to the entrance. The plan worked, but while Ariadne slept on the island of Naxos, Theseus abandoned her.

When sculptors—like the great nineteenth-century Frenchman, Antoine Louis Barye—illustrate this myth, they usually depict the actively heroic episodes of the story (fig. 79). A bittersweet sense of the story's grown-up aspects appealed to Manship. Rather than depicting the charged battle with the Minotaur as Barye had, Manship sculpted the crucial moment of *inaction* when Theseus, as he contemplates perfidy, recounts and weighs his adventures—and Ariadne's devotion. A sculpture lacking apparent outward motion prompts the knowledgeable spectator to relive the myth. Manship's vision was neither a bland bedtime tale nor a mere amusement. The original quality of the narrative, which had prompted ancient Greeks to repeat the myth from one generation to the next, reappeared in Manship's work. Adult sensibility and relationships supplanted "action packed" heroism.

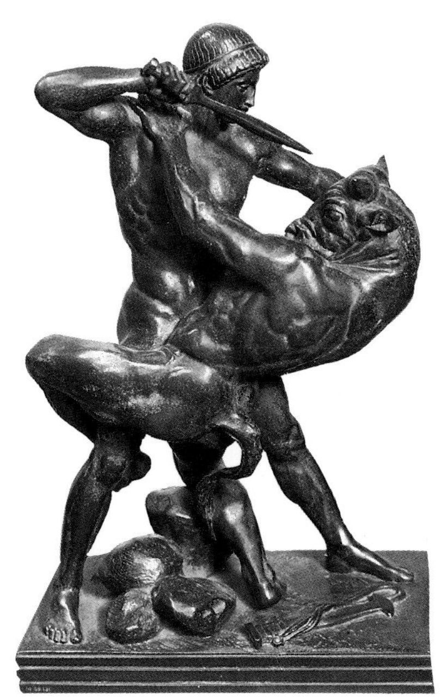

Fig. 79. Antoine Louis Barye, *Theseus and the Minotaur*, 1846; bronze; $17\frac{7}{8}$ in. high. The Metropolitan Museum of Art, Bequest of John Cadwalader, 1914.

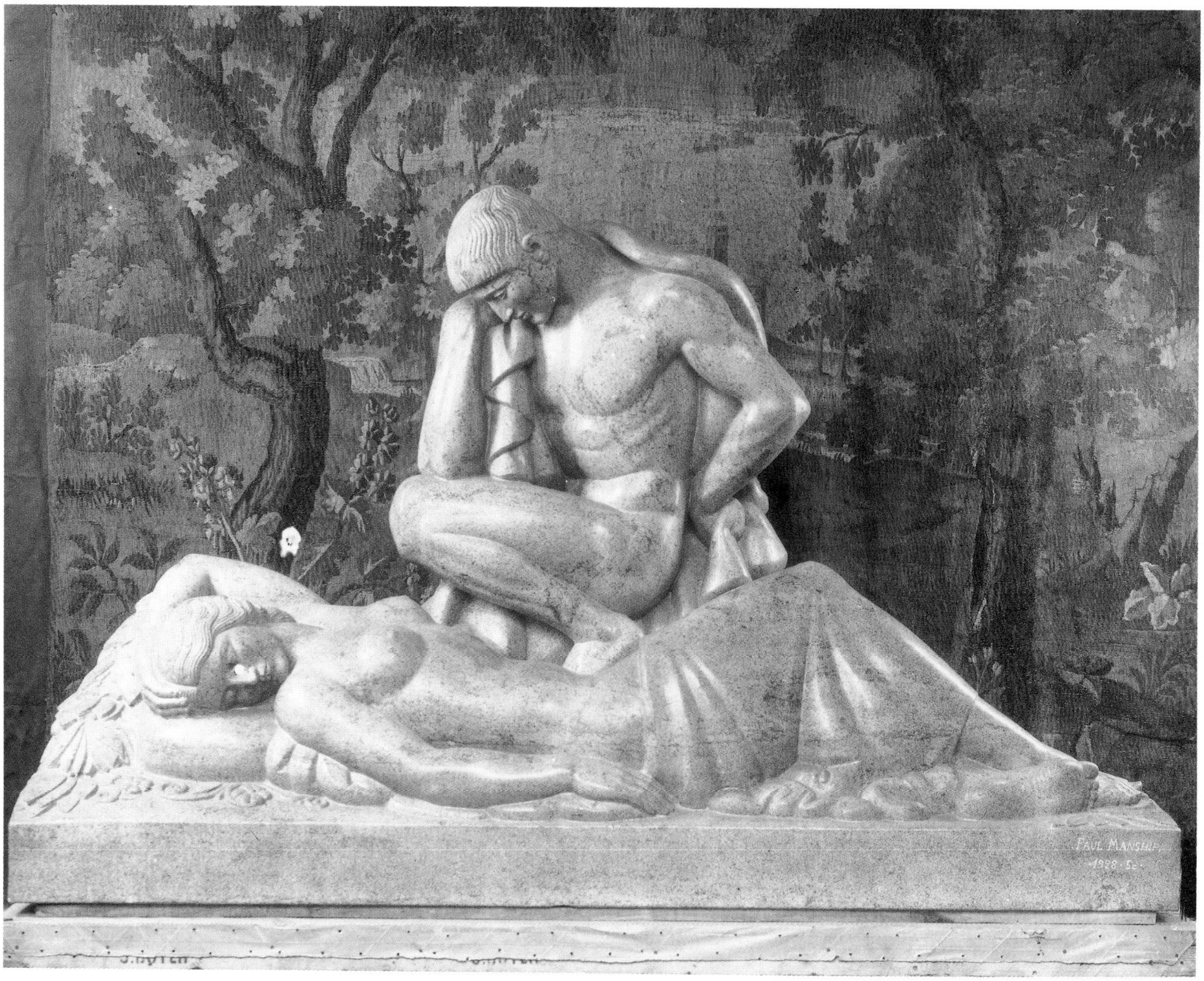

Fig. 80. *Theseus and Ariadne*, 1928; carved limestone; $50\frac{1}{2}$ in. high.

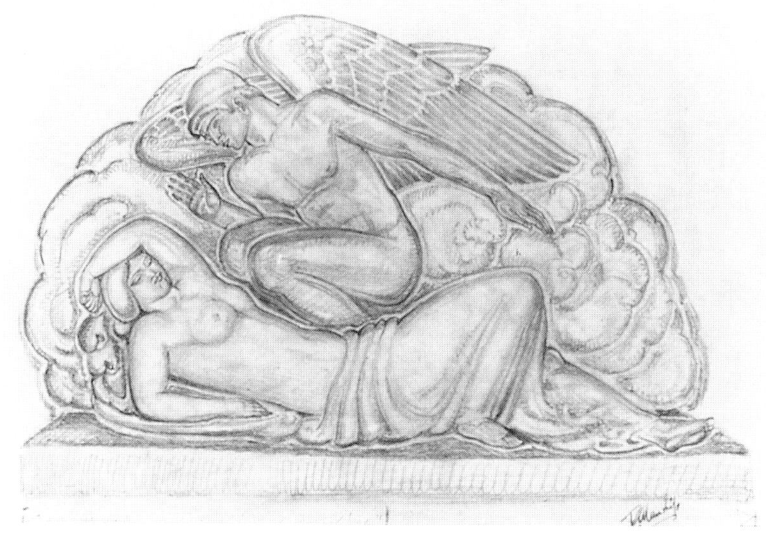

Fig. 81. *Eros and Psyche*, ca. 1925; pencil on tracing paper; $10\frac{9}{16}$ x $15\frac{11}{16}$ in.

Attracted by Manship's reputation, in 1928 Clarence Mackay commissioned a large stone sculpture of *Theseus and Ariadne* (fig. 80) for his Long Island estate's gardens.[9] In a garden surrounded by dense foliage, the figures seemed once more in their mythical world—a superb marriage of site, materials, theme, and scale.

A Manship drawing of *Eros and Psyche* (fig. 81) treated the same theme as *Theseus and Ariadne.* In fact, the stories share a similar, bittersweet scene. The princess Psyche was so beautiful that people began to worship her instead of Venus, and, enraged, Venus ordered her son Eros to make Psyche fall in love with the ugliest creature he could find. When Eros, god of love (*eros* in Greek means sexual love), saw Psyche, he fell in love with her and disobeyed his mother's command. Eros took Psyche to a hidden palace, where he waited on her and spoke to her but remained invisible. He told Psyche that she would enjoy the happiest of lives if only she would refrain from searching for his identity or attempting to see him. Psyche grew to love Eros, and one night after Eros had fallen asleep, Psyche lit a lamp and held it to his face. She was so startled when she saw Eros's beautiful features that a drop of hot oil fell from her lamp and woke him. Eros rose and flew away. Later, desperately seeking his lost wife, Eros approached Jupiter's throne, pleading that Psyche had received due punishment after having served as Venus's slave and that they be allowed to wed lawfully. Their marriage was celebrated by the gods; Venus dismissed her anger; and a daughter, Voluptas, was born. Manship never executed this myth as a sculpture. Manship did produce an ashtray of *Eros and Psyche* in 1937, but the piece had a different composition.

In June 1925 Thomas Cochran commissioned a fountain destined for Manship's hometown of St. Paul, Minnesota, and, late in 1926, Manship installed the life-size *Indian Hunter and His Dog* in Cochran Memorial Park. This work remained a favorite of the artist throughout his life (fig. 82)—it recalled for him his boyhood amid the woods and lakes of Minnesota. (In the spring of 1927 Manship added four life-size bronze *Canada Geese* at the corners of the fountain.) Manship's native subject and his treatment of the theme strongly recall John Quincy Adams Ward's *Indian Hunter* of 1864 (fig. 83). Ward was perhaps the most successful of post–Civil War sculptors; his work displayed a naturalistic spirit that animated the solid forms he favored. Manship's treatment echoes Ward's, although Manship attempted to show greater outward vigor at the expense of psychology. Indeed, the works are so close in their details that Manship's seems a successive frame in a movie of Ward's statue.

Holding a bow in his left hand and arrows in his right, a moccasinned Indian in a breechclout runs with his dog by his side. This traditional new-world theme engendered a lightly buoyant group. Conceptually striking in its

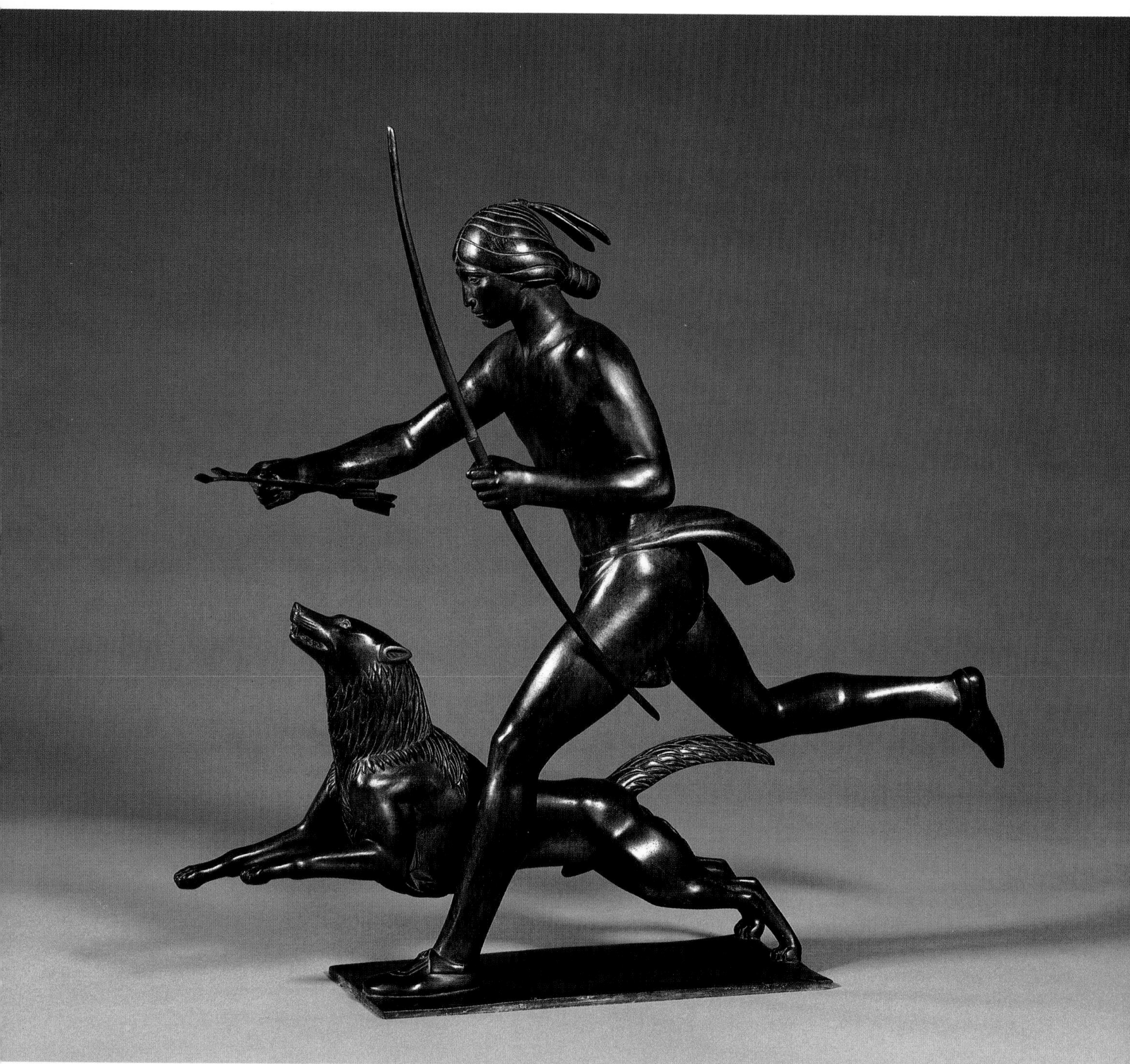

Fig. 82. *Indian Hunter and His Dog*, 1926; bronze; 23¼ in. high.

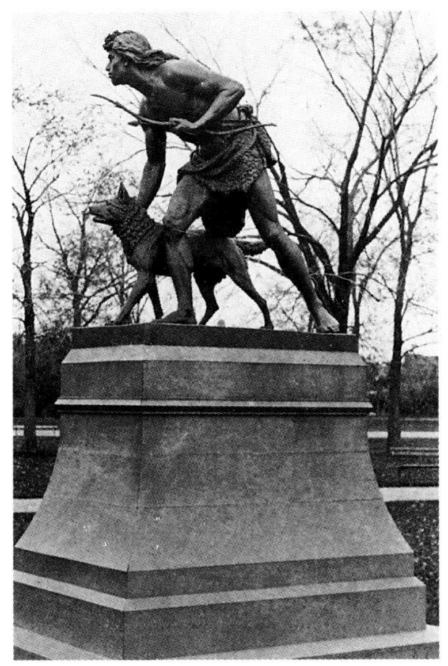

Fig. 83. John Quincy Adams Ward, *The Indian Hunter,* 1873–74; bronze. Central Park.

simplicity, *Indian Hunter and His Dog* is decoratively refined in its parts. Manship must have been very satisfied with this piece, because he issued a reduction of *Indian Hunter and His Dog* that he cast several times, each with a different patina. Relying neither on classical nor biblical references, Manship worked in the smoothly fluid style of the *Actaeon* ensemble. In some respects, this sculpture seems an extension of classical hunting figures, especially meaningful in a historical context. This native subject matter, reduced to elemental forms, identifies a major expression of the Art Deco aesthetic (of which Elie Nadelman and Lachaise were also masters).

Modeled with acute simplification, the dog's head and the Indian's smoothly streamlined body define the limits of Manship's abstraction, although the piece may appear traditional to current spectators. Abstraction itself was not one of Manship's ambitions, and among twentieth-century artists this antipathy distinguished him. In *Indian Hunter and His Dog* we can discern the difference between Art Deco (as the quintessential twentieth-century style) and modernism.

If abstraction was the *telos* of modern art, it held no inherent allure for Manship. Moreover, he seems to have lacked any sense of an overriding progress for art beyond ever more refined dexterity. In just that crucial difference lay the distinction between Manship and his modernist contemporaries. Manship borrowed from the history of art, mined it for invention, and summarized its past, but he did not advance his sculpture's implications, formal or programmatic. For Manship, art did not possess implications; it was a thing made, its forms were inherited to be perfected. Manship's audience neither found, nor would it have reasonably expected, fundamental progress in his art. Nevertheless, Manship evidenced the machine-age aesthetic (identified with the cult of progress) that exhorted evolution. The aesthetic's principal identifiable assumption, shared as a component of all its devotees, was positive change. According to this view, evolution meant social change, but art was simply to undergo shifts of fashion while technology dictated the pattern of life.

History doomed Manship to a terminal position. No major artist assumed the burden of his style to advance or alter what he had accomplished. Just when his sculpture was nearing its apex in the mid 1920s, premonitions of his art's exhaustion were sensed:

> Manship cannot yet claim the title of a great artist, because hitherto he has not shown himself much more than an unparalleled imitator and a most accomplished technician. We must demand of him a further development and expression of his own personality, further technical originality, and a profounder spiritual content.[10]

Particularly, charges that some academic sculptors' works were less contrived and therefore more palatable—regardless of accomplishment, breadth of conception, or skill of execution—were especially sharp. Hearty and companionable, Paul Howard Manship would hardly have thought himself evasive; nor does his art suggest a covert agenda. He seems, simply, to have been incapable of self-revelation. Within the bounds of decorous bearing, Manship was utterly sincere. His upbringing and reticence placed strong artistic gestures of affection or passion off-limits. His art never dissembled or misrepresented his affections or admirations, but he never attempted that degree of self-revelation essential for modernism's characteristic *authenticity*.

Eventually, Manship's formal and historical sources began to wither. Constantly recruited, the past's vitality, glimpsed in youthful rapture, grew more dim and distant with time. Yet in the mid 1920s most observers recognized that his skill had found its just focus and scope of expression.

After his six-year Parisian sojourn, Manship returned to New York in 1927. He established his studio and residence on East Seventy-second Street, where his mature style and career took shape.

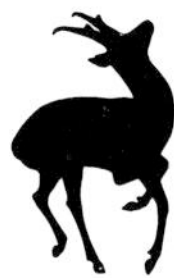

Mature Style and Career

NEITHER RESTRAINED TASTEFULNESS nor an agreeable talent for entrepreneurship accounted for Manship's success as much as dogged labor, cheerful workmanship, and a keen organizational sense. His managerial ability helped account for the torrent of production that issued from his studio. Manship's contributions to modern design and his characteristically clear sculptural conception would not have attracted such attention had Manship been a less productive artist. In addition to being gifted, Manship was prolific, a trait, along with longevity, shared with many artists who leave their mark on history. As sculptor Jacques Schnier noted, "A chronological list of his important sculpture, published in 1927, included more works than any sculptor without assistance could produce in a lifetime."[1] To make his works in great variety and number Manship employed a large staff of assistants.

Perhaps Lachaise—one of his assistants who in 1923 carved two *Dancing Children* in wood—brought to Manship's notice the potential of the "dancing children" theme. With his self-taught erudition and zest for the human side of mythology, Manship invigorated the idea far beyond what he inherited. In the face of his audience's genteelism, Paul Manship's classical studies had taught him that "sculpture, it must be remembered, was not at any time a distinctly serious, grandiose, or heroic mode of expression. The revered ancients were often in lighter mood, hence it is not unseemly that an American artist should be."[2]

Manship was not affected by the genteelism from which some of his clientele suffered. When Manship referred to "the revered ancients," he meant those artists and traditions to whom he looked (more than any of the moderns) as the gauge for achievement in sculpture; "the revered ancients" also gently mocked the conception of a solemnly inviolable past held in sterile (and hence ignorant) esteem by reactionaries. His 1926–27 *Dancing Child* series—in which he used the characteristic poses of the Charleston dance—was at once an amiable chiding of his strait-laced patrons and a charming resuscitation of ancient sources (fig. 84). Animations of ancient or exotic material remained Manship's strongest characteristic; for this series he returned to India as a source.

The favorite, and most human, of the god Vishnu's many incarnations, blue-skinned Krishna is associated with the pleasures of joyful eroticism. To spare his life, Krishna's mother exchanged him for the daughter of a poor cowherd. Soon after his birth, he was already vigorous and given to pranks as well as marvelous heroic deeds. As he grew up to be a playful herdsman, Krishna seized the popular imagination. Despite his presiding over the philosophical *Bhagavad-Gita*, his enchanting of women and the pleasures he gave them accounts for Krishna's vast popular worship. In the form of Balakrishna (*bala*, from the same Indo-European root that yields "ballet" and "ball," a dance) he is adored as the dancing child, whose brother, the lighter-skinned Balarama, helped him defeat the snake-demon Kaliya. Krishna danced upon Kaliya's head in cosmic victory. This enormously widespread theme engendered an image produced in every medium and, as a sculpture, Balakrishna graces the humblest villager's hut and the grandest temple or palace (fig. 85). Manship understood this precedent of the joyful dancing infant and produced his cycle on this subject.

Fig. 84. *Dancing Child* series (*Charleston I–IV*), 1927; bronze; 12 to 12$\frac{7}{16}$ in. high.

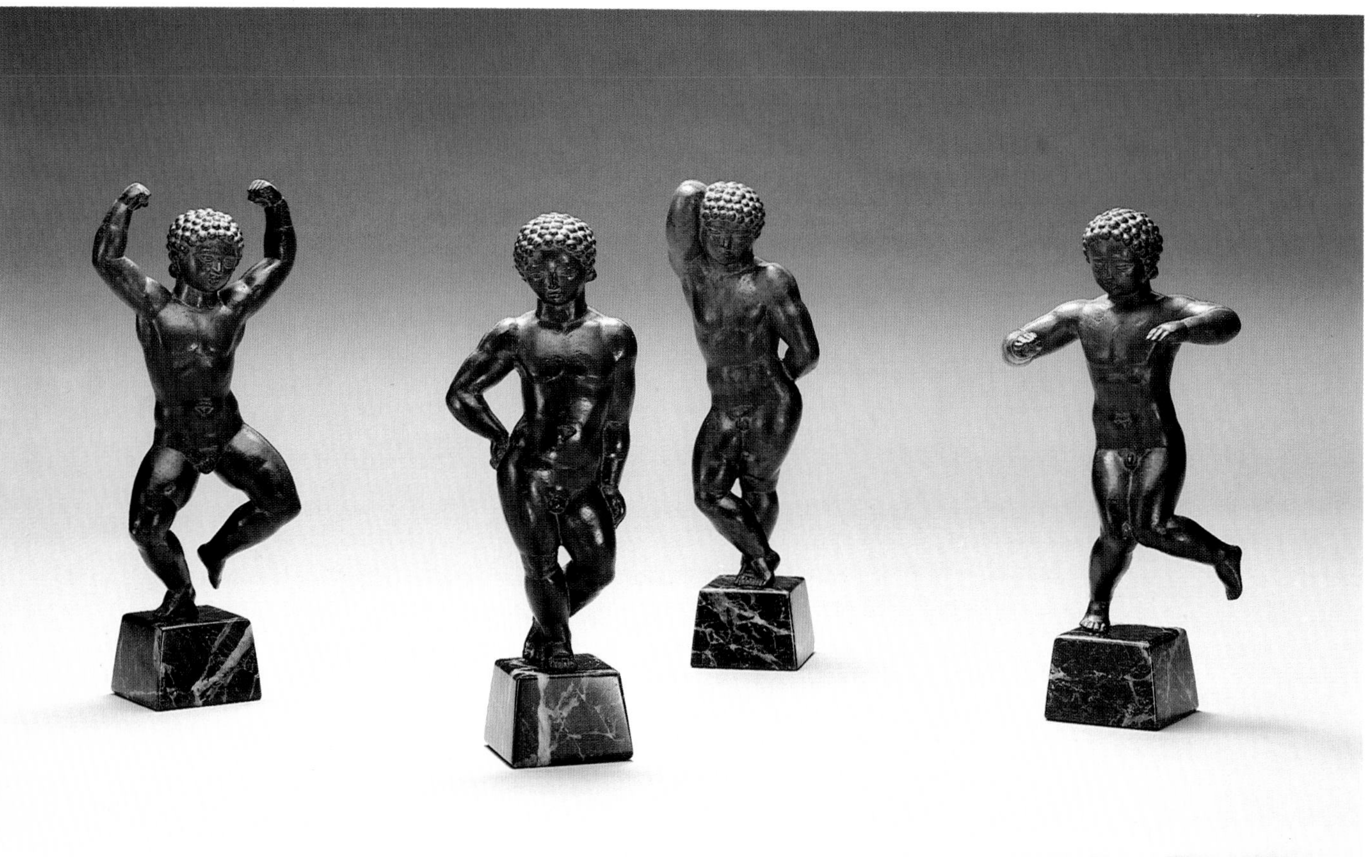

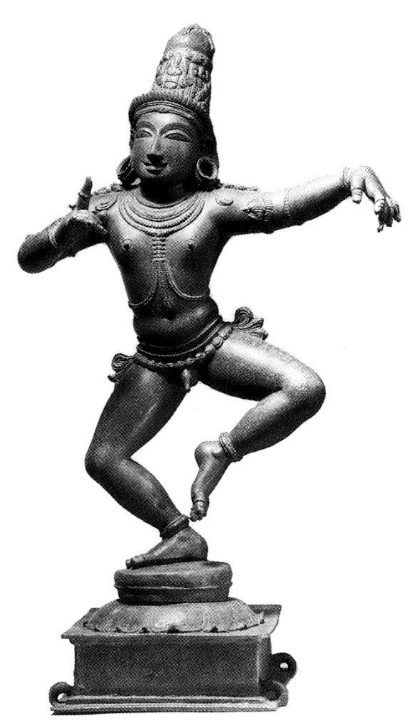

Fig. 85. Indian, Chola Period, 11th century; *Dancing Sambandar* (traditionally, *Dancing Krishna/Balakrishna*); reportedly excavated from Tiruvan Vanpanalur Temple, Tamil Nadu; bronze; 18⅞ in. high. The Asia Society, New York, Mr. and Mrs. John D. Rockefeller III Collection.

Sculpture abandoned to frolicsome and erotic jest was commonplace in Mediterranean cultures during the prehistoric, protohistoric, and classical ages. In addition to the Indic tradition, the figurative terra cottas of Etruria and Latium provide merry precedent for the frivolity of Manship's Charleston figures. His dancing children resurrected a tradition that had lapsed as modernism's high seriousness overcame its protagonists.

Manship's historical influences were not exotic curios gleaned from a mystical and misunderstood past; he respected his artistic sources. His view of the past was not merely a place with the potential for progress, but a wholly independent and authentic world, replete with human incident and developed feeling. For Manship, the arena of the past gave his own emotional range its widest freedom. He shared something of modernism's attraction to pre-modern cultures' formal simplification. Antiquity's high culture possessed a gentleness of feeling, coupled with a complete refinement of expressive range and means, unknown in the modern world.

Conspicuously, Manship eschewed primitivism both for its symbolic incoherence and formal disintegration. Ultimately, incomprehensible symbolism was incompatible with the developed mythologies of those high cultures with which Manship was familiar. The apparently unsystematic formal disposition of primitive art proved unintelligible. (In more understanding hands, primitivism's tendency to an accretion of forms—rather than the *carving* aesthetic at the root of classicism—gave rise to Constructivism, to which Manship's sculpture was anathema.) Just as he found Rodin's unsystematic art unacceptable, the unpredictable characteristics in primitivism were abhorrent and threatening.

The distinction between archaism and primitivism is ultimately the threshold separating Manship from the great mainstream movements of this century. The very traits he rejected beckoned to the youthfully inquisitive modernists (and appealed especially to Picasso and Matisse); eventually, the inoculation of primitivism strengthened the avant-garde, who toppled the edifice of traditional Western art. This was an enterprise in which Manship neither wanted, nor had, any part. For Manship, the recapitulation of the classical world offered too many possibilities for summary rejection. As a late twentieth-century synthesis of classical and moderne, post-modernism allows his work to be viewed in congenial terms once again. History, to which he was faithful, has come to his aid.

By the end of the decade Manship's reputation was secure, if subject to steady reevaluation. Late in 1929, the taste-making *Vanity Fair* devoted a sizeable column to marveling at his achievement: "Still in his middle forties, Paul Manship has attained to distinction and importance not only in the American but in the international world of sculpture."[3]

Whether William Rush or Augustus Saint-Gaudens was the first American sculptor to shake off contemporary Europe's influence and dominate successive generations of the emergent American school, Manship could just as easily represent the start of international respectability for American sculpture. Paradoxically, Manship himself drew succor and inspiration from *ancient* Europe. In this regard, Manship really did break new ground for American culture. Heretofore, our greatest artists—arguably, Benjamin West, John Singleton Copley, James McNeill Whistler, or John Singer Sargent—had been expatriates. While Manship worked outside America for long periods, he was never in danger of being considered an expatriate. A generation before the New York School, Manship represented an artist whose international reputation was as high as his local celebrity. He achieved this stature with a novel formulation.

When the titanic personage of Rodin had threatened to engulf sculpture in Expressionism's confusion, Manship reestablished soundly naturalistic design principles; his early mature style fused antiquity and a distinctly modern naturalism. Rodin's wonderful achievement was beyond emulation and, perhaps, ultimately unsalutary as an example. Manship's serenity could not have appeared more dissimilar to Rodin's turmoil. Manship reemphasized readily perceptible sculptural form; his works' fluent representationalism derived from Konti's and Borglum's insistence on spatial clarity and anatomical accuracy to both bone and flesh. Manship sculpted recognizable plants and animals; his literal-mindedness conceded precision to formal arrangement. His approach rejected nineteenth-century realism or romanticism (as found in Europe and America), which dictated sentimental and unintelligible poses. Sharing the Art Deco sense of an integrated built environment, he united minor decorative elements in major sculpture.

If Manship was not alone, neither did he have an equal. Early in the 1930s, Holger Cahill declared that Manship, more successfully than any of his contemporaries, "has derived from Oriental art a better understanding of formal relations and particularly for a decorative handling of the silhouette."[4] Surpassing any other single quality, silhouette had come to characterize Art Deco, whose designs were distinguished by bold and distinctive shapes or outline as ornamental motif in architectural situations.

In June 1929 Paul Manship was commissioned to design a bronze equestrian statue of Ulysses S. Grant as a part of the monument planned for the president's tomb on Riverside Drive in New York. Following a brief examination of such monuments in Washington, D.C., Manship sailed to Europe to study equestrian statues. He completed a five-foot-high plaster design for a group (and a smaller sketch of about two and a half feet that was cast in 1955). But a lack of funds doomed the commission, and Manship's long-cherished dream of executing an equestrian statue died with this project. (Of course, equestrian statuary did not survive the cavalry, which in a few years fell victim to panzer divisions' *Blitzkrieg*.)

Despite such setbacks, Manship's reputation was firmly established, and in the fall of 1932 he was inducted, along with Walter Damrosch (composer and orchestra conductor) and fellow-sculptor Anna Hyatt Huntington into the American Academy of Arts and Letters.

Interviewed by the New York *Herald Tribune*, Manship was pessimistic about living in "a machine age." He decried the lack of a coherent cultural community with distinct values and, concomitantly, the unintegrated condition of the arts. Instead of the disarray he encountered, Manship (like anthropologist and linguist Edward Sapir) dreamed of a classical community, a model of society in which productive and creative labor were integrated:

> Work done with hands in a machine age is no expression of the age, is personal art, and personal art can hardly be great. I think art is dying already, for the only arts really of our age are the mechanical, the cheap trash of the movies, and so on. Besides an art needs religion, belief in something, and production for a purpose. Always great artists have had it.
>
> Art has lost its integral place in life. Buildings go up and buildings come down, and a sculptor cannot feel that his architect's extra inducements will last more than twenty years. When one thought of the Egyptian temples, of the Acropolis, it made him feel like the decorator of a tawdry, temporary exposition.[5]

Commenting in the *Sun*, Henry McBride failed to grasp the underlying values in what Manship espoused, and how these values just as easily described an ancient *polis* as a modern Art Deco city. Manship fought the alienation of art from life and labor, but McBride assumed only that Manship was lamenting some minor indisposition inherent in his own success. Peevishly, McBride tried to impose his obstinate view:

> Nothing can quite stifle the thought that if an artist be wholly in love with art no amount of isolation and lack of recognition can prevent him from practicing that profession. . . . Mr. Manship himself—the very personification of success . . . has had comparable honors and much more money than Michelangelo ever dreamed of. . . . Artists know nothing of the world and less of philosophy. Your true artist lives in a world of his own fashioning.[6]

MAJOR COMMISSIONS

For many years the officers of the Lincoln National Life Insurance Company thought the firm should have a statue of Lincoln at their national offices in Fort Wayne, Indiana.

> The officers wanted an outstanding creation of art which would be one of the recognized monuments of the world and which, as such, would attract universal

> admiration. . . . Fortunately, the architect of The Lincoln National Life Building, Benjamin Wistar Morris, is a connoisseur of architecture, of sculpture, of painting, of literature and of life. We therefore had recourse to him in the selection of a sculptor. He recommended Paul Manship, whom he considers the world's greatest living sculptor.[7]

The insurance company commissioned Manship to do a heroic bronze statue, and Manship chose to depict Lincoln as a young man. Perhaps more remarkable than the size or the subject of this work was the price of the commission. During the Depression, a car might cost a few hundred and a house a few thousand dollars. Though the insurance company commissioned this piece in the late 1920s, they paid Manship an astonishing $75,000 in 1932, the midst of the Depression.[8] (A little computation suggests an equivalent sum in today's dollars: a number that drives breath from the body.)

Manship chose two separate, and not necessarily harmonious, goals for this large commission. First, he wished to make a successful formal arrangement, and after much experimentation, he arrived at the simple form of an elongated pyramid. This shape derives most clearly from Italian Baroque models (Bernini's homage to antiquity) and French Rococo monuments. Manship's second goal was to present a plausible image of what the young Lincoln might have looked like; he wished to create an insightful and reverential statue.

The first photographs of Lincoln were taken when he was thirty-seven years old. Without photographic records as a guide to his subject's youthful appearance, Manship sought the cooperation of Louis A. Warren, director of the Lincoln National Life Insurance Company and an authority on Lincoln's family and childhood. Together, they researched the genealogy of the Lincoln and Hanks families, and they toured the area of Lincoln's boyhood in Indiana and Kentucky. Glimpses of Lincoln's Kentucky homestead and his childhood haunts excited the sculptor's imagination. The Ohio River recalled old ferryboat days for Manship, who also studied both Carl Sandburg's and Ida Tarbell's biographies of Lincoln. Manship's writings record his impressions of place and his consultations with Lincoln scholars, and his reading enlivened impressions that, as Manship wrote, led

> to the desire to represent the youth as a dreamer and a poet, rather than the material aspect of the railsplitter, as the qualities are more important in view of the greatness of later accomplishment and the influence of the accomplishment of the great which continues after death. Without these qualities of spirit, the idealism and clarity of his future visions would never have been possible.[9]

At first, Manship thought of indicating Lincoln's gentle nature and backwoods scholarship by pairing him with his mother in a tender scene of parental instruction. In a bronze sketch, *Nancy Hanks and the Boy Abraham Lincoln (#1)*, Manship showed Lincoln's mother, book in hand, questioning the boy as they engage in serious talk (fig. 86). This arrangement was rejected, and the plaster waited until 1955 to be cast—even then, it was cast just once. Again and again Manship tried to bring the two figures together; first he placed the boy on one side of his mother, then he tried another arrangement of the motif (figs. 87, 88). Dissatisfied with these compositions of *Nancy Hanks and the Boy Abraham Lincoln* (#2 and #3), Manship waited until 1955 to cast them, and then in only two copies each. In another unique cast, the fourth version of *Nancy Hanks and the Boy Abraham Lincoln* (fig. 89), Manship splayed open the sculpture's mass when he posed the young Lincoln seated at the foot of his mother. Unlike in the other studies, space circulates across the design. Fanned out almost like a high relief, the figures do not seem tubular or vertical, but are richly planar. In this instance, Manship combined the developed formal ensemble with an ornamental surface treatment reminiscent of his *Theseus and Ariadne* from the previous year. Tendrils and vines were meant to suggest a forest setting, but rather than eliciting untamed nature, the carefully placed foliage recalls a classical pastoral. In *Nancy Hanks and the Boy Abraham Lincoln (#4)*, Manship attempted to perfect a compositional idea that grew from his previous work, but which was ultimately unsuited to his ambitions for the monument. Finally, he rejected the Madonna/Pieta constellation of associations in favor of presenting Lincoln as a young David, solitary and independent.

In Manship's final study, *Abraham Lincoln, The Hoosier Youth* (fig. 90), the mother is no longer tutoring the thoughtful boy. Instead, symbols of Lincoln's country life surround him. He reflects, and that inwardness and moodiness appeared that marked the melancholy adult weighed down with responsibility. A completely different agenda for the sculpture had evolved.

In the new study, Manship had the youth leaning against a tree stump; the piece is inscribed: "Study of statue of Abraham Lincoln as a youth of the Indiana period." Manship wanted to represent the young Lincoln as a thoughtful idealist rather than a backwoodsman—the ax sufficed to indicate the latter. Manship explained that he "depicted Lincoln as the brawny youth that he was. . . . The book symbolizes his intellectual faculties; and the dog reminds us of his exceptional love for animals as well as the greater feeling of human sympathy and protectiveness. For clothes I decided on a linsey-woolsey homemade shirt, buckskin trousers, and boots."[10] At first Manship conceived of having Lincoln wear homemade moccasins but eventually remembered that

> by the age of twenty-one, when the Lincolns moved to Illinois, Abraham had already been in contact with the world apart from his locality. He had made the trip from New Orleans on a flat boat and had worked as a ferryman on the Ohio River; it was therefore conceived that, with his greater earning capacity, he would probably wear boots.[11]

Fig. 86. *Nancy Hanks and the Boy Abraham Lincoln (#1)*, modeled ca. 1929, cast 1955; bronze; 15¾ in. high.

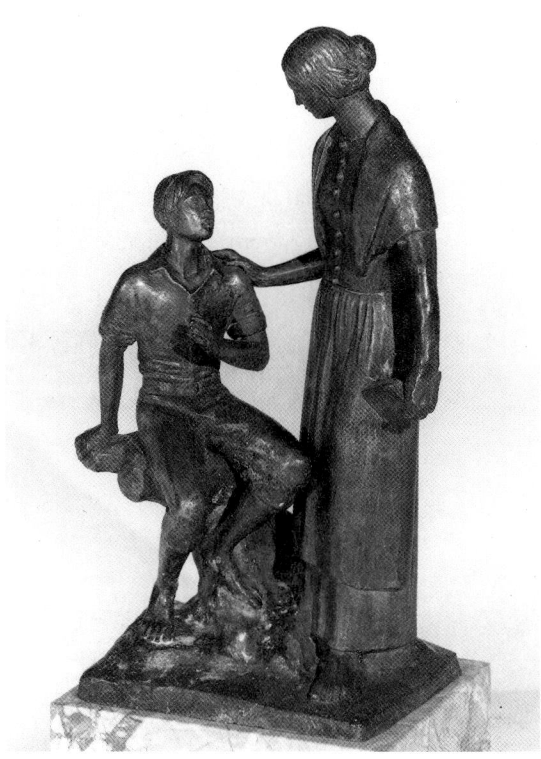

Fig. 87. *Nancy Hanks and the Boy Abraham Lincoln (#2)*, modeled 1929, cast 1955; bronze; 7¾ in. high.

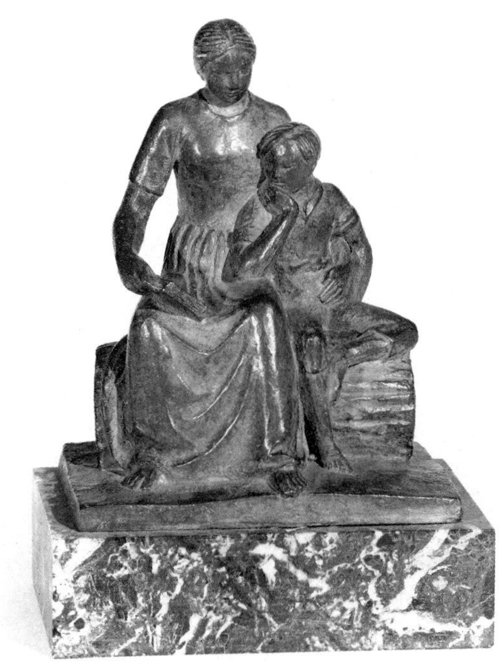

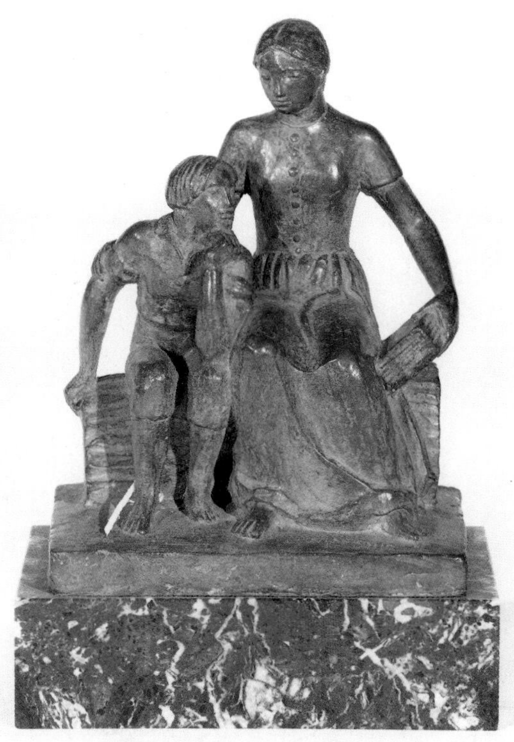

Fig. 88. *Nancy Hanks and the Boy Abraham Lincoln (#3)*, modeled 1929, cast 1955; bronze; 9 in. high.

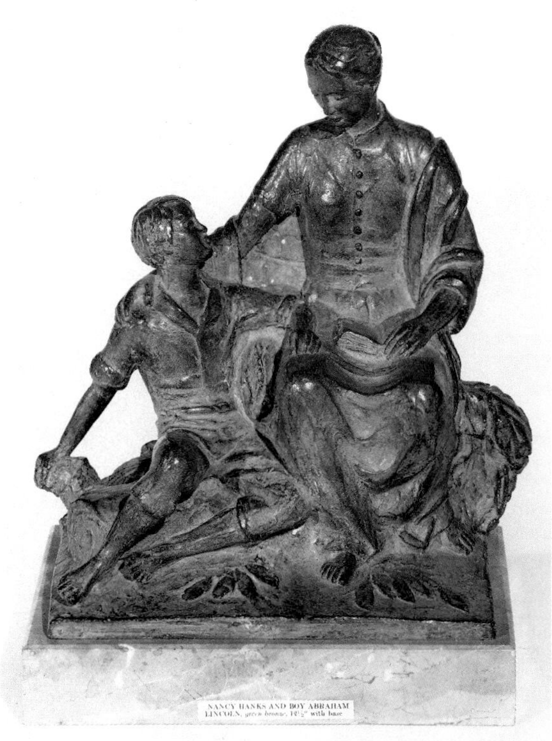

Fig. 89. *Nancy Hanks and the Boy Abraham Lincoln (#4)*, 1929; bronze; 12¼ in. high.

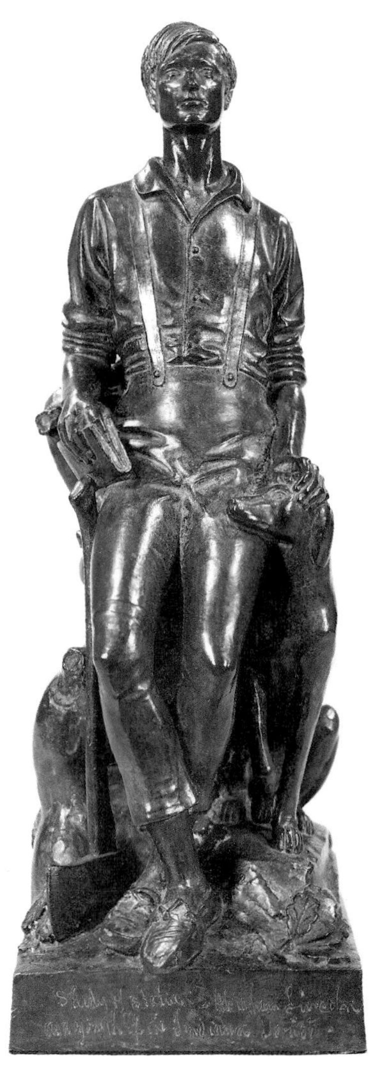

Fig. 90. *Abraham Lincoln, The Hoosier Youth*, 1929; bronze; 18¾ in. high; inscribed: "Study of statue of Abraham Lincoln as a youth of the Indiana period."

In May 1929, after an engrossing year immersed in his subject's life, Manship presented the Lincoln National Life Insurance Company with a plaster sketch. The sketch approved, Manship continued working on the statue in his New York and Paris studios until, in November 1931, a plaster model was finished in Paris. A second plaster model was cast in Brussels, and a third model had been sent to his New York studio. It was there, during the winter of 1931–32, that Manship completed the statue and the four small relief medallions on its base. He thought the base was an appropriate place to represent

> some of the major qualities which Lincoln possessed—Patriotism, Justice, Fortitude and Charity; these I have expressed in the conventional manner, with the exception of Patriotism, which goes on the front of the pedestal and which I have characterized by the American Eagle holding an olive branch and a bunch of arrows. The unity of his country, symbolized by the eagle, was his great patriotic ideal.[12]

In April he sailed for Europe to inspect the finished casting and to supervise the application of a patina (figs. 91, 92). He wrote from Brussels on 8 May 1932: "Via SS 'Minnewaska' sailing May 13th—Antwerp—I am shipping the Lincoln statue with the four reliefs. It is a good casting and I am pleased with the colour of the bronze which I have been working on here for the past week. I have kept the colour light in tone to harmonize with the stone of the building."[13] The giant sculpture was finished at last; it measured twenty-two-feet high, the figure alone standing twelve-and-a-half-feet tall. (*The Hoosier Youth* weighed four and a half tons. Including base and plinth, the total weight came to seventy-nine tons.) On 16 September 1932 the completed bronze was dedicated in the plaza of the Lincoln National Life Building.

The full-size plaster model of the Lincoln figure suggested to some critics that Manship was beyond his art's eclectic and assimilating streak; to these spectators he seemed to have arrived at a genuinely personal expression, a style capping his entire synthetic enterprise. But there was a price to pay. Now naturalism receded in favor of heavy-handed, less sure, theatrical touches. This newly awkward art, however, sprang from serious research that Manship conducted especially for the project. In retrospect, Manship's lack of confidence in his own midwestern experience might arouse suspicion. Where in the past, Manship's robust vitality had invigorated antiquity, now, perhaps awed by his subject, dry facts supplanted living sensation. The sincere reverence for Lincoln that Manship felt and had expressed plastically in the small studies of *Nancy Hanks and the Boy Abraham Lincoln*—all that intimate humanity seemed absent from the completed monument. For the first time, intimations of Manship's increasingly vacant late works could be sensed. The urges to denature his art produced a formal solution, which was more difficult to shed with each

Fig. 91. *Abraham Lincoln, The Hoosier Youth*, 1932; bronze; 24 ft. high; four bronze medallions adorn the base representing: patriotism, justice, fortitude, and charity. Lincoln National Life Insurance Company, Fort Wayne, Indiana.

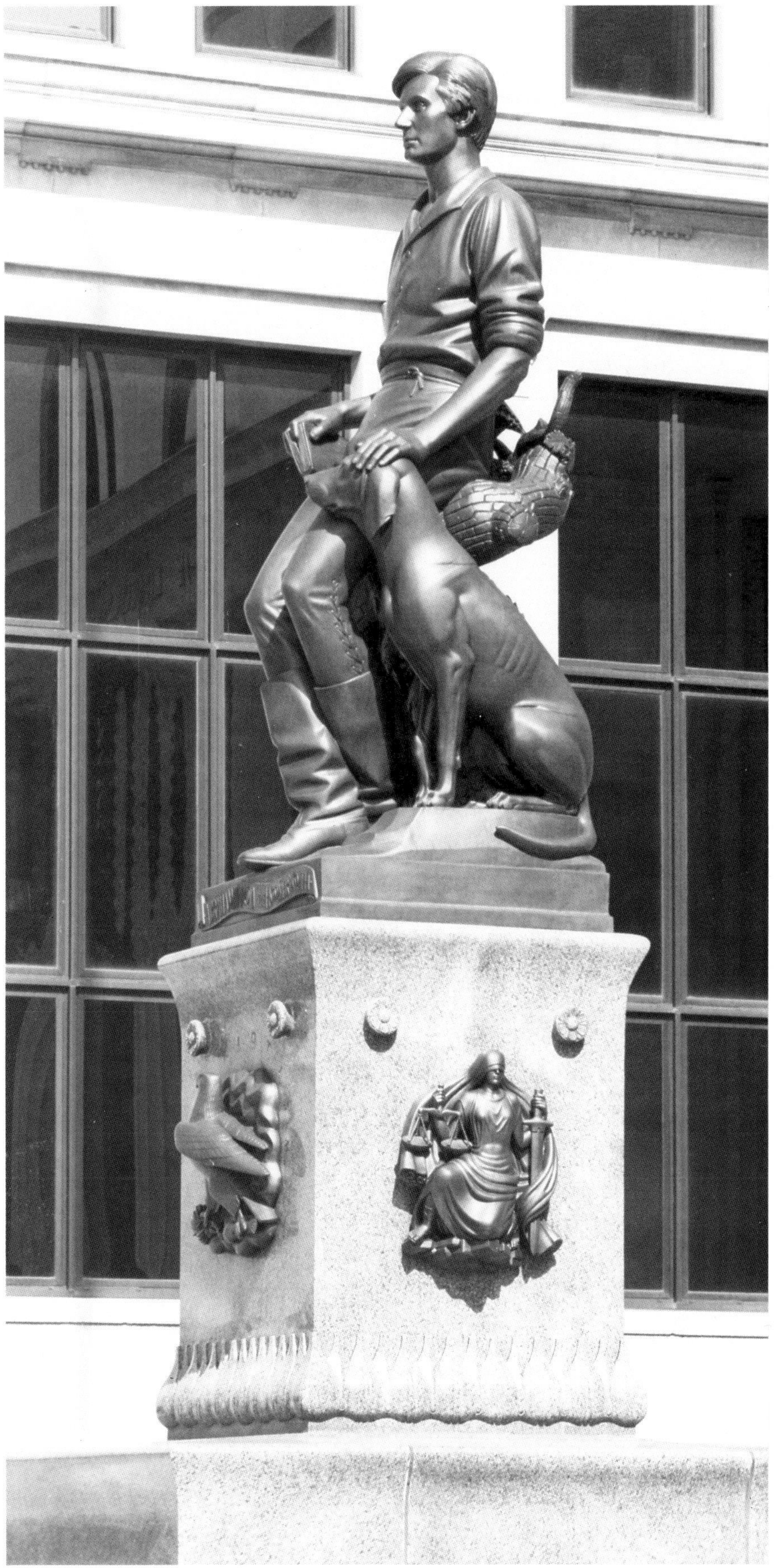

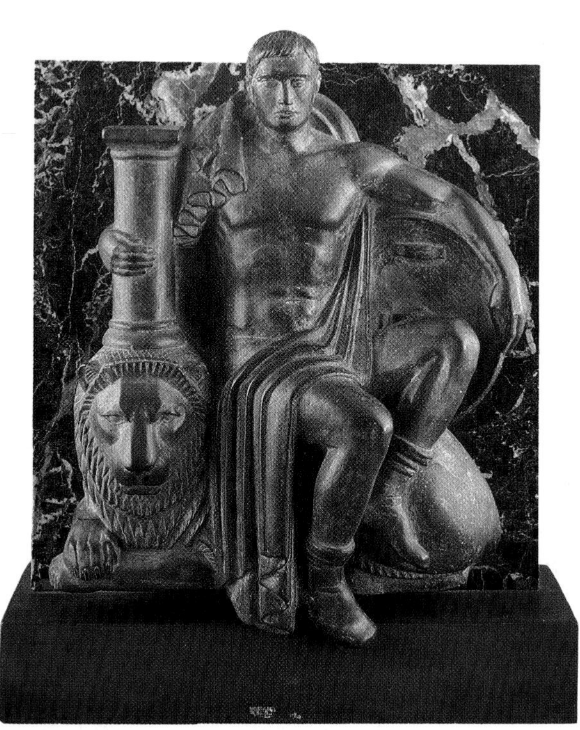

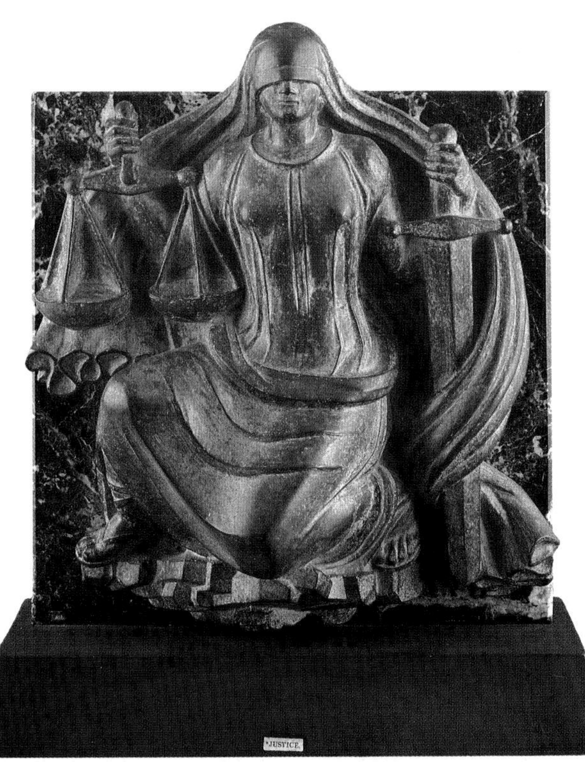

Fig. 92. *Fortitude* and *Justice*, 1955; bronze on marble and wood bases; $14\frac{3}{8}$ to $15\frac{1}{16}$ in. high.

successive piece, although his inventive spark flared intermittently for the rest of his life.[14]

Manship was prominent enough to be attacked by the press; however, his patrons supported him against journalistic diatribes, and warrants for grand commissions carried his art to greater achievements. For New York's Bronx Zoological Gardens, Mrs. Grace Rainey Rogers ordered memorial gates dedicated to her brother, Paul J. Rainey, a big game hunter, explorer, and motion-picture photographer.

Manship received the commission in 1926 for the double gates, which, completed in 1934, ultimately measured thirty-four by forty-two feet. With fifteen assistants, Manship worked in New York, and the casting was done in Belgium. The gates, installed on the zoo's northern border, mark the formal entry to extensive grounds and exhibits, laboratories, and educational facilities (fig. 93). Over its eight-year life, the project cost $250,000—an enormous amount in Depression dollars. Above each of the two gates is a lunette—one contains a group of deer, the other bears—and the gate's central column is a stylized tree surmounted by a lion. In all, twenty-three animals were sculpted for the gates requiring twenty-eight tons of bronze. Moving this huge amount of metal ever so gently caused logistical nightmares. The ships contracted to transport the casts proved too small. On arrival in America the sculpture needed to be moved in special oversize trucks, which were too large to negotiate the Holland Tunnel. The crates had to be barged upriver, replaced on the trucks, and finally delivered.

Manship, who had learned every aspect of his art's technique, could allow himself great flexibility in planning (figs. 93–96). His friends, mostly artists themselves, were awed by his diligence and remarked that "the technical problems of sculpture fascinated Manship and he did not rest until he mastered them and could direct with authority even the bronze founders."[15]

For two years Manship worked on the gate designs, and the working model was only in three-eighths scale. This was the largest size that would fit into the sculptor's studios in New York and Paris; it took almost five years to scale up the work to a full-size plaster version. In 1933 the full-size plaster working models were displayed in New York at a benefit for unemployed architects and draftsmen. The show was not only philanthropically motivated

Fig. 93. *Paul J. Rainey Memorial Gateway*, 1934; bronze; 36 x 42 ft. New York Zoological Park, Bronx.

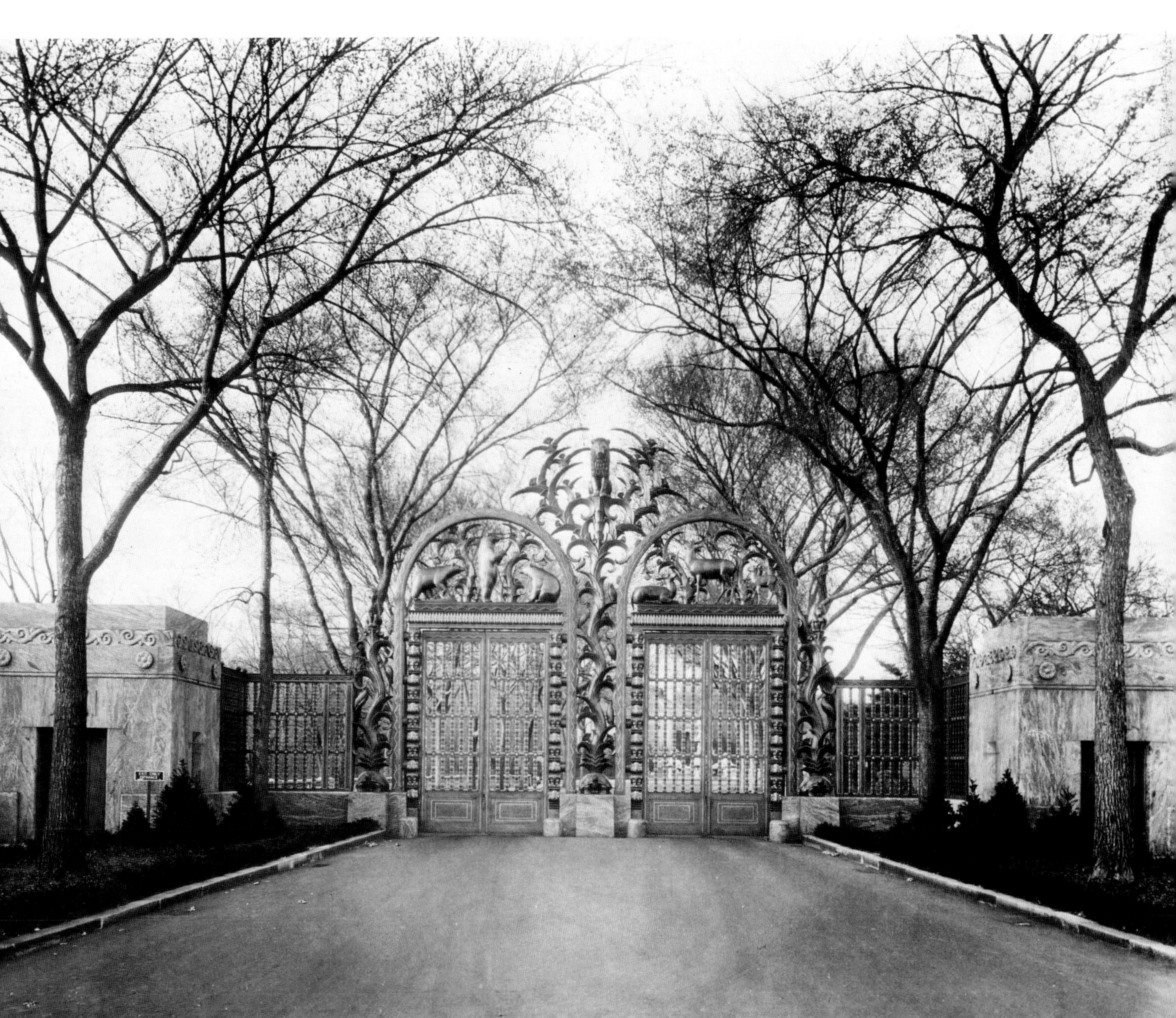

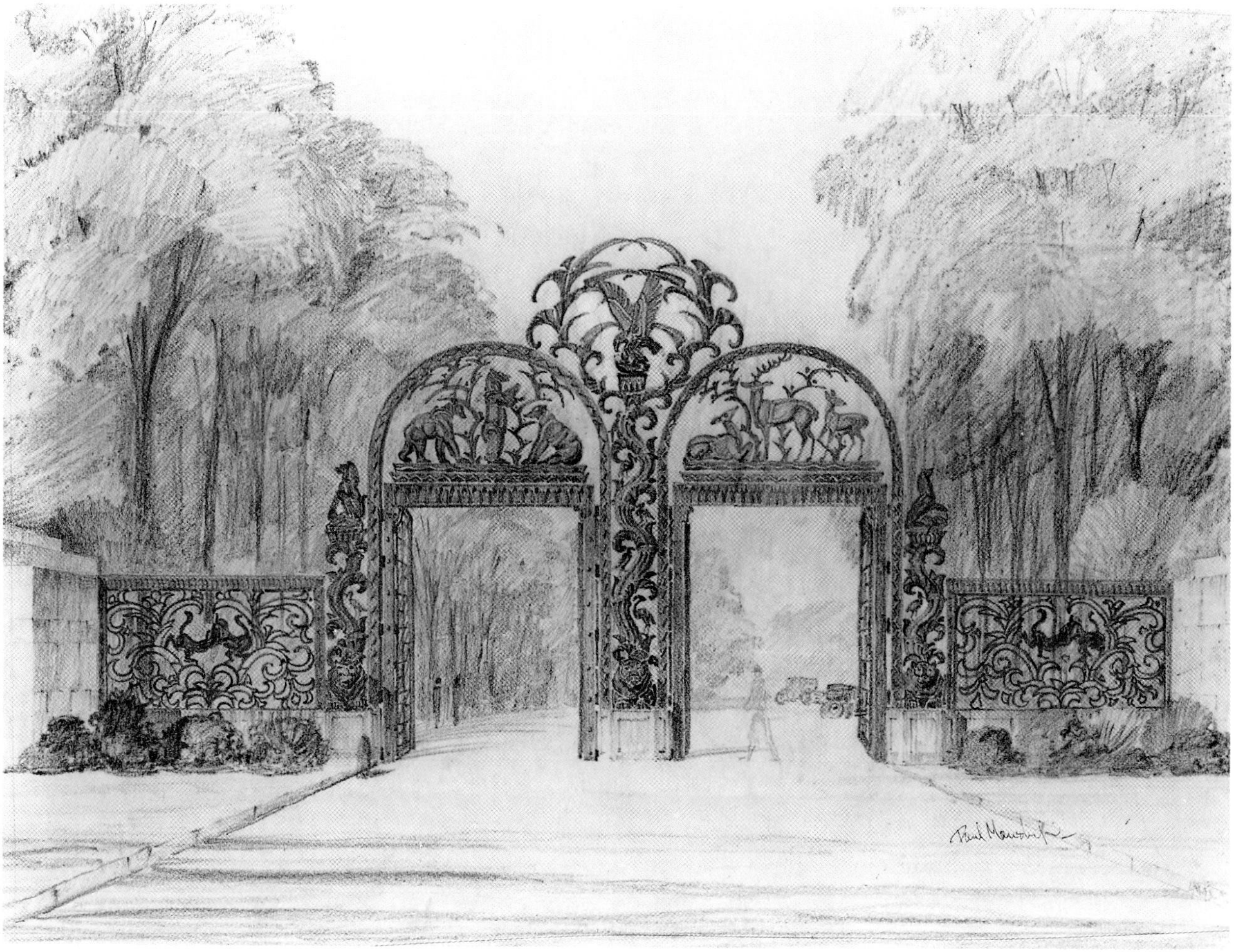

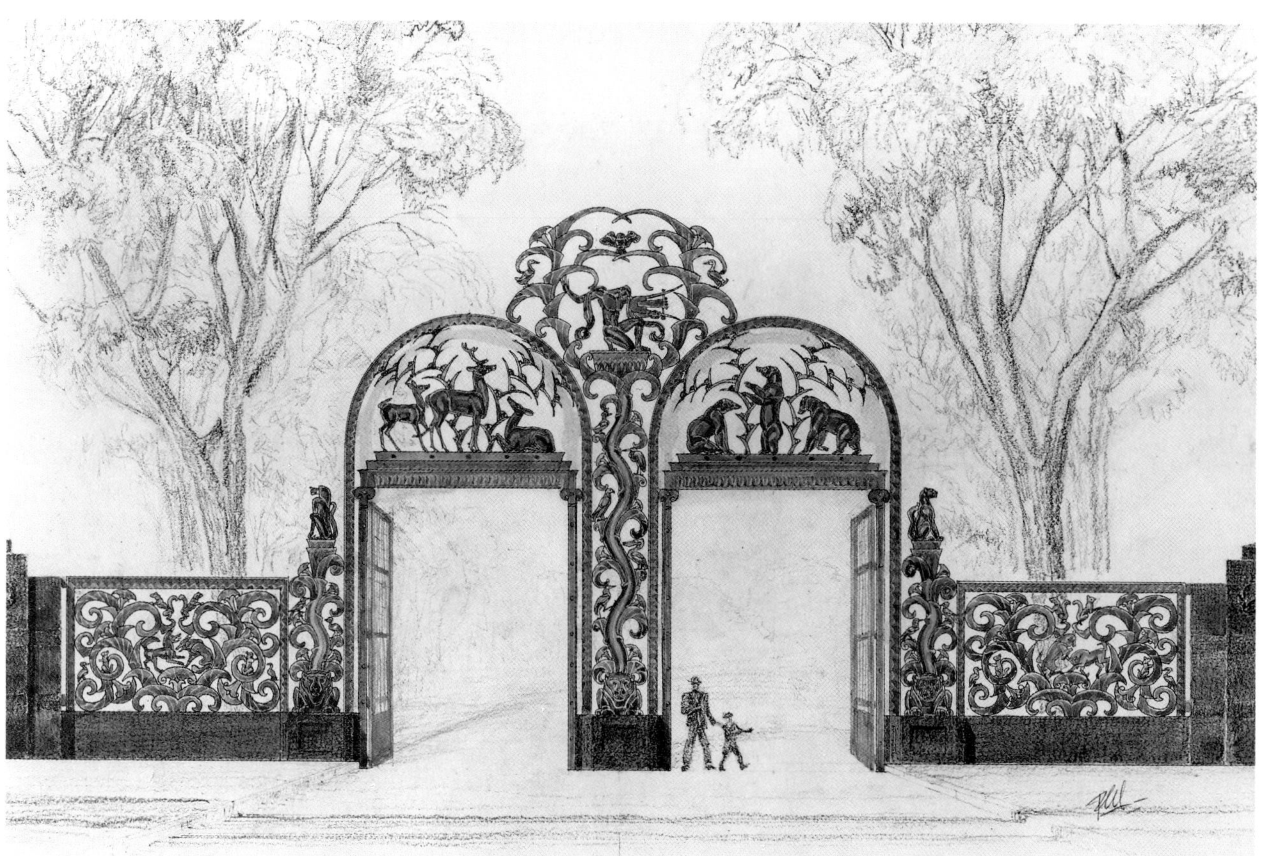

Fig. 94. *Design for the Paul J. Rainey Memorial Gateway*, 1934; crayon, pencil, and gouache on paperboard; $14\frac{15}{16}$ x 19 in.

Fig. 95. *Design for the Paul J. Rainey Memorial Gateway*, 1934; pen and ink, watercolor, gouache, crayon, and pencil on paperboard; $14\frac{7}{8}$ x 20 in.

but also gave Manship the first chance in years to display his works' full range. With over seventy pieces, including the life-size casts of animals for the gates, this show was his first big solo exhibition in New York since 1916.

While it must have been hard to see how the plaster bears, deer, lions, and other animals could be incorporated within the whole design, critics generally were pleased by what they encountered. One wrote waggishly that the animal sculptures seemed "rather arbitrarily inserted into the plant-like supports that wind upward through the various sections of the gate. But the animals themselves are what is so commonly called today—swell."[16] In the zoo gates commission Manship returned to a subject he had learned so well from both Solon and Gutzon Borglum and Isidore Konti—animal sculpture. Murtha, Manship's cataloguer, recalled that "Borglum was executing two heroic size equestrian monuments when Manship worked for him," and that "horses and dogs were dissected under Borglum's instruction, which gave Manship the sound anatomical knowledge that has been revealed in all his animal sculpture, and that is especially evident in the numerous animal details from the *Paul J. Rainey Memorial Gateway*. Several competent animal studies reflected the lessons Manship learned from Borglum."[17]

Originally, the gates were to be of wrought iron, with added details of birds and animals in bronze relief. But when the size of the gates was established, it became clear that details would be lost amid the ironwork, and Manship wished to make the gates a sculptural, not an architectural, statement. (As part of the ensemble, Manship and the architect Charles Platt designed two granite gatehouses flanking the gates.) Sketched from life, each of the animals and groups is modeled completely in the round.

Fig. 96. *Study for Grillwork in the Paul J. Rainey Memorial Gateway*, 1934; pen and ink and pencil on tracing paper; $3\frac{7}{16}$ x $5\frac{3}{16}$ in.

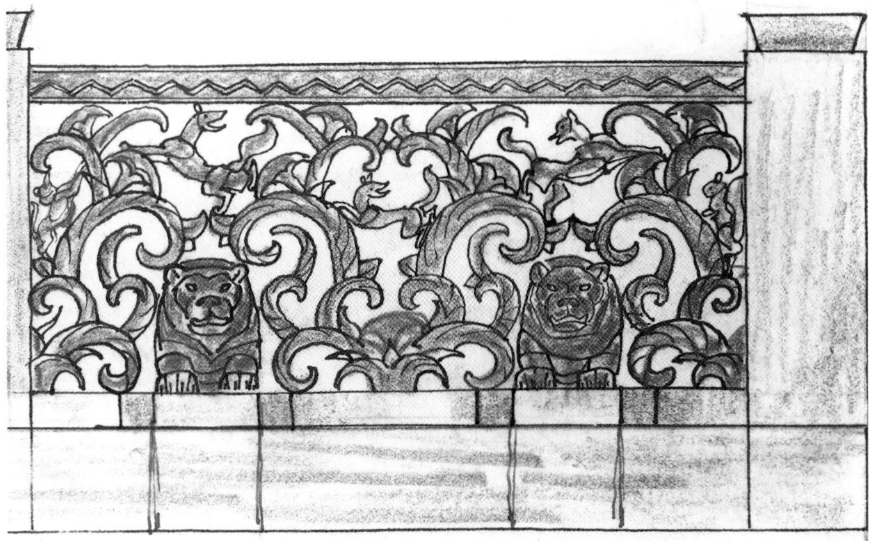

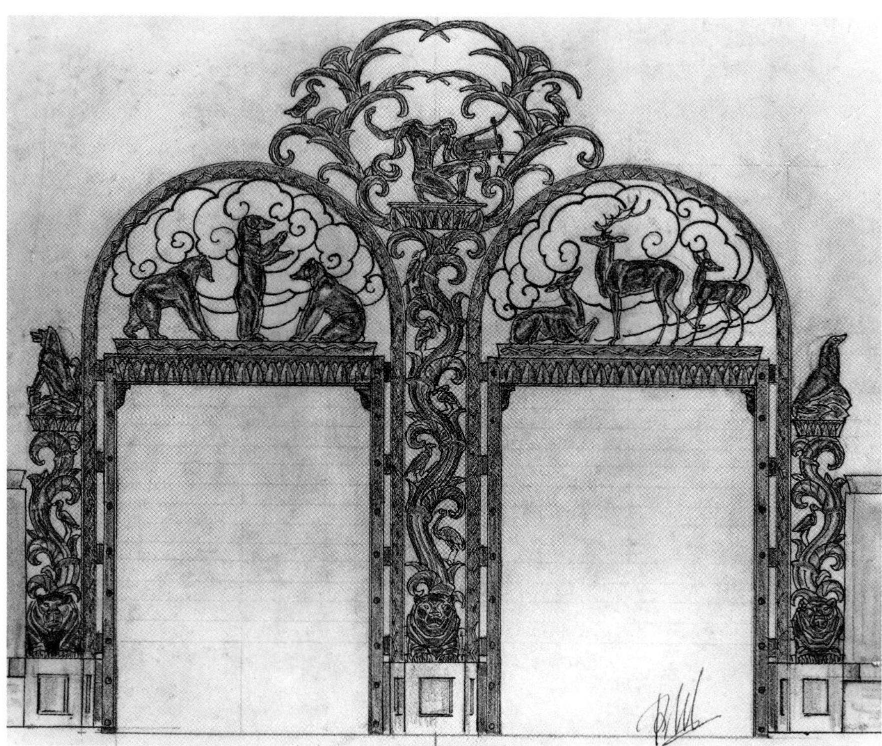

Fig. 97. *Study for the Paul J. Rainey Memorial Gateway,* 1934; pen and ink and pencil on tracing paper; 8 15/16 x 10 1/2 in.

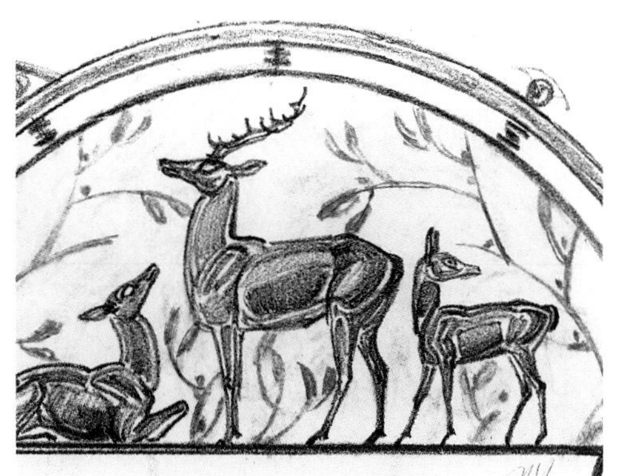

Fig. 98. *Study for the Paul J. Rainey Memorial Gateway,* 1934; conté crayon and charcoal on tracing paper; 7 7/16 x 9 5/8 in.

Manship's group of black bears, for a lunette of the zoo gates, was subsequently issued as independent casts—as was the *Group of Deer* (figs. 97–100). Modeled individually, the bears strike poses characterizing aspects of ursine personality: inquisitive, majestic, lumbering, prowling, deliberate. Set high in the gates, the bears were fitted into a single plane of the least depth to accommodate the surface's sheer ascent. When cast as separate units, the animals were freed from the gates' confining plane; viewing them as freestanding pieces immeasurably heightens their three-dimensionality.

Manship consciously composed the bears in order to display the basic properties of sculptural space. The bears' shapes, the grandest element of sculptural statement, are very distinctive as silhouette; this is the most immediate distinguishing characteristic of one sculpture from another. Manship treated the subordinate elements independently, as clear columnar forms; these tubular units point in various directions, their masses easily legible. Even smaller units that read as rhythmic pattern, such as the bears' toes, invite us to scan the surface for small incidents (fig. 101). In turn, these diminutive components lead to decorative elements (which Manship had long ago mastered in the works of his early maturity), limited to such discrete zones as the bears' manes. (The same careful accounting of every level of sculptural consideration appeared as early as the *Infant Hercules Fountain*'s waterspout *Grotesque Figures,* when Manship gave compact shapes sharp silhouettes, fine details, and a patterned

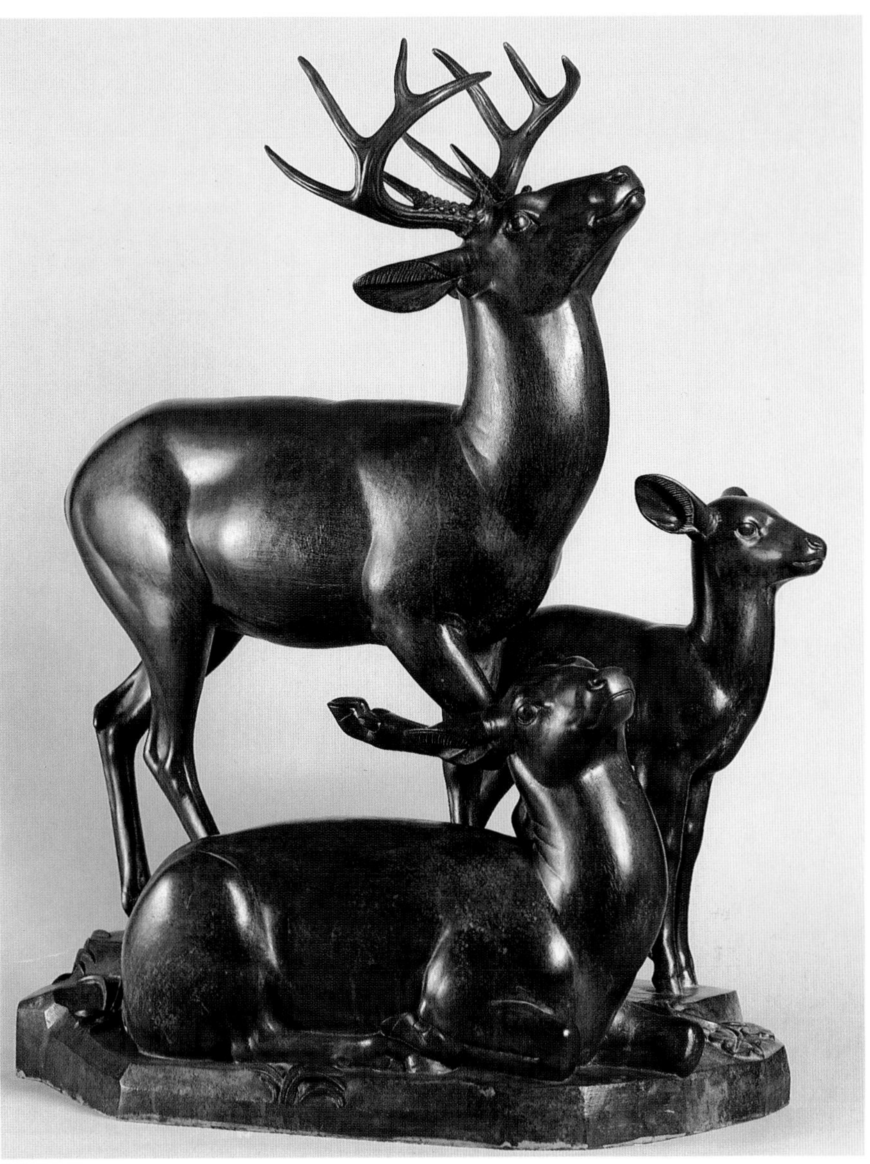

Fig. 99. *Group of Deer*, 1941; bronze; 32½ in. high.

surface.) Gradually, the spectator's gaze moves from the bulkiest forms down to the finest details. Nothing about this orchestration of parts to the whole was happenstance.

Although delimited by an obvious formal agenda, this *Group of Bears* retains a vivacity that bespeaks the figures' origin in careful life studies. Fully satisfied with his resolution of these masses and their ability to express both a formal intelligence about volumes as well as a delightful comment on the nature of bears, Manship resurrected this ensemble when he worked on the Osborne playground some twenty years later.

Manship modeled the *Baboon* for the Bronx Zoo to surmount one of the gates' terminals (fig. 102). The dense, absolutely compact form is covered with

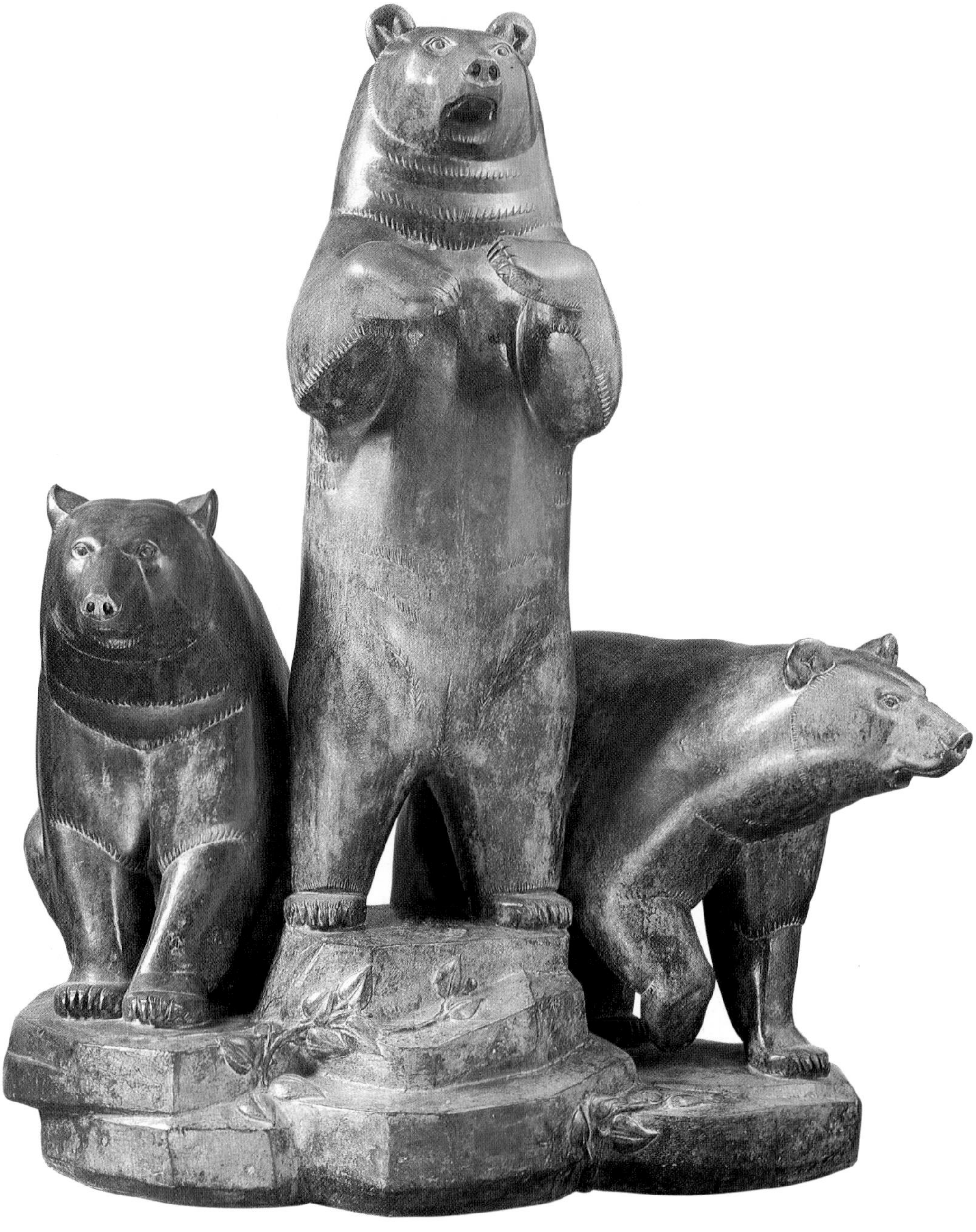

Fig. 100. *Group of Bears*, 1939; bronze; 33 in. high.

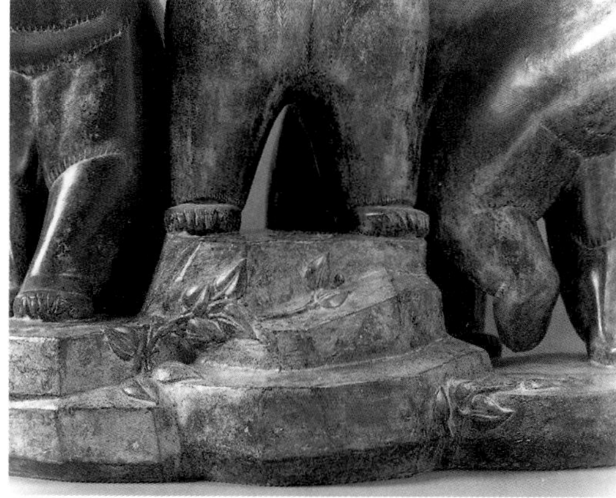

Fig. 101. Detail, *Group of Bears*.

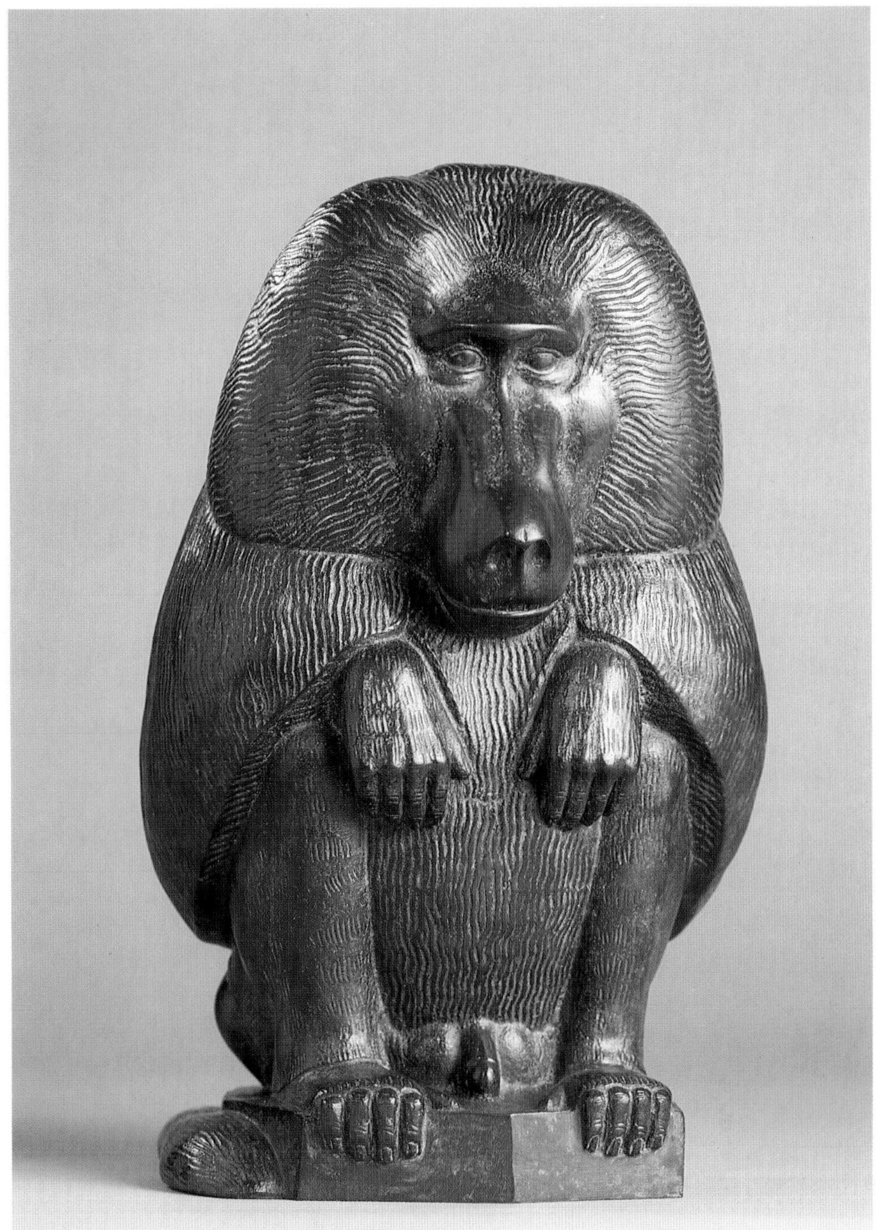

Fig. 102. *Baboon*, 1932; bronze; $11\frac{1}{4}$ in. high.

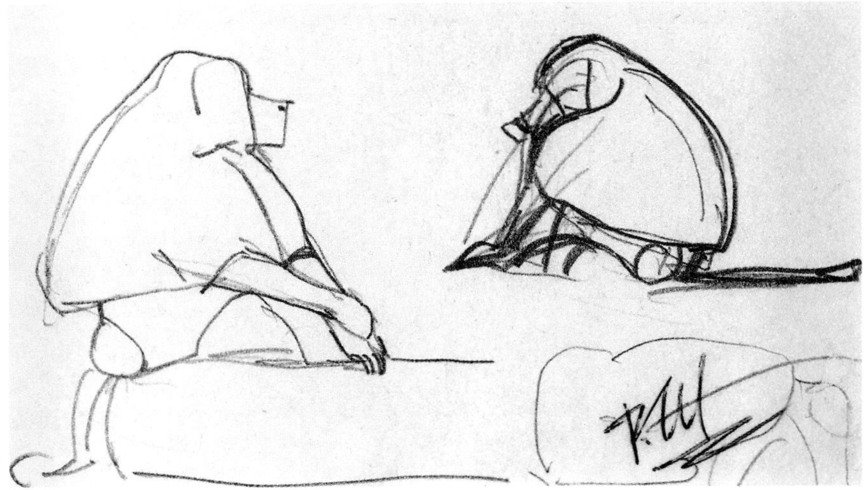

Fig. 103. *Study of Baboons*; pencil on paper; $2\frac{1}{4} \times 4\frac{1}{4}$ in. Minnesota Museum of Art, St. Paul, Bequest of the Estate of Paul Howard Manship.

surface patterns to indicate a monkey's hair and is based on studies that include some of Manship's finest drawings. An unsurpassable sketch, the *Study of Baboons* is breathtaking in its concision, accuracy, and elegance (fig. 103). A few swift lines are all Manship needed to define one animal hunched and withdrawn and another, hands clasped over its knees, inquisitively scanning the world; Manship captured the form and attitude of these animals and their humanly meditative state—qualities that survive in the bronze. The pencil sketch recalls the best sort of drawing by sculptors, those works in which volume assumes an easy familiarity and lines gracefully carve masses out of the air. It can even stand comparison with a Rembrandt animal drawing—just so suavely accomplished and human was Manship at his best.

Among his most elegant works are ten birds, elements of the zoo gates, that Manship subsequently produced in two sizes. Both the small-scale models and the life-size pieces are wonderful in their details, the plumage mediating

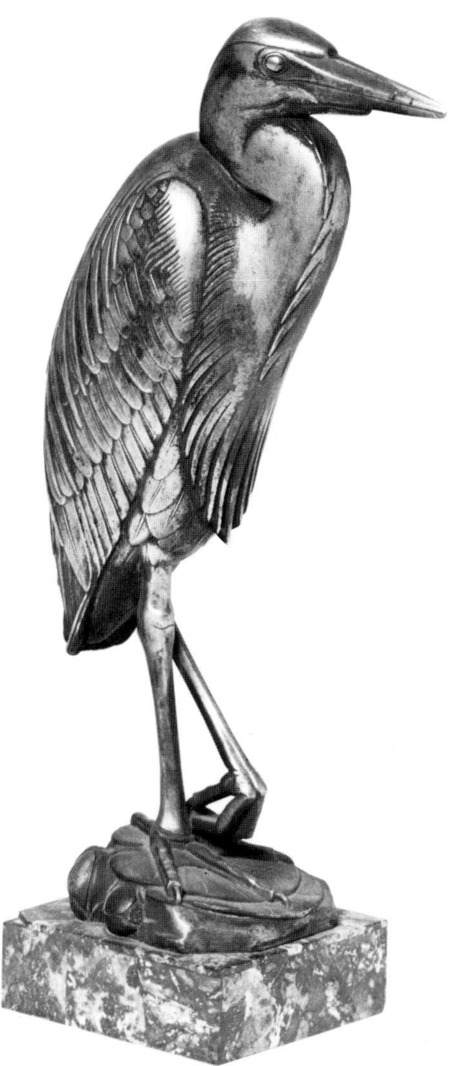

Fig. 104. *Goliath Heron*, 1932; gilded bronze on lapis lazuli base; 12⅝ in. high.

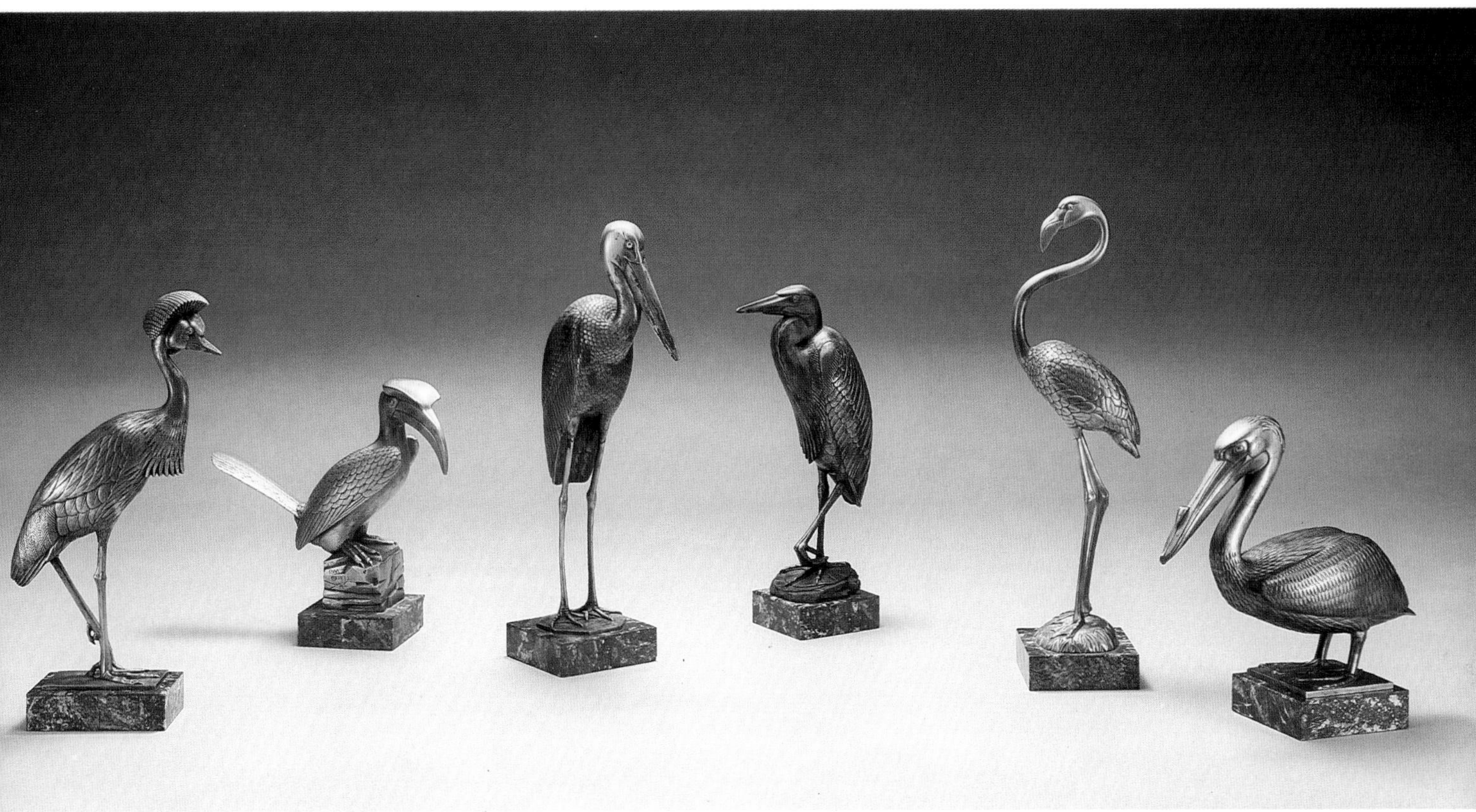

Fig. 105. *Group of Birds*, 1932; gilded bronze on lapis lazuli bases; 9⅝ to 16¼ in. high.

between high realism and the abstract qualities of pure decoration (figs. 104–107). However refined their incidental passages, each of these works feels graceful and at ease. (Unlike the Morgan Memorial, which Lachaise had declined an invitation to sign, the animal figures for the zoo gates were co-signed by Manship (PM) and his assistant, Angelo Columbo (AC)—a mysterious and otherwise obscure artisan who assisted Manship with these statuettes.) All the birds were gilded; the smaller versions rise from bases of semiprecious lapis lazuli, which present them as even more jewellike and intimate than would their size and delicacy otherwise. Despite the number of these birds, Manship did not mass produce them; each is a separate creation, capturing the physiology and something of the personality of each species.

The individuality of every creature was noticed from the beginning. One critic remarked that Manship's "animals are characters, if not portraits; they have a distinctive mark which indicates that they have been understood by their interpreter. . . . None of his sculpture is realistic."[18] Another reviewer noted that "These figures, so tranquil, so sensitively posed, profoundly express that quality in animal life—something large and great, very remote from civilization."[19] The individuation of the *Crowned Crane* was certainly never confused with *Flamingo*; nor did Manship blend one species of *Adjutant Stork*

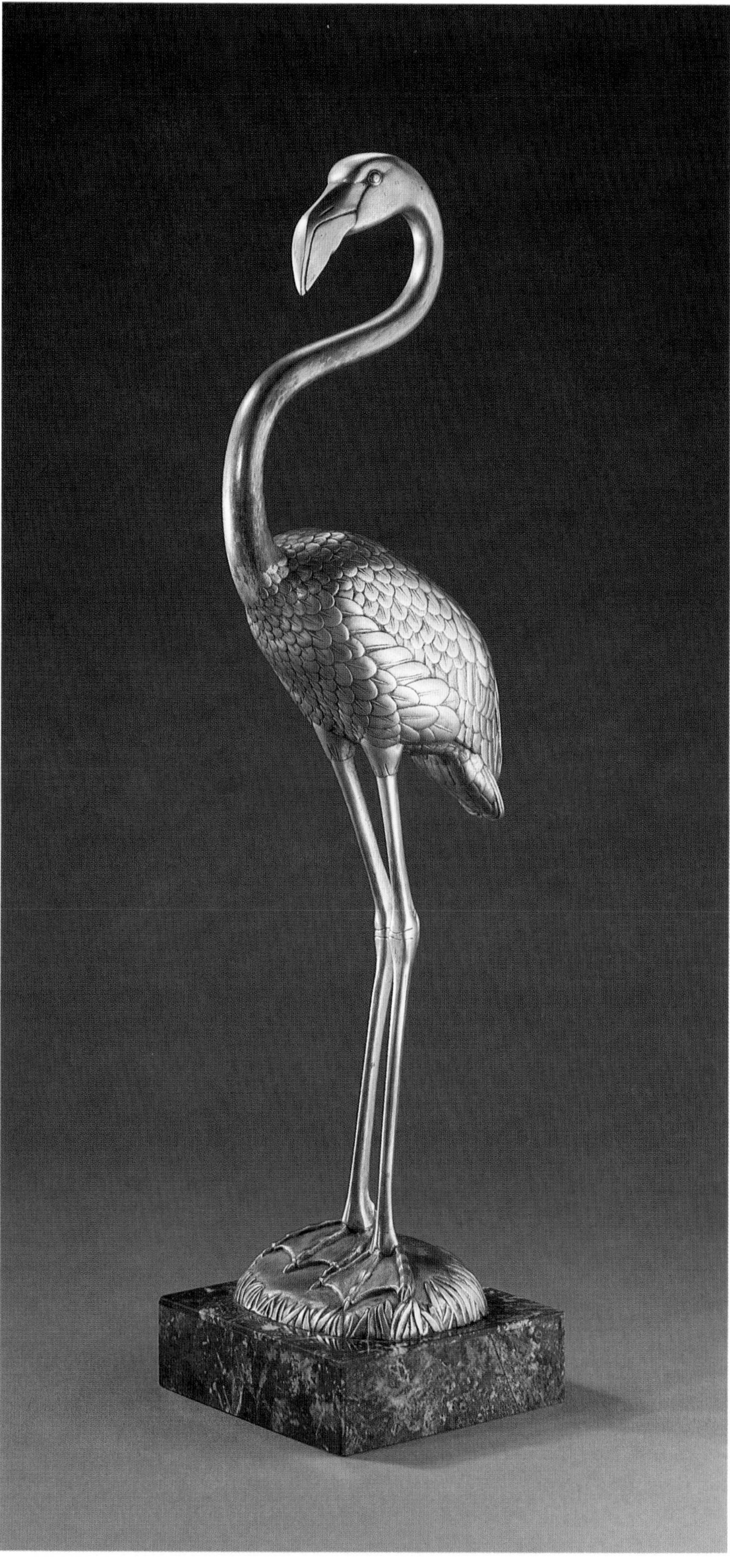

Fig. 106. *Flamingo (#1)*, 1932; gilded bronze on lapis lazuli base; 16¼ in. high.

Fig. 107. *Crowned Crane*, 1932; gilded bronze on lapis lazuli base; 13⅝ in. high.

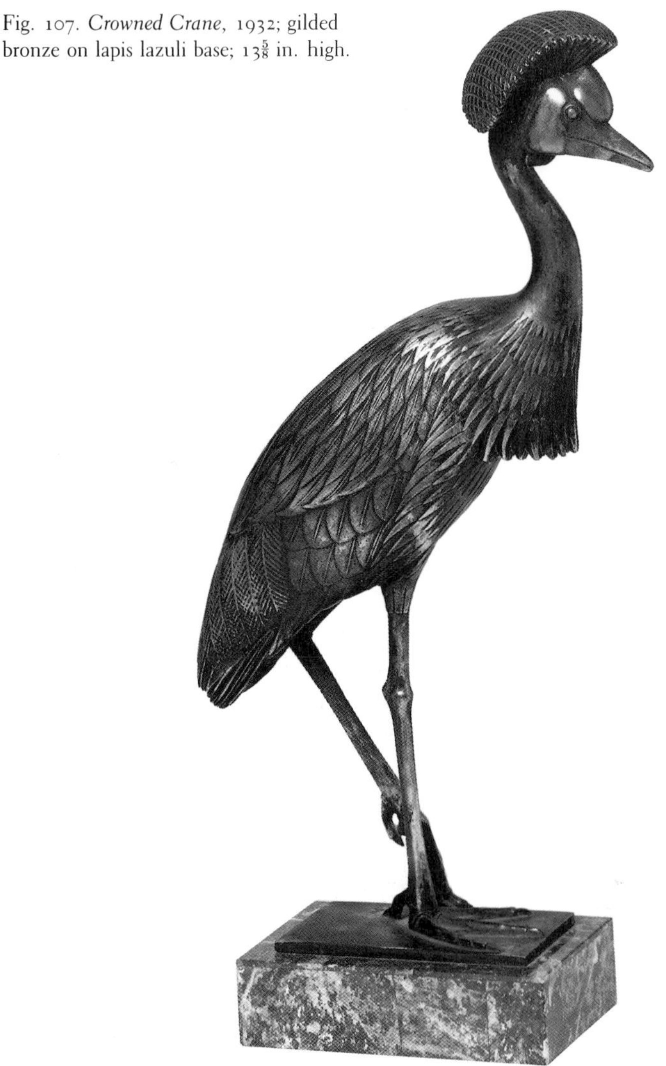

with the attributes of the *Shoebill Stork* (figs. 108, 109) to form a common notion of "stork." With the respectful eye of a naturalist, he assumed the distinguishing characteristics of each species as immutable, and within these bounds he worked his considerable art.

Royal Cortissoz regarded Manship's twenty-year survey at the Averell House in New York dyspeptically, stating that Manship too "soon became a mature craftsman," and that modernism might have deflected the natural course of his development, "because the newer things here show a decided trend toward that 'simplification' that we have all heard so much about. . . . Where he once took simplicity as a matter of course, as though it innately belonged to him, he now seems self-conscious about it and the more recent works tell a new story."[20]

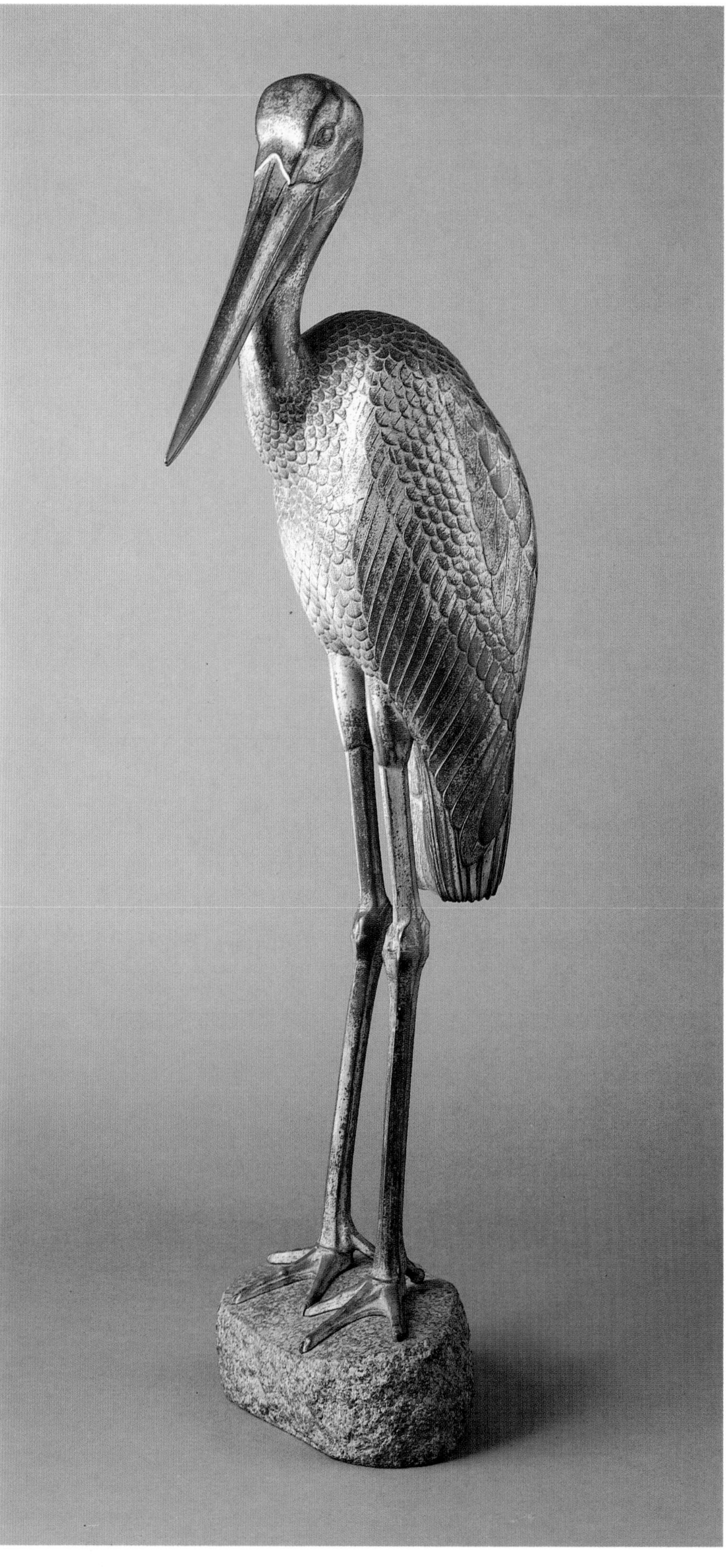

Fig. 108. *Adjutant Stork (#1)*, 1932; gilded bronze on red granite base; 45 in. high.

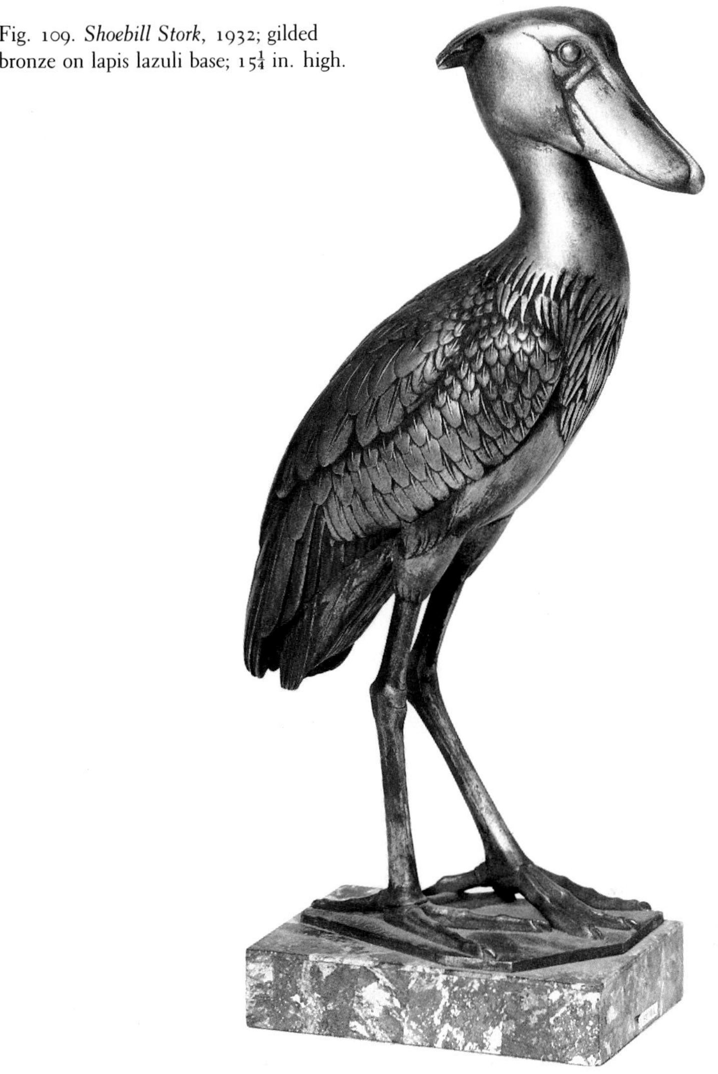

Fig. 109. *Shoebill Stork*, 1932; gilded bronze on lapis lazuli base; 15¼ in. high.

Cortissoz intimated tendencies that were only beginning to appear in Manship's art but which would subsequently dominate. At the time, Manship's ambitions were primarily naturalistic. For example, he avoided symbolic references to the owl and elevated naturalism above symbolism. The wise owl (*glaucus*, "gray" in Greek) is associated with Athena, the daughter of Zeus and the patron deity of war and of many crafts and skills; she is often depicted with an owl on her shoulder. Athena is sometimes called *Athena Glaucus*, either because of her gray eyes or her symbol, the owl. The base of *Owl (#1)*, shaped like a tree stump, places the bird in a quasi-landscape setting as replete as an Audubon study (fig. 110). Simultaneously, a hint of archaism resounds in the bird's plumage, which Manship treated as a repeated pattern whose regularity recalls classical imbrication (the overlapping of tiles or shingles). Years later, when Manship reengaged the mythological owl in 1961, he fared less well (fig. 111). *Owl (#2)* seems leaden and inanimate, a densely rounded form

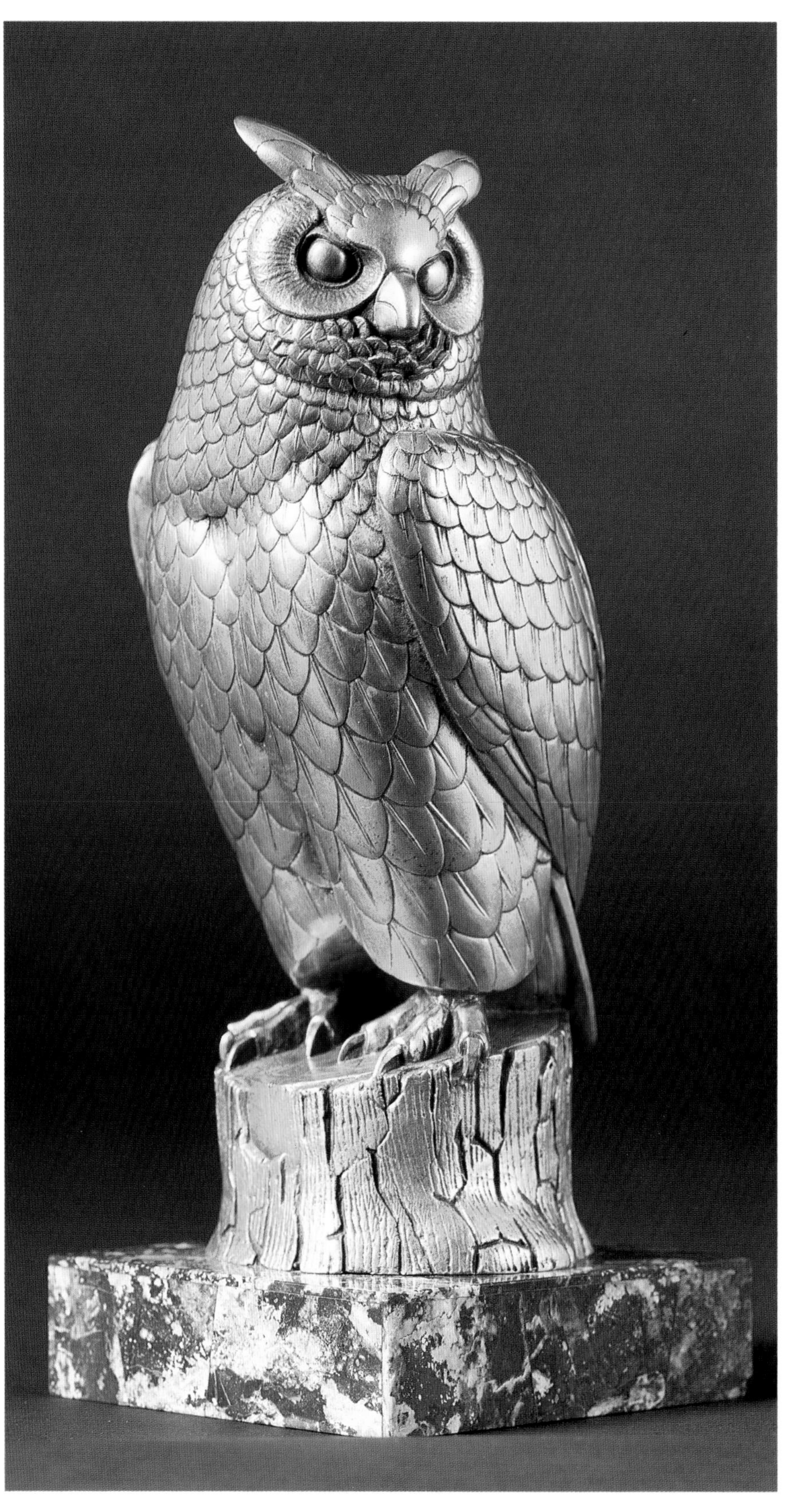

Fig. 110. *Owl (#1)*, 1932; bronze mounted on lapis lazuli; 9⅜ in. high.

Fig. 111. *Owl (#2)*, 1961; bronze on marble base; 10 in. high.

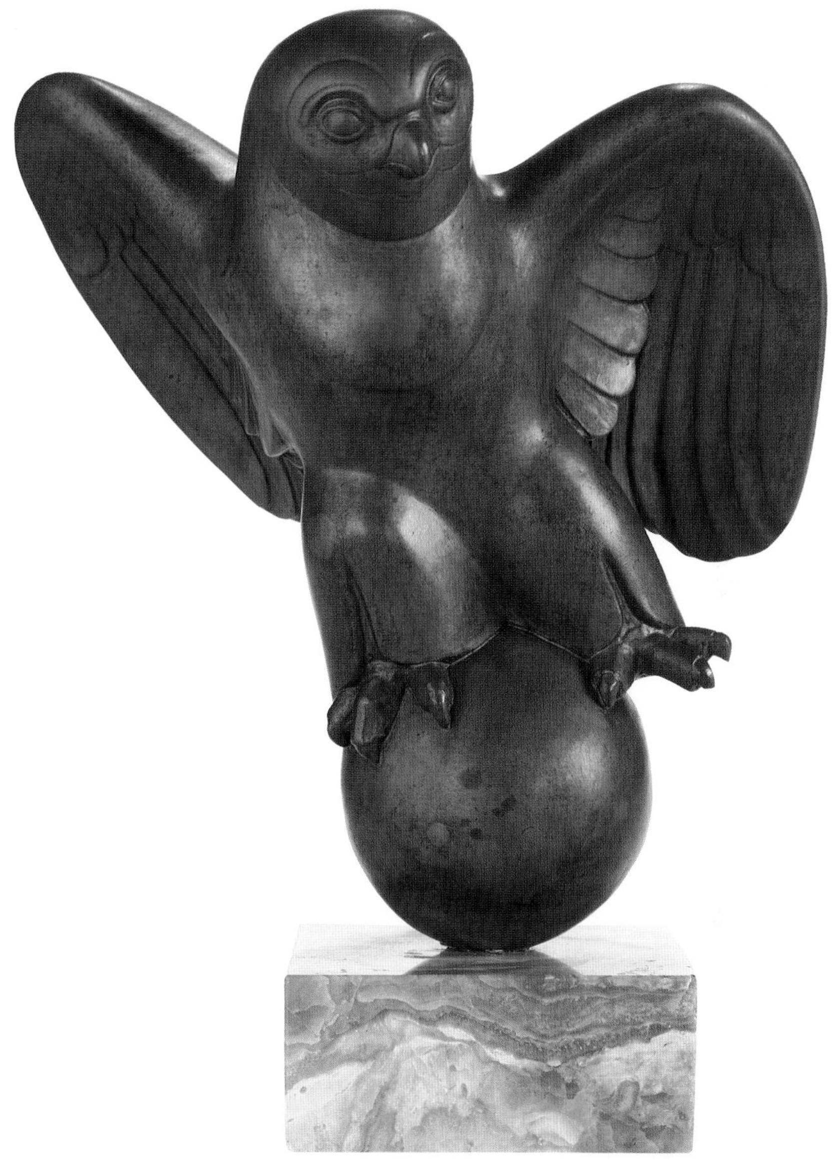

precariously balanced like a circus seal upon a ball. With no capacity for buoyancy, *Owl (#2)* demonstrates the liability Manship faced when he returned to the regalia of mythology with none of its faith. Symbolism prevailed over observation with the most unhappy results. All of the mysterious self-containment of the earlier *Owl* seems exhausted by the later work, which altogether lacks the brilliant counterpoise of small decorative elements with a fresh overall conception. By perching the figure atop a small sphere, Manship tried to revive a means of levitation he had first expounded in 1916 in *Flight of Night* (fig. 112).

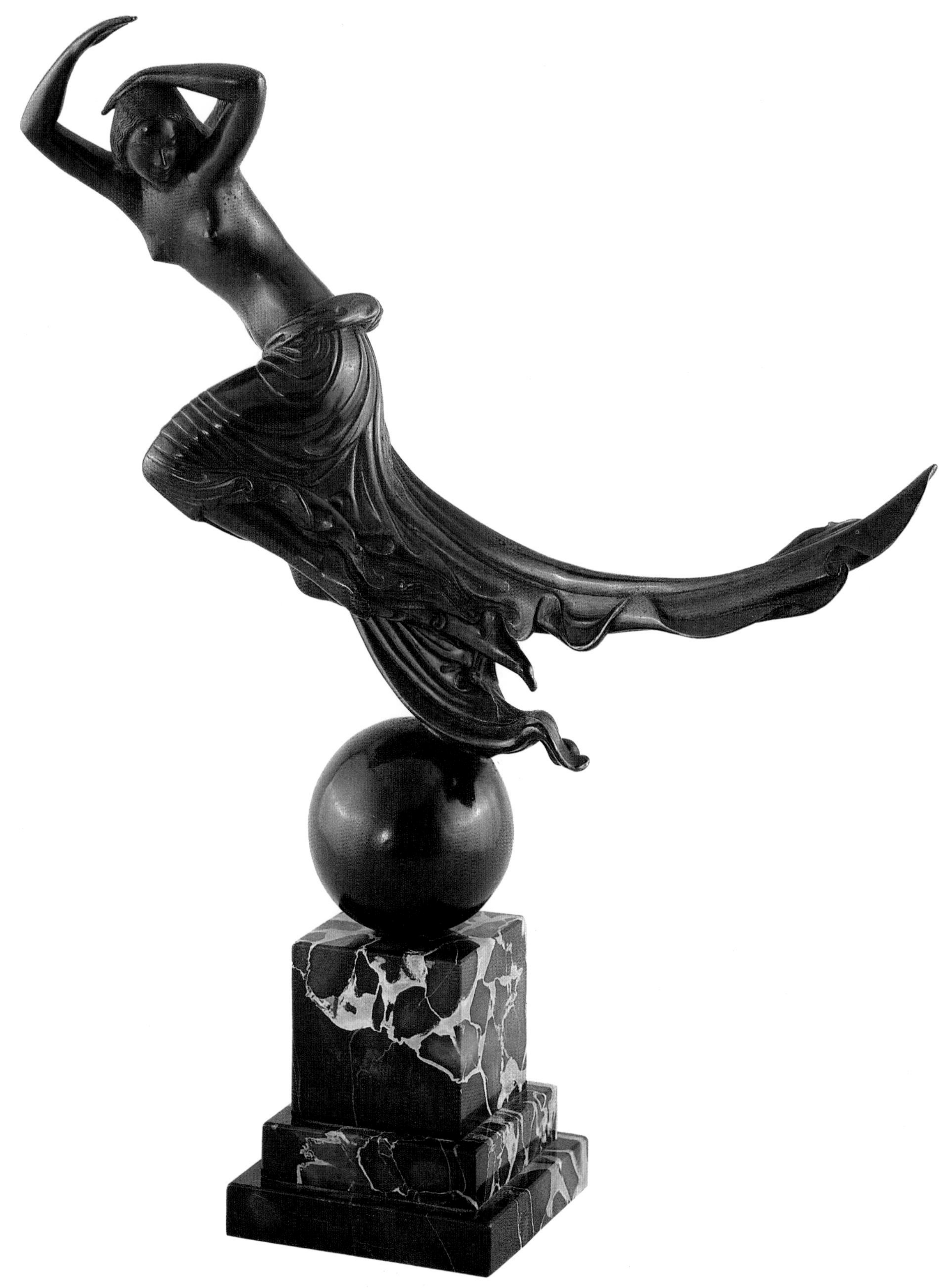

Fig. 112. *Flight of Night*, 1916; bronze; 18 in. high.

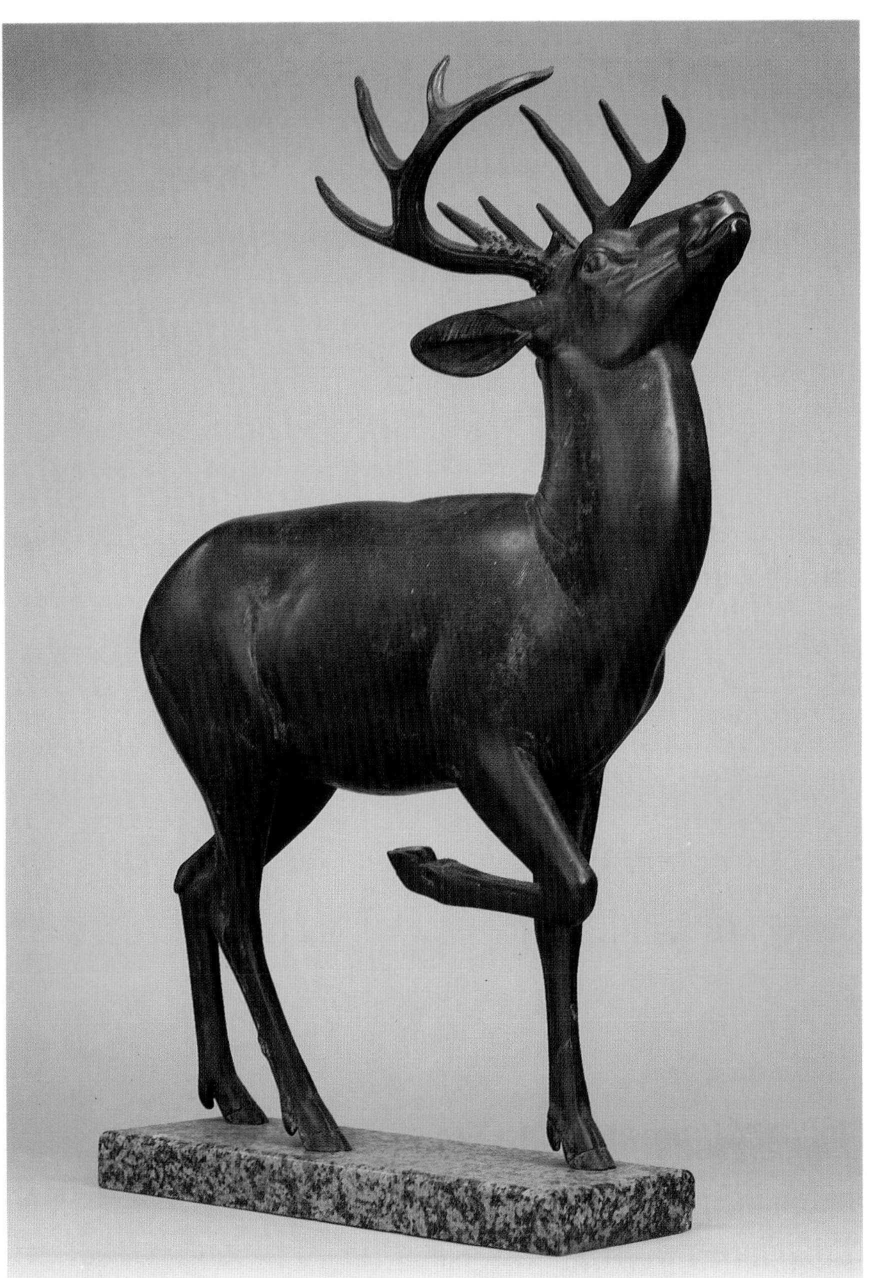

Fig. 113. *Standing Stag*, 1932; bronze on marble base; 28⅜ in. high.

Just as the *Group of Bears* featured an alert animal upright and sniffing the air, Manship chose to show the *Group of Deer* in a state of alertness, a family presided over by a stag. Praise for Manship's zoo gate castings extended across the ocean. When he was honored with an exhibition at the Tate Gallery in 1935, he showed twenty or so animal sculptures. In particular, the formal organization of his animal groups (like the *Standing Stag* [fig. 113] and the *Group of Deer*—which in fact includes the *Standing Stag* in the group) was savored, and the works shown at the Tate Gallery "prove him a modernist alive to progress and all that it implies, yet thoroughly grounded in the classic traditions," noted *Connoisseur* in August 1935. The review applauded Manship's artistic approach:

> These have refinements that bespeak a wide scholarship and display an accomplishment not arrived at by casting to the winds all that can be learnt from past exemplars of a noble art. . . . Often his groups, so spirited and lively in action, are built up by means of elaborately planned connecting rhythms which act as supporting links and reinforcements to the main theme, thus proving him to be a designer of unusual calibre. Delicacy rather than brute strength appears to be the keynote of Manship's thought.[21]

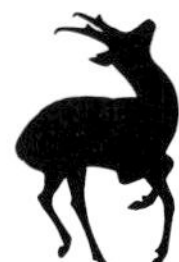

Monuments and Medals

IN 1933 PAUL MANSHIP'S CAREER was marching along. Royal Cortissoz described Manship's reputation as "gaining cumulative force as though it were a thing in nature . . . he has reached the point when he is acknowledged to be the most successful sculptor in the country—the sculptor to whom all the important jobs naturally gravitate."[1]

Manship often thought in terms of the monument. His sound training in the basic techniques of drawing and sculpture allowed him to conceive in three dimensions with a facility and grace that artists of subsequent generations have not mastered. (Of course, for succeeding generations, "authenticity" predicated art that was not rehearsed but discovered in the act of working.) In a sheet of offhand sketches from the mid 1930s, called *Studies of Orpheus and Funerary Monuments*, Manship displayed a phenomenal adroitness, thinking in fully realized forms that he casually rotated in space (fig. 114). Never intended for exhibition—though the artist, obviously pleased, initialed and preserved it—this worksheet demonstrates Manship's patterns of thought and the value of a classical artistic education.

Casually he covered a page with various sculptural ideas for Orpheus with his harp and female figures mourning over both tombs and funerary urns. Beginning in the late 1920s, the Orpheus theme started to occupy Manship, and it became one of his principal concerns during the mid 1930s.

The supreme minstrel of Greek mythology, Orpheus was such a marvelous musician that when he sang and played his lyre, nature itself would listen entranced and all creatures would follow him. When Eurydice, his wife, was killed by a snake, Orpheus, overwhelmed by grief, wandered into the Underworld. There he played his lyre so beautifully that Hades granted him a favor: Eurydice would return from the dead if Orpheus could lead her to open air without looking back at her. According to the oldest version of the story, Orpheus succeeded in this task, but in Virgil's and Ovid's accounts, Orpheus could not refrain from glancing at his wife and through his excess of love, he lost her.

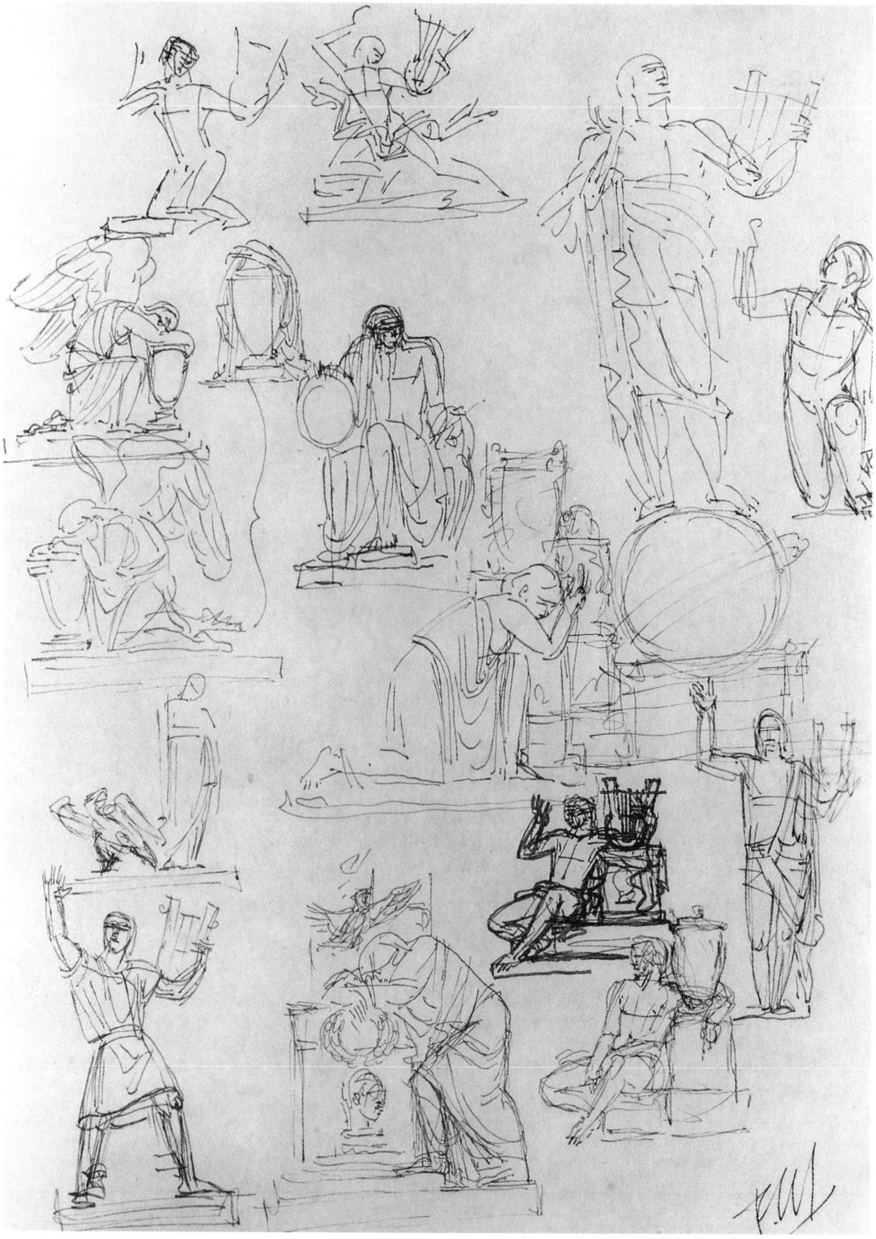

Fig. 114. *Studies of Orpheus and Funerary Monuments*, ca. 1934; pen and ink on paper; $10\frac{1}{2}$ x $7\frac{11}{16}$ in.

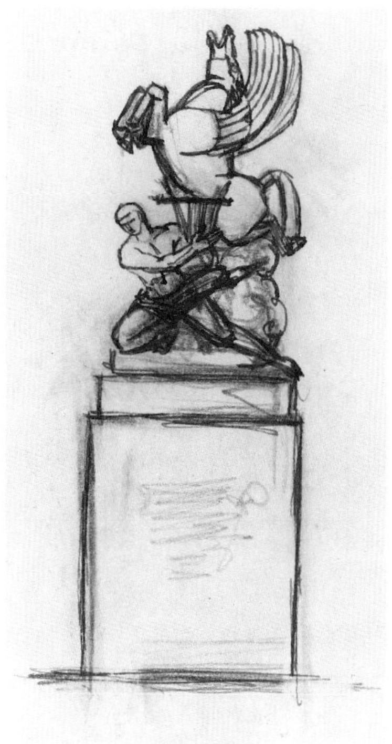

Fig. 115. *Orpheus and Pegasus*, ca. 1930; pencil and pen and ink on paper; $5\frac{5}{16}$ x $2\frac{13}{16}$ in.

Orpheus and Pegasus are not generally associated, and this combination seems to have been an invention of which Manship was especially fond—perhaps for the open form of the lyre in conjunction with the horse's closed cylindrical form (fig. 115). In addition, the vertical column of the man's torso played against the horizontal mass of the flying horse, whose wings supplied flat projections to express the underlying helical structure (figs. 116, 117). This firm geometry rests upon a contrastingly vague cloud.

In the 1930s Manship executed many versions of the *Standing Orpheus with Pegasus (Music)*. All were unique casts modeled in *cire perdu* (lost wax) and all were miniatures; yet the statue's conception could have been better served on a heroic scale. The country's resources strained, Manship seemed to be thinking about monuments.

His ambition, under the circumstances, was not unrealistic. While the WPA was supporting America's artists, Manship had a steady supply of clients;

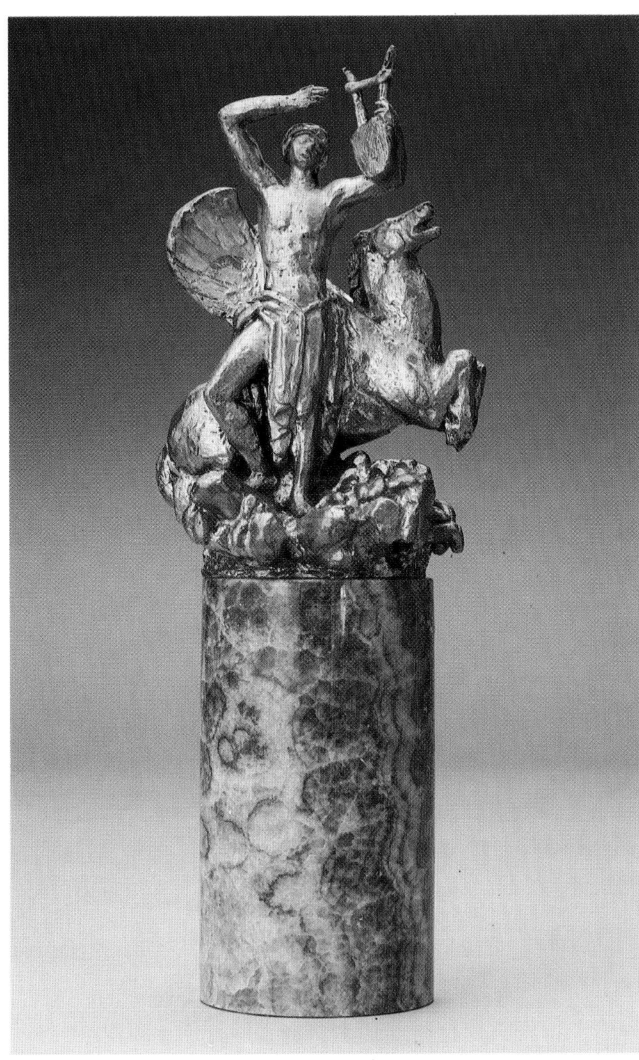

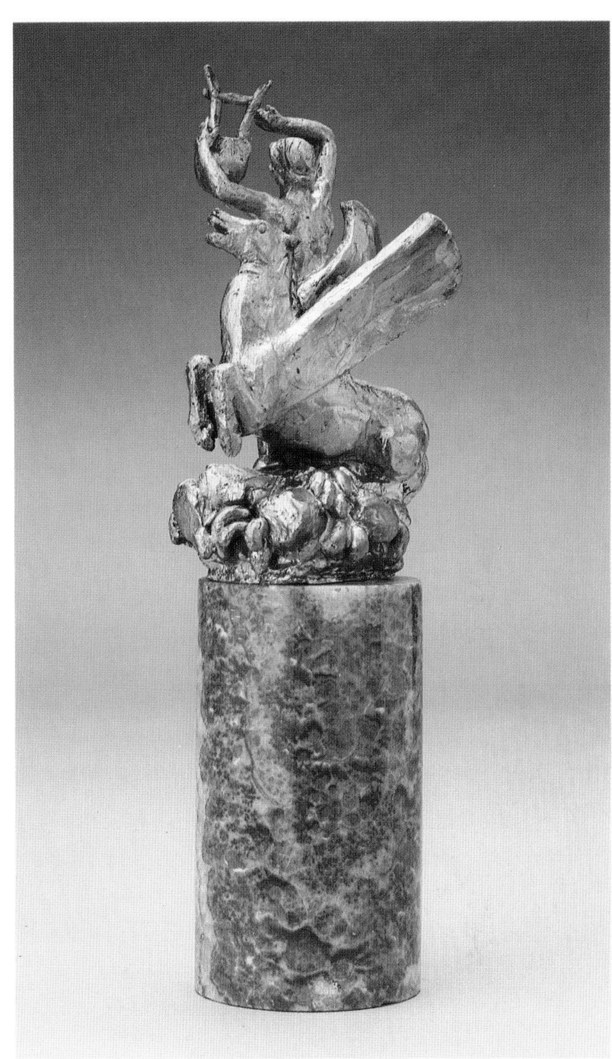

Figs. 116 and 117. *Standing Orpheus with Pegasus* (*Music*), ca. 1932; bronze on marble base; 11½ in. high.

after the enormous zoo gates he was offered the *Prometheus* commission at Rockefeller Center. Henry McBride wrote in the *Sun*: "The elite of this generation almost instantly recognized Mr. Manship to be their sculptor. They get from him what they would get in surgery from the highest priced surgeon of the day, in engineering from the very best engineer, and so on."[2] At the opening of an exhibition of Manship's works at the Tate Gallery in London, the United States Ambassador, Robert Worth Bingham, officiated. This high-level presence implied the dignity of the event, for at that time, the only non-Britons so honored by the Tate in their lifetimes were Manship and Rodin.

In British reviews of the exhibition we hear the same admiration of American objectivity that had long ago become associated with our painting—as if Europeans were once again gaining their first glimpses of Copley. The subdued factuality of Manship's work, tamed by a rigorous formalism and inflected by classical vocabulary, elicited the most appreciation. Of his animal sculptures, the British thought "all of them are simplified in form and static in execution. . . . It is to the good that the Tate Gallery has given a welcome to this accomplished American artist."[3]

Manship took his growing transatlantic celebrity in stride. The authority provided by his looming eminence he dedicated to advancing sculpture as a public activity, albeit one needing affluent patronage. He began to lecture and give demonstrations; he wrote three articles for the *Encyclopaedia Britannica*: "American Sculpture" in 1939 and "The History of Sculpture" and "Decorative Sculpture" in 1940.

When Manship's bronze *Celestial Sphere*—with its gilded constellations, white metal stars, and variously patinated architectural parts—was exhibited at the Averell House, it elicited this excited review:

> In this chamber is seen for the first time the model for the Celestial Globe that is perhaps his most exciting performance to date. It is an intricately devised sphere that will be seen eventually without background, permitting observation of the stars which will be placed on the inside of the figured constellations.[4]

A blindfolded woman representing night supports the sphere. All the stars of the first four magnitudes are shown, as are sixty-six constellations; the perforated sphere turns on its polar axis and can be set for any hour. It was first executed in a height of eight feet, with a five-foot (diameter) sphere for the Aero Memorial in Philadelphia's Logan Square.

In 1934 Manship cast five two-foot-high reductions of the *Celestial Sphere* with a sphere one and a quarter feet in diameter (fig. 118). The *Celestial Sphere* was enlarged to monumental size in a plaster version for the 1939 New York World's Fair (the sphere was destroyed after the fair). Most important, a bronze version was cast in the heroic scale of thirteen-and-a-half-feet high, with gilded constellations, silvered stars, and machinery to make it turn (figs. 119, 120). This enormous work, which derived its imagery from the ancients' notion of the heavens' disposition, lightly rested on four turtles swimming in the primordial sea. These tortoises (fig. 121) were first modeled for the base of the Bronx Zoo gates, and Manship slightly altered their necks—raising them to support the curve of the sphere's rim—when he recalled them to service. Periodically, Manship retraced his steps to masterworks that were key to his career, pieces in which he had the luxury to deliberate forms and their relationships to other forms.

To honor the League of Nations' guiding spirit, this huge rendition of the sphere was installed in Geneva, at the Palais des Nations (now the gardens of the Palace of the United Nations) as the *Wilson Memorial*. At the end of April 1936, word came from Geneva that Manship had been awarded the commission to honor the League's founding genius.[5] The sphere was installed

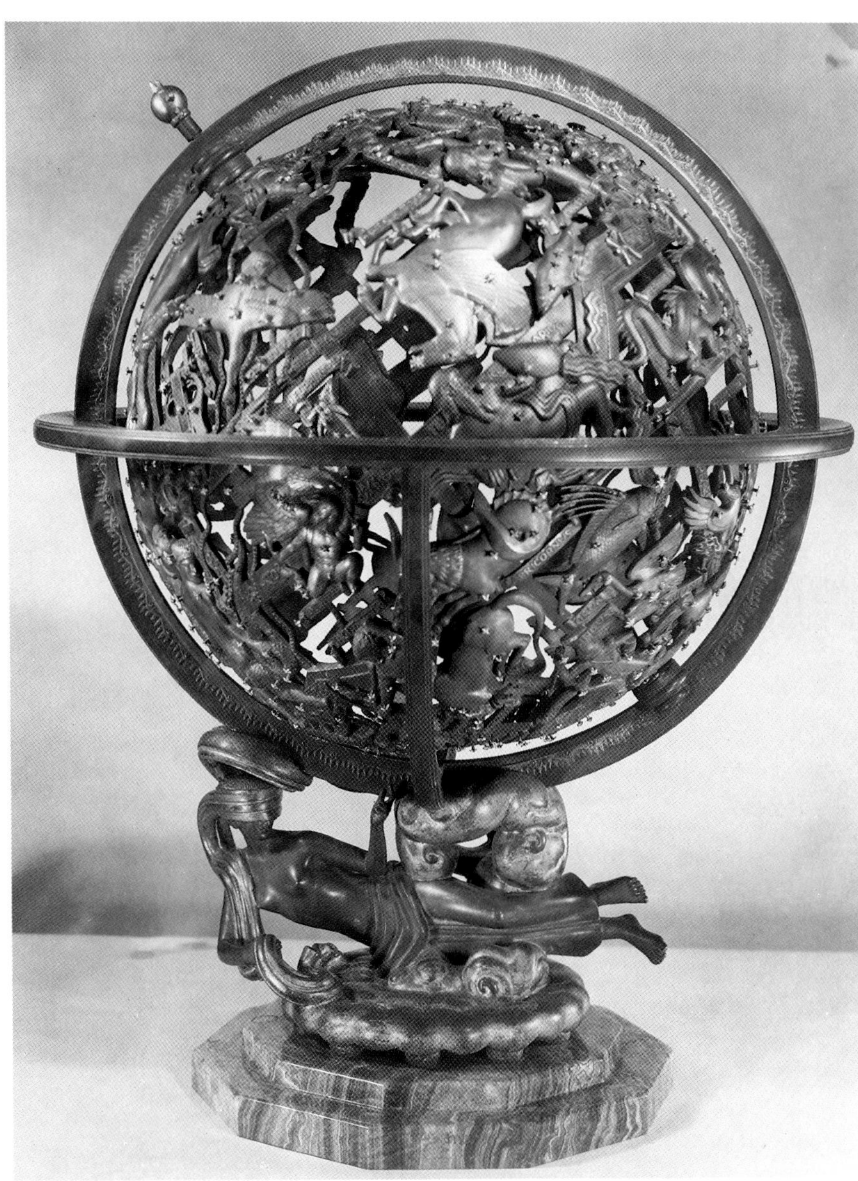

Fig. 118. *Celestial Sphere*, 1934; bronze on marble base; 26 in. high. Fogg Art Museum, Harvard University, Cambridge, Massachusetts, Bequest of Grenville L. Winthrop.

at the League of Nations in the twilight of peace before World War II in August of 1939. Placed on the central terrace facing the lake, the *Wilson Memorial* turned slowly and was illuminated:

> In the execution of this sphere I spent a full three years' work. The representation of the heavenly constellations is derived from Babylonia and Assyria; the Greeks and Latins added their names and gave the constellations a local significance in some cases and I have adhered as closely as possible to the ancient forms. Thus the star, Aldeberan, which represents the eye of Taurus, dictates the character of the design, as is also the case of Regulas, the Lion's Heart, and so with all the constellations the forms and attitudes of the figures have been made to correspond firstly with the positions and the meanings of the jobs themselves, and after that the inter-relationship of the constellations was designed to create a harmonious ensemble.[6]

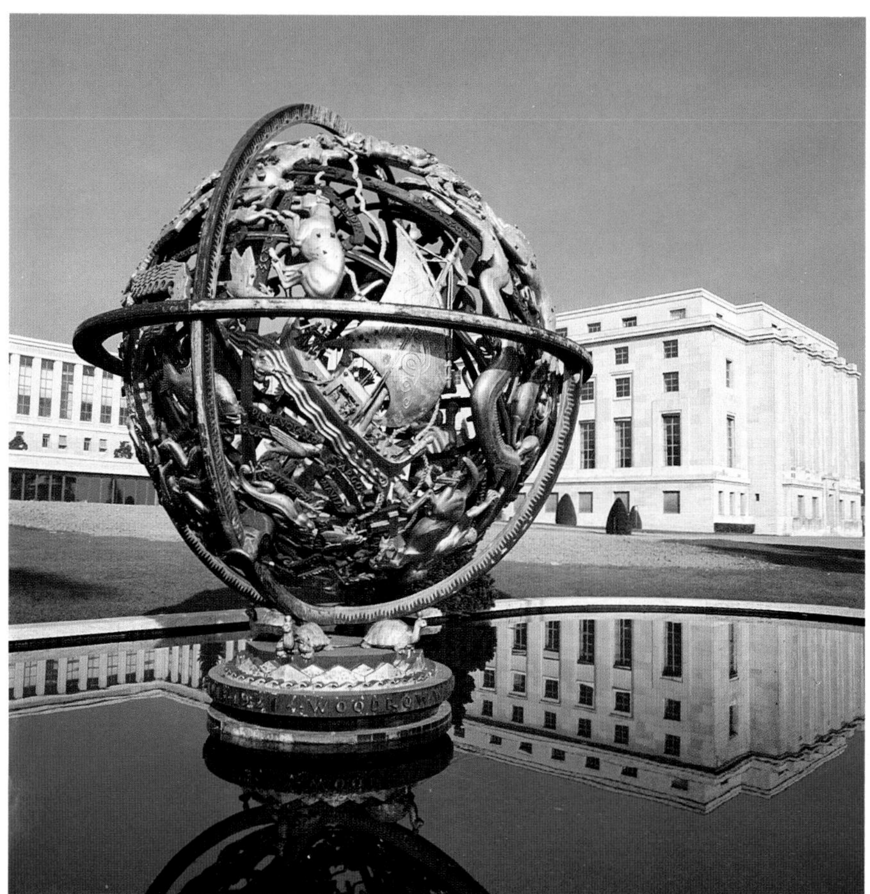

Figs. 119 and 120. *Wilson Memorial (Celestial Sphere)*, 1939; bronze, gilded constellations, silvered stars; 13½ ft. diameter. Palais des Nations, Geneva, Headquarters of the European Offices of the United Nations.

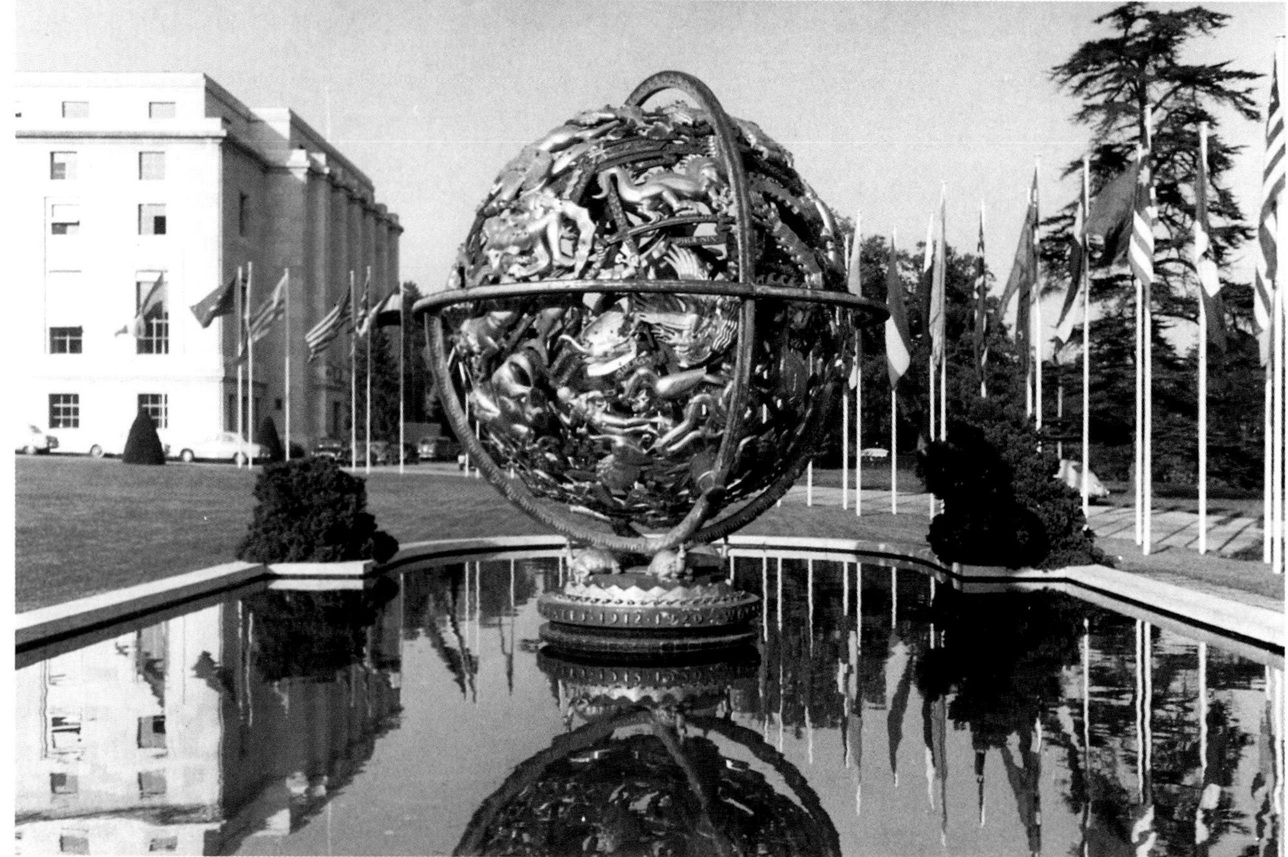

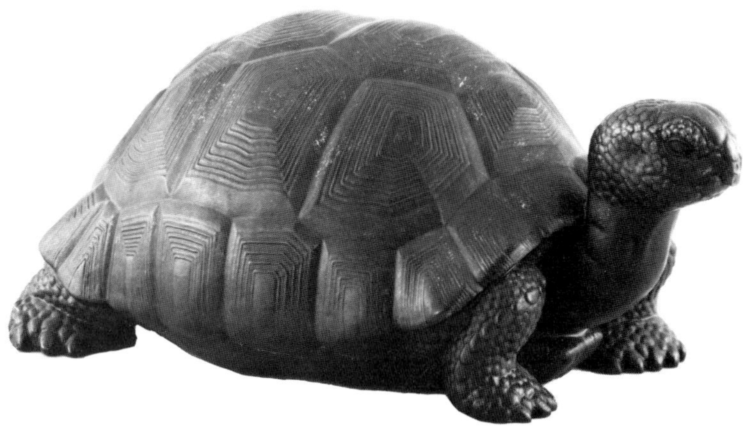

Fig. 121. *Tortoise*, 1932; bronze; $4\frac{3}{4}$ in. high.

The *Wilson Memorial* rises from a rectangular pool overlooking Lake Geneva. Here the sculptor, working on a world stage, produced a glittering performance. For the sake of accuracy, he spent years studying surveys of the heavenly objects. He fixed the positions of the numerous stars and the constellations, which he located exactly. Superb ornament reconciled astronomical precision, astrological legend, the iconography of classical myth, and naturalisitic renditions of numerous figures. He blended all the varied constituents of the work harmoniously on the grandest scale. Sparkling details were subsumed into the conception of the whole, as Manship achieved the appearance of effortless and graceful monumentality against the memorial's striking setting. The huge sphere floats, buoyant against gravity, the smallest refinements articulate amidst the immensity of the undertaking.

MEDALS

Every sculptor dreams of working on a public scale, in heroic sizes impossible to ignore. Gutzon Borglum carved Mt. Rushmore into a monument perdurable as the pyramids, and Walker Hancock shaped one face of Stone Mountain, Georgia, into a gigantic cavalry tableau. (While conservative artists labored on their great commissions, modernist sculpture also tended to gargantuan growth, which paralleled how modernist painting stretched its boundaries.) Although Manship gained monumental commissions, he did not scorn small work, and whatever the size in which he worked, Manship's sculpture exhibits an appropriateness of scale. With equal fervor he embraced the chance to execute monuments and pocket-size sculpture; varying formats sharpened his dexterity and sculptor's skills.

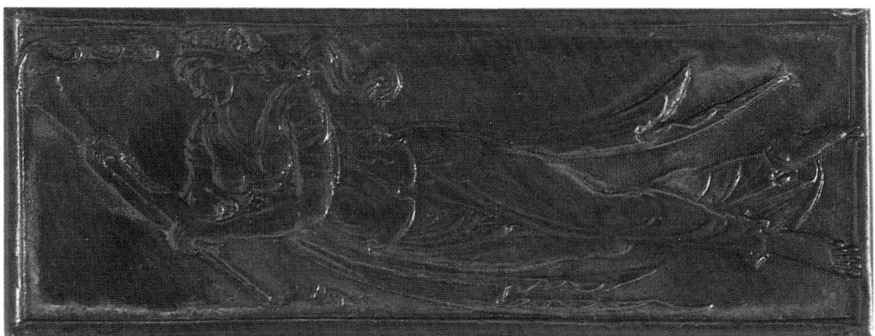

Fig. 122. *Figure With Torch*; bronze relief; $2\frac{1}{2}$ x $6\frac{7}{8}$ in.

Throughout his life Manship prolifically executed medals, which are the most diminutive form of sculpture. Like the rest of his art, his medals were technically innovative and thematically conservative.

Beginning with Petrarch himself, Renaissance collectors sought small, beautifully made artifacts echoing the elegant taste of well-to-do ancients who, in turn, had adorned their pagan homes with statuettes and medallions. The first modern medal dates from the last decade of the fourteenth century. These small bronzes came to epitomize both antiquity as we view it and the Renaissance humanists, who revivified the ancients. Manship, an admirer of both classical ages, produced commemorative and honorific medals redolent of these two periods.

Augustus Saint-Gaudens convinced President Theodore Roosevelt to aesthetically reform American coinage, and this campaign coincided with a renewed interest in the medal as a miniature art object—of which coins partook as the everyday medals we pocket and exchange. Manship helped restore this noble artistic tradition.

Manship's framed relief plaque, *Figure With Torch*, is a lyrical composition that seems to coincide with no occasion, nor to celebrate any event (fig. 122). The horizontal draped figure holds her torch as she flies to the left, and no apparent purpose is served but sheer sculptural joy. Occasionally, as in *Amoris Triumphus*, he used the coin's intimacy to celebrate a private joy—in this case, the birth of his first child (fig. 123). To commemorate persons or events, Manship designed hundreds of medals during his career. His son, John, recalled the format Manship preferred for his medals and the tradition from which those assumptions arose:

> Although Manship's imagery was derived from Greek mythology and art, the format and design were influenced greatly by artists of the Renaissance. Medalists such as Benvenuto Cellini and Antonio Pisanello used the obverse of the medals for the portrait and inscription of the person or event. The reverse of the medal referred to the symbolic meaning or significance of the person or event.[7]

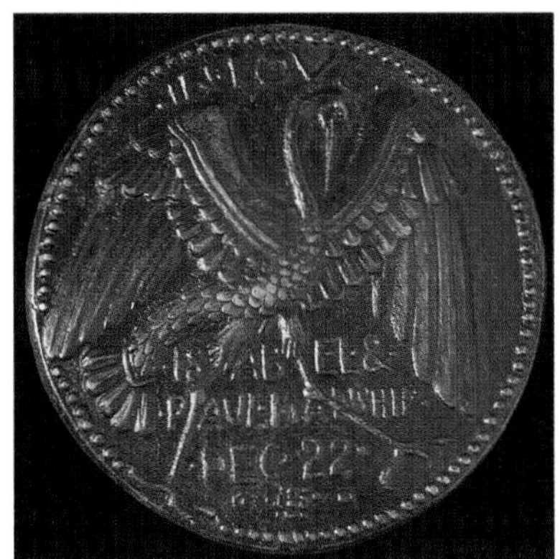

Fig. 123. *Amoris Triumphus Medal* (reverse), 1914; bronze; 3 in. diameter; inscribed "IN LOVE - ISABEL AND PAUL MANSHIP - DEC 22."

This was a formula Manship followed in his 1914 bronze *Civic Forum Medal of Honor* (fig. 124). The medal's obverse bears the image of a classical female figure carrying a torch in her left hand and a winged statue in her right hand, while the reverse shows an American eagle. The medal is inscribed, "For Distinguished Public Service"; it was awarded in 1914 to George Goethals, in 1915 to Thomas Edison, in 1917 to Alexander Graham Bell, and in 1920 to Herbert Hoover. The Greek coins Manship so admired were produced by cutting directly into the die from which the coin was struck. Although Manship's medals were produced by casting in bronze from a wax model, as they did in the Renaissance, Manship felt the Renaissance had revived the classical perfection of medallic craftmanship.

One of Manship's most complete recapitulations of the Renaissance medal was in his *Jeanne d'Arc* (figs. 125, 126). The medal's obverse displays the right profile of an armor-clad Saint Joan on horseback. Her legs straight forward from her saddle, she carries a long banner with her left hand. The horse prances with its right front leg raised high above a ground line and a hovering angel offers a heavy broadsword. Two *fleurs-de-lis* flank the inscribed "Jeanne d'Arc." All this heraldry, so compactly displayed, is counterpoised by the grim terseness of the reverse, where a border of small dots in relief encircle Saint Joan at the stake. As the flames rise around her, a hand descends from heaven to crown her with laurel—as once an angel proferred a sword—and the border carries the inscription: "La Vierge Heroique et Martyre MCCCCXXXI."

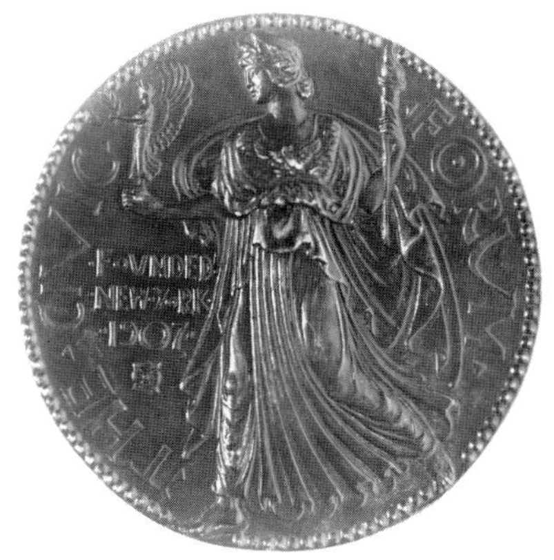

Fig. 124. *Civic Forum Medal of Honor* (obverse), 1914; bronze; 3¼ in. diameter.

In real deference to the solid lyricism of Italian archetypes, the formal treatment of the *Jeanne d'Arc* medal resembles Renaissance cast medals. To achieve his effects, Manship first formed a rough plasticine model from which was taken a plaster mold; a considerable amount of detail was carved into this plaster before a positive cast was taken and corrections were also made in the second cast. This process was repeated—possibly through several molds and casts, with continual refinements introduced to sharpen the clarity, composition,

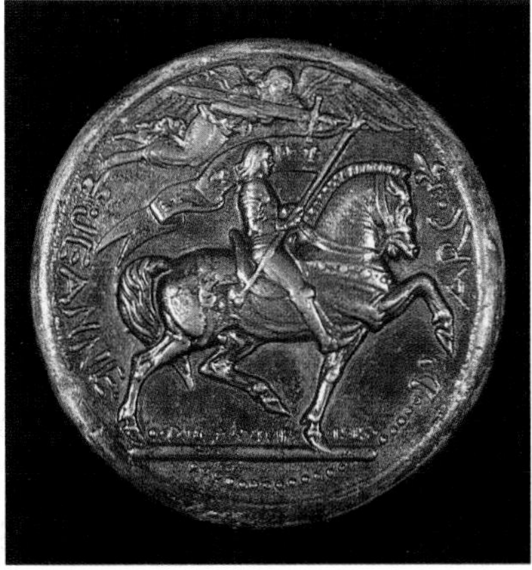

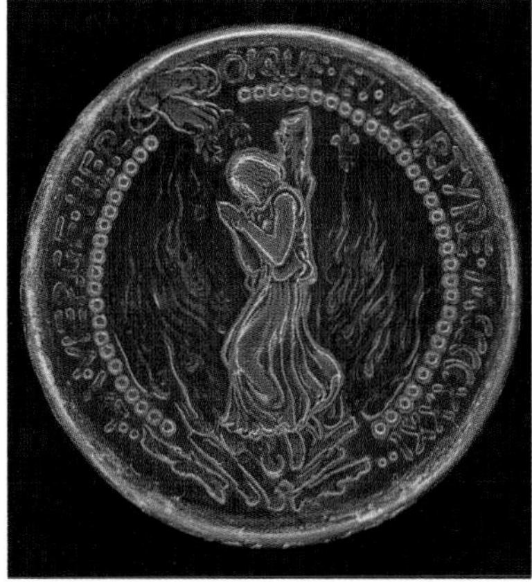

Figs. 125 and 126. *Jeanne d'Arc*, 1915; bronze; 2¾ in. diameter.

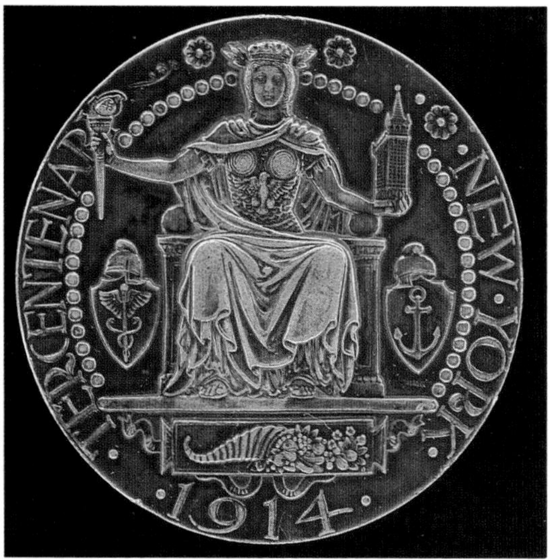

Fig. 127. *New York Tercentenary Medal* (obverse), 1914; bronze; $2\frac{5}{8}$ in. diameter.

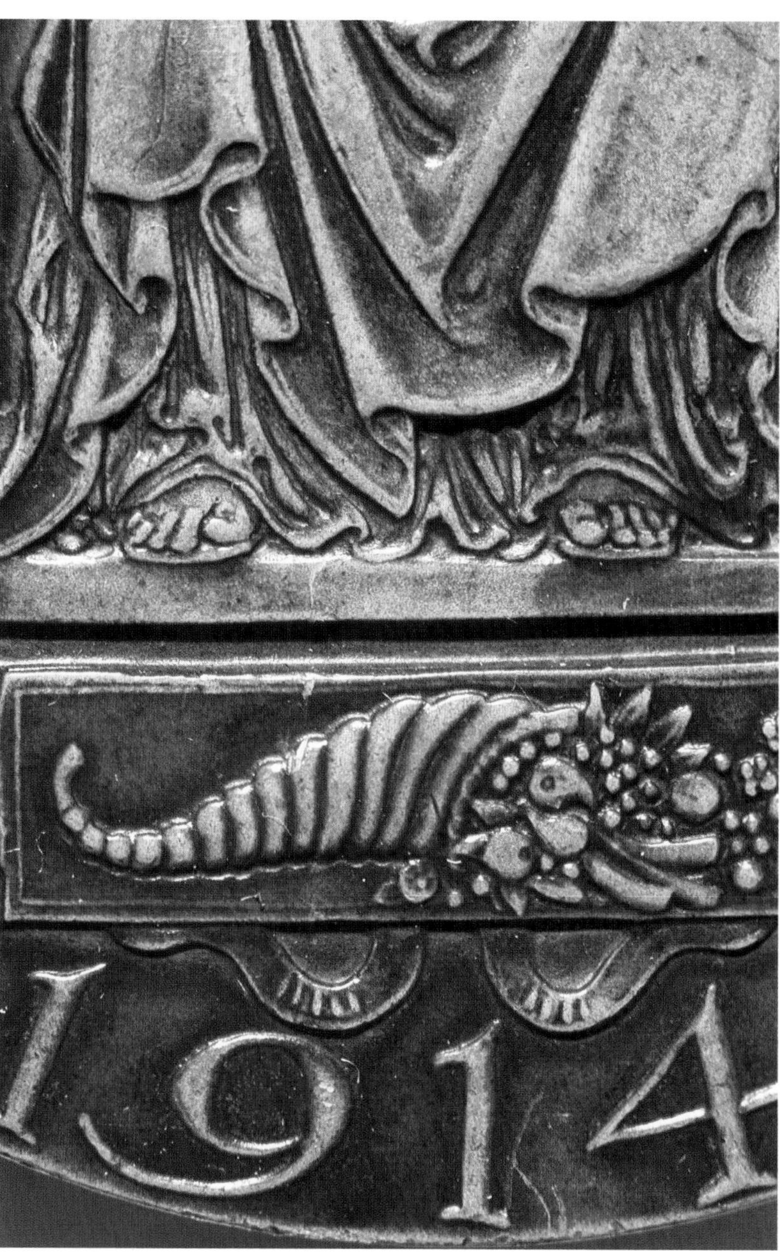

Fig. 128. Detail, *New York Tercentenary Medal.*

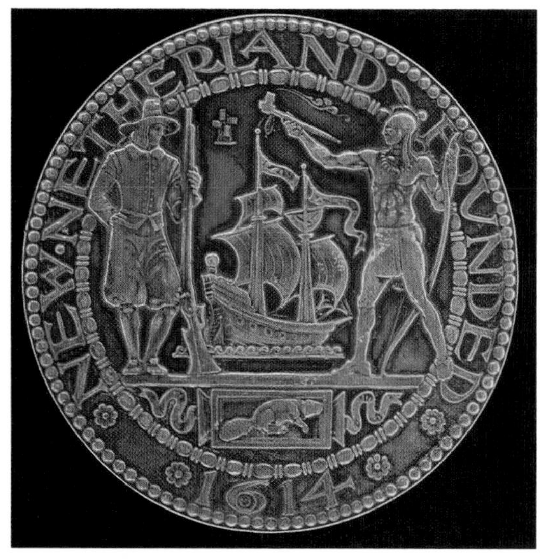

Fig. 129. *New York Tercentenary Medal (reverse).*

and details of the whole—before a model was presented to the founder for casting in bronze. In order to impose the discipline of forcing concentrated details into a restricted area, Manship used smaller models than other sculptors had, even though his models were to be reduced mechanically for striking. Walker Hancock recalled that "the model for the *Jeanne d'Arc Medal*, for example, was only six inches in diameter. The effect of technique upon style was a constant concern."[8]

Details of the *New York Tercentenary Medal* reveal Manship's concern for scale and for the potential of such diminutiveness to suggest real monumentality (fig. 127). The enthroned woman, who represents New York, holds a torch in her right hand and a skyscraper (which resembles the Woolworth Building) in her left. This figure is possessed of a presence and gravity altogether beyond her actual size (fig. 128). Working in the shallowest space, the fine effect achieved by minor, indeed exquisitely small, details of the drapery in the woman's lap contribute to a dramatic foreshortening. The distance between her knee and torso seems a deep ledge, but in fact the space is extremely narrow. Such an adroit rendition delights the attentive spectator with virtuosic accomplishment.

Walker Hancock describes how "following the invention of the Janvier machine for cutting dies from larger models, medallists had departed from the appropriateness of scale that had been imposed upon the ancient die cutters by the exigencies of their materials and tools," and it was not long before a certain cavalier loss of attention appeared. "Manship revived the clarity of design and treatment that had been the charm of the Greek gems and coins."[9] Well into the period of the early Renaissance, obdurate materials and relatively primitive cutting tools determined the limits of style, which Manship admired and emulated even when modern technology had bequeathed him the means to be microscopically delicate.

Besides scale and the balance of detail, the other elements of the *New York Tercentenary Medal* are equally accomplished and effective presentations of an American iconography. Flanking the throne are two shields, one with an anchor, another with a caduceus. On the reverse (fig. 129), a colonist with rifle stands to the left of a seventeenth-century sailing ship, and an Indian with bow and pipe appears on the right. Beneath these figures, within a square cartouche, ambles a beaver—symbol of the early settler's wealth. A windmill, part of New York's coat of arms, nestles just within the inscription: "New Netherland Founded 1614."

For another diminutive exposition of the medalist's art, the *St. Paul Institute Medal*, Manship returned to images of classical mythology (figs. 130–132). On the reverse, a laurel-wreathed outer edge is broken by Pegasus rising from the globe. In the background a pattern of vertical rays rises into space, a

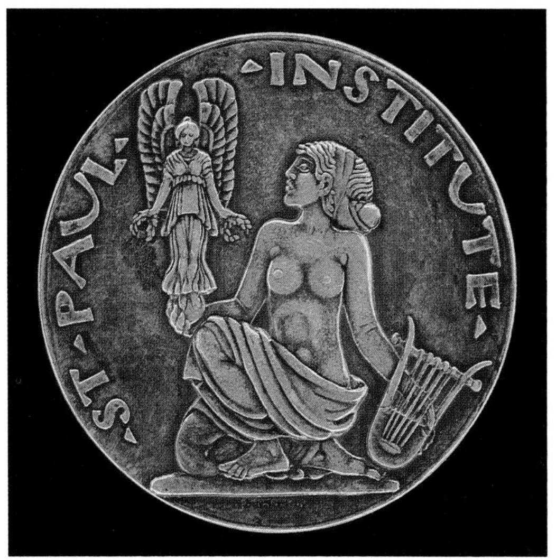

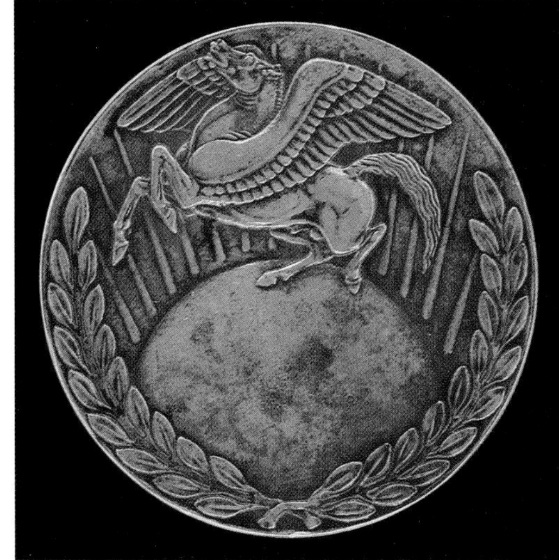

Figs. 130 and 131. *St. Paul Institute Medal*, 1916; bronze; $2\frac{1}{8}$ in. diameter.

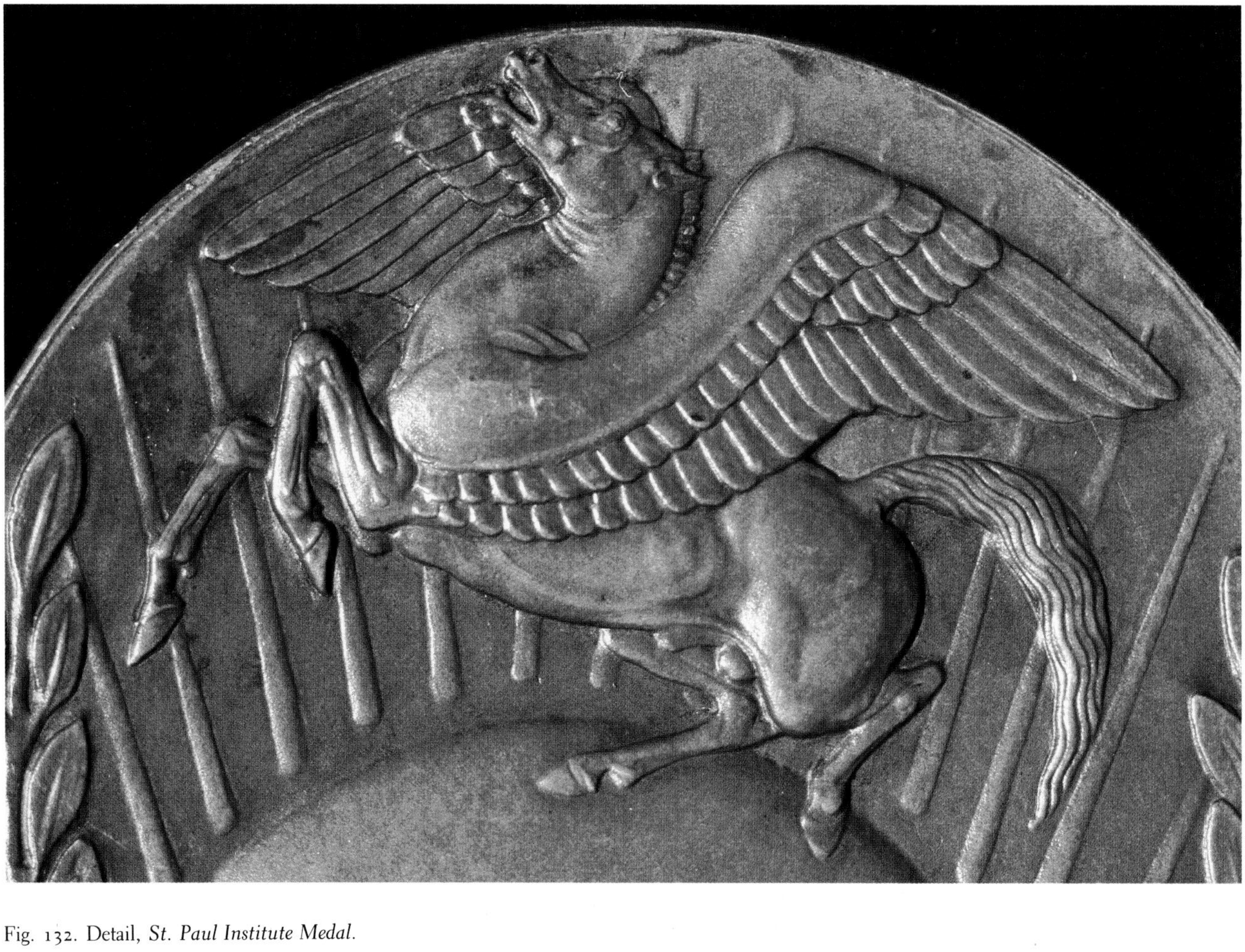

Fig. 132. Detail, *St. Paul Institute Medal*.

hallmark design of Art Deco (and this in 1916). The obverse features a half-draped muse kneeling before winged Victory, whom she carries as a statue in her right hand while in her left hand is a lyre. Manship envisioned this work, which to contemporary eyes seems a wholly conservative enterprise, as a radical departure for him. From his statement, we can glean exactly how cautiously he considered such matters:

> I have thought to get away from the stereotyped models . . . and to suggest the whole idea in an abstract manner. So instead of representing the figure of Art with a palette in one hand and a work of sculpture in the other, I have pictured . . . the Muse that inspires and extols, kneeling before the figure of Victory, who bestows recognition and artistic accomplishment . . . the Pegasus rising from the Globe is, of course, suggestive of the flight of fancy, and its vehicle of transport to the Higher Realms.

Perhaps only Manship could have thought that such an elaborate program was a flight from "stereotyped models" and an excursion toward the "abstract." Herein, we also learn just how literary were his conceptions.

Manship circulated medals of general interest relating to World War I. The most arresting of these was undoubtedly his bitterly titled *Kultur Medal* (figs. 133, 134). The obverse bears a bust of the Kaiser, who wears a necklace of skulls from which was suspended an iron cross. The brutal visage is crowned with a helmet and flanked by a bayonet. The inscription reads: "The Foe of Free Peoples—His Rosary." On the reverse, a German soldier is abducting a helpless woman while a child lies on the ground. The inscription on this side declares: "Kultur in Belgium—Murder Pillage." Intensified by the war, public sentiment about the enemy propelled this grisly piece into fashionable store windows.[10] A later generation—which witnessed the invention of horrors once inconceivable—found their spokesman in David Smith and his *Medals for Dishonor,* which "celebrated" the achievements warfare visits on humanity (fig. 135). For Smith, a more cynical artist, the foe was the human penchant for war—and not a nationality or a figurehead (such as the Kaiser).

Art's evolution and the gloomy political realities twilit before World War II conferred on Manship's successors certain hard-won freedoms. The brutality Manship wished to convey was limited to his agitprop subject matter; however, Smith's *Propaganda for War* presented the theme with an almost forced clumsiness, a coarseness that he used to express how politicians' sleek phrases belie the ends of policy. Manship would never have allowed his feelings to produce intentional ugliness. Thus, as early as the *Kultur Medal* of 1918, we can begin to discern Manship's conflation of eloquence with passion—slowly, but with accelerating rapidity he mistook the difference. Manship replaced feeling with formal precision. For him, beauty was truth—any truth he wished to convey, however inherently ugly. Accordingly, we might think of Manship as a Neo-Hellenistic artist, rather than simply academic or Neoclassical. Despite

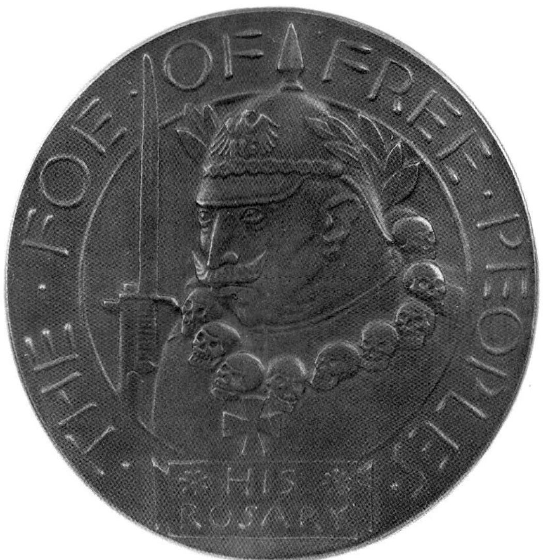

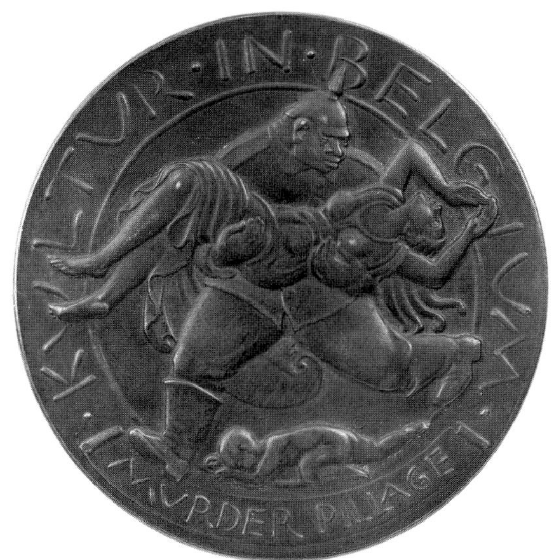

Figs. 133 and 134. *Kultur Medal*, 1918; bronze; $2\frac{1}{2}$ in. diameter.

his attraction to archaic Greece's leaner forms and the arts of simpler dawn cultures, Manship showed a distinct bent for the ornately reasoned, the elaborately contrived emblemology of a ripe world.

In 1927 Manship fashioned the bronze *Carnegie Corporation Ashtray* as an object both ceremonial and in harmony with his notion that the goods with which people surrounded themselves ought to be of the highest quality and of integrated design (fig. 136). Rearing on hind legs, Pegasus, a symbol of knowledge, rises from crystal rocks, and around him an inscription reads: "Carnegie Corporation for the Advancement and Diffusion of Knowledge and Understanding." If, given its function, this ashtray's motto seems a bit grand, we might recall that Manship's audience was composed of quite normal poseurs, who required a public expression of distaste at what to anyone else would be inoffensive—in order that observers would be sure to recognize rectitude.

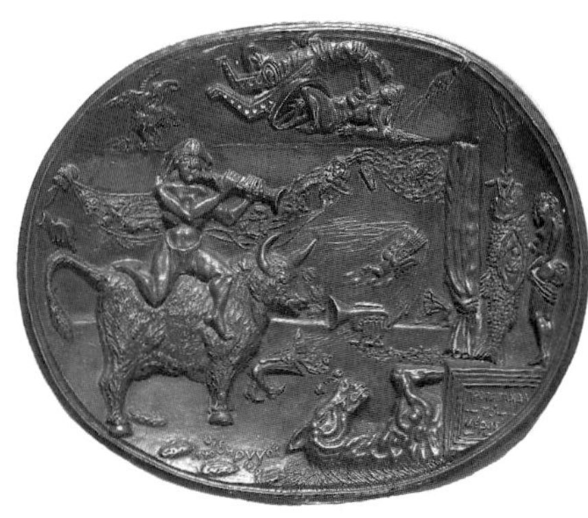

Fig. 135. David Smith, *Medal for Dishonor: Propaganda for War*, 1939–40; bronze; $9\frac{1}{2}$ x $11\frac{7}{8}$ x 1 in. Hirshhorn Museum and Sculpture Garden, Smithsonian Institution.

The Society of Medalists' second issue produced an uproar, caused by the gentlest tempest in an otherwise occupied teacup. Manship's 1930 salute to Bacchus presented the god of wine and debauchery rather too attractively for some of his viewers. Protests were received from members of the Society of Medalists, and one member threatened to resign if "any more insults to the Constitution are perpetrated in the name of art."[11] But the disagreement could not

> be attributed to any controversy between "wets" and "drys" within the society regarding the design of [the] medal. . . . An officer of the society said . . . the medal, bearing the inscription "Hail to Dionysus who first discovered the magic of the grape," aroused the ire of some of the 1,500 members of the organization. This was denied yesterday by a representative of the society.[12]

Manship, who loved antiquity as epitomized by the medalist's art (for which he hoped to revive public enthusiasm), also was a connoisseur of fine wines. (Manship's well-stocked cellars boasted the best vintages—which he, always the warm host, shared heartily with his friends.) In the robust god Dionysus, Manship saw a chance for one of his sculpture's happier conjunctions; the miniature's hostile reception must have caught him off-guard.

For the first time since his 1913 *Centaur and Dryad*—and particularly the frieze on its pedestal—Manship celebrated abandonment to the pleasures of wine and the flesh. He paid homage to what must have been one of his favorite deities. The coin's obverse (fig. 137) bears a head of Dionysus rising from a kylix (a classical Greek drinking cup). In the middle of Prohibition, Manship boldly inscribed the medal: "Hail to Dionysus Who First Discovered the Magic of the Grape." On the coin's reverse, flanked by bunches of grapes, two fauns dance out the vintage, and the work is signed: "P. MANSHIP, 1930" (fig. 138). The work's more dour recipients collided with Manship's whimsy. Reactionaries failed to see in the Dionysus medal that Manship was not an advocate of "wets," and they believed that he had skirted the issue of Prohibition.

The Dionysus medal exalted the complexity of normal human appetites rather than rendering them invisible or seemingly unnatural. The Dionysus

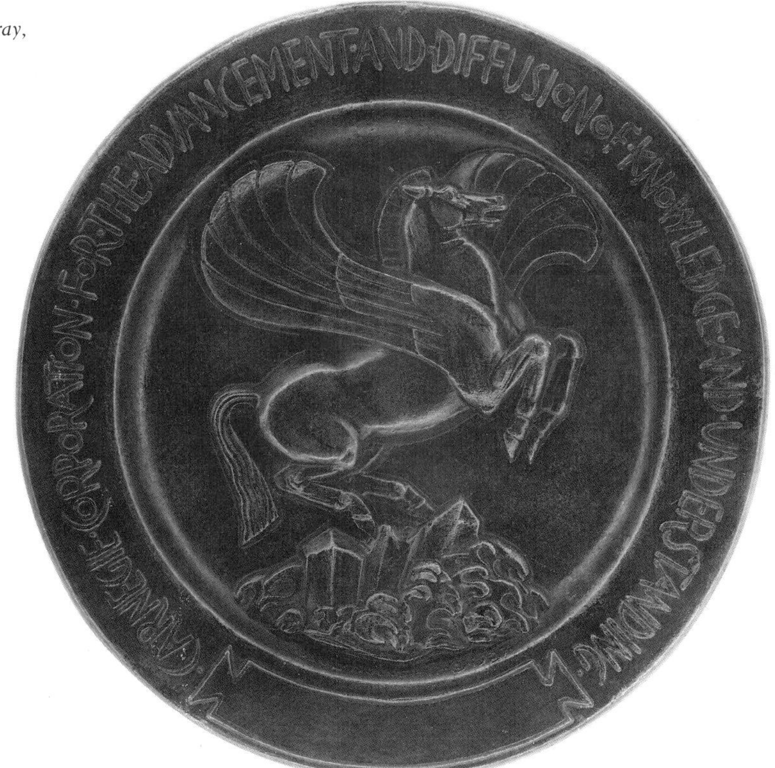

Fig. 136. *Carnegie Corporation Ashtray*, 1927; bronze; $5\frac{5}{8}$ in. diameter.

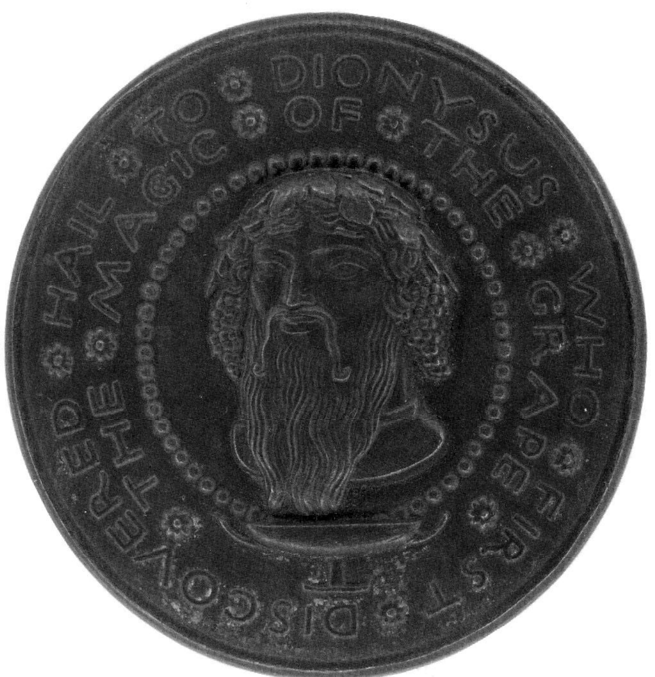

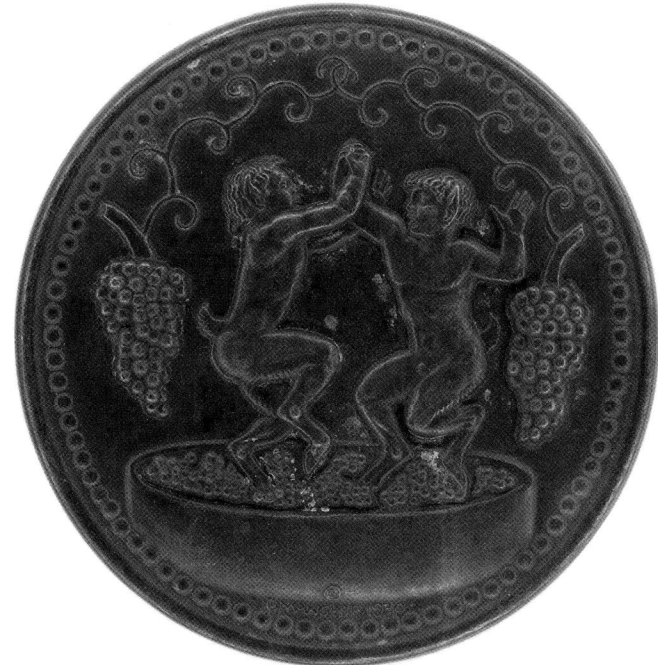

Figs. 137 and 138. *Hail to Dionysus Who First Discovered the Magic of the Grape,* 1930; bronze; $2\frac{7}{8}$ in. diameter. Gift of the heirs of Albert Laessle.

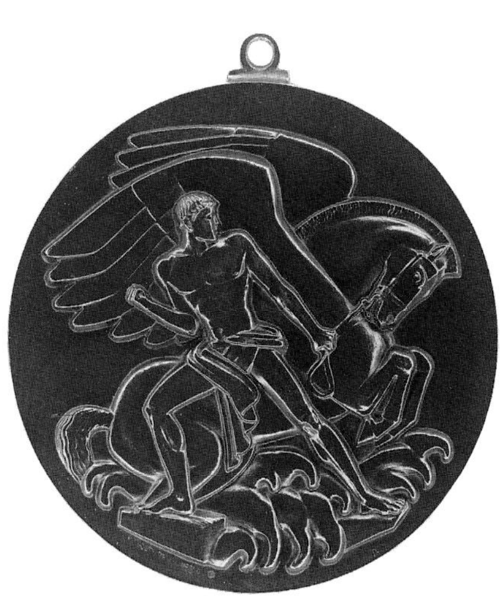

Fig. 139. *Carnegie Corporation Medal* (obverse), 1934; bronze; 4 in. diameter.

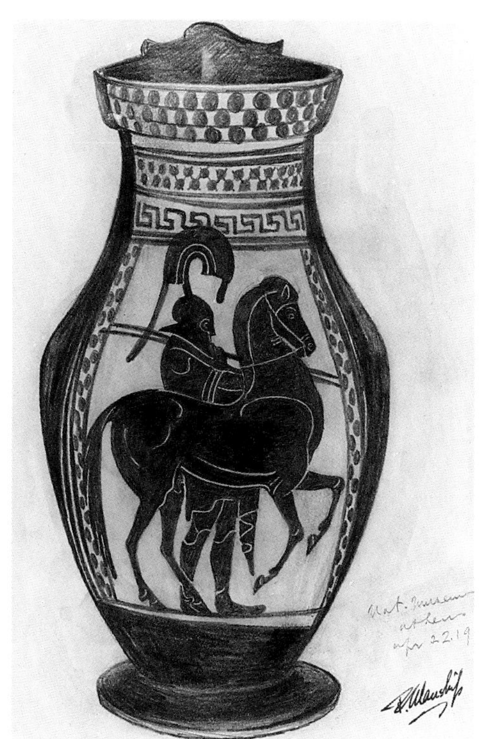

Fig. 140. *Greek Vase,* 1912; pencil on paper; $8\frac{1}{2}$ x 6 in.

medal accepted the full reality of human desires and neither scorned them—or worse—made them the object of charade. By the time Manship issued this medal, his classicism was admired and perfectly understood; yet the very heart of that classicism, its spirit and variety, was rejected in some quarters. Using this work as a gauge, we can measure the difference between those who falsely supported Manship as the hope of a revived (and stultifying) academicism and those who grasped the real vitality of his effort.

Exemplifying Manship's human and artistic personality, the Dionysus medal displayed his rare talent for reading contemporary events in the language of classical forms. Accordingly, he was awarded many medallic occasions, such as the commission for the Franklin Delano Roosevelt inauguration medal.[13] The furiously occupied president-elect gave the sculptor only two sittings. (Manship charged a nominal $500 fee, as he had known the president since 1919 when Roosevelt had been secretary of the navy and had consulted Manship about a redesign of the navy's Medal of Honor. The Manships had called on Governor Roosevelt in Albany, and Eleanor Roosevelt returned the visit, taking tea at the Manship's New York home—a major social achievement for Mrs. Manship.) The medal

> has a bas-relief of Roosevelt's head on one side and a full-rigged sailing ship, the old Constitution conventionalized, in slightly lower bas-relief, on the other. The reverse was suggested by Mr. Roosevelt himself, and is reminiscent of his old hobby, the navy.[14]

His friends recalled that, in addition to his public medal commissions, Manship found it relaxing to model "small portrait medallions of his friends and [he] decorated the reverse side with humorous designs symbolic of their tastes or character. The study of Oriental Art in the museums was another relaxation but he believed his early and best inspiration came from the study of Greek vases in Italy."[15]

For the *Carnegie Corporation Medal* (fig. 139) Manship reached back into his notes and drew upon his recollections of classical Greek horses as depicted on the ancient vases he had seen in Athens in 1912 (fig. 140) or in the Panathenaic frieze of the Elgin Marbles. The firm, clean lines of these Greek horses emblemized strength, as in the story of Bellerophon and Pegasus. One of classical mythology's great youthful heroes, Bellerophon aspired to tame the immortal winged horse, Pegasus, who was said to have sprung from Medusa's severed neck when Perseus killed her. A seer told Bellerophon to lie for a night upon the altar of Athena. When he awoke, Bellerophon found a golden bridle on the ground beside him; then he found Pegasus calmly waiting at a spring in Corinth. Manship depicts Bellerophon placing the bridle on the beast's head.

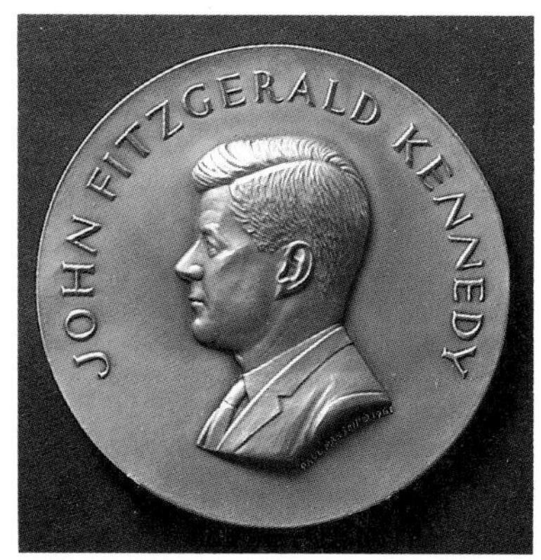

Fig. 141. *John F. Kennedy Inaugural Medal,* 1961; bronze; 9½ in. diameter.

Manship's semi-official status as America's medalist-laureate continued nearly to his death. His last effort was on behalf of President John F. Kennedy. The president-elect's wife, Jacqueline, had written a college term paper on Paul Manship's sculpture, and she suggested Manship to the inaugural committee.

In the midst of pre-inauguration hubbub at the Kennedy household, with future cabinet secretaries coming and going, campaign workers and dignitaries paying respects, and political transition teams meeting, the old artist made his call on the young president.[16] The president surprised Manship by inviting him to join the Kennedys in Florida; later, Manship regretted his hasty refusal. The quick sketch he made in forty-five minutes sufficed to capture a dour likeness. Nevertheless, the work was a huge success, outselling any previous presidential medal (fig. 141).

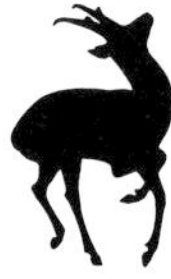

Celebrity

IN JULY 1932 the board of directors of Rockefeller Center approved employing Manship to create a sculpture for the main axis of their epochal development. The choice of Manship for this job derived from his growing respectability as an artist of genteel taste and his reputation as a sculptor possessed of a businesslike reliability. Since the late 1920s, Manship had been considered the leading candidate for monumental and architectural commissions.

When one of Rockefeller Center's architects was asked why Paul Manship had been selected to execute the central fountain, he answered, "Because Manship is the only man we can count on." While some could have argued that another artist might produce nobler or more moving concepts better integrated with the architecture, no one could match Manship's technique. "We know," the architect continued, "that he'll turn out a 100% professional job, capably modeled, brilliantly cast, in scale, and with waterworks that work. And furthermore, on the opening day Manship will be there with the cord in his hand all ready to unveil."[1]

Manship received the commission for the *Prometheus Fountain* in January 1933, and, astonishingly, the huge ensemble was dedicated only a year later in January 1934. The speed of execution was not Manship's idea:

> I made my designs for the Plaza fountain guided by the architects' drawings of the RCA Building behind it. Now sometimes in studying such a drawing, no matter how accurate it may be, perspective plays tricks on a man. In my imagination I saw the building—which was to be the background of the fountain—as much wider than it actually turned out to be. Then, too, in any vast building enterprise like that one, other factors inevitably come in. There's the question of time. Schedules are essential. Things must be pushed on and on relentlessly. . . . There's a sense of rush and push in the very atmosphere . . . this is in no sense a criticism of this particular job. It's a criticism of the times. . . . The owners and builders were generous to a fault. . . . But there was time to consider. There was money. There was engineering practicability. . . . I could wish—perhaps everyone concerned does—and did—that there had been more time to devote to a study of all the sketches I submitted. I could wish—and perhaps the others do also—that the figures had first been put up in plaster instead of bronze. This was suggested, but

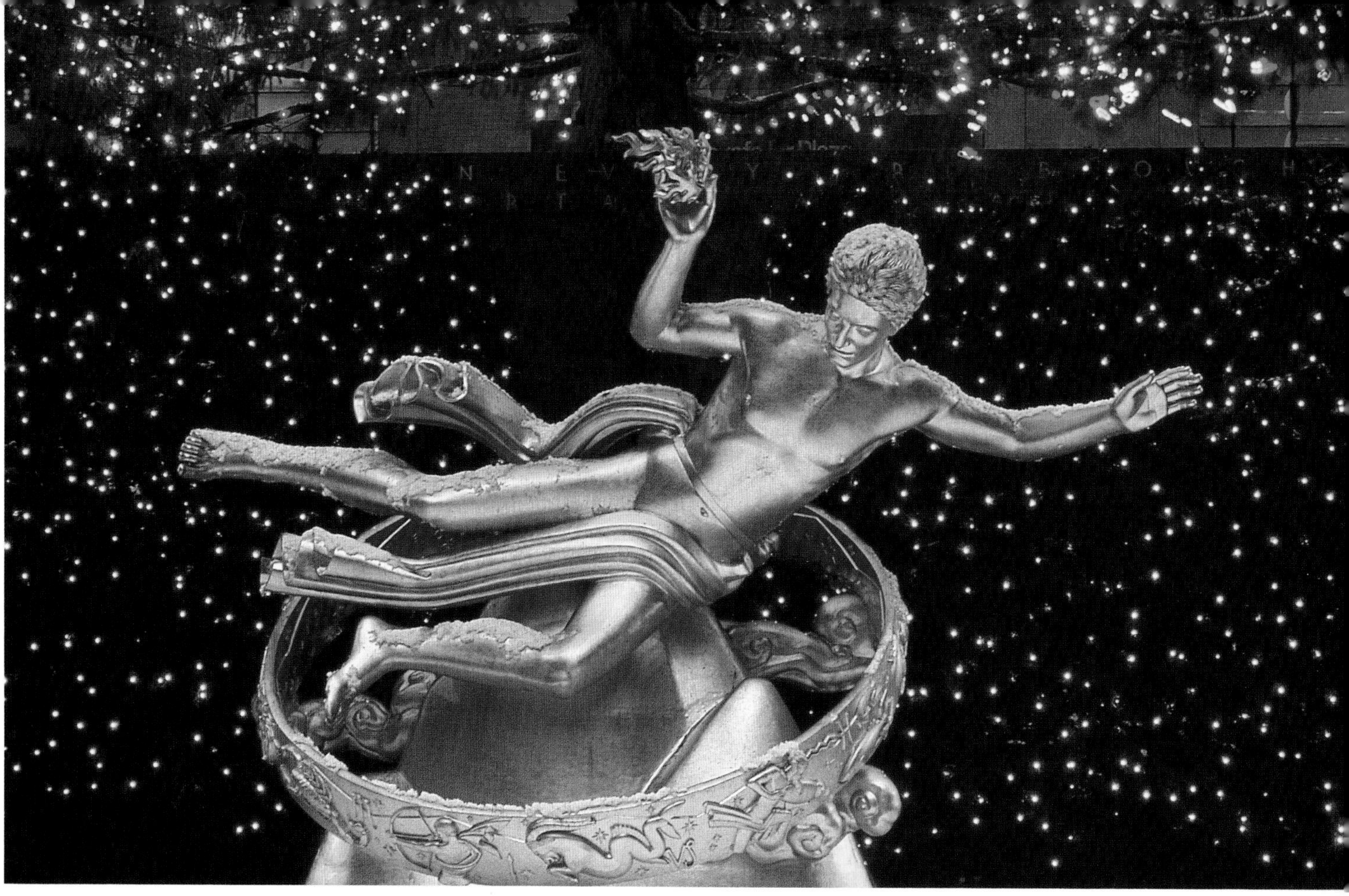

Fig. 142. *Prometheus Fountain*, 1934; gilded bronze; Rockefeller Center.

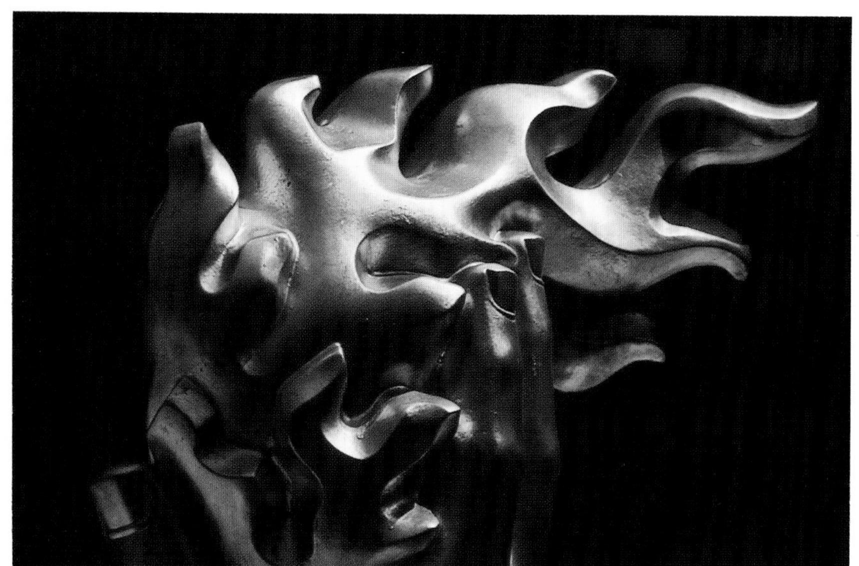

Fig. 143. Detail, *Prometheus Fountain*.

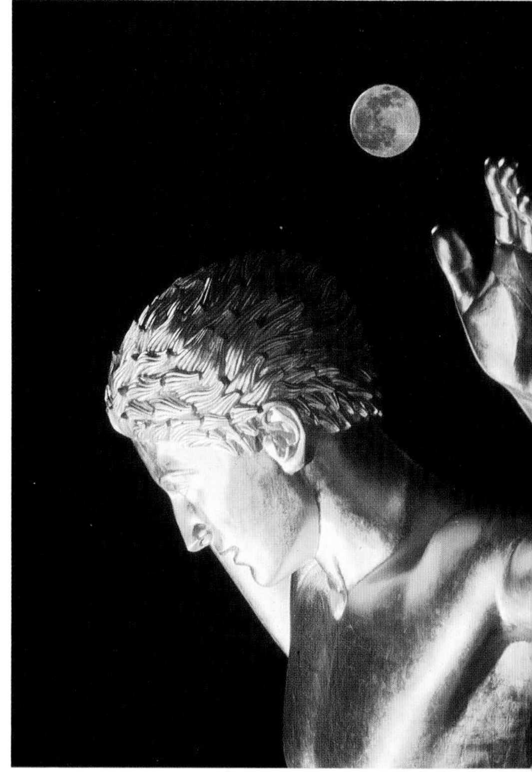

Fig. 144. Detail, *Prometheus Fountain*.

> there was the desire—almost the necessity, perhaps—to keep going to the finish. No artist is ever entirely satisfied with the work he creates. I'd naturally welcome the opportunity of doing the whole fountain group over again.[2]

Thus, Manship's best-known work is a sculpture he more or less dismissed. The situation recalled Herbert Adams's warning to Oliver La Farge in 1913 that Manship might "do American art an incalculable good," if, as Adams had cautioned, fate didn't "let the architects ruin him by giving him a lot of big work which must be hastily executed."

Set against the west wall of a sunken plaza in front of the RCA Building, and visible from Fifth Avenue, the *Prometheus Fountain* became the main feature of Rockefeller Center's exterior decorative program (figs. 142–144). In time it also became a central attraction of the city's promenading. With its attendant restaurants and ice skating rink, this fountain and surrounding space succeeded beyond the most optimistic expectations of its planners, architects, or the artist to provide a focus for respite and relaxed socializing in the midst of the city (fig. 145). Two and one half times life size—and weighing nearly eight tons—the nude figure of the Titan who brought fire to mankind surmounts a ring of the zodiac signs in low relief. Supported by a mountainous mass that suggests his cosmic size, Prometheus is shown descending to earth carrying the primordial fire (fig. 146).

Mankind's creator, Prometheus was the mythical arch-rebel who fashioned man out of clay and championed mankind against the gods' hostility. Prometheus also stole fire from Olympus and taught man the use of it. For this he suffered the punishment of being tied to a mountain and having his liver devoured every day by an eagle (fig. 147). Manship's *Prometheus* floats above the fountain's main basin (the present lighting and sheet of water were designed in 1958, while the original plan called for sprays and jets of water arching against the wall behind the sculpture). To Manship, the exalted setting in the very heart of the designed city—the quintessential Art Deco statement—must have seemed irresistible as the site for this god, the fashioner of mankind, the first sculptor. A gleaming sign, *Prometheus* advertises both archaism and the sculptural enterprise itself.

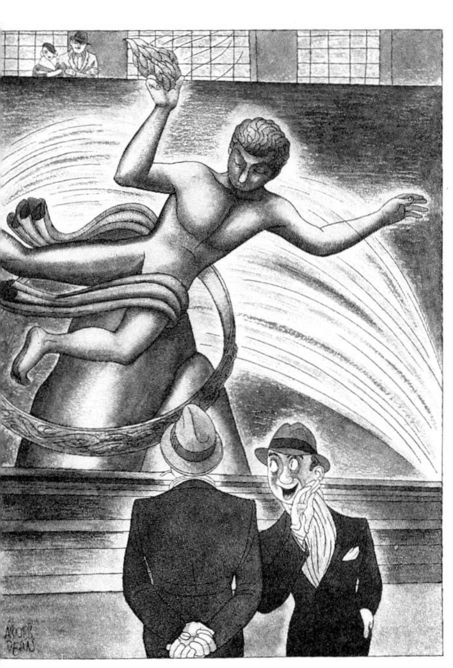

"Let's tie up the rights for radiator caps!"

Fig. 145. Abner Dean, cartoon, 1934.

Prometheus's hair and the fireball he carries are patterned passages setting off the rest of the smoothly stylized body. Although it sits at the foot of one of the greatest of skyscrapers, *Prometheus* possesses a decorative charm that is not overwhelmed by its surroundings. Indeed, the sleekly debonair vacancy—perhaps the result of an accelerated work schedule or an attempt at enormous monumentality to match the encircling buildings—promoted decoration over sculptural potency. As in the *Flight of Europa*, Manship used gilding to levitate an opaque mass.[3]

Fig. 146. *Prometheus Studies*, 1933; pen and ink and pencil on tracing paper; $4\frac{3}{16}$ x $4\frac{1}{4}$ in.

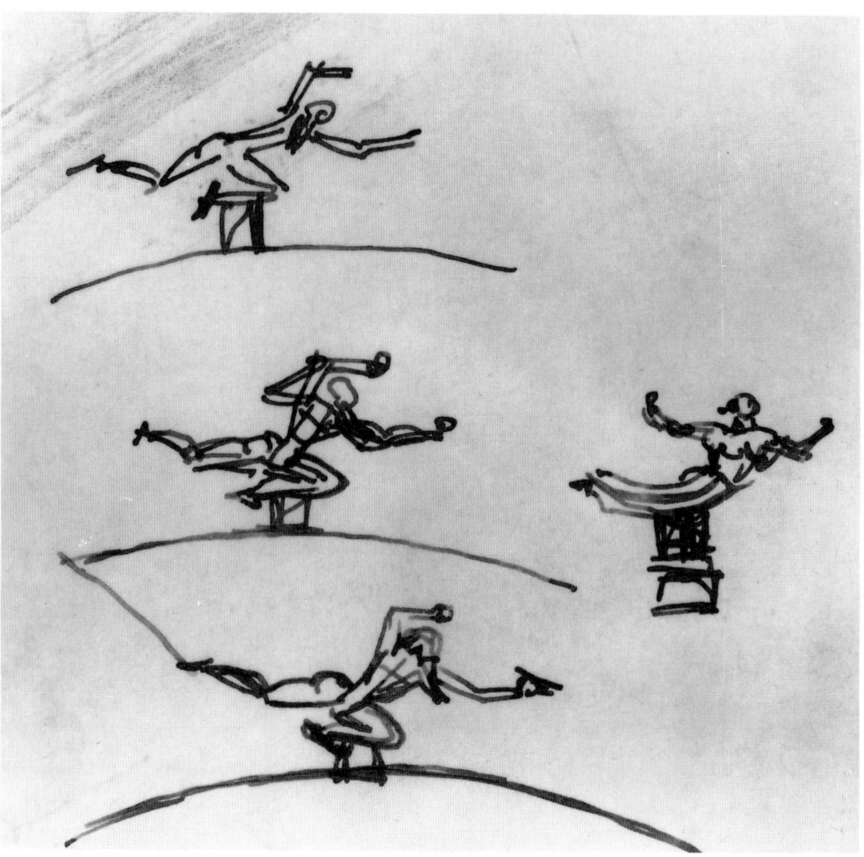

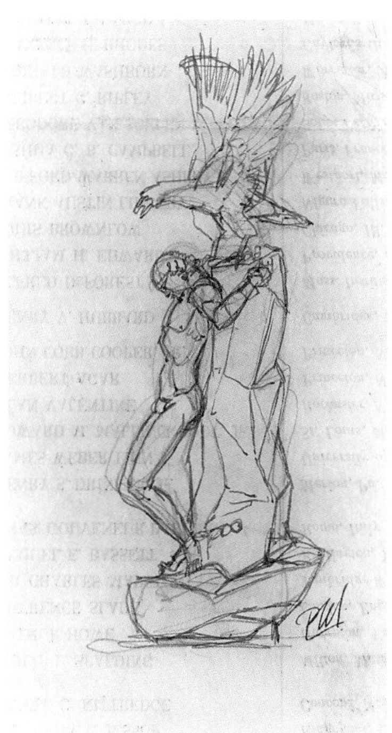

Fig. 147. *Prometheus Sketch*; pen and ink and pencil on paper; $7\frac{1}{8}$ x $4\frac{3}{16}$ in.

In time, *Prometheus* received three additional coats of gold, which softened and obscured the statue's original lines. Details were lost. By the late 1960s the old coating had to be removed and discarded—almost 7 pounds of gold leafing too uneconomic to reprocess. Workers built a wood and plastic enclosure around the entire sculpture, in order to maintain a temperature of at least fifty degrees while they stripped *Prometheus* down to the bronze. Repairs were made to the sculpture, and the undercoating was completely sanded before applying new gold leaf. Only 1.2 pounds of new gold were required for the entire surface, but considering the lost gold leaf, this project cost a handsome sum of money.

In addition to the colossal central *Prometheus*, two figures—one male, one female, representing mankind—were originally placed on either side of the gilded fountain. A year after the ensemble was installed, Manship came to have misgivings about these figures and felt that they "were out of proportion, that they should be removed and replaced with something else." His suggestion was taken.[4] Between 1935 and 1984 these figures decorated the Palazzo Italia's roof garden (facing Saint Patrick's Cathedral) in the Rockefeller Center complex (fig. 148). (When the "RCA Boy and Girl" figures were reinstated in 1984,

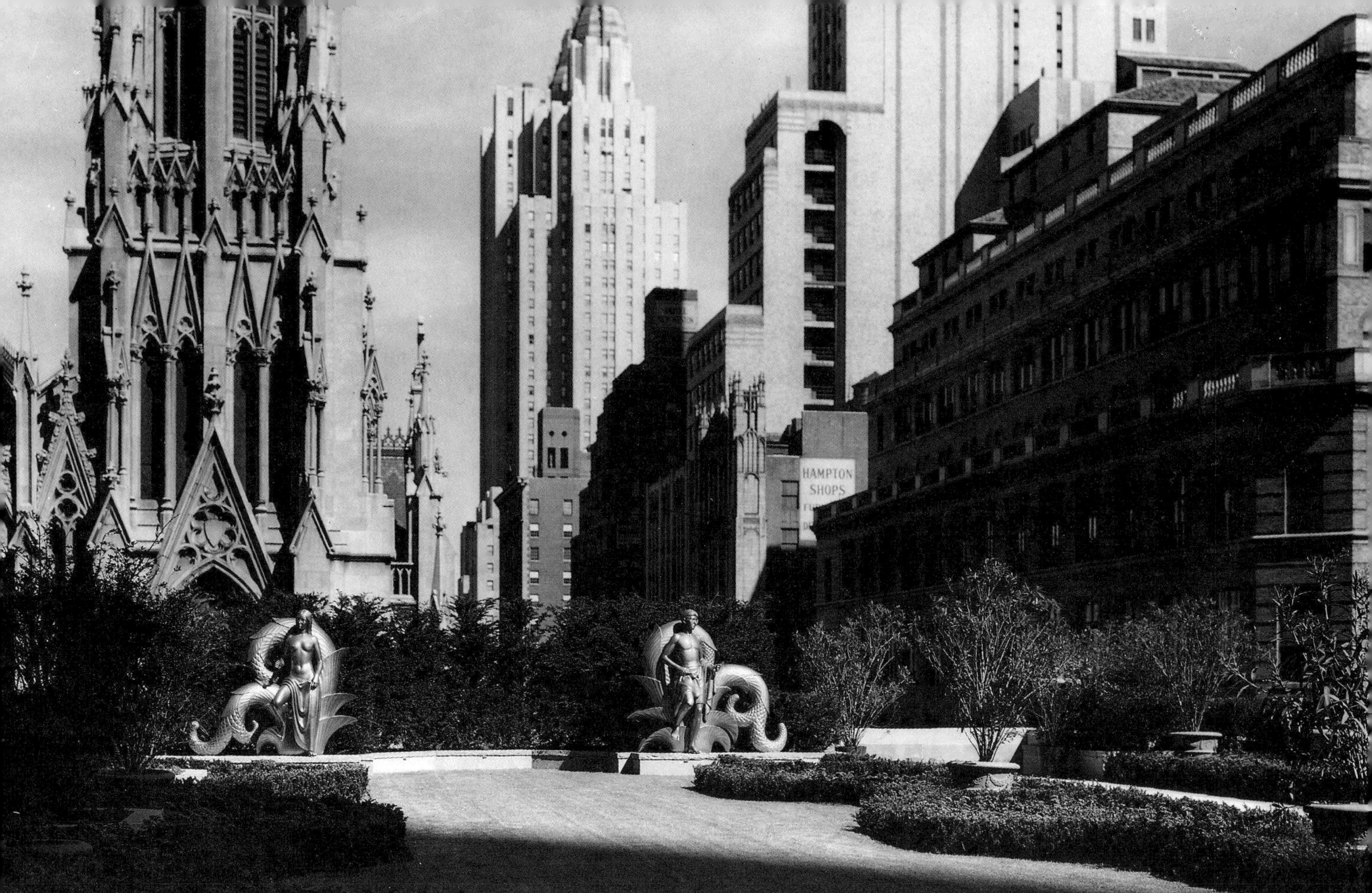

Fig. 148. *Male and Female Figures,* from *Prometheus Fountain,* 1934; bronze; Rockefeller Center.

they were not set on flanking ledges in proximity to *Prometheus*. Instead, the two sculptures were placed at ground level, in the midst of the cafes and adjacent to the central plaza used as a skating rink.) The first humans created by Prometheus, the figures each present one hand to receive fire from the Titan (fig. 149). Partially clothed—the boy in shorts, the girl in a loose drapery—they stand before richly curving vegetative ornamentation.

Beneath his heavy brows and receding hairline, Paul Manship had dancing light blue eyes. He was given to wearing a bow tie, and his low-pitched voice carried his booming laugh across the room. He could quite naturally charm his patrons (fig. 150). The wealthy felt comfortable around him. He radiated none of the anxiety of the bohemian whose livelihood depended on individual sales, and, consequently, Manship could ask for, and did get, the highest prices for his work.

Amid the plaster models and plans for projects, clients were made welcome. In his studio in Italy, assistants would produce roast kid and lots of Chianti. In Paris a light lunch of a salad, an omelet, and some delectable wine would appear. Manship would cock his head, tell a wonderful story, and tell it well. Another sale.

He had the knack for living with zest, for living well, with fine wine, a large studio, a corps of assistants. In New York, one day a week he had an

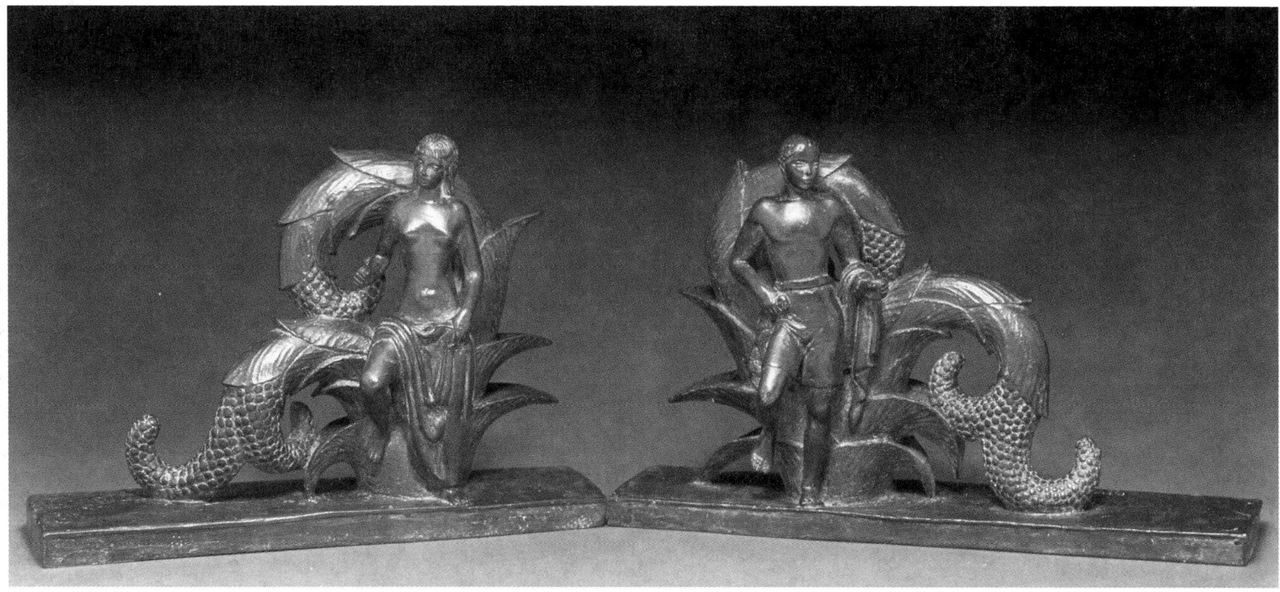

Fig. 149. Study for *Male and Female Figures*, from *Prometheus Fountain*, 1934; bronze; 9 in. high.

open house for people to gather at his place; in Paris, his marvelous studio at 6 rue du Val de Grace was in a convent garden. Such genial success made him a target. During the 1940s Manship became the sculptor against whom the modernists reacted—although he had always been generous with his time, advice, energy, and shared his patrimony.

Manship's wealth of invention allowed him to pursue a path between the rear guard (who were consciously, even adamantly, the ultraconservative realist-academics) and modern art's avant-garde. His work embodied something of the reactionary as well as the progressive adventurer, yet he was eventually adopted by the more conservative faction. The monied class's ability to commission works did not automatically place Manship in their camp. Finding no welcome with the modernists, he was drawn ever more compactly into a world of reaction not necessarily fated as his native bent. Manship's subjects and exposition relied upon antique precedent, which he saw as the wellspring of Western art, and would, therefore, not casually jettison. And so Manship's sculpture was readily, perhaps too readily for his own good, embraced by misunderstanding academics. Other factions failed to see that his work embodied some of the simplification and abstraction of modernism and that it arose from the same urges and necessities.

The genuine academic, Manship produced truly derivative work; he had studied the sculptors of other ages firsthand, and the distillate of his observations formed the elements of his personal style. The process Manship went through was the same "as any Greek artist who had been taught to accept the 'canons' of art formulated by the Masters and adhered to by many subsequent generations. In a word 'academic' means simply the acceptance of certain conventions of

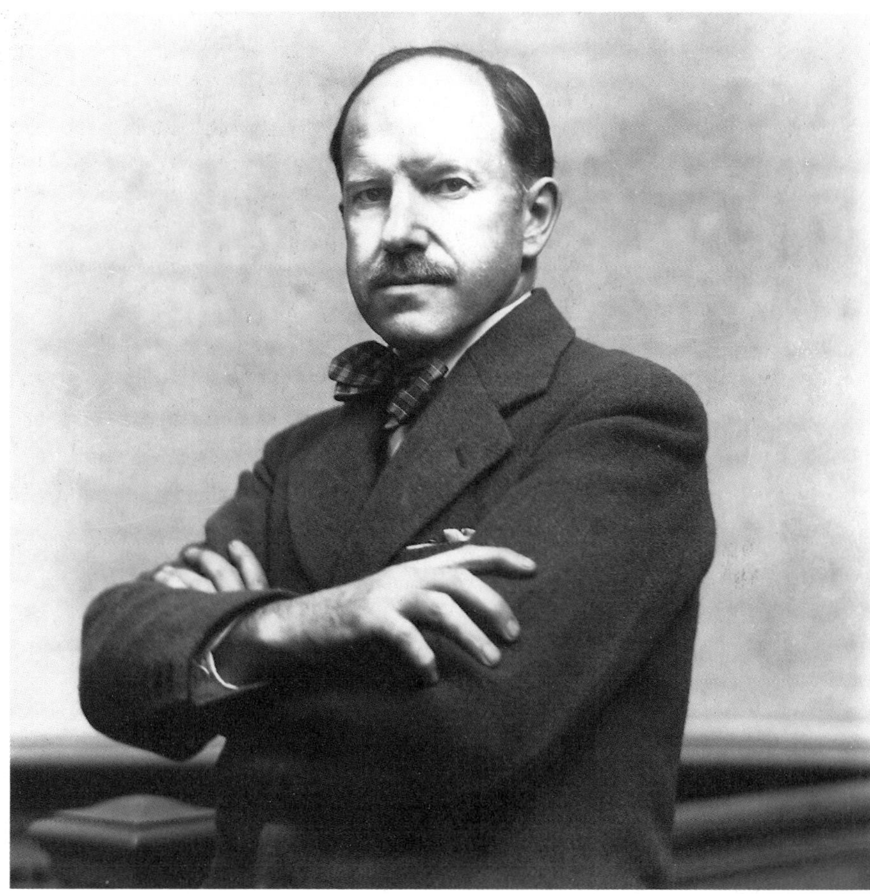

Fig. 150. Paul Manship.

method and technique, certain methods of construction and systems of proportion which experience has shown to be satisfactory."[5]

Manship's unexpected response in the dialogue of modern art branded him an academic in the pejorative sense. Those in power appreciated his work and expressed that admiration, which Manship relished (welcoming praise from whatever quarter). Awards showered upon him.

By 1916, just four years after his return from Rome as a student, he had been elected to the National Academy of Design. Throughout the 1920s he garnered numerous medals and awards for his individual works and for overall accomplishment. In 1931 Manship was appointed a successor to Daniel Chester French as a member of the National Gallery of Art Commission, so named because what is now the National Museum of American Art was first called the National Gallery of Art. In 1938, when the museum changed its name to the National Collection of Fine Arts, this commission was renamed the Smithsonian Art Commission. The commission kept this title when the museum became the National Museum of American Art. Manship remained a commissioner until his death, and his loyalty to the Smithsonian extended to a major bequest. In 1932 he was elected to the American Academy of Arts and Letters. The Paris Exposition of 1937 awarded Manship the *Diplome d' Honneur*. Following Lee Lawrie's term, Manship served between 1937 and 1941 as a member of the congressionally established Commission of Fine Arts, which guides the architectural planning and growth of the Federal City (Washington, D.C.), whose appearance today is mainly the result of the commission's continuing supervision. The National Sculpture Society gave him its Medal of Honor in 1942, and in that same year, Manship became vice-president of the National Academy of Design—a position he held until 1948.

Distant countries elected Manship to their national academies. Argentina named Manship a Corresponding Member of its National Academy of Fine Arts in 1944, and the next year he was elected a Corresponding Member for sculpture of the Academy of Beaux Arts of the Institute of France. America's National Institute of Arts and Letters (to which he had been elected in 1920) in February 1945 awarded its gold medal—given to a sculptor only once every nine years—to Paul Manship.[6] Not surprisingly, given Manship's penchant for hard work and good living, this acclaim translated into a very comfortable existence.

Manship's Massachusetts studio was large and beautifully situated near water (fig. 151). Throughout the house and its grounds Manship displayed his sculptures. Amid foliage and under the open sky as well as in a pergola, the sculpture gardens showed his pieces to good effect (fig. 152).

In the heart of midtown Manhattan's most fashionable district, Manship bought a row of three townhouses on Seventy-second Street. He opened continuous spaces in the connected buildings to form a restful and cozy home for his family. For this extraordinary house he crafted all the major decorative elements. (The family moved out in 1941 when Mrs. Manship became ill and in the war-depleted labor market, they were unable to secure servants. But they did not move far, just to an apartment next door.) At home he could show his own work while displaying a vision of the integrated decorative arts. This large decorative program afforded him the adventure of making ornamental and useful pieces (figs. 153, 154). For example, Manship had fashioned two candelabra in 1916, which decorated the artist's library (fig. 155). One featured *Adam and Eve*, the other *Venus and Vulcan*; both were gilded, gleaming down to the four crouching lions that decorate the bases. Each of the figures surmounts straight standards, and each figure supports a candle collar or bobeche. In 1920 Manship again tried his hand at making collars for candles in a coffee house. Later, he cast candlesticks for his own table. Manship made two other candelabra in 1931. These have serpentine standards of gilded bronze that rise from a foliage-ornamented base (fig. 156). One of the candelabra,

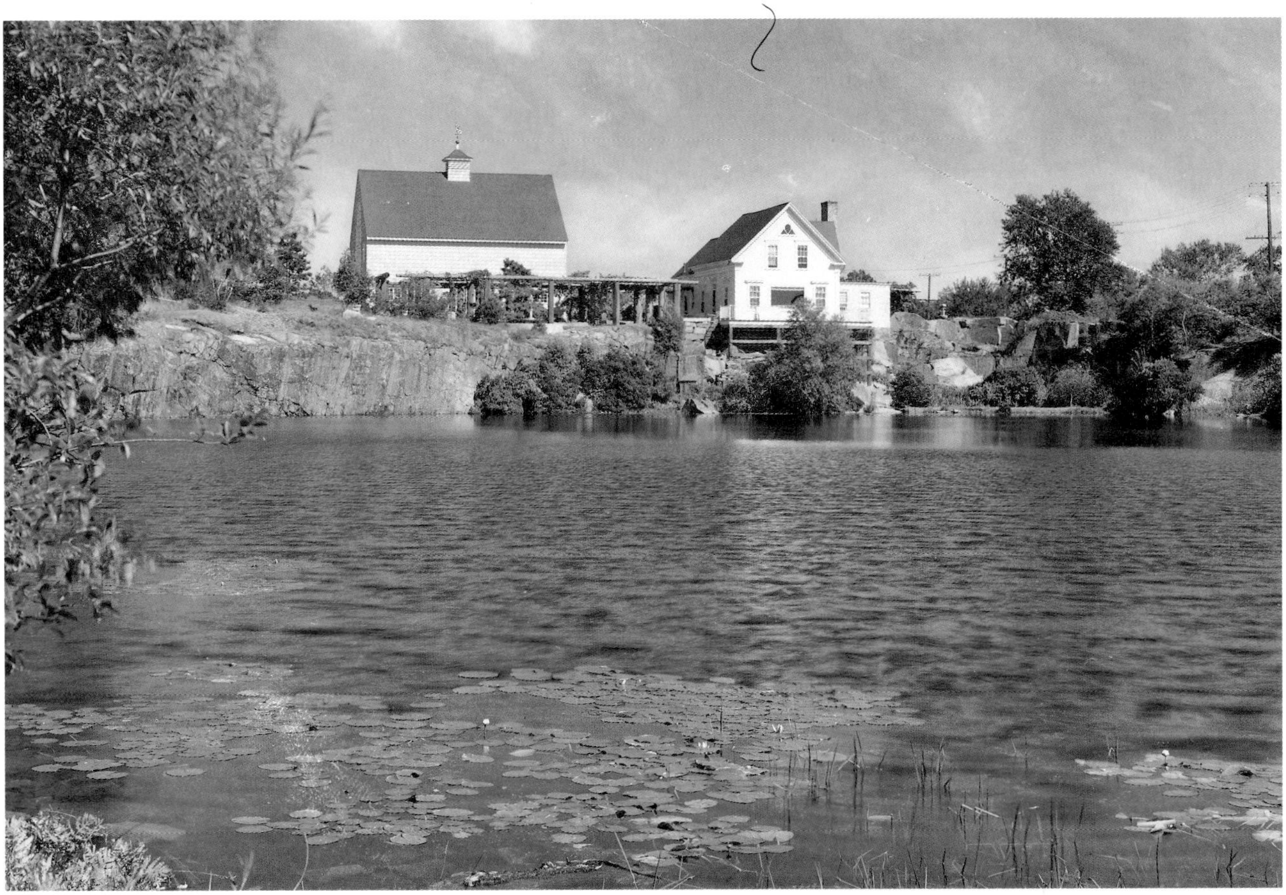

Fig. 151. Manship's Massachusetts studio.

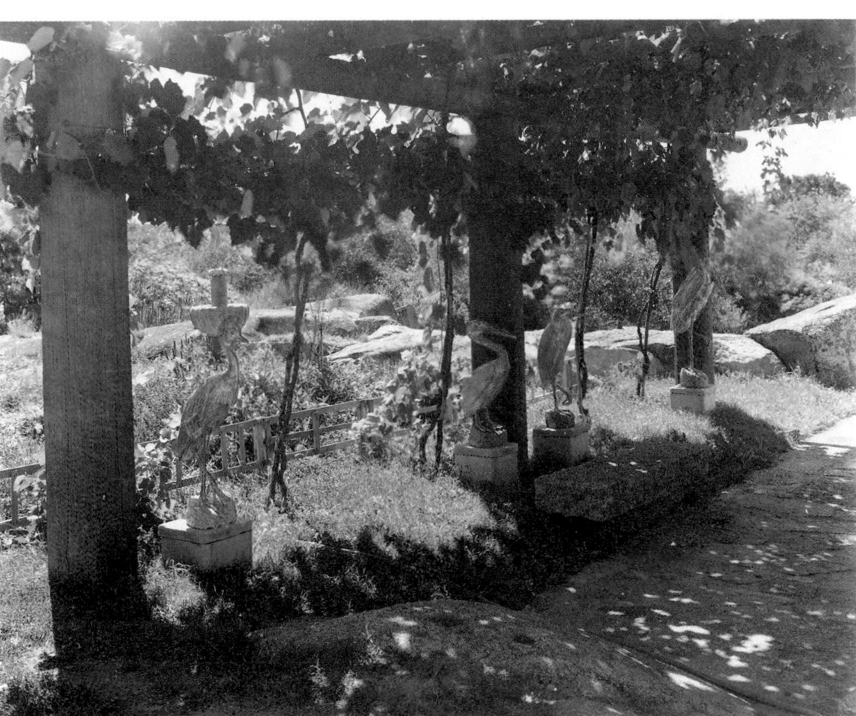

Fig. 152. Manship's Massachusetts studio, sculpture garden.

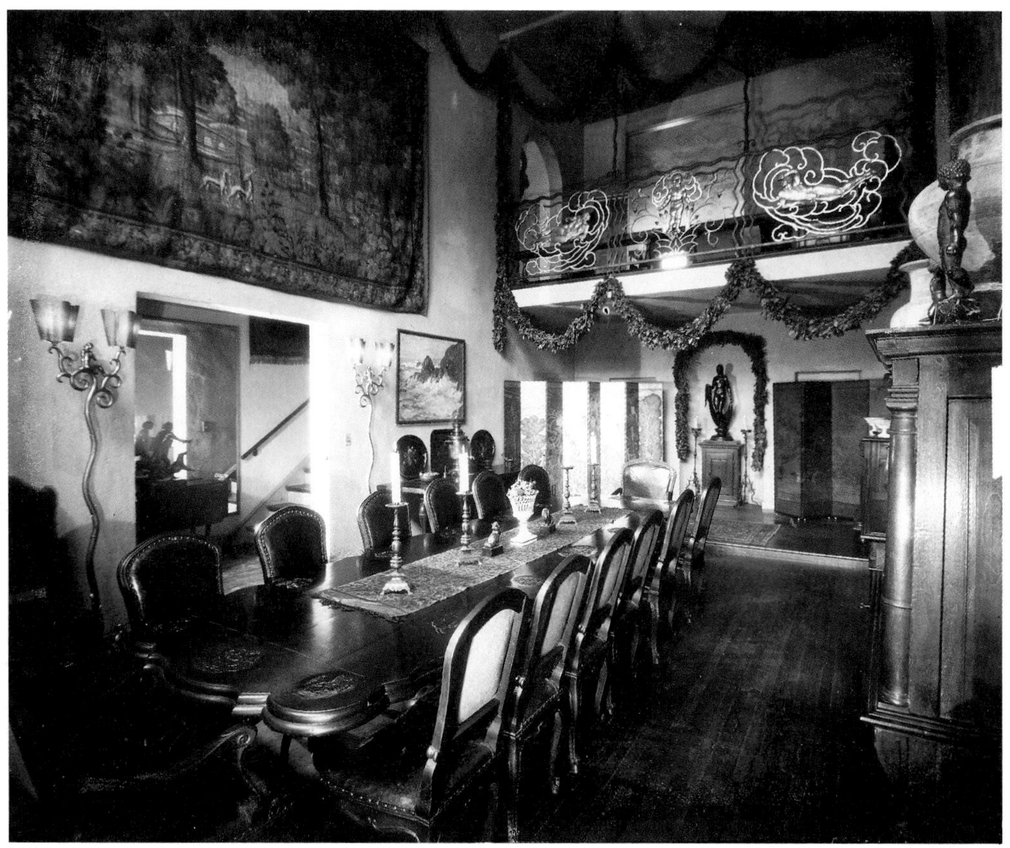

Fig. 153. Manship's Manhattan townhouse, dining room.

Fig. 154. Manship's Manhattan townhouse, library.

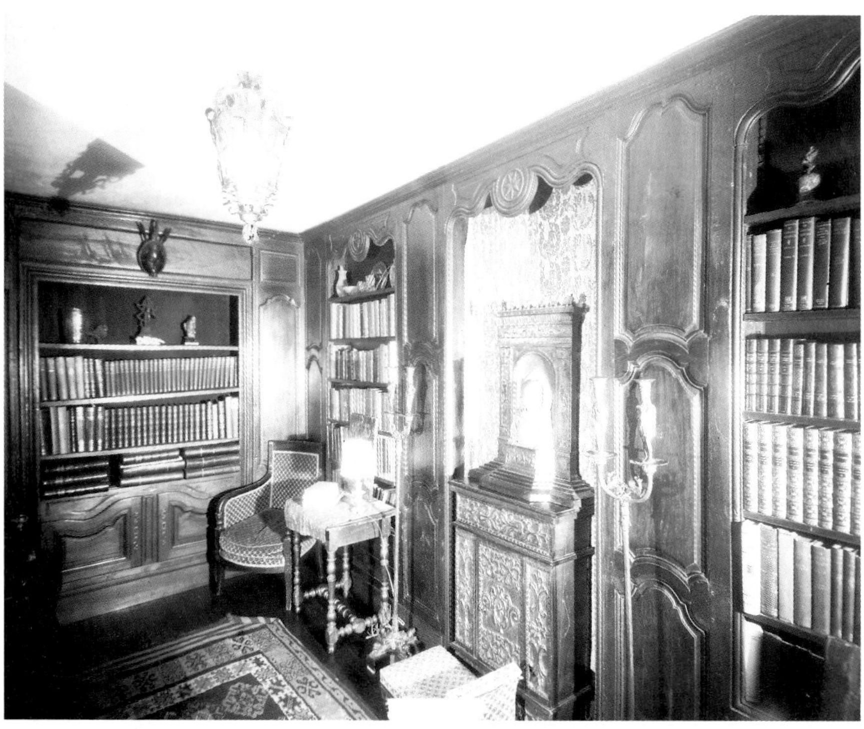

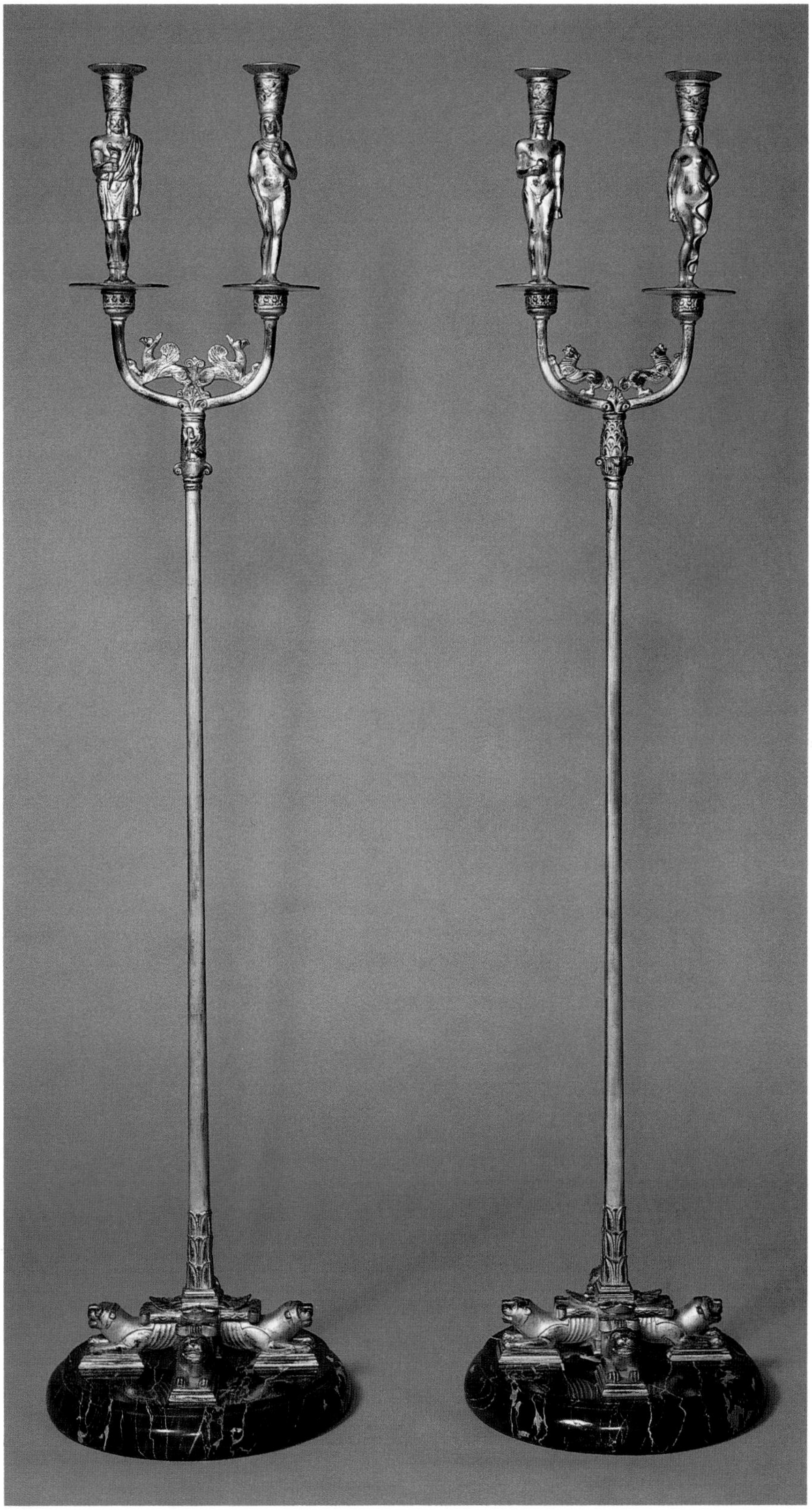

Fig. 155. Candelabra: *Adam and Eve*, 1916; *Venus and Vulcan*, 1916; gilded bronze; 57¾ in. high. Collection Walda and Sydney Besthoff.

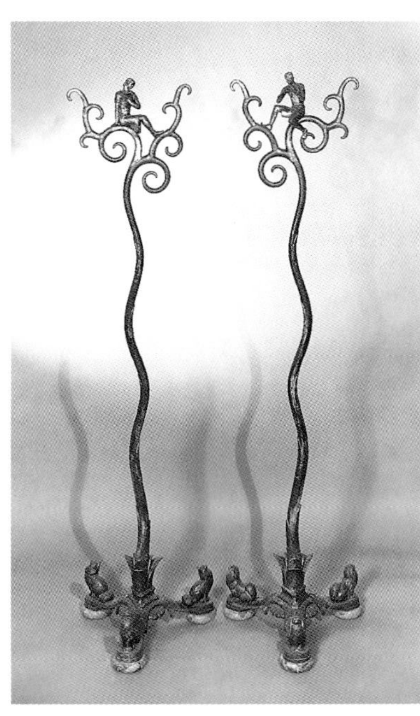

Fig. 156. *Candelabra*, 1931; gilded bronze; 79 in. high.

whose base is ornamented with Persian cats, terminates in a seated nymph (wearing, essentially, a modern boat-neck dress). The other candelabra, whose base is ornamented with three Pekingese dogs, terminates in a figure of Pan (in walking shorts) playing pipes. Both figures rest in a rough thicket of branches, abstracted in the Chinese style. The figures' clothing, their activities, and the foliate theme suggest a pastoral motif for these candelabra-as-trees. Manship also designed the folding screens in the dining room. As much as possible, with the exception of the oil paintings, Manship was responsible for everything notable in the house.

An ornamented wrought iron and gilded bronze railing, which Manship designed in 1928, screened the dining room's balcony (see fig. 153). The railing's three divisions featured gilt figures buoyant in the left and right sections, and in the center a child stood on the equivalent of a foliated throne. The outer male and female figures (supported by clouds that blend Chinese and Minoan qualities) both recline and direct worshipful attention to the child; the whole seems a playful metaphor for Manship's family life amid his artistic influences. The railing touched the ceiling in four twisting supports topped by sculptures from the *Dancing Children* series. The entire ensemble floated above the dinner guests. In these capacious rooms Manship's hand was everywhere. In 1930 he fashioned the cherrywood dining room table (now in the St. Louis Art Museum), which he ornamented in carved low relief with medallions of the signs of the four seasons and the zodiac; this table is over thirteen feet long and four feet wide (see fig. 153). To complete the ensemble, he also carved the dining room chairs.

Here, surrounded by his family in the decorative climate he had fashioned, Manship passed his happiest and most successful years.

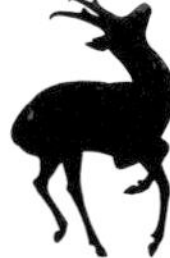

Social Responsibility and Public Visibility

MANSHIP EXPERIMENTED with different materials, yet all his energies and experiments served a few concentrated effects. His small number of marble pieces were carefully rubbed to enhance the quality of solidity and simplicity that carved sculptural forms do not usually approach. The solidity of the figure—the opacity of its form—was a trait that eventually dominated his work. When this formal proclivity controlled his forms, the work became leaden and uninspired. From the early to the late 1920s, Manship had wrestled with one such obdurate sculptural problem.

EVE His small nudes and formal studies of *Eve* and *Adam* hardly evolved. Occasional bursts of intensity (passages of dramatically highlighted gesture) erupted in works of evident synthetic character. In the early version of *Eve* (see fig. 75) Manship played subtle variations on high relief and symmetry; the sculpture was basically limited to front and back views. His 1935 *Eve* refined the thoughts of over a decade before (fig. 157). Where once he crossed *Eve*'s right hand over her body, now Manship turned that gesture inward—the horizontal movement restrained as the right arm was raised—ending in a clenched fist that expressed the tension of an inner struggle. *Eve*'s left arm, downturned in the earlier work, now turned up, also terminating in a fist as she looks down at the serpent demon, Lilith (fig. 158).

An economical sculptural invigoration no longer served Manship's ambitions or the requirements of an expressive anatomy. Trying to create fully realized figures turning as a cylinder in space, he repaired to art history. His son recalled that Manship wrestled with "a problem that he had. In every woman's body the spinal column is evident in the lower back but it is never indicated by the Greek sculptors. Should he therefore follow the example of nature or that of the Greeks? He chose the Greeks."[1] It might seem that Manship relied exclusively on antique paradigms to guide his combinations of sources and references; we have only to look at one of his drawings from the model (see fig. 52) to grasp the vigor of the living figure before him, its singular

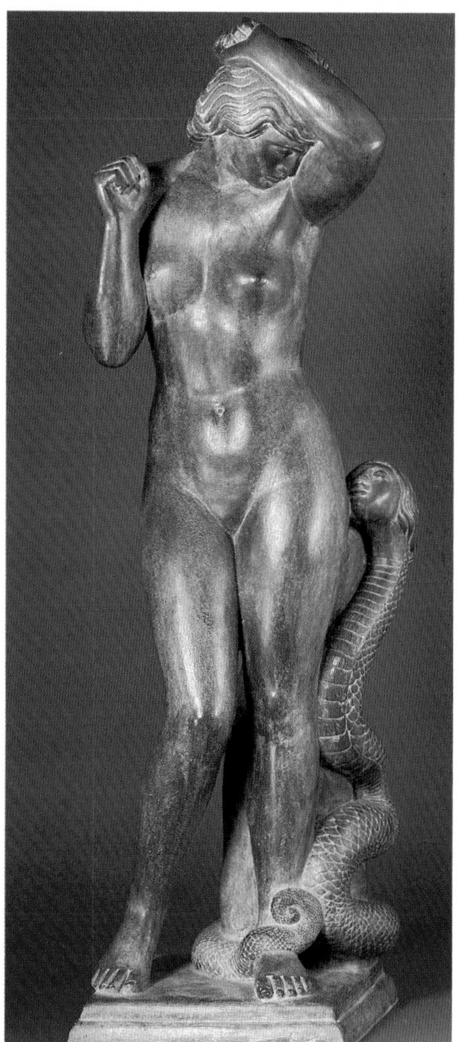

Fig. 157. *Eve (#1)*, 1935; bronze; 44 in. high.

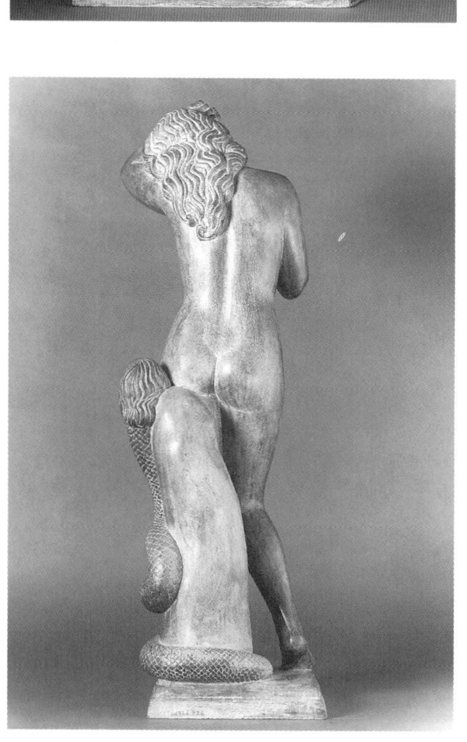

Fig. 159. *Eve (#1)*.

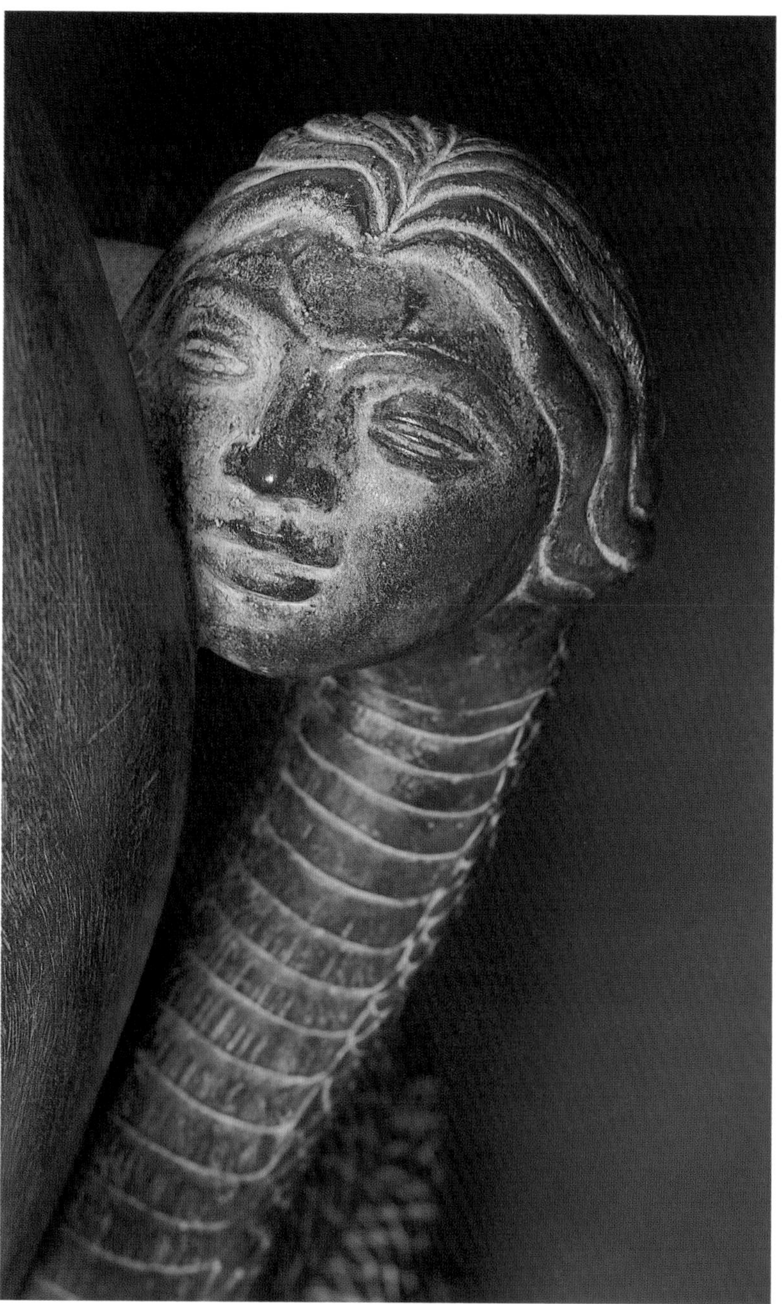

Fig. 158. Detail, *Eve (#1)*.

grace and individual manner of draping as a body supported against gravity. The 1935 *Eve* convinces us, not only of its tri-dimensional sculptural conception but also of the pendulousness of flesh as form, and most important (and rare for Manship), its source in a living body (fig. 159). This *Eve* might have walked, and the vivacity of the sculpture only heightens the work's psychological freight.

Manship recited the pose of Michelangelo's dying slaves for his 1935 *Eve* (the weight of the figure channeled to one leg, knee raised to create a helix that moves up the body from her right knee to her left hip, from her right elbow to her left). He even added a support in the back, as if the figure had been carved. Such a support was irrelevant to a cast bronze; Manship was mimicking and reminding us of carved stone. With remarkable virtuosity, Manship used form to remind us of iconography; the figure of Lilith that curls dangerously at *Eve*'s side derives from Romanesque stone sculpture (probably from Provence). Just this sort of blunt face peers from innumerable column capitals, corbels, lintel decorations, rain spouts, and other ornamental locations in Romanesque architecture.

The sculpture's declaration of its source in carving is heightened by the surface treatment, which retains the marks of the chisel in plaster. Manship was exquisitely aware of the variety of effects that could be achieved by working in the plaster. He avoided the loss of control and immediacy of the usual method, which required: modeling in clay, casting the clay model in plaster, executing a bronze or a terra cotta or even a subsequent marble carved by an artisan. "But I often prefer to work directly in plaster. . . . I have developed this technique because it makes for simplification and an enrichment of form at the same time."[2]

ARTISTS' CONGRESS STATEMENT

In the middle of February 1936, the American Artists' Congress Against War and Fascism was held in New York, and Manship addressed the first public session. Unlike many other speakers, who had overt Communist allegiances, Manship was more politically pragmatic than dogmatic. His clients were wealthy, his commissions numerous, and the courage he showed by addressing this meeting (where he was likely to be despised just because of his relative affluence) redounded badly years later, when this appearance raised the ridiculous specter of his possible Communism. Manship's ideas about society's betterment were intimately bound to the societal condition of art—which was stronger than any party affiliation. Ultimately, he was as humane in his approach to the here-and-now as he was committed to the classics as a means of expression.

Manship's speech "Why Established Artists Should Oppose War and Fascism" was revealing and moving. He began forcefully:

> The purpose of the Congress is to organize artists in the interests of peace and in the defense of culture. We have seen in Europe the working of forces to destroy this culture. By united action we may do much for the preservation of this peace and culture which is of such inestimable value to us all.[3]

This implied that the culture Manship had in mind was shared with his audience—an unlikely notion—and that America, the recent heir to this ancient culture, was a legitimate inheritor who could invigorate Europe's failed vitality. Then Manship revealed his own mandate for art:

> From time immemorial the struggle for freedom of expression has been part and parcel of the accomplishment of great art. In relation to his environment the artist of all times has been the exponent of spiritual and social concepts and ideals and in large measure has been a prophet and interpreter of popular aspirations.

The first freedom, of expression, was the province of the arts. Manship made it clear that he shared little with the avant-garde; he saw his mission as the extension of the artist's historical role and not as a revolutionary profession. Yet, he did not denigrate the revolutionaries and spoke—not as an ersatz member of the avant-garde but as the wealthy and successful conservative he was—of the common responsibility of artists of all stripes, and of Fascism's threat to all art:

> There are artists today who live in comparative economic security. That they may be threatened with the loss of that security as well as their artistic independence is not obvious to them. It may not occur to them that their economic condition, as well as their spiritual freedom, is subject to the tendencies of political forces. They are not politically minded and their education probably is against their being so. . . . It is mainly in the group of those who are economically affected that the awareness takes place.

Manship's warning, based on first-hand experience of the years he had resided in Europe, was clear:

> When people say there is no danger of Fascism in this country it seems to me to mean that they are not conscious of the great and inevitable shaping of forces in that direction going on in the world today. They think America is isolated and uninfluenced politically by those forces. In Europe we have seen the beginnings of those movements which have ended in the seizure of power, then the militarization and regimentation of the people, with the accompanying stifling of democratic cultural liberties. . . . The forces of Fascism so confuse the fundamental issues that the unthinking man risks to be herded like sheep into the corrals of a Fascist state unless consciousness of the danger of loss of his freedom is brought before his eyes.
>
> The artist, through organization, will serve culture and may do much to keep the beacon of warning alight to show the threat to liberty, democracy and peace.

Manship's appearance at the American Artists' Congress Against War and Fascism did not damage his reputation; a year after Manship delivered his speech, President Roosevelt appointed him (and two other New Yorkers, Eugene F. Sarange and William Lamb) a member of the Fine Arts Commission. In 1939 Manship was elected to succeed John Gregory as president of the National Sculpture Society.

His life, however well-regulated and productive, was not without bizarre events. In 1939 one could have read of the following incident:

> Paul Manship's 250-pound bronze statue *Actaeon*, which on Oct. 7 was stolen from the grounds of the Yonkers (N.Y.) estate of Samuel Untermyer, was recovered last fortnight from one John Real, dealer in metals and junk. Police located the missing work of art in the shack of Mr. Real, who refused to tell how he had come by it. The present international demand for scrap metal may have something to do with the case.[4]

The rising tide of war accounted for the "international demand for scrap metal," and so Fascism, against which Manship had warned, took its temporary revenge on him.

WORLD'S FAIR

Gradually, the first youthful vision that infused Manship's gracefully exuberant work of the 1920s vanished. His figures assumed more solidity; a simplification of the sculptures' contours accented their substance. Details were eliminated as Manship focused attention on form alone. Perhaps this penchant reflected a sense of economy or streamlining (but the effect was sometimes less than dignified or monumental). In such works, bereft of animating details and despite the fluidity of action, some of Manship's genius was lacking. Rockefeller Center's *Prometheus* fountain verged on the solemn, where, previously, Manship had invigorated mythology with a humanly compelling empathy.

For the New York World's Fair, Manship shed sobriety in a return to his youthful inventiveness. His enormous and lavish fountain group and sundial were conceived with radiant zest. Manship believed that the world's fair was "not only to be a commercial enterprise of great interest but devoted also to the spiritual, artistic and cultural glories of American life."[5] This statement summed up Manship's credo for his own work as well.

Manship's view of the 1939 fair may have been shared by its planners or public—who saw the chance for educational entertainment. The occasion for enormous public display, for creating on the grandest scale, brought forth from Manship some of his balanced work. With sufficient time for reflection, he weighed the merits of gargantuan size with delicate detail, solid massing with animated gesture, antique references with current and everyday concerns and introspections. The fair was a great opportunity for him—one that he used to its fullest extent—for his large-scale work to regain some of the balance between

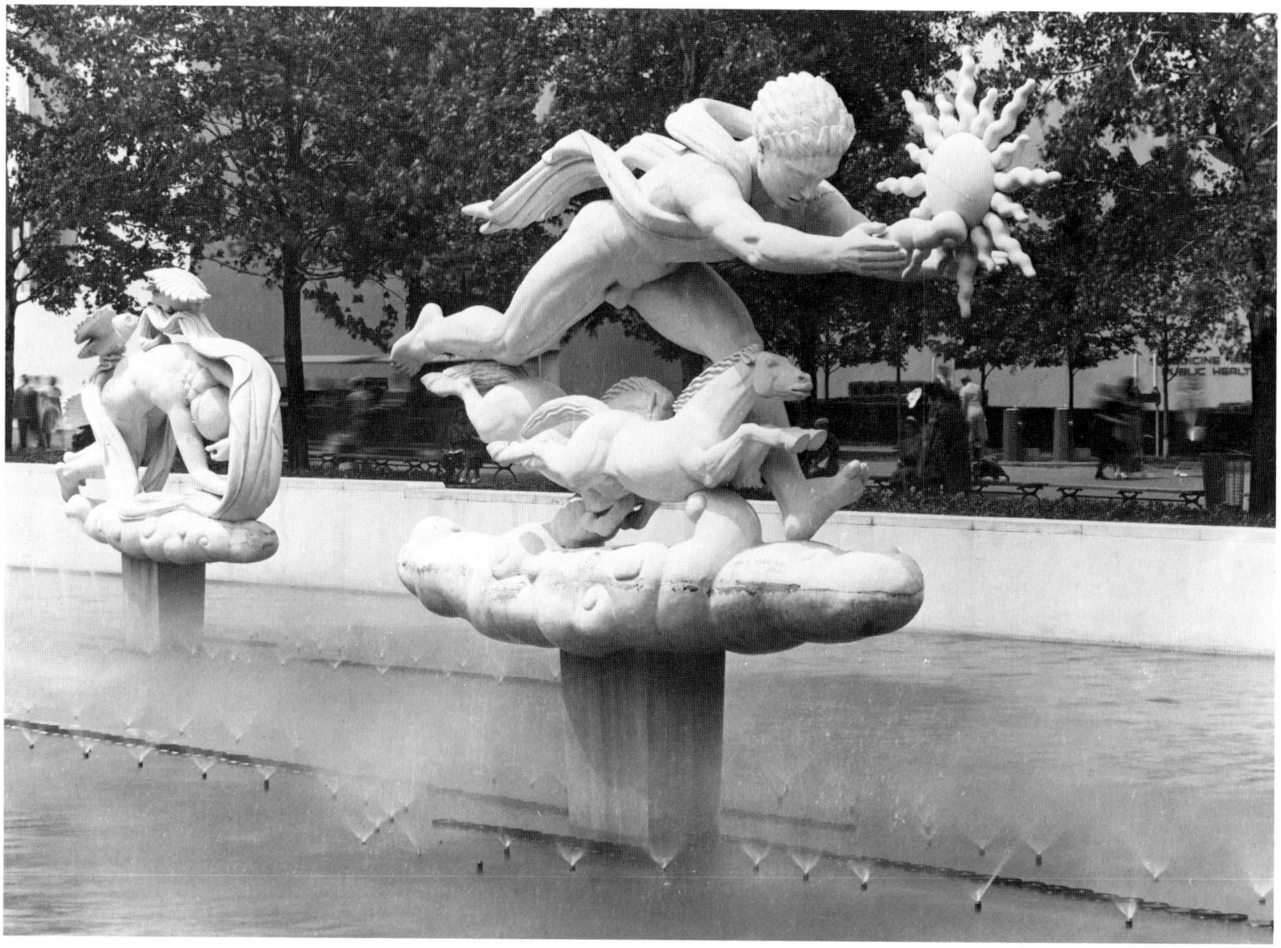

Fig. 160. *Moods of Time*, showing *Day* and *Evening*, 1939 New York World's Fair.

Fig. 161. *Time and the Fates Sundial*, 1939 New York World's Fair, in front of the Trylon and Perisphere.

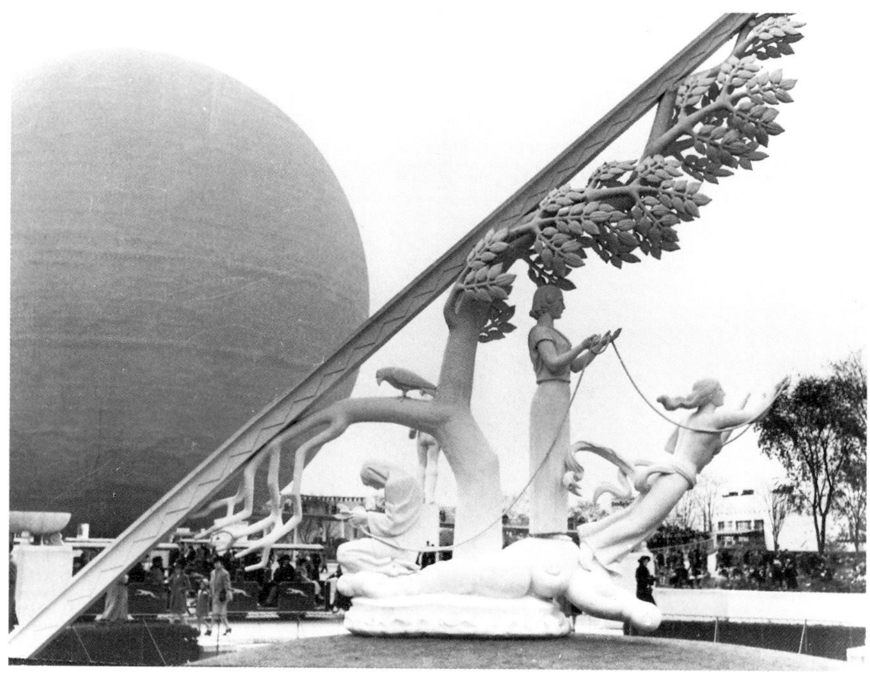

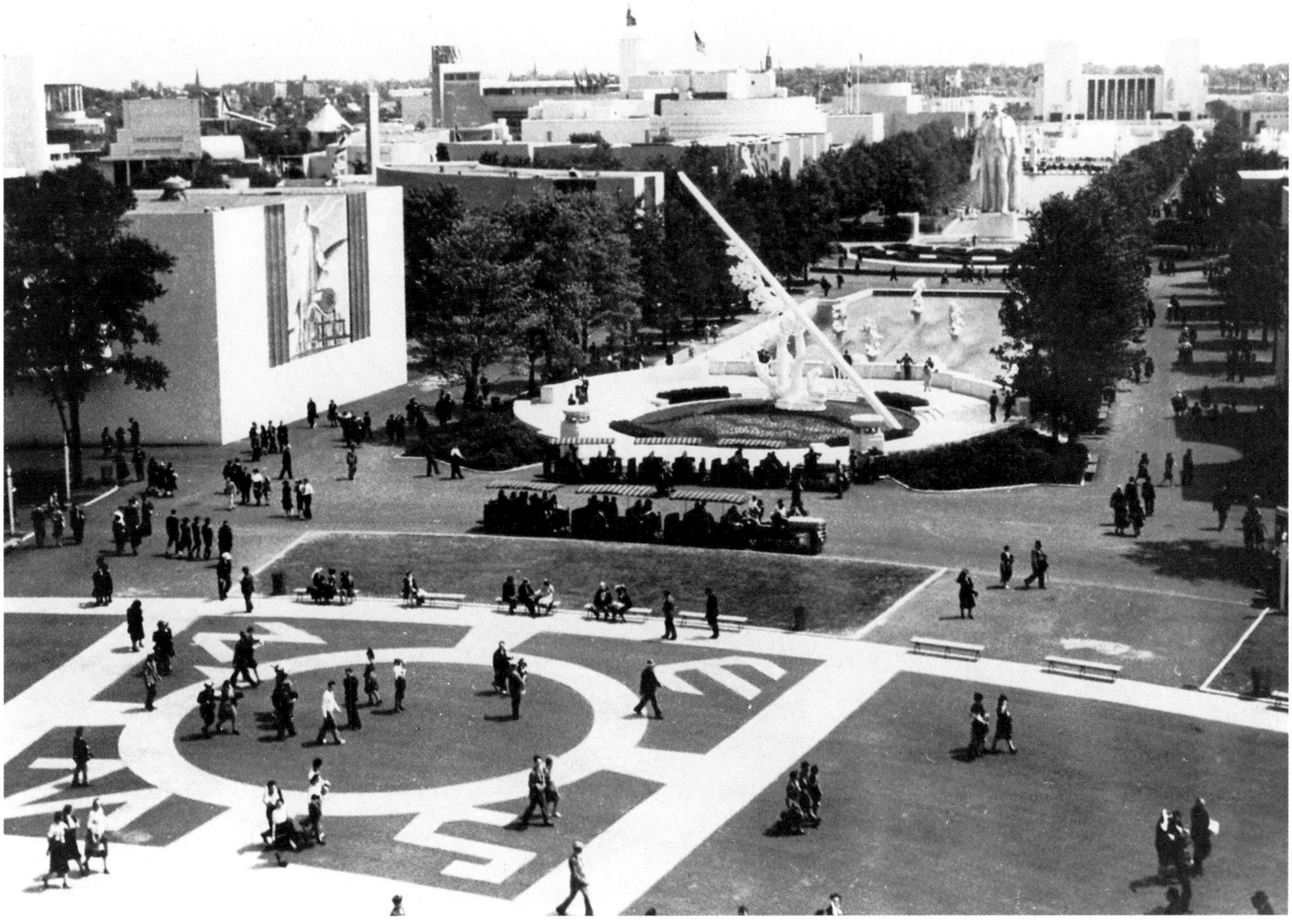

Fig. 162. *Time and the Fates Sundial* and *Moods of Time*, 1939 New York World's Fair, seen from entrance to Perisphere.

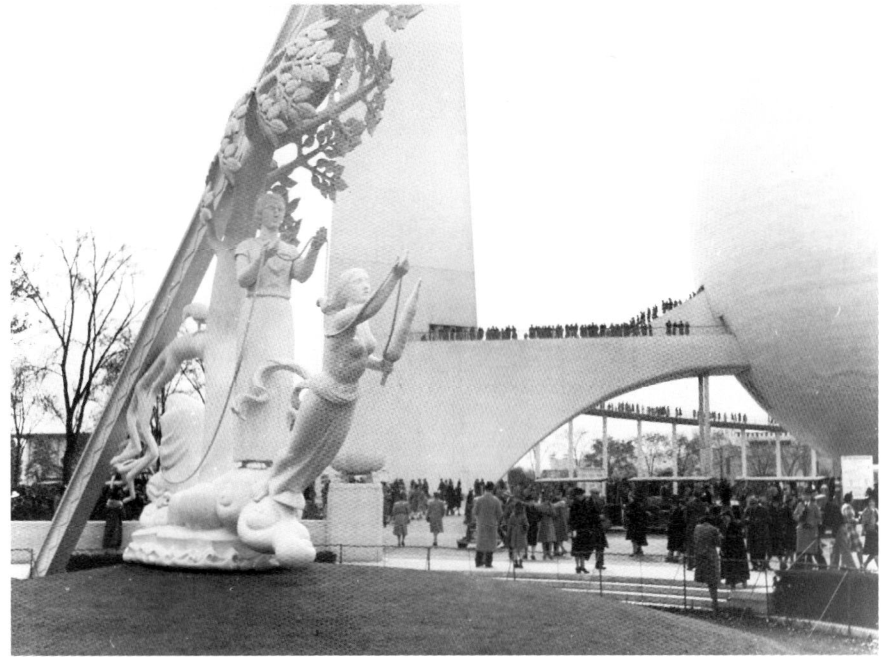

Fig. 163. *Time and the Fates Sundial*, 1939 New York World's Fair, in front of the Trylon and Perisphere.

overall massing and applied pattern that was absent from the *Prometheus* fountain.

Major works by four sculptors—Paul Manship, Donald DeLue, Theodore Roszak, and Marshall M. Fredericks—were commissioned by the New York World's Fair, which instituted a policy of issuing no statement on these works until the fair opened on April 22. Amid an air of expectation, Manship created the large sculpture groups *Four Moods of Time* and *Time and the Fates Sundial* (figs. 160, 161). Both ensembles treat fleeting time, and though he clothed them in antique garb, Manship obliquely addressed the fair's theme, "The World of Tomorrow." The two ensembles were placed in close proximity to the fair's motific emblems, the Trylon and Perisphere (figs. 162, 163).

Manship explained his program for the work within the ensemble of the fair:

> The Perisphere and Trylon at the World's Fair suggest to me symbols of measurement of time and space, so my sundial-time, the Fates and the Thread of life, relates to the background of the central motif of the fair—the Perisphere and Trylon.
>
> *Sundial* The gnomon casts its shadow on the platform dial surrounding it and registers sun time. The gnomon is upheld by the Tree of Life, which grows out of a rocky, insular base. The Three Fates—Clotho, the Future, holds the distaff and is the motif of the forward curve; Lachesis, the Present, is vertical and looking ahead and is measuring the thread as it passes through her hands; and Atropos, the Past, the curved line which returns within itself, symbolizes the end of things as she cuts the thread. Over her head the branches of the Tree of Life have lost their foliage and the Raven—the Bird of Doom—sits watching her.[6]

After completing the enormous *Prometheus* fountain and the huge, technically challenging Bronx Zoo gates, Manship felt sufficiently the master of his materials to take on a breathtaking project. Unfortunately, it is a project that no longer exists in its original size. *Time and the Fates Sundial* was the largest sundial in the world, with a bronze gnomon (the pointer on a sundial, which by the length of its shadow indicates the hour of the day) over eighty feet in length. The work currently survives in reductions (fig. 164).

The Fates are usually conceived as three female deities who preside over the birth of human beings and supervise their individual and immutable destinies. The Fates are identified as Clotho, the spinner, who personifies the thread of life (and who in Manship's work thrusts like a ship's figurehead into the future); Lachesis, chance or luck; and Atropos, the inescapable fate, who cuts off the thread of life and against whom there was is no appeal. The sundial's gnomon rests on the Tree of Life, which is leafy and fecund above the future and present but unfoliated over the barren past. In the tree's naked branches sits a raven, a symbol of death who watches cloaked Atropos cut life's thread.

Lachesis, standing stiffly erect and virtually tubular in conception, recalls the *Charioteer of Delphi*, whose form was also made to accommodate reins

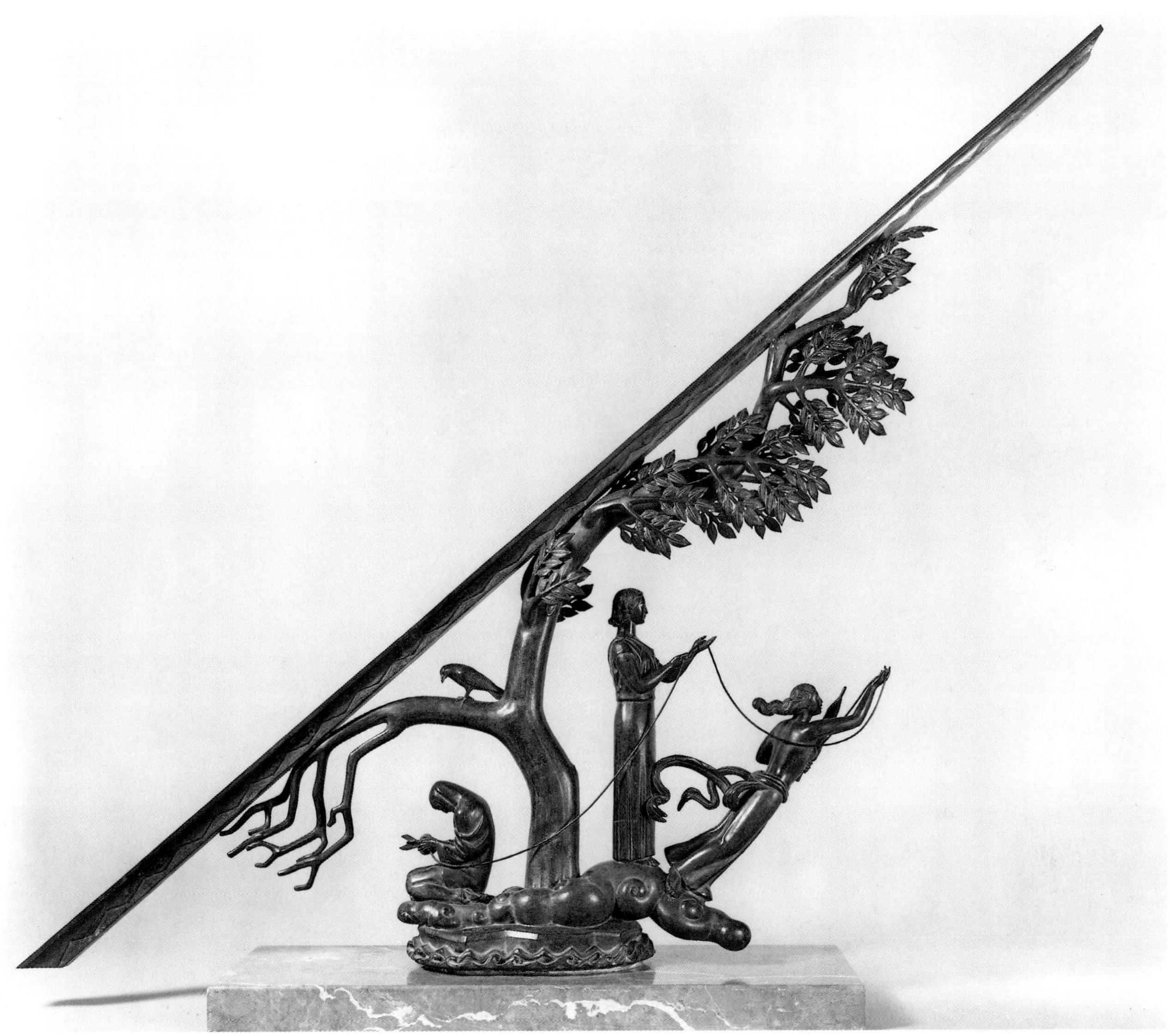

Fig. 164. *Time and the Fates Sundial*, 1938; bronze on marble base; 54½ in. high.

passing through its hands (figs. 165, 166). In 1896 the bronze sculpture of a charioteer, now in the museum at Delphi, was excavated in the Delphic sanctuary of Apollo. The *Charioteer of Delphi* was originally part of a large ensemble, which has survived in fragments. The group, which stood on a terrace of the Temple of Apollo, displayed the complete regalia of a chariot team including horses, a chariot, and a groom. An inscription found on the stone base blocks dates the austere ensemble of Doric sculptures to about 475 B.C., but the most complete work of the group, as well as the most important is the *Charioteer of Delphi*. A masterpiece, the work derives its power, in part, from its reserve and the extraordinary clarity of outline. The pensiveness that seems to pervade the work issues as much from its quietude as from the piece's masklike face. Manship himself commented on how forcefully it moved him:

Fig. 166. Greek, ca. 475 B.C.; *Charioteer of Delphi*; bronze; 71 in. high. Archaeological Museum, Delphi.

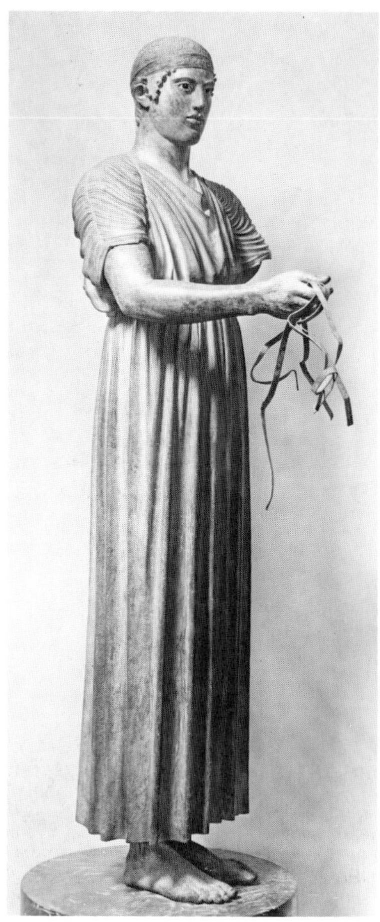

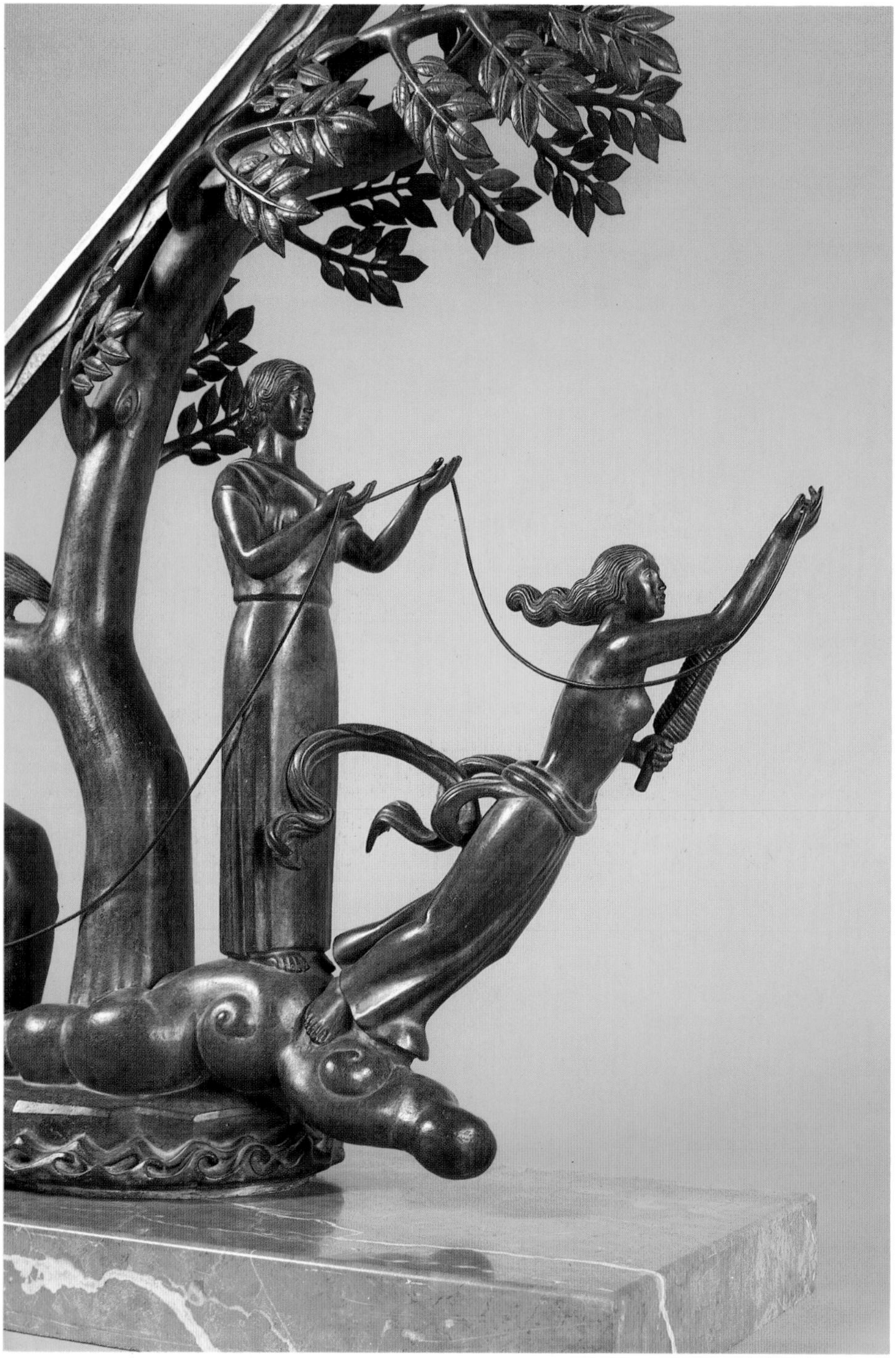

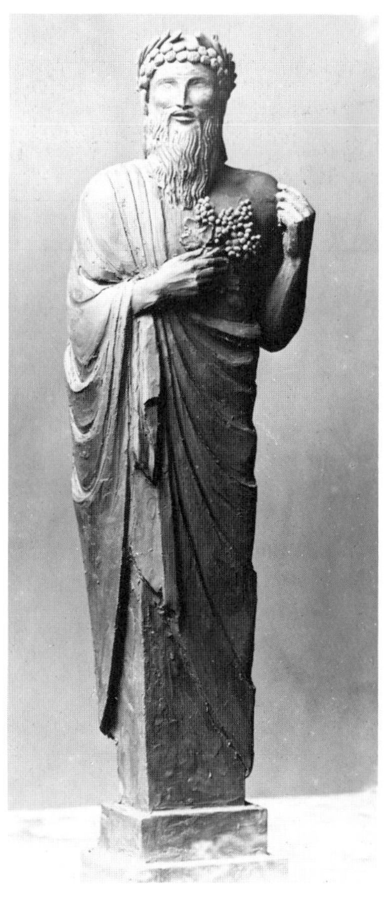

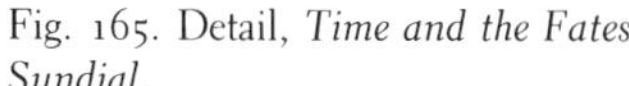

Fig. 165. Detail, *Time and the Fates Sundial*.

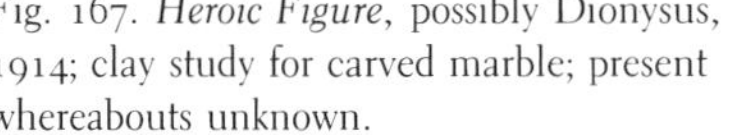

Fig. 167. *Heroic Figure*, possibly Dionysus, 1914; clay study for carved marble; present whereabouts unknown.

"Of the Bronzes of Archaic Greece there is one that stands out with special emphasis—the Charioteer at Delphi. I remember returning again and again to this figure. . . . The wonderful bronze treatment of this sculpture mark it as one of the finest extant examples of bronze sculpture."[7]

The two figures are so close in conception that it would be conceivable that Manship had based his *Lachesis* directly upon the *Charioteer of Delphi* without any intermediation or deliberation. As early as 1914, when commissioned by the architect Charles Platt to make twelve marble garden sculptures for one of his clients, Manship seems to have been considering the *Charioteer of Delphi*. These now unlocated sculptures were mainly in the form of herms, terminal busts of heroically sized figures (treating Greek gods and heroes: Calypso, Hermes, Theseus, Silenus, Odysseus, Heracles, Dionysus, Orpheus, and so forth); photographs suggest their tight outlines were surmounted by identifying emblems and limited hand gestures (fig. 167).

By suffusing his pieces for the world's fair with classical references and careful craftsmanship, Manship presented his values for the huge audience that would stream by his work. He tried to place public sculpture within the life of the community, as it had been in antiquity and as the Art Deco aesthetic had hoped it would be once more. True to his sentiments in his address to the American Artists' Congress Against War and Fascism, Manship remarked that "when art is removed from the snobbish and specialized patronage of the few and brought more into contact with the broad masses, it will become fundamentally the expression of our common culture and will gain in its

Fig. 168. *Sketches for Moods of Time*, ca. 1938; pen and ink on tracing paper; $8\frac{1}{8}$ x $11\frac{3}{8}$ in.

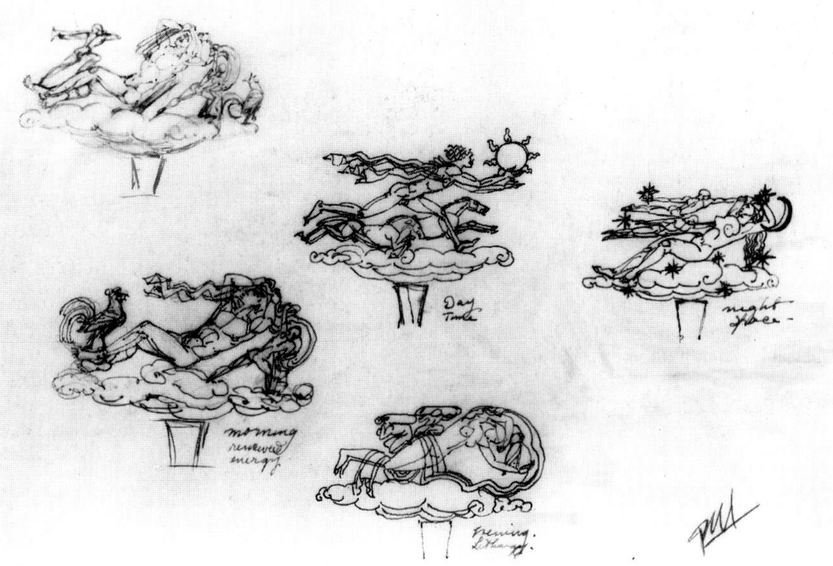

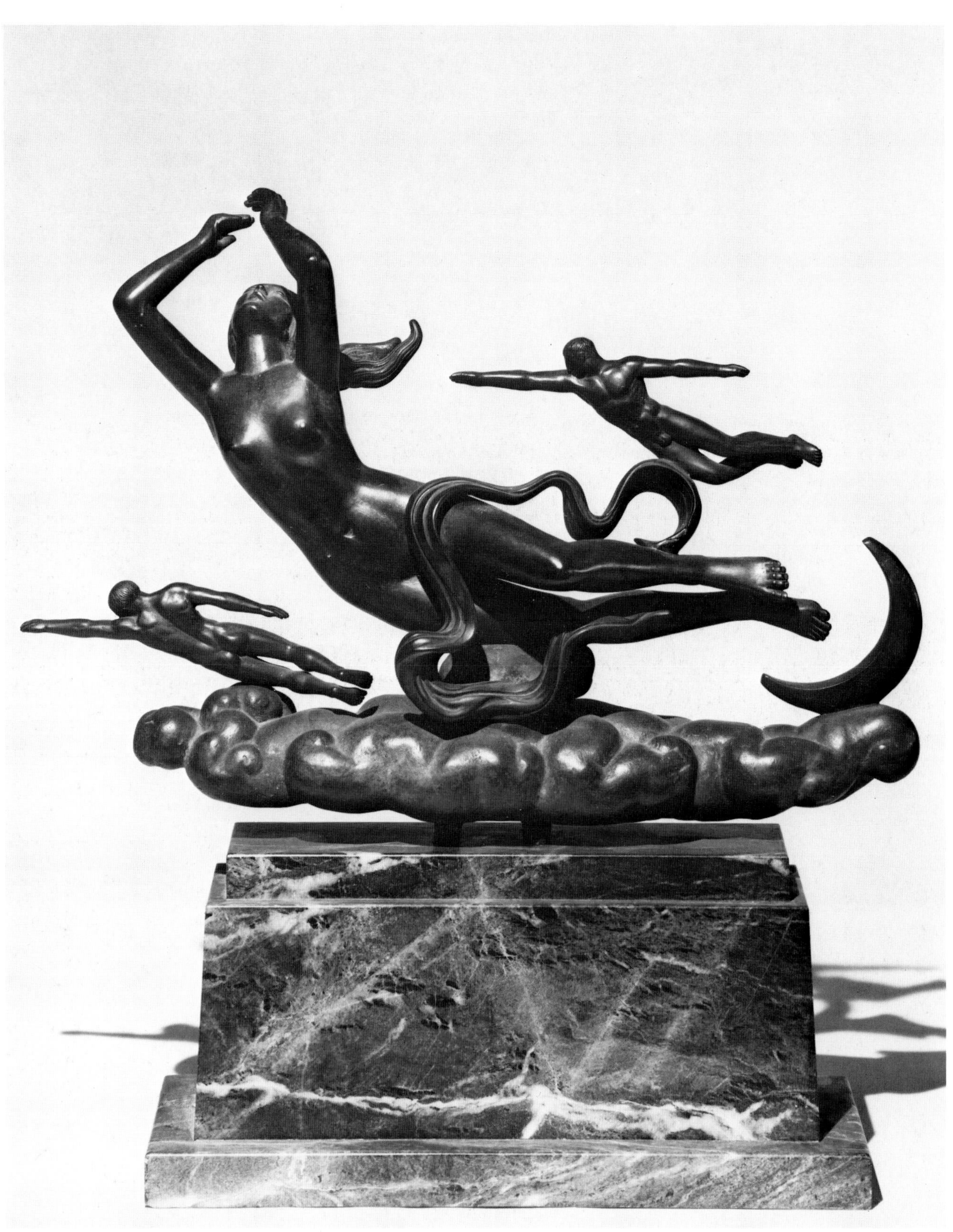

Fig. 169. *Night*, from *Moods of Time*, 1938; bronze on marble base; 16½ in. high.

Fig. 170. *Evening*, from *Moods of Time*, 1938; bronze on marble base; 22½ in. high.

spiritual content."[8] It may be hard to imagine so esoteric a scheme speaking directly to the "broad masses," but Manship saw himself as one of their number, a hard-working midwesterner, a craftsman whose life and works expressed both the period and the best of the popular temperament.

Near the great sundial were four groups symbolizing times of day, *The Moods of Time*, situated in a large rectangular pool (see fig. 160). The fountain figures rose from the water and carried the spray's movement through their bodies; they seemed to fly, racing with the hours. This element of speed was appreciated as the link to the "World of Tomorrow":

> The *Moods of Time* are part of this larger [theme of fleeting time], they particularize man's earthly concept of time in relationship to the movement of the sun [fig. 168].

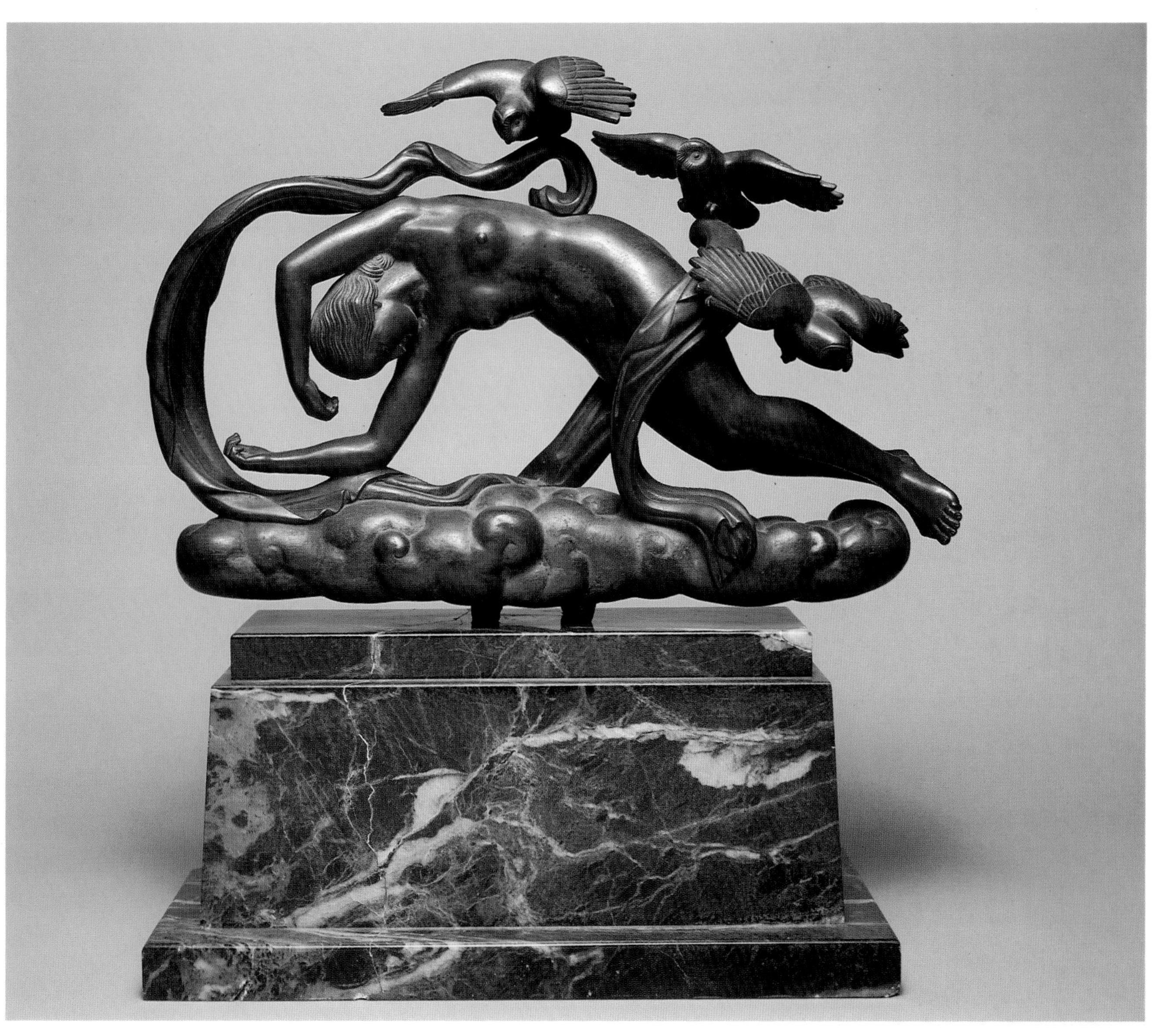

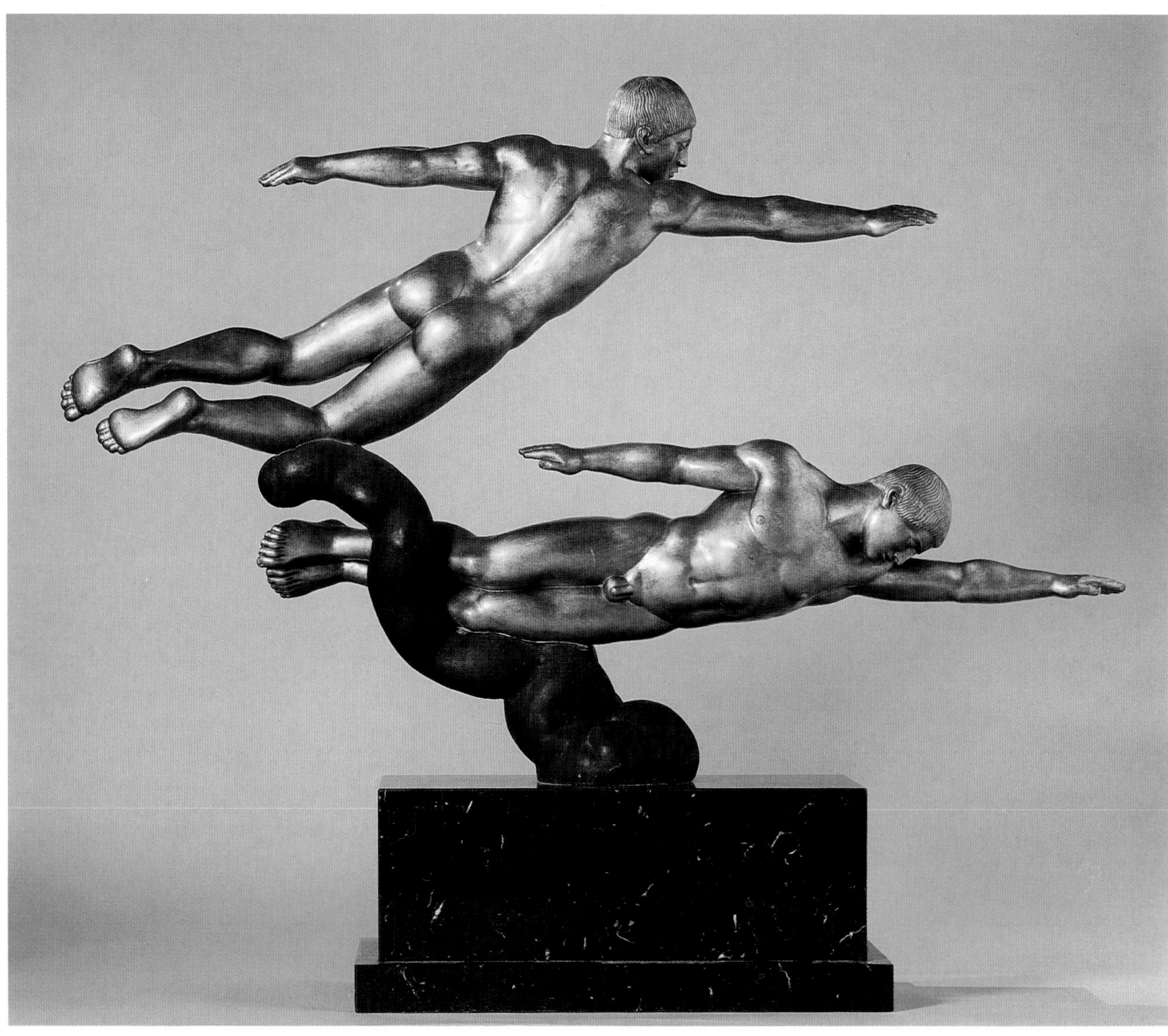

Fig. 171. *Figures of Night*, 1938; gilded bronze on marble base; 23 in. high.

> DAY Onrushing Day, with the sun typifies the day of Helios, with energy, radiation, speed.
> NIGHT On the other hand, Night, with the moon as its symbol, suggests the movement of the world of dreams and intangible things. The little figures accompanying the major nude figure of Night typify those things that reach out into space [fig. 169].
> *Morning* Have tried to make these groups understandable to morning—which is awakening energy, the use of the cock, the trumpeter and the throwing aside of the veil of night is rather obvious.
> *Evening* Symbolizes inertia—that time of inactivity before the movement of night begins, and the figure is falling asleep, with the shadows of evening over it [fig. 170].[9]

The figure of *Morning* rises sleepily, his limbs heavy with drowsiness amid the active messengers of Dawn (Aurora). *Day*, symbolized by the Sun (Helios) races against the arc of the sky, drapery and hair flying. *Evening* declines

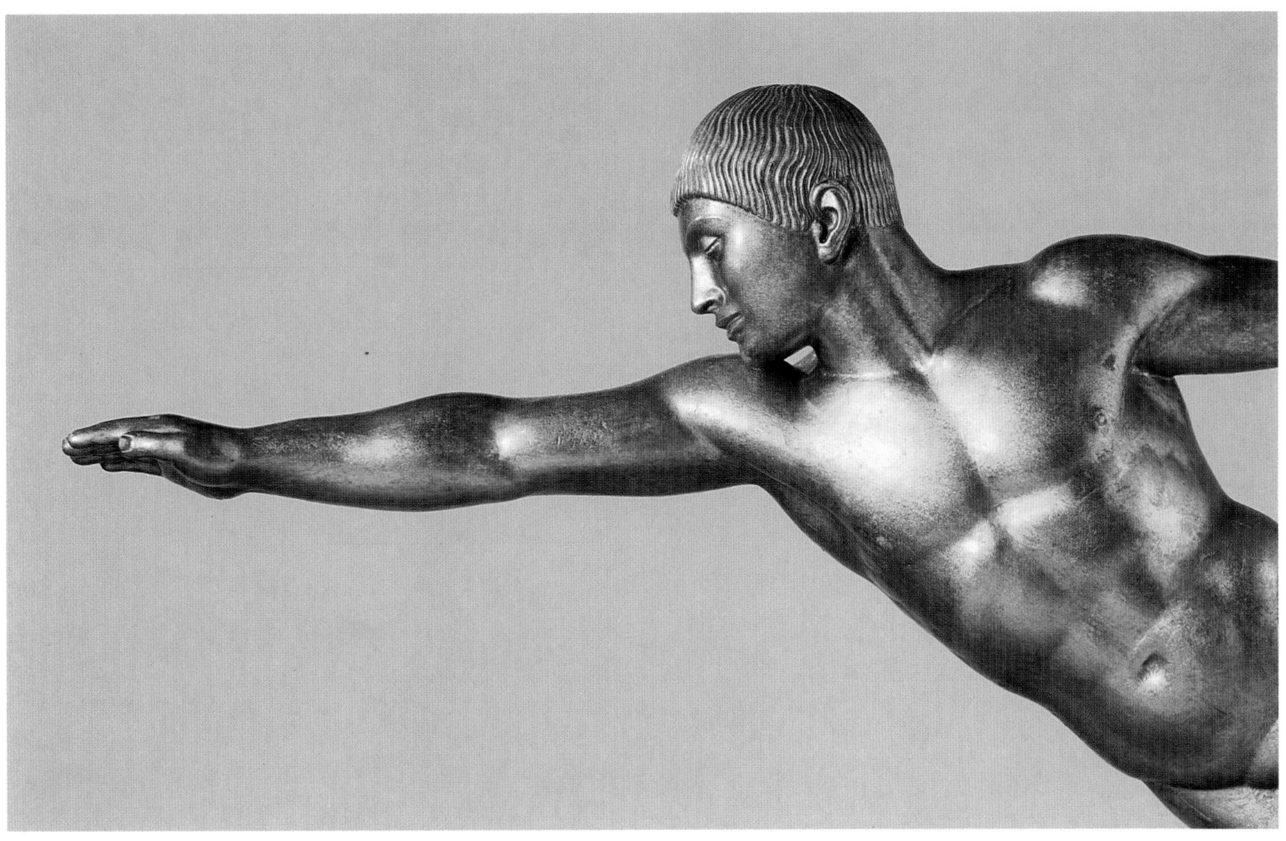

Fig. 172. Detail, *Figures of Night.*

toward inactivity, while the splendid *Night* floats a levitated figure above the clouds and crescent moon (figs. 171, 172).

Manship had explored the theme of the floating figure in his 1916 work *Flight of Night* (see fig. 112), a statuette that pointed to many of his later accomplishments; also in 1916, Manship cast ten copies of a sundial *Day and the Hours,* which is most closely allied to the world's fair ensemble in subject matter.

The world's fair's over-life-size figures and the sundial were executed in plaster; none was cast in the original heroic size. Manship cast some lovely reductions in different sizes, many apparently more successful than the hulking originals (figs. 173, 174). His beautifully crafted reductions of the *Time and the Fates Sundial* equilibrate refinements against overall form. The work's smallest and largest elements read with equal clarity. Manship applied a beautiful green patina to enhance the overall sculpture; the color also sets off the balanced masses and their elegant details. The largest of these reductions, modeled in 1938 and cast in 1952, features a gnomon twenty-seven feet long. The care and thought inherent in the world's fair works were almost washed away by the tide of change but for Manship's forebearance and belief in the merits of the pieces.

Figs. 173 and 174. *Time and the Fates Sundial*, 1938; plaster; photographed in Manship's garden; present whereabouts unknown.

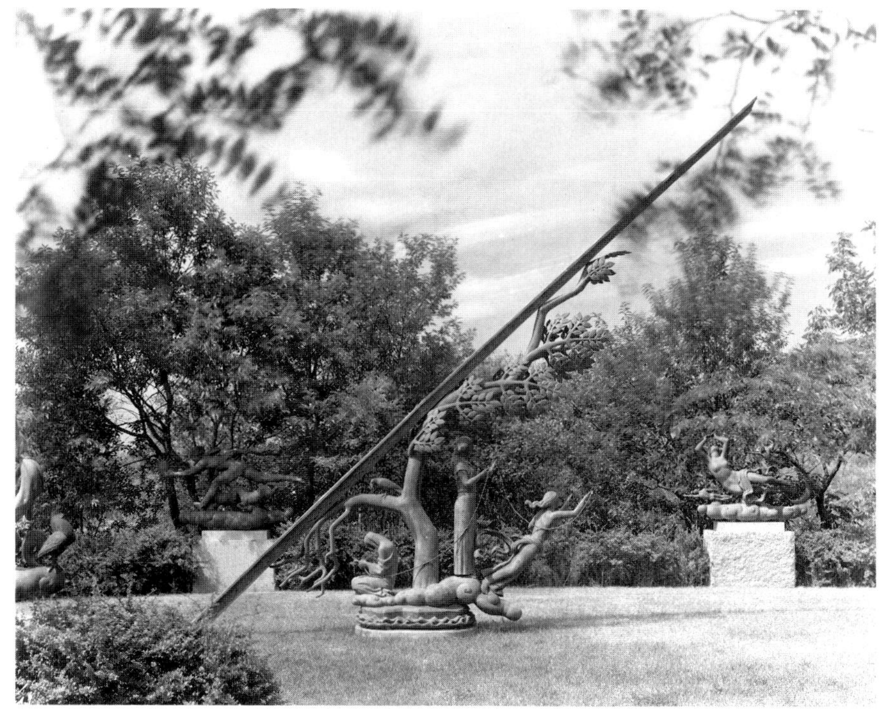

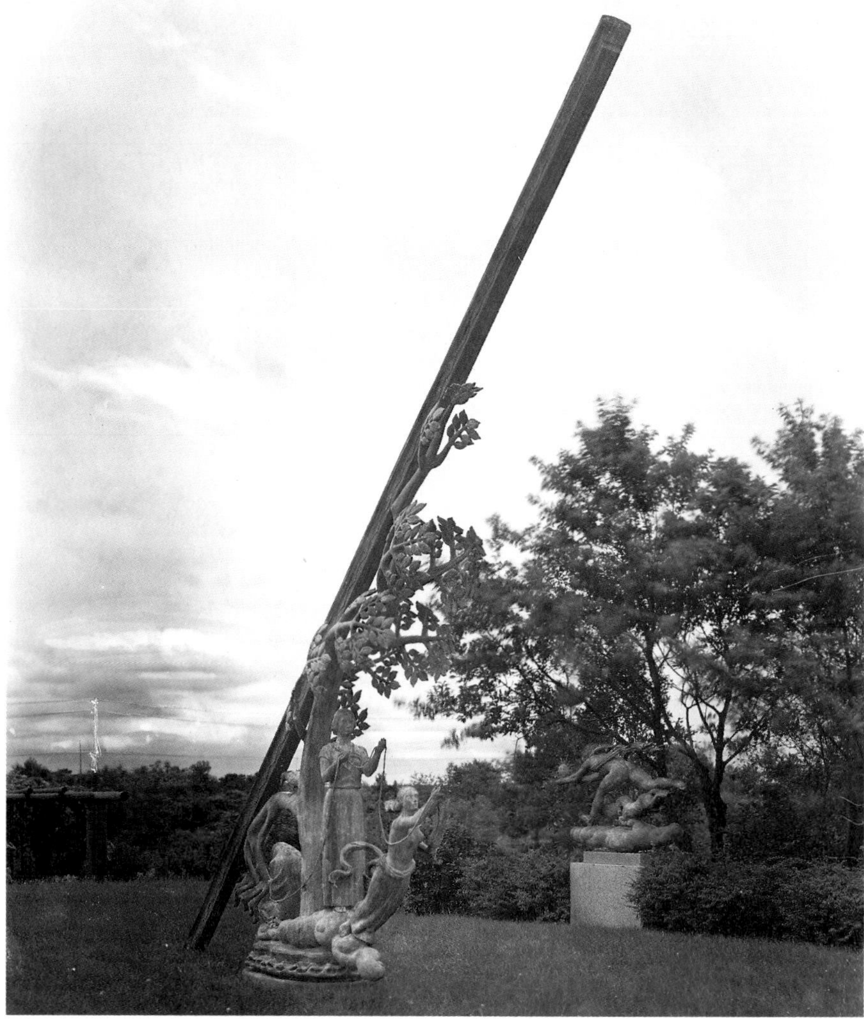

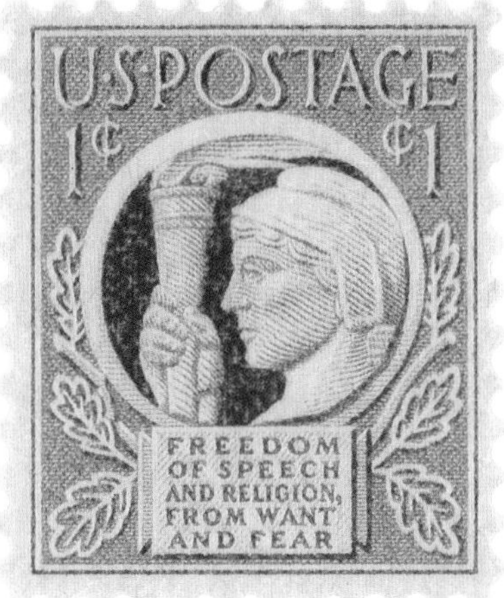

Fig. 175. *Four Freedoms' Stamp*, released 12 February 1943.

While the New York World's Fair would completely vanish, existing only in the memory of its visitors, Manship had hoped to create a public sculpture garden from the remnants of the fair. He had "a suggestion. . . . [He] expressed the hope that if the grounds are transformed into a public park the sculpture will remain."[10] This happy idea did not, unfortunately, prove to be the case, and the fair was dismantled in time to make war.

Manship maintained his own theory of monuments:

> *A Monument should be permanent.* The life of the monument should measure the life of the memories and the ideals which raised it. Anything less permanent is unworthy and betrays the lack of faith in the high impulses of our children's children.
>
> *A monument should be fit for high moral and devotional purposes.* A monument to commemorate an ideal should rank second only to the House of God in the community. It should be dedicated to the high uses of contemplation and self-consecration. It should be set apart from the humdrum affairs of everyday life, lest its chief function be forgotten.
>
> *A monument should be beautiful.* Ideals can be worthily expressed only in terms of beauty. Ugliness in monuments is proof of ignorance of the builders. Beauty insures permanence. The world will cherish and protect beauty. It will neglect, or even destroy, an ugly monument no matter how costly. Without beauty there can be no lasting appeal to the uplifting forces of reflection and consecration.[11]

In accordance with his ideas about monuments, and in harmony with the facts of commercial life, Manship was offered another chance to produce a statue of a founder of the republic. In 1942—ten years after Manship had finished his commission work for the Lincoln Life Insurance Company—the John Hancock Insurance Company commissioned an eight-foot statue of the company's namesake for their new home office in Boston. That summer Manship sailed to Italy to supervise the casting of the statue in bronze with gold-leaf patina.

The next year, Manship was one of the group of artists and sculptors who volunteered drawings for stamps on the themes "United Nations" and "Four Freedoms"; their sketches for stamps were placed in the Office of War Information during January. Originally designed as a three-cent stamp, the *Four Freedoms* was issued as a one-cent green stamp released on 12 February 1943 (fig. 175). Across the top is "U.S. Postage" in white architectural Roman on a shaded background, and underneath "1¢" is mirror-imaged at both left and right. The design features, within a circular panel supported by oak-leaf clusters outlined in white, a low relief profile of Liberty (or Columbia) holding the lighted torch of freedom and enlightenment. In a rectangular plaque below appears "Freedom of Speech and Religion, From Want and Fear" in five lines of solid Gothic. To the modern eye, the effect is not particularly striking; however, the production of the stamp offered the artist new opportunities.

Manship, having never prepared a postage stamp before—although early in his Minnesota days he had run a small design firm—proceeded quite differently from any other previous method. He made a five-by-seven-inch plaster mold into which he carved in reverse; when cast, this showed the stamp design in a raised form or bas-relief. He then colored the background around the torch and the face of Columbia, and he had the painted plaster photographed to produce the final image—a process that did not endear Manship to graphic designers, who saw in his technique an avoidance of all the challenges of their profession.

Paul Manship and Leon Helguera—who made the designs for the concurrent "United Nations" two-cent stamp—donated over $200 to Mme. Chiang Kai-shek for Chinese War Relief. The artists raised the money by autographing copies of the two stamps for collectors, at one dollar per signature.

The zenith of popularity Manship enjoyed during the 1939 New York World's Fair started to wane following World War II. His work was cast aside in the flurry of activity that heralded the appearance of Abstract Expressionism, a movement that more and more monopolized critical attentions—if not popular sentiment. The sudden shift in judgment and taste, although it had been building for some time, broke furiously on the scene. Manship's academic art was rejected wholesale, along with his emphasis on craftsmanship. His explicit representationalism could no longer survive undefended; now, instead of abstraction needing explanation, figurative work had to plead the cause of its creation. Manship, who had never achieved much psychological depth in his pieces, was regarded as a superficial artist; rather than ornamenting and beautifying the world, he seemed to be avoiding reality. For the first time he was not merely a conservative—with something worth *conserving*—he was outmoded.

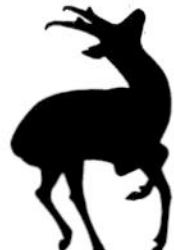

Late Works and Legacy

AFTER THE WAR, and until the time of his death, Manship executed a wonderful series of small sculptures, mainly of mythological groups. He modeled these works in wax, and all were cast directly in bronze by the *cire perdu* method. Each, therefore, is a unique cast. In these statuettes we can feel the direct handling of the artist; the immediacy of his touch speaks to us with an intimacy akin to drawing. Revisions and quick reconsiderations are all visible in Manship's immensely dexterous and accomplished miniatures.

His friends recalled the pleasure Manship took in modeling these diminutive masterpieces, which are among the best of his works. "While 'resting' on Sundays, or on the way to see a museum, on plane or train, or overnight in a hotel, there were born the marvelous succession of lively little waxes for direct bronze casting . . . classic themes, themes of classic persistence, 'slices of life,' all were ennobled with his profound sense of design, an engaging decorative playfulness, and the careful clarity of his feeling for form."[1] These sculptures, despite their size, are in no way "preliminary," though some may have been studies for unexecuted sculptures he may have envisioned. Although they address us with the intimacy of drawings, these are not sketches. Independent works, these miniatures exactly match the level of gesture and incident to their size. They invite us to handle them, to see them from the viewpoint of the artist as they once revolved in his grasp, his hands altering and adjusting their poses.

Late in his life Manship found a new poignancy. With these independent works, he had, it seems, come upon that plateau reached by few artists, a grand late style, an old-age style. Now, all that had moved him was summarized in the most graceful and offhand manner, without intellectualization or grandiloquence, and more forcefully than in any previous exposition.

Perhaps even more than in his sketch of the subject (fig. 176), Manship's bronze *Reclining Nude with Children* (fig. 177) effortlessly mingles godly serenity and maternity, temporalness and timeliness. The fullness of the *Swimming Figure with Fishes* (fig. 178) belies its tiny size; it could be a study

Fig. 176. *Reclining Female Nude with Child*, ca. 1955; pen and ink on tissue paper; $3\frac{3}{4}$ x $6\frac{1}{2}$ in.

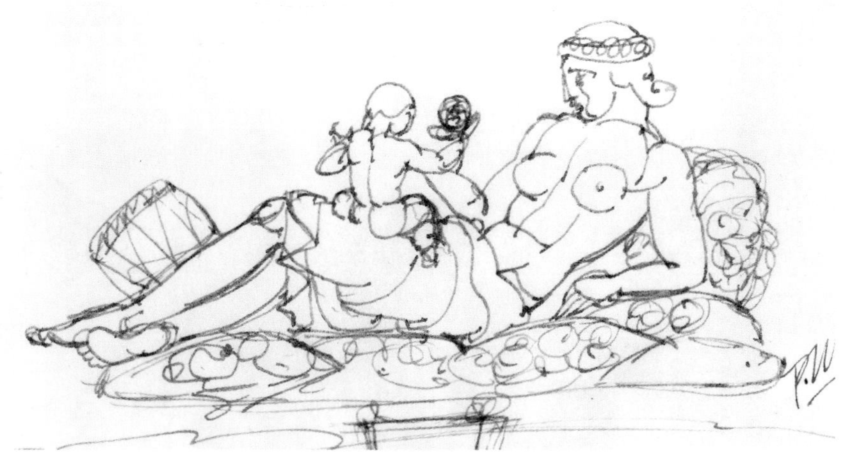

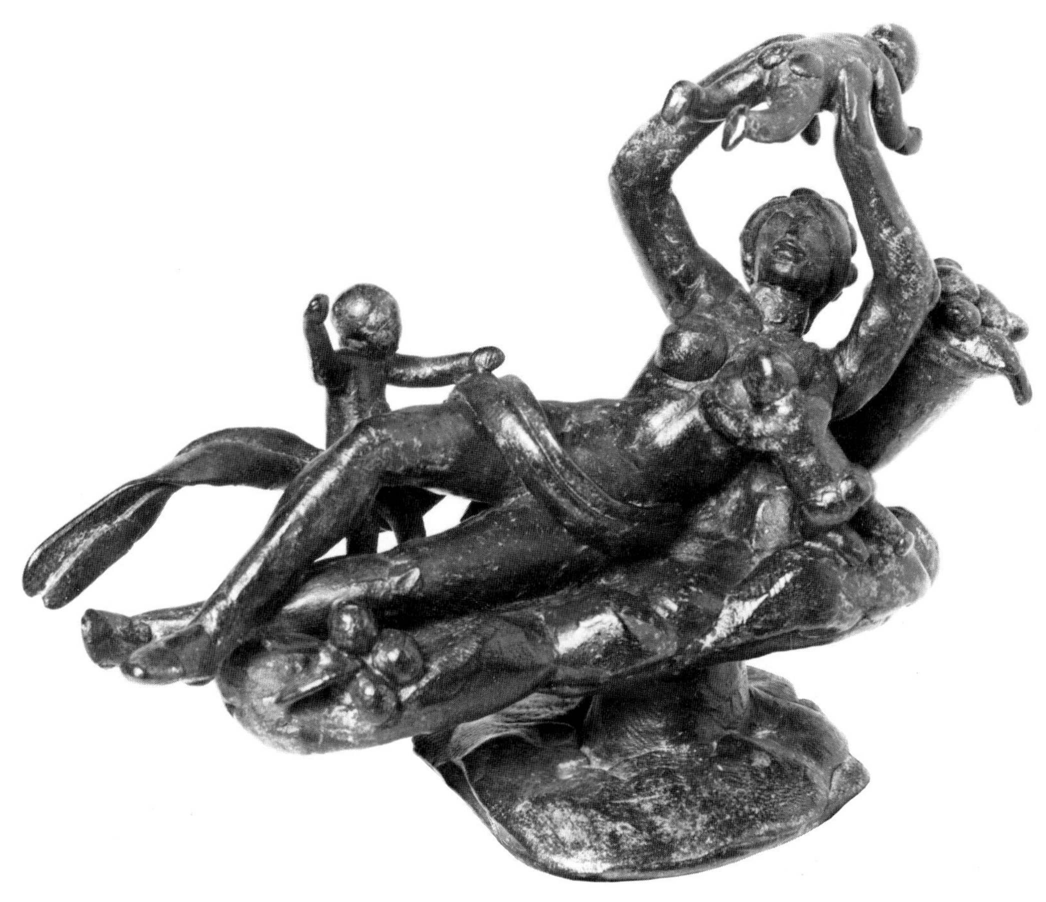

Fig. 177. *Reclining Nude with Children (#1)*; bronze on wood base; $3\frac{1}{2}$ in. high.

Fig. 178. *Swimming Figure with Fishes*, ca. 1950; bronze; $2\frac{7}{16}$ in. high.

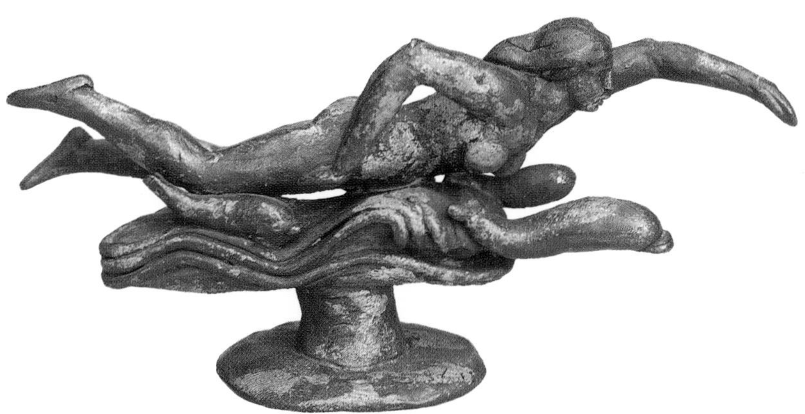

for some great monument (such as Lachaise attempted in his *Floating Women* sculptures). In fact, the swimming woman, as a theme, has a venerable history with specific precedents—as we know is the case for much of Manship's work. A more tubular and conceptual treatment of the swimming woman, *Mermaids* (fig. 179) apparently predates *Swimming Figure with Fishes*. The probable sources for the *Swimming Figure with Fishes* combine both the famous "Boy on a Dolphin," an image from Hellenistic antiquity, and a much earlier Egyptian precedent. This Egyptian type, the "Swimming Girl Unguent Spoon" (fig. 180), from the eighteenth dynasty, features the prone figure of a woman with arms outstretched (originally to hold the cupped end of a spoon for which the body serves as a handle). These lovely little utilitarian objects survive in great numbers from antiquity, and Manship could have seen examples in many of the world's museums.

Manship's *Hercules and the Cretan Bull* (fig. 181) depicts one of twelve seemingly impossible tasks that Eurystheus, Hercules' bitter enemy, ordered him to perform. This bull—which Minos had failed to sacrifice to Poseidon and which had become the lover of Minos's wife—was taken alive by Hercules.

According to medieval Christian legend, Lucifer, a rebellious angel, was expelled from heaven and hurled from the brightness of God's presence into darkness, there to rule the underworld. One of only an occasional foray into Christian themes, Manship's exposition of this powerful story, though miniature, was faultless (fig. 182). Manship used the purple quartz into which *Lucifer* plummets to serve multiple functions in this exquisite sculpture. The stone's color heightens the hue of the gold that covers the figurine and the base. The natural smoothness of the rock crystal amplifies the surface texture of the bronze, thereby conferring a richness on the piece that only a finicky injection of detail could otherwise have produced. Like a cloud bank with light streaming from below, the stone supports the falling figure. The quartz, translucent at

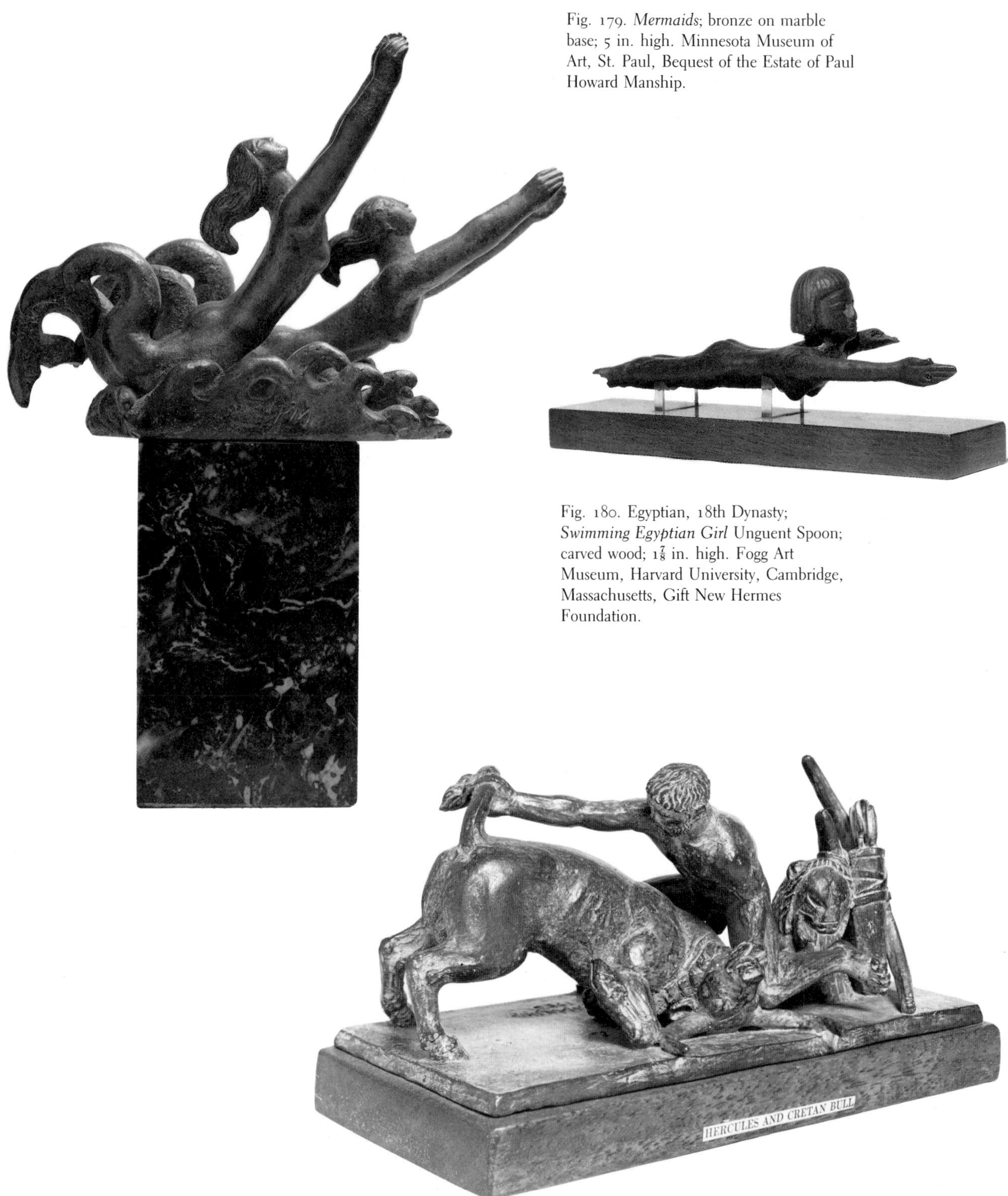

Fig. 179. *Mermaids*; bronze on marble base; 5 in. high. Minnesota Museum of Art, St. Paul, Bequest of the Estate of Paul Howard Manship.

Fig. 180. Egyptian, 18th Dynasty; *Swimming Egyptian Girl* Unguent Spoon; carved wood; $1\frac{7}{8}$ in. high. Fogg Art Museum, Harvard University, Cambridge, Massachusetts, Gift New Hermes Foundation.

Fig. 181. *Hercules and the Cretan Bull*, 1956; bronze on wood base; $4\frac{1}{16}$ in. high.

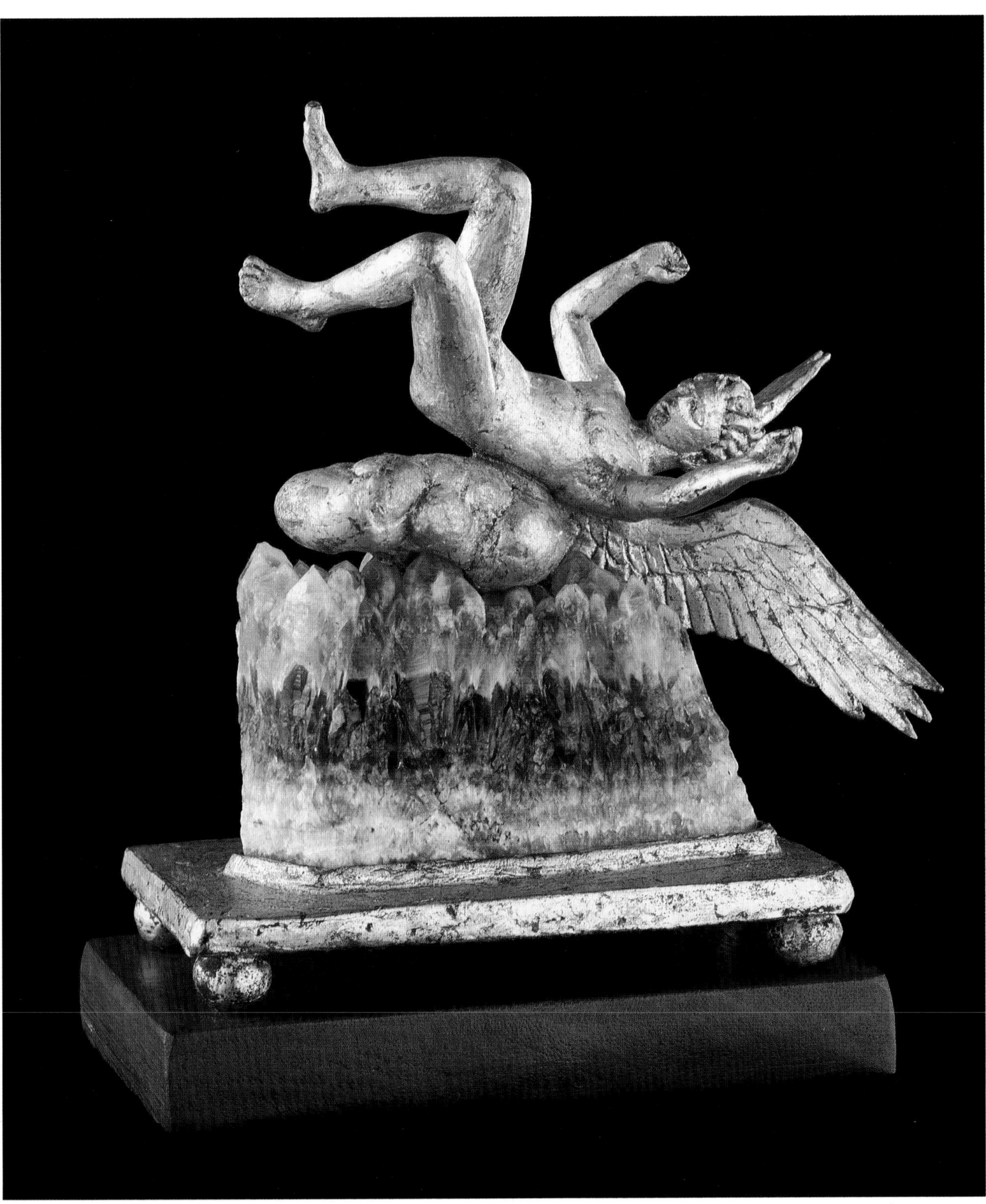

Fig. 182. *Lucifer*, 1956; bronze and quartz on wood base; $7\frac{3}{4}$ in. high.

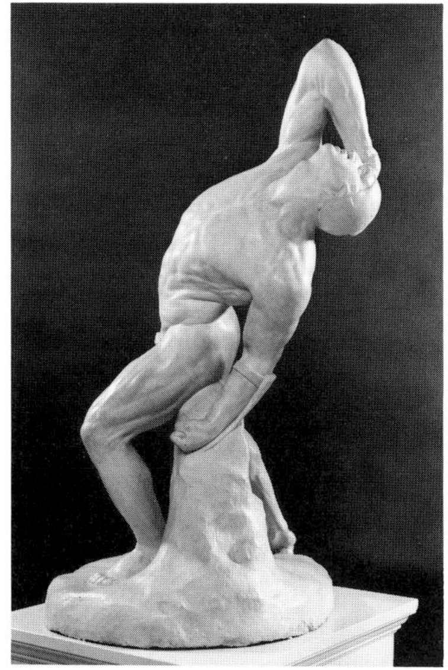

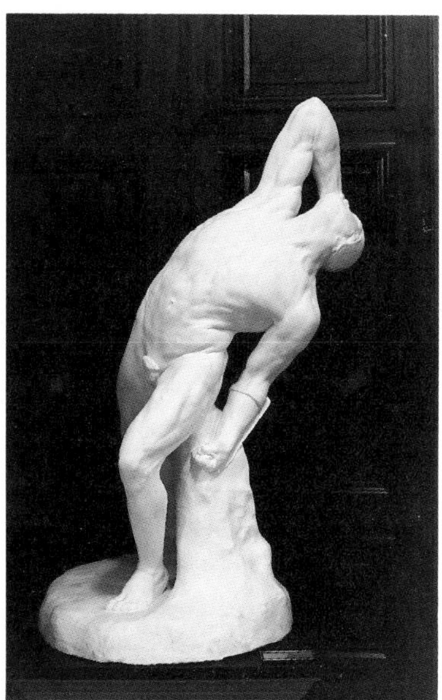

Figs. 183 and 184. William Rimmer, *The Falling Gladiator*, 1861; plaster; 64 in. high. Gift of Caroline Hunter Rimmer.

the tip of the crystals and growing more opaque near the bottom, helps describe the cascade of the falling angel into darkness. Manship illustrated a specific section of narrative—rather than a symbol for the story, or its attributes—and the choice of moment was ambitious.

The selection of this moment in the story suggests not only narrative potency but also that Manship may have heeded William Rimmer's claim that a sculptor's greatest challenge is to capture the effect of a falling figure. The demand to render the uncharacteristic behavior of tensed muscles and skeleton freed from counteracting gravity is not common to all periods. Although the figure falling or floating is a frequent component of painting, the levitated images on Baroque or Rococo ceilings do not have equivalents in period sculpture. In *Lucifer*, Manship recapitulated ideas of the straining figure that first appeared in his early "wrestlers" theme, although the wrestlers struggle against visible forces. The falling figure labors against an invisible force. More closely than any classical precedent, Rimmer suggested the challenge Manship faced, and Rimmer himself attacked the problem in his remarkable (if too little celebrated) career, most notably in *The Falling Gladiator* (figs. 183, 184).

Another example of Manship's selection of a narrative moment in this series of works is his *Circe Enchants Ulysses' Sailors* (fig. 185). Circe was a

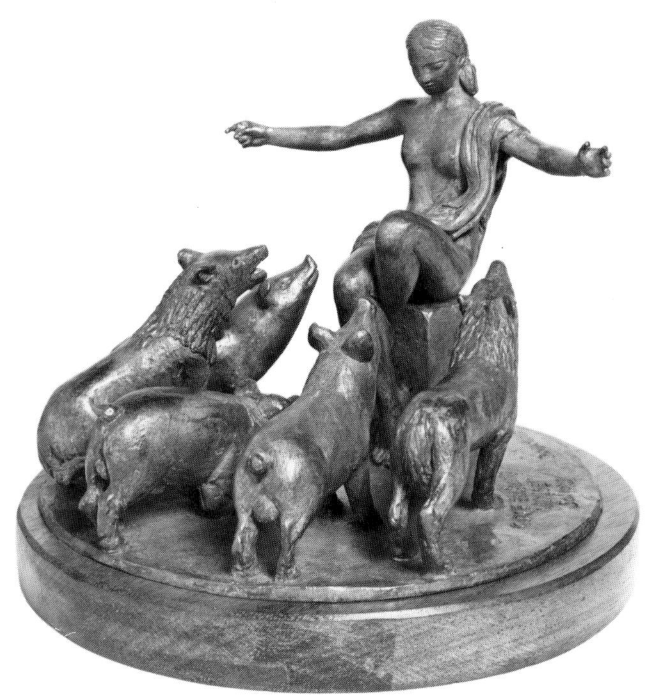

Fig. 185. *Circe Enchants Ulysses' Sailors*, 1957; bronze on wood base; $5\frac{1}{2}$ in. high.

powerful enchantress who lived on the island of Aeaea. She turned the members of Ulysses' advance party into swine, and before Ulysses set out to rescue his men, Hermes taught him how to counter Circe's sorcery with the magic herb *moly*. Ulysses spent one year in Circe's company, and when he chose to leave, Circe gave him instructions for his homeward journey. Just as in his *Theseus and Ariadne* (see fig. 80), Manship rejected the heroic or erotic aspects of the story—Ulysses is not even present in the work. Instead, Manship depicts Circe with a captivated audience of swine. Circe gathers her retinue together for this pose, encircling them from above with her open arms.

LAST PUBLIC WORKS

In May 1943 Manship wrote to thank his friend Booth Tarkington for sending a copy of his new book. In the course of that letter, Manship fretted about his position in the postwar art world, and he confessed misgivings and self-doubt. Tarkington replied on 15 May 1943:

> "Always fearful that the old reputation will slump," you say. . . . Taxes and the advance of State Socialism have pretty well wiped out that unfortunate feller [the private collector]—he doesn't control enough votes to save himself. After the war, however, the sculptor should "come back." Monuments and Memorials . . . you're undoubtedly the "most famous" American sculptor: your name has gone over the land for years and carries more weight than any other.[2]

Tarkington based his counsel on experience. After World War I the American Battle Monuments Commission chose Manship to execute the memorial at Thiaucourt, France. Erected in 1926, the monument consists of a relief of Fame and a statue of an American soldier in limestone. After World War II Manship did receive some major commissions; unfortunately, they resulted in pieces that are far from his best work. The critical climate having changed, no one winked at these failures; they were not well-received.

Together with his friend Eric Gugler, an architect, Manship planned many projects. They collaborated on the National Memorial to Theodore Roosevelt in Washington, D.C., and the American War Memorial at Anzio near Rome. In the interior court of their long, low, and white monument in the Anzio military cemetery stand twin figures of youthful soldiers, *Comrades in Arms*, a heroically scaled bronze group within a grove of pines. Manship decorated the monument's exterior with allegorical reliefs suggesting memory and immortality. The whole character of this work was rankest reaction and the once-friendly critics turned on him. In December 1951, Emily Genauer (critic for the *New York Herald Tribune*) singled out the Anzio memorial, repudiating it as "so bad, it's downright embarrassing. It depicts two barechested American doughboys as expressionless and about as sculptural as a pair of department store dummies."[3] The *New York Times*'s Howard Devree agreed, writing that Manship's soldiers resembled "the monstrous figures in that clothing advertisement display on Times Square."[4] The critics also excoriated Manship's contribution to the 1951 American sculpture exhibition of the Metropolitan Museum; opinions that might have quietly circulated for some time now burst into the open.

Manship had witnessed a revolution in abstract art that assigned him the role of archconservative. He reviled abstract sculpture, and his vehement foredoomed objections won him little against the tide of history. To postwar artists, Manship seemed a looming figure who, although a giant in his own time, could easily be side-stepped or ignored. For younger artists, Manship's career did not have to be reconciled with the development of modern sculpture. Personal art histories, by which artists navigate toward their goals, less and less frequently featured Manship.

On 7 August 1953, the front page of the *New York Times* announced plans for a gigantic granite shrine, where the history of the United States would be carved in figures and words. Designed by Eric Gugler, the shrine would measure 415 feet in length, 253 feet in width, and be as tall as a nine-story building. The shrine was to be erected in central Georgia, with inscriptions of imperishable phrases from our past on granite walls and, in high relief, groups of figures and episodes of American history. The memorial—a huge, roofless, open rectangle with terraces, fountains, and gardens forming a park—to be known as *The Hall of Our History*—was to be built over the following ten years at a cost of $25,000,000. The funds for the monument, which were to be raised in voluntary public subscription, never materialized. To continue the project, in August 1954, Congress created a National Monument Committee (which changed its title in 1960 to the Freedom Monument Commission and proposed a new location for the project). Congress, however, was hardly about to authorize building a controversial freedom shrine next to Arlington National Cemetery, and the Arlington County Board described the proposed shrine as a "monolithic monstrosity" that would be the "antithesis of freedom." "A tired cliche" is what Ada Louise Huxtable called the building, and she wrote that

> although the roofless walled court, set in a grove of trees, has been an agreeable form since the open Greek peristyle, it is executed here in a flaccid, watered-down classic style, innocuous and uninspired. The sculptured reliefs are carried out in that peculiarly artificial and specialized manner that might be called "historical realism" which relies heavily on groups of explorers, patriots and Indians [to be sculpted by Manship]. . . . It would be unfortunate, indeed, if Congress were to approve the construction of a monument that offers neither truth nor esthetic excellence. Its empty pomposity is a poor substitute for one visit to original documents of freedom.[5]

For fully a generation, the public, if it recalled Manship at all, thought of him as a footnote, or as a lovely and impressive curiosity. In recent years a reconsideration of Art Deco has revived his reputation. Respect for craftsmanship predominated in Manship's life; however, the tradition of the artisan in the modern era did not fare well. Precisely the distinction between the artisan and the modernist experimenter separated Manship from the most advanced thinking of his age. On numerous occasions he achieved genuine formal innovations, which only confused the issue.

Manship held young artists accountable to succeed within the same artistic standards he had set for himself. His sculptural agenda had arisen in response to a specific artistic situation that no longer prevailed after the earliest days of his career—and certainly had no bearing after World War II.

The awards and recognition continually showered upon Manship made him seem an establishment figure to be attacked by the new generation of artists. After Walter Damrosch's resignation as president of the American Academy of Arts and Letters in March 1948, Manship served as acting president. In November the academy elected Manship president (and Archibald MacLeish secretary); Manship was reelected the next year. In 1954 Paul Manship was chosen as a director of the American Academy of Arts and Letters. He had ascended to the very pinnacle of the academic system in America.[6]

The gateway to the William Church Osborne Memorial Playground in Central Park was commissioned to honor a president of the Metropolitan Museum of Art. Manship created the gates as a set of six perforated bronze panels with Aesop's Fables shown in low relief. He made the gates in sections and had to assemble them for installation.

Mingling sculpture with gardens, fountains, and pleasant walks represents a paradisiacal blend to soothe the senses. The controlled and amended quality of the garden, a civilized ideal as old as culture, rested at the core of Manship's artistic vision. In America, untouched wilderness had always been worshiped as a paradigm of the Garden of Eden, but now the romanticism of soaring buildings was vaunted as well. Neither the skyscraper nor the park, however, had been satisfactorily blended into a new amalgam to replace the garden. Manship's ideal of civic responsibility envisioned an art-pervaded world in which utensils, all the contents of houses, and whole cities were well-designed and artistically made. That this preference coincided with the style and philosophy of Art Deco's built environment tied his fortunes to that movement. The built and designed Art Deco environment was different from previous attempts to orchestrate all human activity in its historical self-consciousness and its celebration of the future and the past. As he had discovered himself in the right place at the right time early in his career, one more time the stars aligned for Manship: in the ripe moment of postwar America's optimism, the geographic occasion of the Central Park commission—with its then perfect combination of Art Deco possibilities, urban vistas, park, and garden—offered Manship's late style a last moment of glory.

Although confined to a thin plane, Manship's animals in the *Osborne Memorial Playground Gateway* are modeled in the round, and for the most part, they are shown in naturalistic poses set amid decorative screens of abstracted foliage. Cartouches with the names of the stories recall Manship's early fondness for lettering, and here the lettering is handled with affectionate creativity and variation. Manship topped the gates' marble posts with the ensembles of the *Group of Bears* and *Group of Deer* originally conceived for the Bronx Zoo gates.

The subject of the six panels offered Manship the possibility to exercise his talents to the fullest. Aesop's Fables are believed to have been written by a Phrygian slave who lived in the sixth century B.C. Aesop was said to be a hunchback, born dumb, but given the gift of speech by the goddess Isis for his devotion to her. His didactic fables most often involve two animals talking and acting like humans—a narrative device that somewhat blunts these tales' humanly political points. For Manship, Aesop's Fables blended mild editorial comment on the human situation with an opportunity for superb animal sculpture—all under the pretense of telling children's stories (figs. 186, 187). In one tale, for example, a fox flatters a crow in order to trick the bird into talking and, thus, dropping the cheese it holds in its beak. The moral: be wary of the motives of those who flatter you.

The gates were warmly received, and when the Municipal Art Society of New York "presented its annual awards . . . for 'the most outstanding work of art erected in New York during 1953' the society presented its certificate of merit to Paul Manship . . . in recognition of a gate designed by Mr. Manship for a playground in Central Park."[7] This combination of public space, grand scale, and critical admiration was probably the last such happy conjunction Manship was to know.

As late as fall 1957, Manship was cited as a preeminent artist, one who had helped forge the texture of the modern world. The New York Board of Trade awarded him a silver medallion. They also honored architect Wallace K. Harrison; choreographer Agnes de Mille; *New York Times*'s drama critic Brooks Atkinson; general manager of the Metropolitan Opera, Rudolf Bing; poet Joseph Auslander; director of the Metropolitan Museum of Art, James J. Rorimer; and painter Edward Hopper—the only other visual artist to receive this recognition.[8] In July 1946 in Florence, the San Lucas International Art Prize was awarded to Manship "in recognition of his outstanding career in American Art."[9]

Fig. 186. *The Fox and the Crow*, Gateway to the William Church Osborne Memorial Playground, Central Park, 1952; bronze; $40\frac{1}{8}$ in. high.

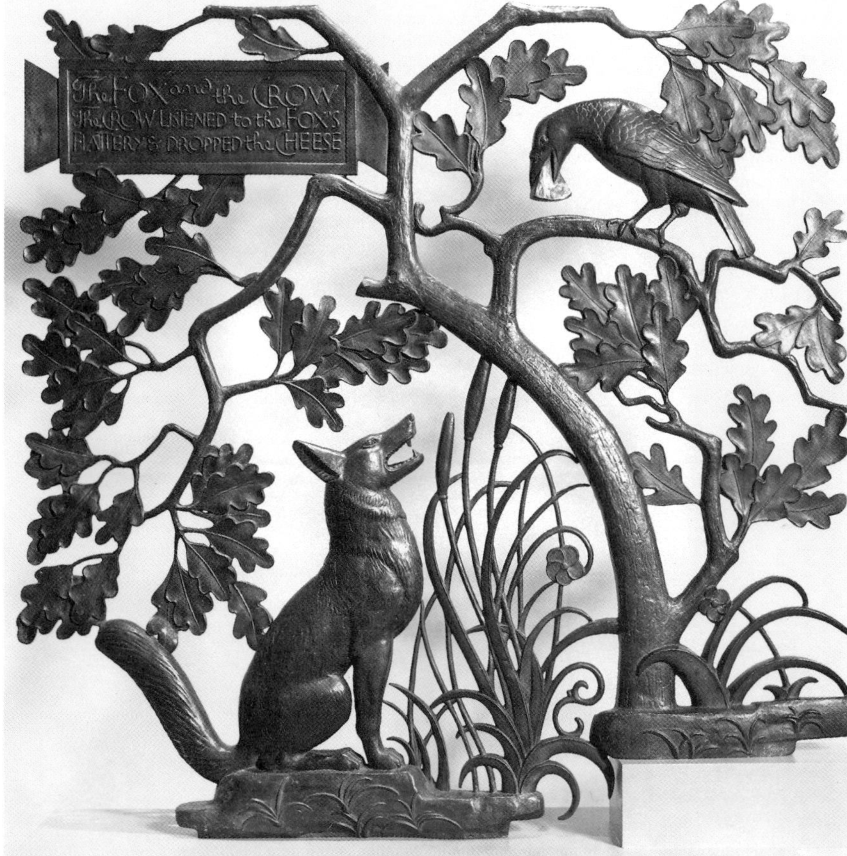

Fig. 187. *The Crane and the Peacock*, Gateway to the William Church Osborne Memorial Playground, Central Park, 1952; bronze; 29 in. high.

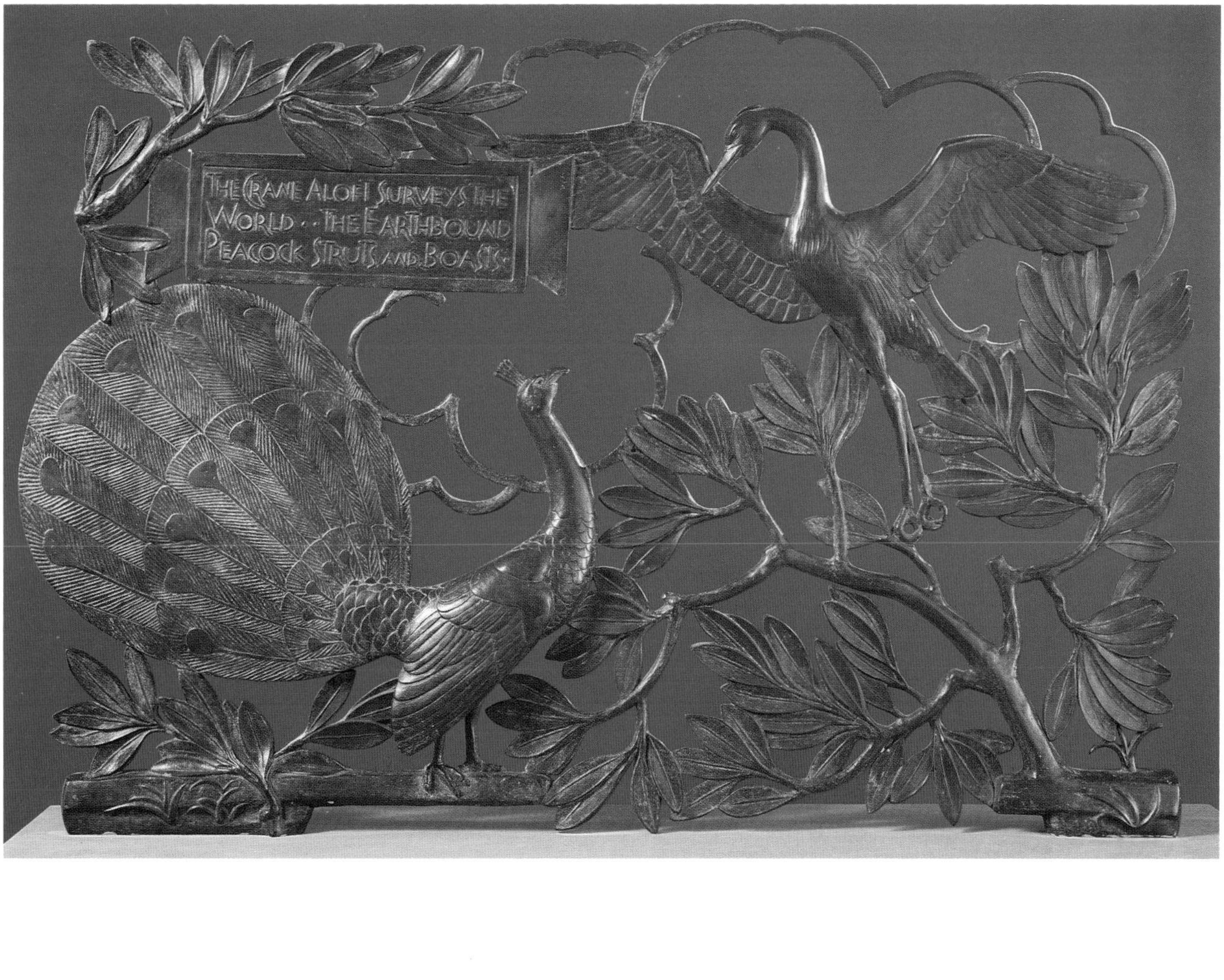

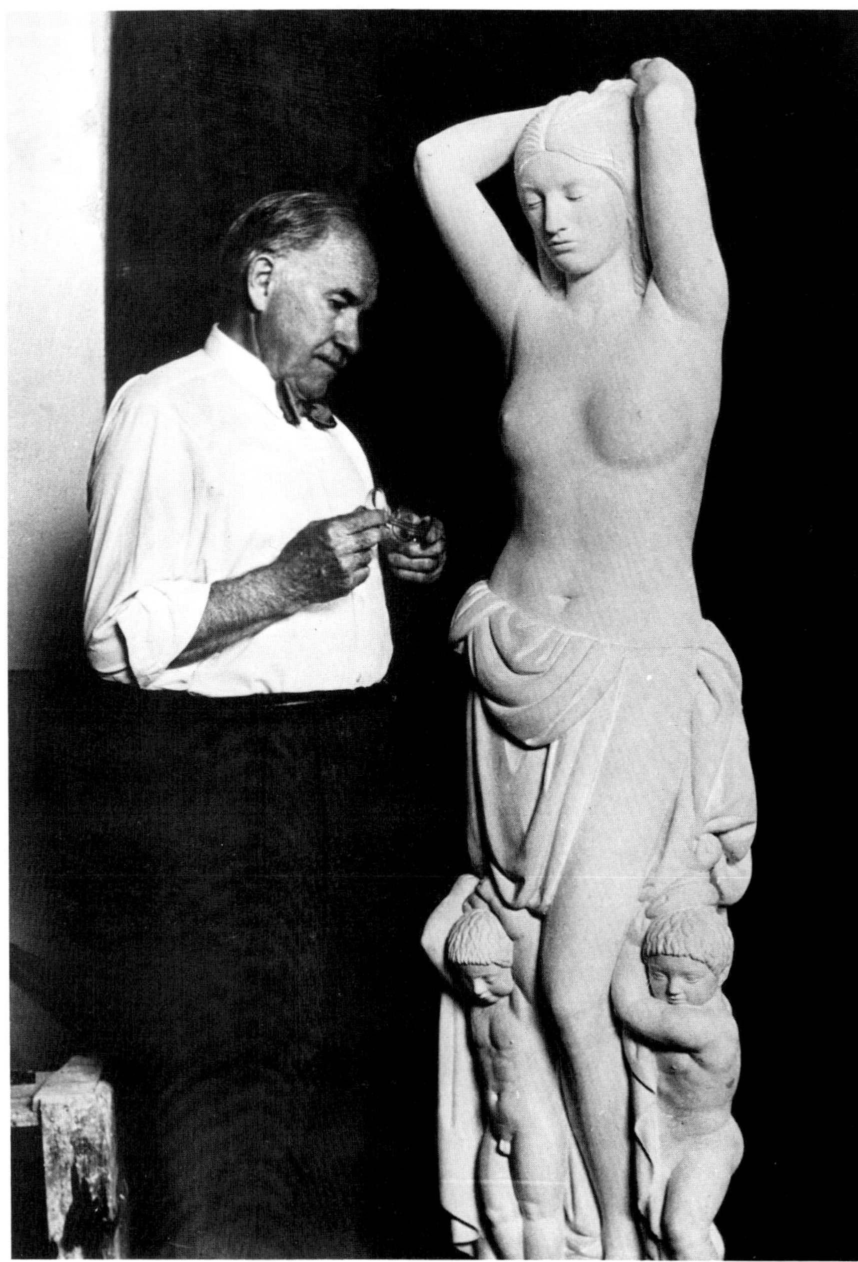

Fig. 188. Paul Manship.

Fig. 189. *Nude (Caryatid)*; pencil on paper; $2\frac{15}{16}$ x $1\frac{1}{16}$ in.

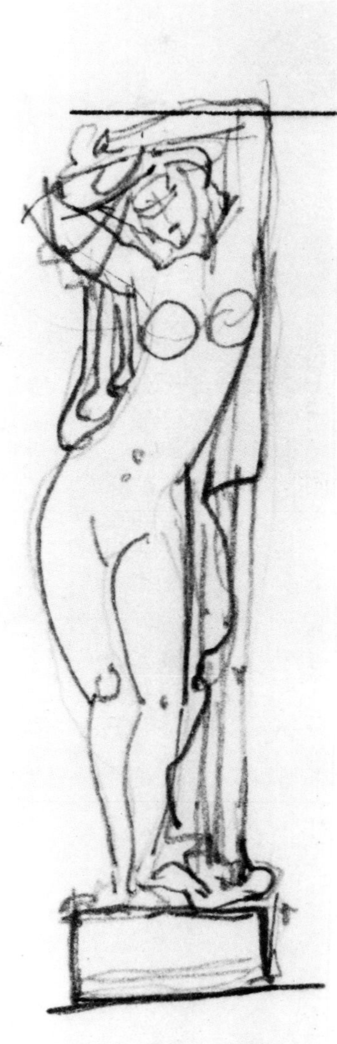

A man deeply concerned with his family, Manship lived for his sculpture (fig. 188). His conversation brimmed with references to all he had seen and thought over a lifetime, "ideas expressed not only in words, but in small expressive drawings on any handy scrap of paper, envelope, menu or matchbox [figs. 189–191]."[10]

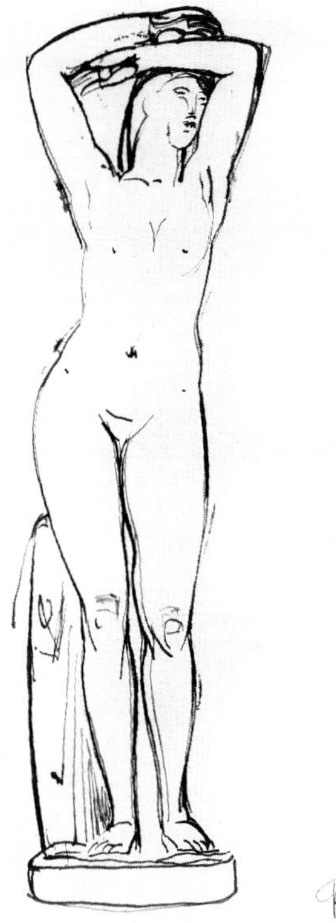

Fig. 190. *Standing Nude Statue (Caryatid)*; pen and ink on paper; $10\frac{11}{16}$ x $8\frac{5}{16}$ in.

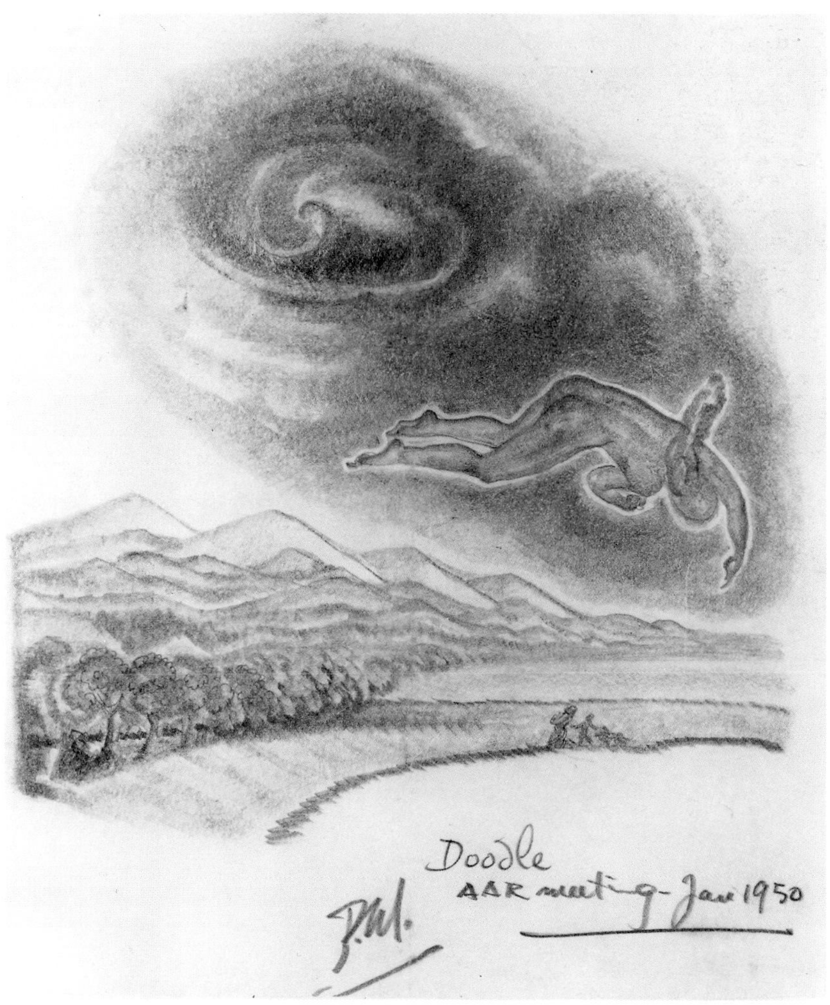

Fig. 191. *Flying Figure, Doodle*, 1950; pencil on paper; $6\frac{13}{16}$ x 6 in.

THE ROOSEVELT MEMORIAL

Almost immediately following the death of Franklin D. Roosevelt, discussions began about a monument to him. FDR had an avowed reluctance to any markers to his memory; the only exception Roosevelt allowed is an inconspicuous marker at the foot of the National Archives. The discussion was still continuing in 1965, when President Johnson signed a bill adding $100,000 to the $25,000 already budgeted for the study of such a monument and extending indefinitely the time for its selection. For a designated site in West Potomac Park, government officials considered a design proposed by architect Eric Gugler. In Gugler's plan, Manship was to supply the monument's main feature: a statue of Roosevelt three times life size, with legs crossed and right arm outstretched.[11] Ultimately, no FDR memorial was built, in accordance with Roosevelt's wishes. But Theodore Roosevelt was so honored, and earlier Manship had been chosen to embody Teddy's spirit and character.

Posthumously unveiled, the *President Theodore Roosevelt Memorial* was Manship's last great commission for the United States government. Theodore Roosevelt Island, the memorial's site, is a green oval in the Potomac River; its only access is a narrow pedestrian causeway. Purchased by the Roosevelt Memorial Association a dozen years after Roosevelt died, the island (formerly called Analostan Island) was donated to the public as a park. The island was to remain pristine except for the memorial; the rest of the thickly forested land would serve as a bird sanctuary and a spot for the contemplation of nature amid the sprawling government metropolis—a fitting conception for the naturalist-hunter-explorer-president.

Manship envisioned the twenty-sixth president as a frock-coated figure with his right arm flung upward and his left extended; this energetic and aggressive stance represented a characteristic speaking pose (fig. 192). In 1964 Manship took a six-foot-ten-inch model of the memorial to Florence to be enlarged. The Italians had sculpture studios with ceilings twenty-five to thirty feet high, and Manship's intention was to have the *Theodore Roosevelt Memorial* finished at a scale of three times life size—seventeen to eighteen feet. Manship was trying to produce a work that would command attention in the monument's open-air setting, a placement which, in the midst of a wilderness retreat, reflected the values of the man being memorialized.

An opening to the sky was cut in the forest; there, amid three acres of cleared land, Roosevelt's huge bronze figure arises before a 30-foot-tall granite shaft. Surrounding the statue, an oval plaza, 264 by 220 feet and paved with flagstones and granite, contains two large fountains. Four 20-foot-high marble tablets display quotations by the former president. This is the largest presidential monument since the Jefferson Memorial was dedicated in 1943.

On 6 May 1966 the statue arrived from Italy, where it had been cast. It stood forlornly in a wood crate until it was unveiled and dedicated on 27

Fig. 192. *Theodore Roosevelt*, 1966; designed by Eric Gugler and part of the Theodore Roosevelt Memorial; bronze; 17 ft. high. Theodore Roosevelt Island, Washington, D.C.

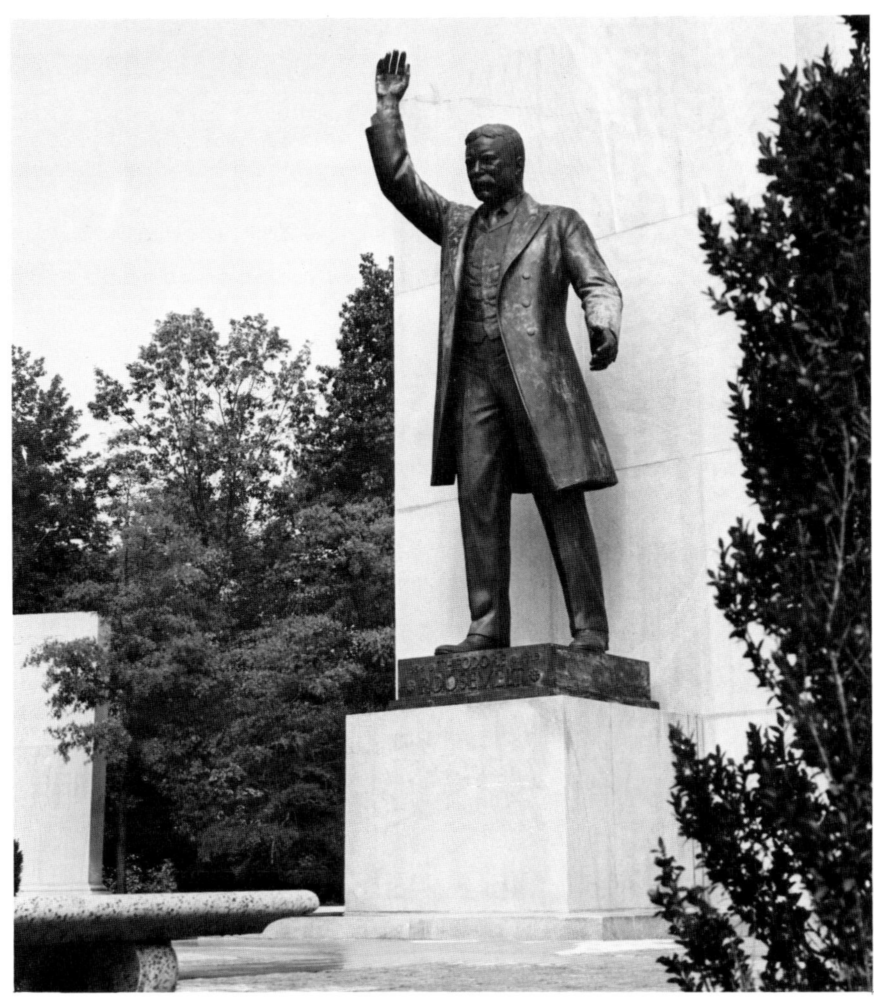

October 1967. Only Teddy's raised hand stuck out of the box, which stood in front of a granite pillar on a raised point near the island's center. Before the statue arrived in Washington, Manship was dead.

Manship was lucky not to have witnessed his work's reception, for—between the time of the commission and the unveiling of the Roosevelt memorial—his reputation had slid into oblivion. Indeed, his previous reputation had become, by this time, a real disadvantage. The huge memorial ensemble was criticized as an intrusion on the natural setting of the island. Teddy's daughter Alice Roosevelt Longworth, eighty-three at the time, remarked that none of her family was urging the dedication. "I only wish there were nothing there but the island itself," she said. The National Park Service, which was in charge, would not say when the crate would be opened or when the memorial would be dedicated. At least the site met with approval, even if the sculpture seemed an afterthought, and an unwelcome one at that. President Johnson remarked, "If Theodore Roosevelt had wanted any memorial at all, . . . he would have wanted it here—in this wild little island in the center of an historic river—where his statue is sheltered in the trees."[12]

Even this was not the worst indignity suffered by Manship's reputation. His life contained the usual measure of travail as well. A sixteenth-century bronze figure of a Benin tribesman and other pieces he owned were stolen, only to be discovered in the possession of two junk dealers nearly five months later. The case against the junk dealers as receivers of stolen goods was eventually dismissed.[13]

At the 1964–65 New York World's Fair, instead of the huge ensemble he had been invited to make in 1939, Manship was commissioned to make but a single work. Adjacent to the fair's symbolic theme, the "Unisphere," he created an *Armillary Sphere and Sundial* (fig. 193). Made of bronze and gold, the sculpture, set in the center of a pool and garden, depicted the signs of the zodiac. Manship's work was stolen, presumably sold as junk to an unscrupulous dealer who melted it for scrap metal; the *Armillary Sphere and Sundial* has never been seen again.

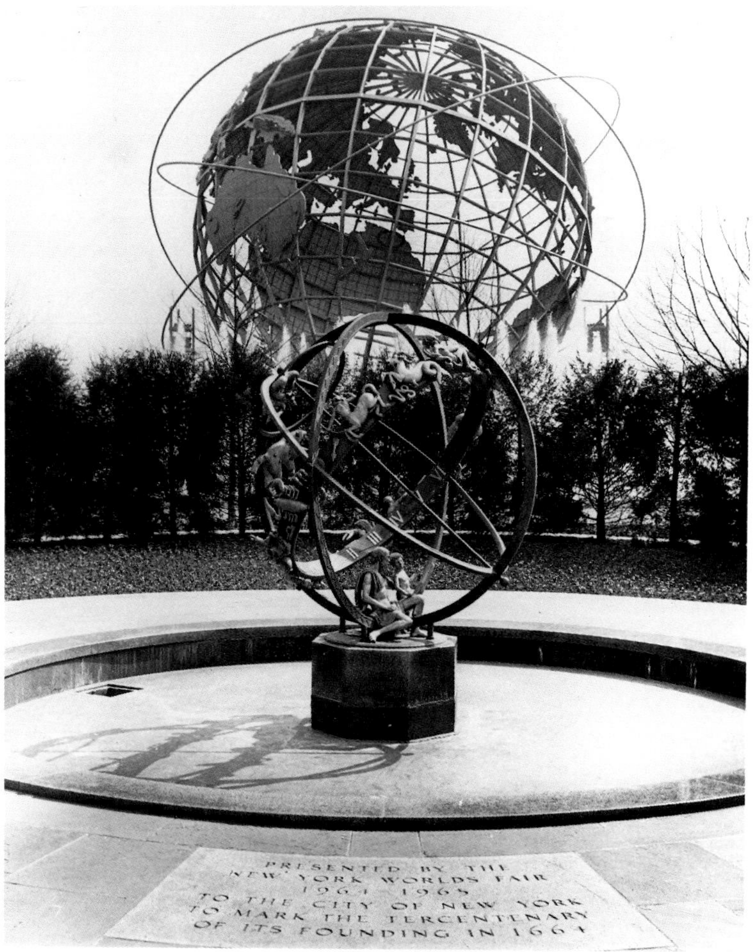

Fig. 193. *Armillary Sphere and Sundial,* 1961; bronze and gold; 1964–65 New York World's Fair; stolen, presumed destroyed.

INFLUENCE AND LEGACY

Manship moved from his great row of connected houses on Seventy-second Street; he spent the end of his life at the National Arts Club in New York. There, while preparing his breakfast, Howard Manship died in January 1966. He was eighty years old.[14] Walker Hancock, bemoaning Manship's loss, called him "perhaps the last American master craftsman in sculpture, equally skilled in every branch of the art from the medal to the monument."[15] Manship had survived into a period in which he was a stranger, and it took time for his work to be shown again, let alone be seriously reassessed.

Six years after he died and the usual legal knots attendant to any large estate were cleared up, Manship's work was seen in New York in his first one-man show since 1933. The show was a survey that included small bronzes, portraits, plasters, drawn sketches, and studies. Reviewers noted that "most of the small bronzes . . . are being shown for the first time, casts having been ordered by Manship before his death . . . [and] after so short a time, Manship's style has already taken on a strong period flavor, recalling the Art Deco vogue for bookends. . . . It also has less the air of an exhibition of sculpture than a collection of objects d'art."[16] Some reviewers were even harsher; the critics "murdered him, and by the time he died was not even forgotten; he did not have that good fortune."[17] Where his work had once radiated glory, it now occasioned derision.

Despite the huge body of work Manship produced, something was lacking from his accomplishment. Manship founded no tradition, had no obvious imitators, spawned no school. His real artistic legacy was carried on by his assistants: Beniamino Bufano, Gaston Lachaise, and Reuben Nakian. In the sculptures of these artists the possibilities of Manship's work flowered (figs. 194–196). Particularly, in Nakian's lyrical use of the figure, Manship beckoned to a future beyond the hegemony of abstraction. Nakian's reliance on lusty figuration tethered his ever more abstract works to nature. Along with Lachaise, Nakian refreshed the mythological figure, which other artists bypassed as exhausted material. Manship had been the principal champion of a bountiful nature as a source of forms. Naturalism, not realism, was Manship's legacy. Critics still friendly to Manship's art perceived him as "the leading sculptor of the 1920s, by far. Powerful backers have tried to puff up Elie Nadelman and Gaston Lachaise, but Nadelman was nobody and Lachaise was Manship's assistant for seven years."[18]

Manship took as his charge the reinvigoration of myths that had become mere mythology. He attempted to bring back to life stories that had descended to nothing more than schoolroom rote (or worse, to shopkeeper's tales that identify an object with a once-vigorous story).

In place of romanticism's ethic of authenticity, Manship offered the eternal life of myth, which was largely mistaken by his genteel patrons for

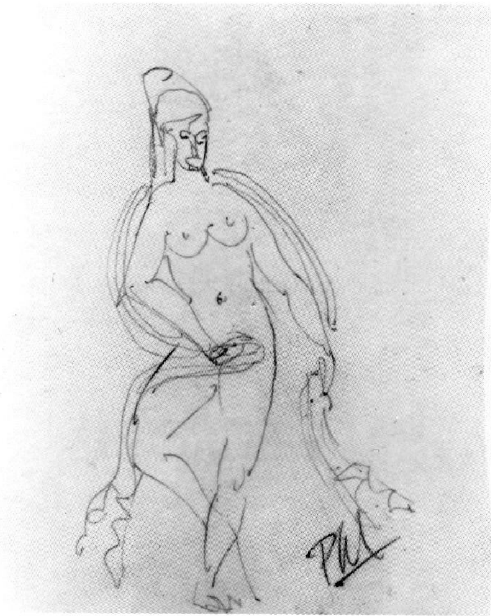

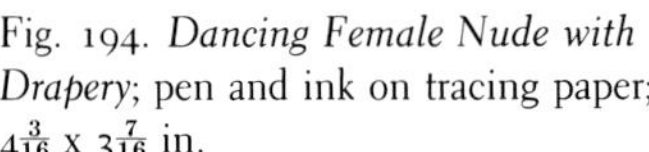

Fig. 194. *Dancing Female Nude with Drapery*; pen and ink on tracing paper; $4\frac{3}{16}$ x $3\frac{7}{16}$ in.

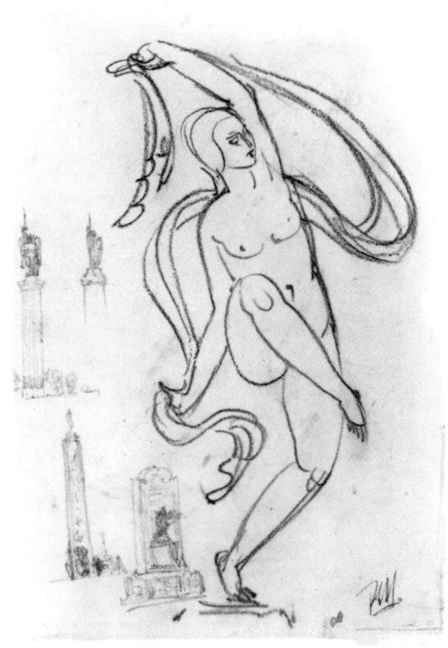

Fig. 195. *Female Nude with Flying Drapery (Maenad)*; pencil on paper; 10 x $8\frac{5}{16}$ in.

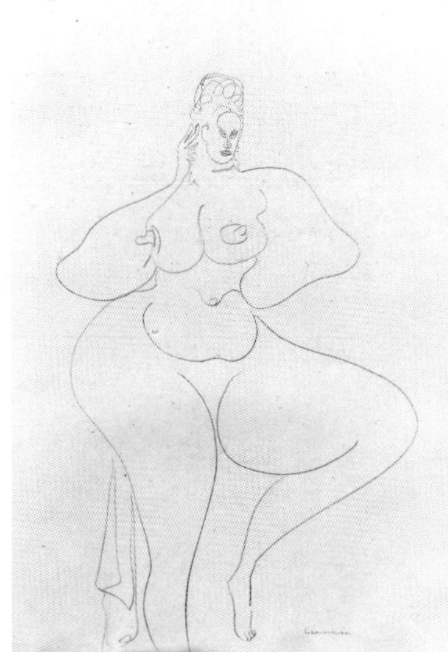

Fig. 196. Gaston Lachaise, *Nude Dancer with Drape*, ca. 1933; pencil on paper; $24\frac{1}{4}$ x $19\frac{1}{16}$ in.

stability. The less affluent thought Manship purveyed good taste or genteelism. They missed a crucial point: Manship never simply appropriated ancient Greece's formal curls of the hair, its sharply folded garments, or the sinuously graceful postures of oriental art; his work was distinguished from the average, or even the accomplished, "archaizers who directly copied Greek archaic works for a market that had begun to realize the beauty of the primitive. But Roman archaistic work was based upon a slender study of the archaic originals and seldom entrusted to artists of the first rank. Quite simply, Manship is better informed, more soundly equipped, and more deeply inspired than the Romano-Greek archaizers."[19]

Of course, Manship was not limited to archaizing, nor to willfully distorting nature. Expressing mere individualism through exaggeration was unsympathetic to all he respected. He believed that despite any intellectual or historical pedigree, sculpture ultimately had to find its rhythms in the organization of natural forms. (For Manship, architecture's formal and geometrical considerations were also secondary to human qualities, harmony, and the movement of life.) Manship professed his duty as an artist was not "to painfully record appearances, but . . . [to create] ideal and abstract representation which is due to the artist's memory of familiar things."[20]

It is doubtful that Manship could have evolved into a more abstract artist than he was; "abstraction" to Manship could not mean nonrepresentation. He conserved the figure's expressive and formal possibilities. Those figurative possibilities, anathema for a generation, now rival nonobjective art. His urge

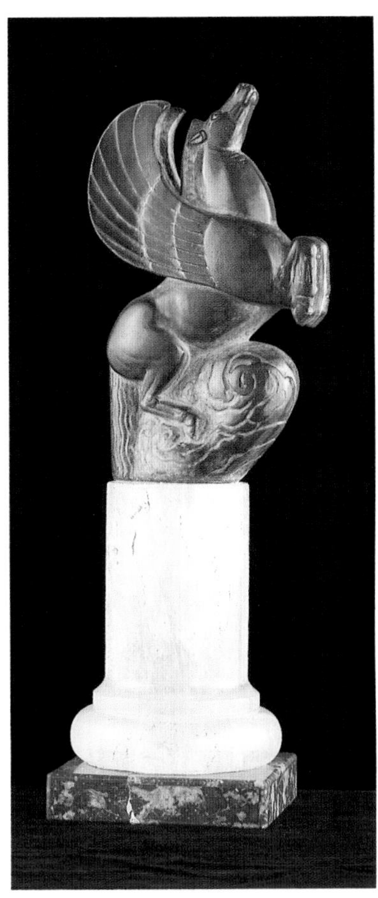

Fig. 197. *Pegasus*, 1937; bronze on marble base; 8 in. high.

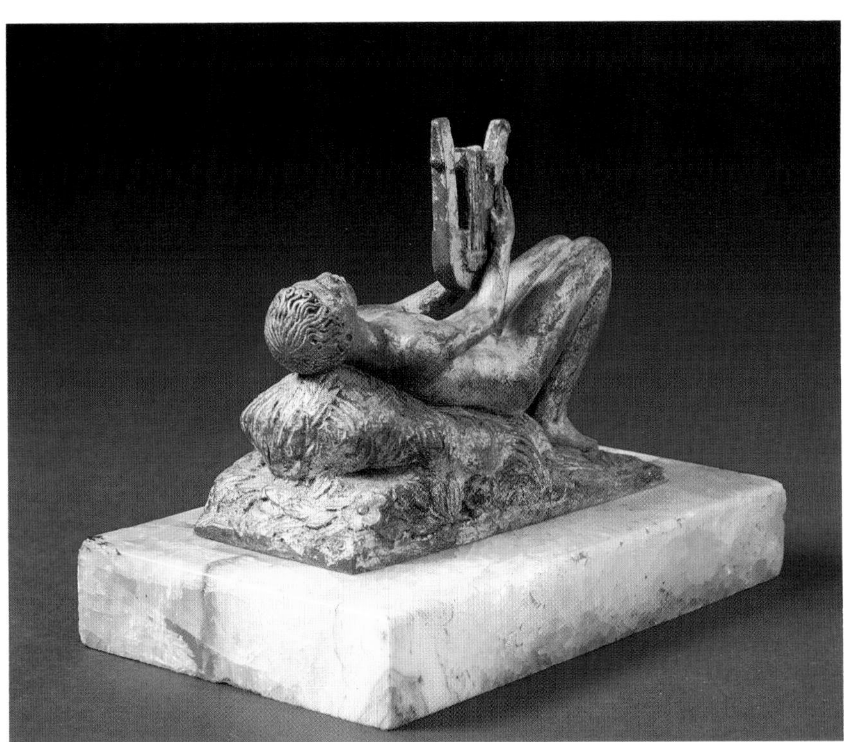

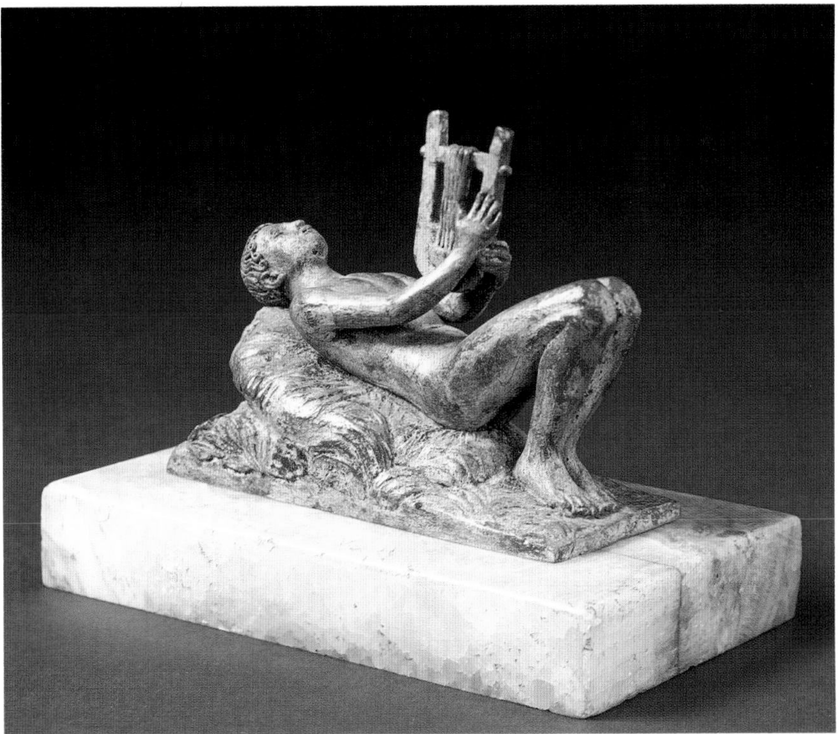

Fig. 198. *Orpheus*, 1954; bronze on marble base; 3½ in. high.

to place art at the center of the public's moral life was realized by the designers of the Art Deco environment, whose revival at the end of the twentieth century marks a new interest in an integrated plan of modern culture. Manship himself, an astute (if inflexible) historian of style, understood the contextuality of his position, writing, "I regret my limitations; I regret that the people about me are not conscious of art's eternal appeal and that art is not part of the everyday lives of these people."[21]

After Manship's death, his son John found two pieces of paper in the pocket of his dressing gown. One read: "The Genius is the Brute with the Delicate Touch"; the other: "The primary impulse in the arts is to give permanence to the fleeting moment, to bid it stay, because we cannot bear to lose it."[22]

A robust man with hearty appetites and a love of good-natured camaraderie, Paul Manship was hardly the "Brute." Nor did he see himself as such. The "Brute with the Delicate Touch" might better describe John Singer Sargent, his friend, benefactor, and perhaps something of a model to Manship. The "Delicate Touch" characterizes Sargent's deft genius better than Manship's method of careful accretions. In this motto we can sense Manship's ideal. The second motto, "to give permanence to the fleeting moment," echoes a major nineteenth-century notion that lingered well into the twentieth century. Claude Monet wrote, "My only merit lies in having painted directly in front of nature, seeking to render my impression of the most fleeting effects, and I still very much regret having caused the naming of a group whose majority had nothing impressionist about it."[23] Written by Monet in 1926, this letter was addressed to John Singer Sargent's biographer.[24] Sargent's genial lifestyle and suave virtuosity vied with both Impressionism's immediacy and modernism's rigor for preeminence in Manship's imagination. Manship's art clusters these three values.

Beginning with the *Portrait of John D. Rockefeller,* we can sense the balance Manship sought between rendering a truthful report of perception and demonstrating his command of technique. If Paul Manship's ultimate place in history depended upon his formal competence, even his technical virtuosity would appear unnoticeable.[25] Unfortunately, Manship practiced his art backlit by the titanic contemporary development of cubist sculpture—the greatest deflection in the course of Western sculpture's evolution since the Renaissance. This least predictable and subsequently most fecund achievement of modern sculpture was Picasso's triumph. Relative to the gigantic accomplishments of European modernists and later, American Abstract Expressionists, the chronicle of this century might well disregard Manship.[26] Rightfully, Manship's work could be relegated to the ranks of first-rate artisans were it not for the art historical importance of the synthesis that he forged. Manship's sculptures were a

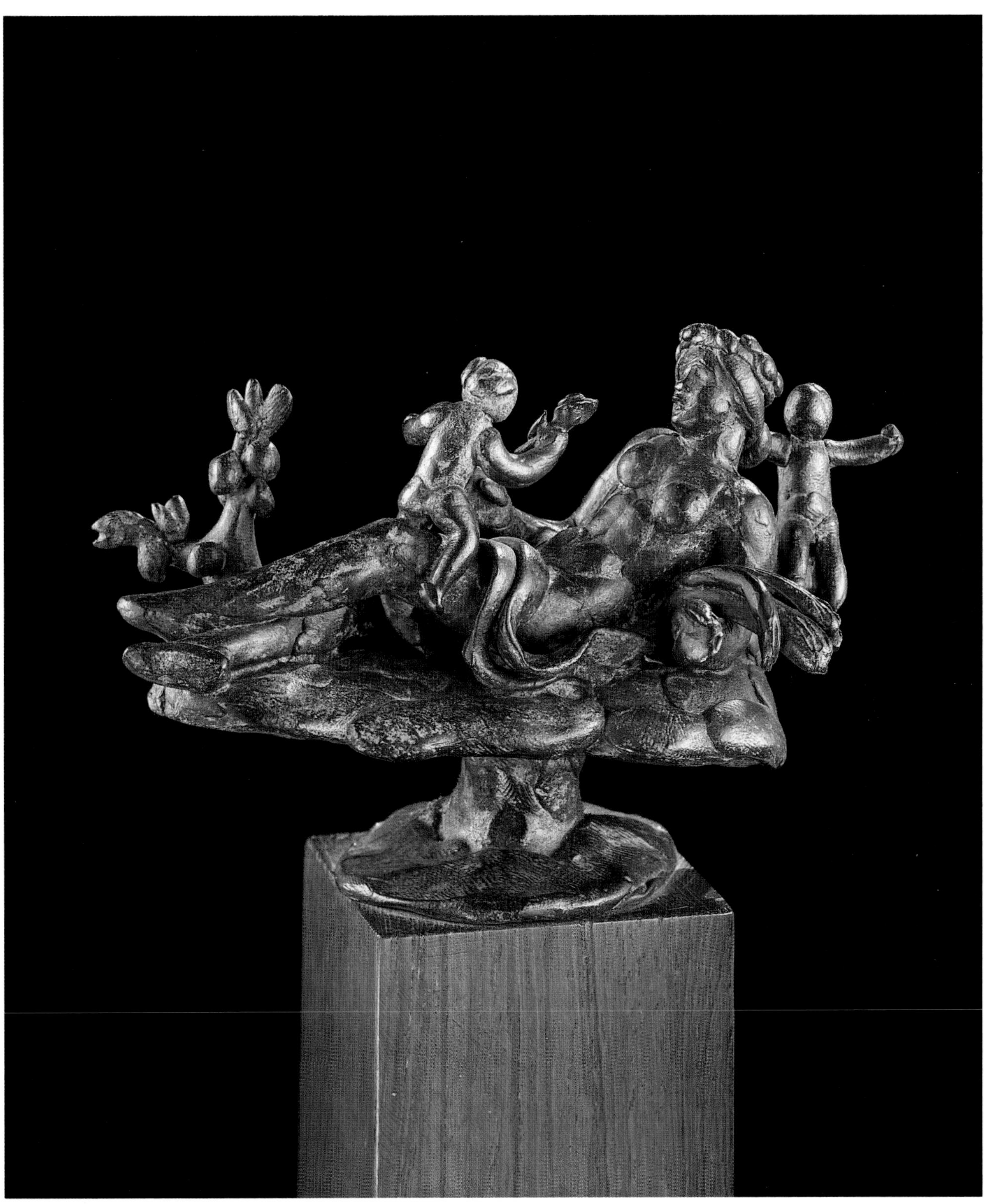

Fig. 199. *Reclining Nude with Children* (#2); bronze on wood base; $3\frac{1}{2}$ in. high.

legitimate response to the conditions that propelled modernism itself. The assessment of Manship as merely an artisan proves incomplete, failing to credit the most meaningful contribution of his art—formal originality almost without peer.

The rigorous, hermetic, and rationally formal realm of Cubism (even its humor concerns reflexive jokes about art) produced a serenity akin to, but different from, that for which Manship strove. He viewed himself as a legitimate heir to the legacy of all Western art. So ordained, Manship produced a synthesis that concluded the history of pre-modern art, even while offering an alternative. His was a sculpture about sculpture's history, as much as Cubism produced a sculpture about sculpture's possibilities. Manship's art represented a memory of sculpture rather than a discovery. His was a metasculpture, peculiarly suited to, and a victim of, that moment when sophistication first characterized the aspirations of art's general public (figs. 197–199).

Manship's work might have summarized the character and development of art from the eighteenth century to his own day, except for his conspicuous exclusion of the major contemporary intellectual and artistic developments. So much of modern art—generated by the Cubists, Surrealists, modern formalists, Dada theoreticians, psychoanalytic investigators—found no welcome in his sculpture, and cut off from so many fresh streams of inquiry, he found it difficult to keep his art vital. Manship worked from an essentially fixed agenda that altered little during his long career. His sculpture, which fully addressed the great questions of the new century, paralleled the other expressions of our time as a response to the art of the nineteenth century. Manship's art represents an alternative channel, if a limited one, to the other grand artistic explorations of our age. But within these self-imposed limits, he succeeded to the fullest possible extent.

Surpassing academic norms, Manship was no atavism, but a genuine, if unexpected, personality in the stream of twentieth-century art. As such, an unprejudiced evaluation must result in an admiration and appreciation of his often breathtaking accomplishments.

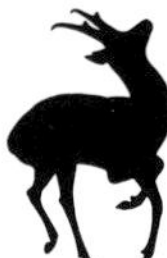

Notes

Boyhood and Family Background

1. Paul Manship Papers, Archives of American Art, Smithsonian Institution, roll NY59–15, frame 387.
2. Ibid., frame 398.
3. Ibid.
4. *Horses in a Storm* is listed as "destroyed by the artist" in Edwin Murtha's catalogue of Manship, where the plaster high relief is described: "Group of three wild horses facing to the left, one of them mounted by a nude male figure" (Edwin Murtha, *Paul Manship* [New York: Macmillan, 1957], p. 149, no. 5). In fact, the work is pictured in Frederick Leach's exhibition catalogue and cited as being in the collection of Paul K. Manship (Frederick D. Leach, *Paul Howard Manship, An Intimate View: Sculpture and Drawing from the Minnesota Museum of Art* [St. Paul: Minnesota Museum of Art, 1972], p. 9).
5. William Sener Rusk, *William Henry Rinehart* (Baltimore: N.T.A. Munder, 1939), pp. 83–84.
6. George Breck, quoted in Susan Rather, "Paul Manship and the Genesis of Archaism," in *Paul Manship: Changing Taste in America* (exh. cat.; St. Paul: Minnesota Museum of Art, 1985), p. 64.
7. Manship Papers, frame 329.
8. Paul Manship, "The Sculptor at the American Academy in Rome," *Art and Archaeology* 19 (February 1925): 89–92.
9. Paul Manship, quoted in Murtha, *Paul Manship*, pp. 11–12.
10. Ibid.
11. See: Jacob Rothenberg, *"Descensus ad Terram": The Acquisition and Reception of the Elgin Marbles* (New York: Garland, 1977).
12. Susan Rather, "The Past Made Modern: Archaism in American Sculpture," *Arts Magazine* 59 (November 1984): 111–19.
13. Ibid.
14. Manship, "Sculptor at American Academy," pp. 89–92.

Overnight Success

1. Frank Owen Payne, "Noted American Sculptors at Work," *Art and Archaeology* 21 (March 1926): 119–28.
2. Walker Hancock, "A Tribute," in *Paul Manship: 1885–1966* (brochure; Washington, D.C.: National Collection of Fine Arts [National Museum of American Art] and St. Paul: St. Paul Art Center, 1966).
3. Kenyon Cox, "A New Sculptor," *Nation* 96 (13 February 1913): 162–63.
4. Herbert Adams, quoted in Joseph Bailey Ellis, "Paul Manship in the Carnegie Institute," *Carnegie Magazine* 11 (September 1937): 110–13.
5. As is true for all artistic inventions, this subtle archaic suggestion of life and breath was borrowed and exaggerated beyond its original intent. Baroque sculpture magnified this gesture of faintly parted lips as an exploitation of the antique. Particularly in Italian Baroque sculpture, figures gape, open-mouthed, without indicating conversation but rather overstating the suggestion of heightened

vitality; but the *Lyric Muse* is actually singing. Only in comparison with the feverish emotions of the Baroque and late Romantic can Manship's accurate return to sources and his toning down of the emotional range be understood.

6. Their name, akin to the Latin "mens" and English "mind" denotes memory. In earlier times, poets (in the Germanic tradition called "minesingers"), having no books to read from, relied on their memories. Hence, they served as the communal memory of their tribe, as did artists.
7. Cox, "A New Sculptor," pp. 162–63.
8. Stanley Casson also commented on Manship's integration of the utmost classical refinement without restriction to specific citations. Commenting on the *Centaur and Dryad* he delighted in the "subject and style alike . . . derived from the work of early fifth-century Greek and Etruscan artists. The group is a small bronze executed in 1913. Five copies exist. . . . The basis is decorated with bronze panels in low relief with a dance of Satyrs and maenads. It is almost a perfect example of what a good basis should be; it finishes off the group in a way that could never be achieved with a plain rectangular basis, for it has gently tapering sides and a very finely worked moulding at the bottom. Its architectural formalism harmonizes with the archaic folds of the Dryad's drapery.

   Although directly dependent upon Greek work the group is in no way a copy of the Greek" (Stanley Casson, *Twentieth Century Sculptors* [London: Oxford University Press, 1930], p. 53).
9. Manship, "Sculptor at American Academy," pp. 89–92.
10. "Friends of American Art," *Bulletin of the Art Institute of Chicago* 9 (1 January 1915): 11.
11. "French Prints and Some American Sculpture: The Work of Paul Manship," *New York Times*, 20 February 1916, section 5, p. 15.
12. A. E. Gallatin, "The Sculpture of Paul Manship," *Bulletin of the Metropolitan Museum of Art* 11 (October 1916): 218–22; "New Bronzes in the George G. Booth Loan Collection," *Bulletin of the Detroit Museum of Art* 11 (November–December 1916): 20.
13. "Manship was certainly sympathetic to the cause of recognition for Indian art, which only began to receive serious art historical attention around 1910. One of several important events that occurred in that year was the foundation of the India Society, by Ananda Coomaraswamy and others. . . . By 1917, Manship had become one of only seventeen American members of this organization, along with Arthur B. Davies and Charles Lang Freer. . . . Between 1910 and 1919, for example, Coomaraswamy alone was responsible for books on Indian drawings (1910, 1912) and sculpture (1912–14, with a preface by Eric Gill); Rajput painting (1916, the same year as Manship's *Dancer and Gazelles*); gesture (1917, a translation of a Sanskrit treatise on Indian dance); and a collection of essays entitled *The Dance of Siva*, his most popular work (1918). He also wrote numerous articles, even for such popular and accessible magazines as *Vanity Fair*" (Susan Rather, "The Past Made Modern," pp. 111–19).
14. Gallatin, "The Sculpture of Paul Manship," pp. 218–22. Gallatin also writes: "Mr. Manship has found his inspiration now in the works of the great Greek sculptors, now in the creative period of Indian art, now in the glorious art of the Italian Renaissance; but always these arts have inspired him to create, not to produce lifeless interpretations, as was the case with such artists as Canova and David . . . with their pseudo-classicism. His work is invariably full of vigor and fire. . . . Early in his career Manship was attracted by Rodin, but this influence, fortunately, was of short duration. Rodin is a rock which has shipwrecked many a young sculptor."
15. "A Modern Primitive in Art," *The Literary Digest* 52 (6 May 1916): 1278–79.
16. "The Greatness of Paul Manship?" *Arts and Decoration* 6 (April 1916): 291. This article's title indicates that Manship's supporters had already made a potent case in his behalf, and the magazine was claiming a revisionist position as early as 1916. The article continued, contending that, "In this they are like the works of that other once popular idol, Bouguereau—neither better nor worse." Thus, Manship was allied to the (at the time) least savory of academics.
17. e. e. cummings, "Gaston Lachaise," *The Dial* 68 (February 1920): 194–204.
18. Frank Owen Payne, "Two Amazing Portraits by Paul Manship," *International Studio* 71 (October 1920): 74–77; Murtha, *Paul Manship*, p. 159.
19. "Notes on Current Art: Paul Manship's Bust of J. D. Rockefeller," *New York Times*, 11 April 1920, section 6, p. 8.
20. Payne, "Two Amazing Portraits," pp. 74–77. Even in Manship's most "abstract" passages, ones that seem pure invention and pattern, he never strayed far from observation. We know of his endless study of the human figure—which produced a wealth of beautiful drawings from every period of his life—but he seems also to have unceasingly studied the auxiliary elements of his work, such as the folds in drapery, that contribute so much of the surface animation to his pieces. To the degree that he rendered what he saw in an idealized manner according to artistic precedent, Manship was always something of a portrait artist—he was always "portraying." As Walker Hancock recalled, Manship sometimes "felt that he had gone too far in the abstraction of certain forms. He

spoke often of the 'anatomy of drapery' and preferred to base his interpretation of it upon the actuality rather than upon the use of arbitrary or conventionalized forms" (Walker Hancock, "Paul Manship," *Fenway Court* 1 [October 1966]: 1–7).

21. Martin Birnbaum, *Introductions* (New York: F. F. Sherman, 1919), pp. 53–54.
22. A. E. Gallatin, "An American Sculptor: Paul Manship," *Studio* 82 (October 1921): 137–44.
23. Ibid. Gallatin continued: "If the artist does not attain these qualities he will almost inevitably occupy a lesser position, for all the sculpture considered great is possessed of at least fire enough to stir the emotions; one does not demand the power to summon ecstasy possessed by Rodin, Byron and Wagner. The figure of the nymph in his group entitled *Centaur and Dryad* shows us that the sculptor is capable of introducing pulsating life into his work. In addition, one would like to see Manship introduce a more decided note of modernity into his work."
24. Manship's work did not fare very well among English critics who reviewed an *Athenaeum* exhibition in London: "Messrs. Brown & Phillips, most enterprising of dealers, have introduced an American sculptor, Mr. Paul Manship, who has had something in the nature of a triumph in the States. He is a curiously unequal artist; some of his exhibits . . . are about as bad as sculpture can possibly be; others again, such as the bronze *Dancer and Gazelles*, are perfectly charming in feeling and design, and most delicately executed. The explanation of this inequality is to be found, firstly, in the evident eclecticism of Mr. Manship's studies, and, secondly, in the nature of his aesthetic impulse. . . . Mr. Manship's aesthetic sense is of a special character; it is, in fact, almost entirely restricted to a feeling for line. The beauty of his successful works is essentially the beauty of line. . . . In other words, his bronzes have no three-dimensional existence. Seen from any but the central point of view, they become a mere haphazard bundle of weak and straggling forms with no beauty or significance. They are, in effect, bas-reliefs cut out of their backgrounds. Set against a light wall, the *Dancer and Gazelles* and *Diana* constitute silhouettes conveying something of the grace and balance of figures on a good Greek vase, because this is how their creator originally conceived them. But when Mr. Manship departs from the strictly two-dimensional conception he fails most lamentably, because he is faced at once with three-dimensional problems which neither his erudition nor technical ability has so far enabled him to solve" ("An English Estimate of Manship," *Arts and Decoration* 15 [October 1921]: 384).
25. "Actaeon: A Recently Modelled Bronze, by Paul Manship," *Vanity Fair* 24 (March 1925): 41.
26. A precedent for Gaston Lachaise's massing of forms in *The Mountain* can be found in Alexander Archipenko's even earlier work, *Repose*, from 1912 (Tel Aviv Museum).
27. Casson, *Twentieth Century Sculptors*, p. 53.
28. "New Manship Sculpture: Recently Completed in Paris," *Vanity Fair* 26 (April 1926): 68.

Art Deco

1. Manship Papers, frame 448.
2. Ibid., frame 458. Manship's phrase, "temperament of the racial group," did not have the same hideous implications of racist pseudo-anthropology that it must possess for sensibilities formed after World War II and the worldwide movement for civil and national rights. Manship used the term benignly, according to current humane thinking and the latest popular anthropology, which viewed the world as populated by dozens of distinct racial types.
3. Subsequently, a similar assumption about the salutary role of art in a society would be embodied in the WPA's Federal Art Program—of which Manship never needed to avail himself. Yet, the WPA's position was in advance of the public's in that the government program placed the artist on equal footing with other workers and did not ghettoize painters and sculptors with any notions of finery.
4. Paul Manship, quoted in Leach, *Paul Howard Manship*, p. 24.
5. Hancock, "Paul Manship," pp. 1–7.
6. Manship Papers, frame 390; Gallatin, "An American Sculptor," pp. 137–44. As usual in Manship's sympathetic reviews, Gallatin noted "the artist's perfection of craftsmanship and wealth of exquisite detail, which enhances rather than detracts from the ensemble. The superb patina on both Manship's bronzes and marbles also plays its part in bringing about the realization of his aims."
7. "Art: Exhibitions of the Week: Paul Manship's Work," *New York Times*, 1 February 1925, section 7, p. 11.
8. Manship Papers, frame 390.
9. The work was made a gift to New York State, which maintained Mackay's estate when it became a park. Concern about both the sculpture's deterioration out of doors and Mackay's intent that the

work remain on public view prompted *Theseus and Ariadne* to be transferred to the National Museum of American Art in 1982.

10. George Henry Chase and Chandler Rathfon Post, *A History of Sculpture* (London and New York: Harper and Bros., 1925), p. 521. The authors continued: "We must ask of him what we find in Minne, Metzner, Mestrovic, however disagreeable their message and however inferior to his their skill."

Mature Style and Career

1. Jacques Schnier, *Sculpture in Modern America* (Berkeley: University of California Press, 1948), p. 9.
2. "Paul Manship in a New Mood," *Vanity Fair* 28 (July 1927): 42.
3. "Paul Manship, American Sculptor," *Vanity Fair* 33 (September 1929): 54. The article continued: "Yet his growth has not in any sense been hurried by precocity or an undigested acceptance of revolutionary dogmas. He has been accused at times of an excessive artistic caution: the very respectability of his reputation has irritated and dismayed the critics. The point is that Mr. Manship has proceeded at his own speed. His early career gave the critics a sufficient clue to bracket him definitely among the classicists. With his eventual mastery of form and the consummation of his self-confidence, he has adventured along a wider frontier."
4. Holger Cahill, "American Art Today" in *America as Americans See It*, ed. Fred J. Ringel (New York: Harcourt Brace & Co., 1932), p. 264. He continued: "Academic sculptors of past generations—Daniel Chester French, Paul Bartlett, Frederick MacMonnies, Gutzon and Solon Borglum, Herbert Adams, Augustus, and Charles Grafly though thoroughly trained did not so fire the imagination. (Nor did some of Manship's contemporaries such as John Gregory, Paul Jennewein, or Wheeler Williams.) Classicism also beckoned to George Gray Barnard, who, some believed, never lived up to his early promise."
5. Paul Manship, quoted in "Pessimism," *Art Digest* 7 (1 March 1933): 4.
6. Henry McBride, quoted in "Pessimism," p. 4.
7. Franklin B. Mead, *Heroic Statues in Bronze of Abraham Lincoln, Introducing the Hoosier Youth of Paul Manship* (Fort Wayne, Ind.: The Lincoln National Life Insurance Company, 1932), pp. 13–15.
8. "Orders Lincoln Statue: Indiana Co. Gives $75,000 Commission to Paul Manship," *New York Times*, 7 June 1928, p. 16.
9. Paul Manship, quoted in Mead, *Heroic Statues*, pp. 20–24.
10. Paul Manship, quoted in "Paul Manship Models Lincoln for Indiana as *The Hoosier Youth*," *Art Digest* 6 (1 August 1932): 7.
11. Paul Manship, quoted in Mead, *Heroic Statues*, pp. 20–24.
12. Ibid.
13. Ibid.
14. When the full-size plaster model of the Lincoln figure was shown in New York, critics recognized that "it is at once apparent that the sculptor has finally assimilated those earlier strains into the unmistakable fiber of his own aesthetic being. . . . I like it tremendously, except for the theatrical looking stump with its clusters of property leaves, and its rather superficially arranged scroll and inscription" ("Exhibitions in New York: Paul Manship: Averell House," *Art News* 31 [15 April 1933]: 5).
15. Barry Faulkner, quoted in Robert Cushman Murphy, *Paul Manship* (a brochure of the eulogy delivered on 8 February 1966 at Grace Episcopal Church, New York).
16. "Paul Manship: Averell House," p. 5.
17. Murtha, *Paul Manship*, p. 12.
18. "Paul Manship at the Tate Gallery," *Apollo* 22 (August 1935): 107.
19. This reviewer continued in awed appreciation: "If you have at all vividly in mind Manship's earlier work, those Blake-like, mystical figures flying through space, as remote from life as smoke drifting out to sea, yet with the power to influence feeling, you come to this new expression of his definitely startled. These animals are presented with such clarity and simplicity that they have not only the beauty and humor inherent in wild life, but are so modeled, with such a sense of sculptural form that they are great art" ("Sculptured Bronze Animals: Paul Manship's Designs for the Tall Gates to the Main Entrance of New York Zoological Park," *Arts and Decoration* 39 [July 1933]: 52–53).
20. Royal Cortissoz, quoted in "New York Criticism," *Art Digest* 7 (1 May 1933): 16.
21. H. Granville Fell, "From Gallery and Mart: American Sculptures in London," *Connoisseur* 96 (August 1935): 101–102.

Monuments and Medals

1. Royal Cortissoz, quoted in Leach, "Paul Manship: Artist, Time and Place," in *Manship: Changing Taste,* pp. 49–51.
2. McBride continued: "The best surgeon and the best engineers do fine jobs, and they achieve a kind of handsomeness in their work that subtle thinkers in Europe have for some time been hailing as art. But the American elite did not wait for European approbation before adopting Mr. Manship. They joined forces with him the moment he swam into their ken. It was a case of instinct, and instinct is always swifter and more unerring than intellect" ("New York Criticism," p. 16).
3. The bulk of this review consists of perceptive descriptions of the works: " 'The North American Black Bear' is neither complex nor compound, he is a bare statement of form and excellent at that. Quiet, too, compact and ornamental, the 'Baboon' is nearest to naturalism in the whole of the little sculptural Zoo, he is a fine fellow. The 'Stag,' with uplifted right leg, is a good specimen, while the group of two 'Deer and a Fawn' is the most impressive of all the works exhibited" ("Manship at the Tate Gallery," p. 107).
4. "Paul Manship: Averell House," p. 5. Consisting of more than seventy pieces, the Manship show that occasioned this review was deemed "one of the outstanding exhibitions of the year."
5. "League Makes Agreement on Memorial for Wilson," *New York Times,* 9 April 1936, p. 12.
6. Manship Papers, frame 363.
7. John Manship, "Paul Manship: A Biographical Sketch," in *Manship: Changing Taste,* p. 150.
8. Walker Hancock, "Paul Manship," pp. 1–7.
9. Ibid. Hancock continues: "In his medallic work, as in most of his relief, lettering played an important part. For him it was as alive and sensitive a form of design as any other. Youthful experience in sign painting had given him great facility and freedom with it. He loved the 'living line' with its apparently accidental irregularities, despising the formal, stereotyped letters that were usually designed in architects' offices."
10. "In some of the shop windows on Fifth Avenue, New York, is now to be seen a bronze medal designed and executed by Paul Manship representing the outrages perpetrated by the German army upon women and children in invaded territory, particularly in Belgium. This is offered for sale at $10 a piece and puts into permanent form those things which if possible should not be remembered, but if remembered not visualized" ("Mr. Manship's Kultur Medal," *American Magazine of Art* 9 [June 1918]: 336).
11. "Manship Medal a Bone of Contention," *Art Digest* 5 (1 January 1931): 6.
12. "God of Wine Stirs Medalists' Society: Distribution of Bas-Relief of Dionysus, by Paul Manship, Arouses Protests: Wet-Dry Row is Denied," *New York Times,* 8 January 1931, p. 48.
13. "Will Design Inauguration Medal," *New York Times,* 12 January 1933, p. 14.
14. The medal's legend was also suggested by President Roosevelt: "Thou, too, sail on, O Ship of State,/ Sail on, O Union strong and great." The article continues: "The model has been reduced from one foot in diameter to three inches. Two examples in gold will be struck for the new President and the Vice-President, some in silver, for the members of the new cabinet, and 2,500 in bronze for the public. The medals will be struck at the mint in Washington, and the bronze ones will be sold for $2.50" ("Manship's Roosevelt Medal," *Art Digest* 7 [1 March 1933]: 4).
15. Barry Faulkner, quoted in Murphy, *Paul Manship.*
16. "Other callers to the Kennedy house today included Paul Manship, the New York sculptor who is working on a traditional Inauguration medal" (Russell Baker, "Goldberg Post Discussed," *New York Times,* 10 December 1960, p. 14).

Celebrity

1. Rosamund Frost, "Manship Ahoy!" *Art News* 44 (June 1945): 28.
2. Paul Manship, quoted in Harold Lucien, "What Paul Manship Thinks of Prometheus," *Rockefeller Center Weekly* 2, no. 3 (1935). See also fig. 145, from *Rockefeller Center Weekly* 1 (25 October 1934): 6.
3. Manship's commission fared better than some of his contemporaries'. Wayne Craven noted that *Prometheus* "became one of the spectacular sights of New York City in the 1930's. . . . Only a few years earlier, however, William Zorach and Robert Laurent had experienced bitter disappointment when the manager of the [Radio City] Music Hall [in Rockefeller Center] had refused to accept their heroic nude abstractions" (Wayne Craven, *Sculpture in America from the Colonial Period to the Present* [New York: Thomas Y. Crowell Co., 1968], pp. 565–68).

4. Harold Lucien, "What Paul Manship Thinks of Prometheus."
5. Casson, *Twentieth Century Sculptors*, pp. 42–43.
6. In other years the institute presents the medal for accomplishment in poetry, history or biography, music, drama, architecture, painting, fiction, and belles-lettres. Former recipients in sculpture were: Augustus Saint-Gaudens, 1907; Daniel Chester French, 1917; Herbert Adams, 1926; George G. Barnard, 1936.

Social Responsibility and Public Visibility

1. John Manship, "Paul Manship," *Manship: Changing Taste*, p. 147.
2. Manship Papers, frame 392.

   Walker Hancock admiringly described Manship's technical advances achieved by his attention to the plaster state of the sculpture: "Much of the work for bronze that other sculptors would have done in clay he did by carving the clean, resistant surface of the plaster. He became tremendously skilled in carving in the plaster mold, the unique quality of his reliefs resulting largely from the application of this technique."

   Hancock explicitly stated that Manship's manner of working his plasters was unique and unrivaled, and that "no important American sculptor, with the possible exception of Karl Bitter, had attempted to treat stone as if it were anything but a copy of a clay model, and none had treated bronze as a hard material, revealing the craftsman's hand in chastening the metallic surfaces. Manship had done this, and his bronzes further suggested in their flow of line the flow of molten metal" (Hancock, "A Tribute").
3. All excerpts of Manship's statement are from *Artists Against War and Fascism*, introduction by Matthew Baigell and Julia Williams (New Brunswick, N.J.: Rutgers University Press, 1986), pp. 87–89.
4. "Manship in Junk Yard," *Art Digest* 14 (1 November 1939): 9.
5. Manship Papers, frame 360.
6. Ibid., frame 362.
7. Ibid., frame 549.
8. Ibid., frame 459.
9. Ibid., frame 362.
10. "Leave the Sculptures," *Art Digest* 14 (1 September 1940): 20.
11. Manship Papers, frame 645.

Late Works and Legacy

1. Herbert L. Kammerer, "In Memoriam—Paul Manship," *National Sculpture Review* 14 (Winter 1965–66): 7.
2. Manship Papers, roll NY–59–17.
3. Emily Genauer, quoted in Leach, "Artist, Time, and Place," in *Manship: Changing Taste*, p. 55.
4. Howard Devree, quoted in Leach, "Artist, Time, and Place," in *Manship: Changing Taste*, p. 55.
5. Ada Louise Huxtable, "$24,000,000 Shrine is Proposed for Capital: Critique of Project, Question Its Style," *New York Times*, 3 June 1960, p. 1.
6. "Academy Elects Four to Membership: Arts and Letters Institution Honors Faulkner, Steinbeck, Kroll and Mark Van Doren," *New York Times*, 24 November 1948, p. 44; "American Academy Elects Sherwood," *New York Times*, 3 December 1949, p. 3; "Four New Members Elected to American Academy," *New York Times*, 17 December 1954, p. 28.
7. "Two Get Art Group Awards: Architect and Sculptor are Honored by Municipal Unit," *New York Times*, 29 April 1954, p. 34.
8. "Eight Cited for Culture: New York Board of Trade to Present Silver Medallions," *New York Times*, 15 September 1957, p. 80.

   The awards dinner at the Waldorf-Astoria Hotel marked a turning point for American arts; the awards signaled the first moment since the WPA when official recognition surfaced for the arts as part of a healthy and integrated society, and the event, and particularly John D. Rockefeller III's speech, initiated the start of what became the corporate participation in funding performances, museum exhibitions, and thoughts of "corporate collecting." Even the creation of the National

Endowments precipitated from that evening. (See: Russell Porter, "Arts Are Saluted by City's Business: Rockefeller III, Griswold of Yale and Eight Others Honored by Board of Trade," *New York Times*, 11 October 1957, p. 32.)

9. "U.S. Sculptor Wins Prize," *New York Times*, 16 July 1961, p. 68.
10. Herbert L. Kammerer, "In Memoriam," p. 7.
11. Popular critics at this time were not eager to see the project develop along these conventional lines; they referred to Manship as a sculptor "not known here as a man to shatter tradition" (Grace Glueck, "Keeping Up With the Rear Guard," *New York Times*, 7 November 1965, section 2, p. 22). Of course, that is precisely the point, that Manship saw himself as an extension of the great tradition of Western art and not as its destroyer or deflector.
12. Willard Clopton, Jr., "Rough Rider 'Rides' Again," *Washington Post*, 28 October 1967, B1.
13. "Stolen $6,000 Statue Regained After $2 Sale," *New York Times*, 26 February 1958, p. 29; "Two Junk Men Cleared: Charge in Theft of Manship Statuette is Dropped," *New York Times*, 5 March 1958, p. 25.
14. "Paul Manship, Eighty, Sculptor, is Dead: Designed Many Monumental Works in Fifty-Year Career," *New York Times*, 1 February 1966, p. 31; see also: "Obituaries," *Art News* 65 (March 1966): 8.
15. Walker Hancock, "Paul Manship," *Fenway Court*, pp. 1–7. Hancock's observation is bitterly ironic in historical context because Manship's most likely challenger, David Smith—a man much younger than Manship—had predeceased him the year before.
16. John Canaday, "Art: 'Bestiary'—Show Full of Delight," *New York Times*, 8 January 1972, p. 25.
17. "Art Across North America: Outstanding Exhibitions: Prix de Rome," *Apollo* 118 (November 1983): 441–42.
18. Ibid.
19. Casson, *Twentieth Century Sculptors*, p. 50.
20. *Paul Howard Manship, An Intimate View*, p. 20.

    Manship's friend Herbert Kammerer observed that "Paul almost single-handedly returned the course of American sculpture to its classic origins in the Federal style and the pure forms of the 'Yankee stonecutters', Horatio Greenough and Hiram Powers, . . . away from the course of French-influenced Renaissance eclecticism provided by Augustus Saint-Gaudens, Daniel Chester French, Lorado Taft, Frederick Ruckstull and the other sculptors prominent in the latter half of the 19th century, so evident in the Columbia Fair, 'Classic' in architecture and so 'Renaissance' in sculpture" (Herbert Kammerer, "Paul Manship," *National Sculpture Review* 15 (Fall 1966): 28).
21. Manship Papers, frame 451.
22. Murphy, *Paul Manship*.
23. Claude Monet to Evan Edward Charteris, 21 June 1926, quoted in Steven Z. Levine, "Monet's Series: Repetition, Obsession," *October* 37 (Summer 1986): 65.
24. Evan Edward Charteris, K.C., *John Singer Sargent* (London, 1927).
25. On the occasion of a small show of Manship's sculpture and drawings at the National Museum of American Art in 1983, one critic remarked: "His craftsmanship seems wondrous still, and, in our eclectic age, his gracefulness and elegance no longer seem so frivolous. This well-timed show suggests that Manship's reputation may soon rise again" (Paul Richard, "The Streamlining of an Ancient Art," *Washington Post*, 15 August 1983).
26. In the late 1960s, some years after Manship died, Walker Hancock recalled sitting as a member of the selection committee of the American Academy in Rome as another member of the committee, José de Creeft, was excoriating the poor draftsmanship of the candidates' submitted work. De Creeft pointed at a cast of *Dancer and Gazelles*, which was placed on a table behind the committee. "Look at that *thing*" de Creeft said, vehemently accenting the last word, and Hancock recalled, as de Creeft's own works were so different from Manship's, no one quite knew what he was going to say. "In one hundred years," de Creeft continued, "any museum in the world would give anything for that *thing* . . . because of the craftsmanship!" (Walker Hancock, in conversation with the author, 4 December 1986).

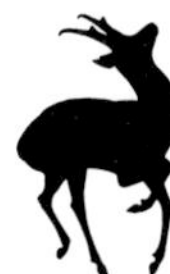

Bibliography

Writings by Paul Manship

The Paul Manship Papers, Archives of American Art:
N 714 Personal calendars (tiny appointment books with lecture and travel dates) 1925–35, and 1937–61. N 715 Personal calendars 1937–61, cont. N 716 Personal calendars 1937–61, cont. N 717 Personal calendars 1963–65. N 62 Paul Manship scrapbooks. NY–59–15 Paul Manship photographs, exhibition catalogues, clippings, writings, lectures, articles on sculpture, etc. NY–59–16 Writings on art, family records, and correspondence 1933–57. Also correspondence A through N, 1940–47. NY–59–17 Correspondence O through Z, 1940–47.

Letters from Paul Manship, Archives of American Art:
D 42 Letters of Frederic Newlin Price: Calder, A. to Wiles, Irving. D 195 Correspondence of Sidney C. Woodward; K (cont.) to S (cont.). D 100 Philip Leslie Hale correspondence: miscellaneous letters, 1885–1935.

"The Sculptor at the American Academy in Rome." *Art and Archaeology* 19 (February 1925): 89–92.

"Why Established Artists Should Oppose War and Fascism." Speech delivered at the public session of the First American Artists' Congress Against War and Fascism. Reprinted in *Artists Against War and Fascism,* with introduction by Matthew Baigell and Julia Williams. New Brunswick, N.J.: Rutgers Univeristy Press, 1986.

Monographs

Gallatin, A. E. *Paul Manship: A Critical Essay on His Sculpture, and an Iconography.* New York: John Lane, 1917.

Lincoln National Life Foundation. *Abraham Lincoln: The Hoosier Youth.* Fort Wayne, Ind.: Lincoln National Life Foundation, 1932.

Murtha, Edwin. *Paul Manship.* New York: Macmillan, 1957.

Books

Agard, Walter Raymond. *Classical Myths in Sculpture.* Madison, Wis.: University of Wisconsin Press, 1951.

American Sculptors: Scrap Book of Reproductions. New York: New York Public Library, 1931.

Averell House. *Sculpture by Paul Manship.* New York, 1933.

Biographical Sketches of American Artists. 5th ed. Lansing, Mich.: Michigan State Library, 1924.

Birnbaum, Martin. *Introductions.* New York: Frederic Fairchild Sherman, 1919.

Brookgreen Gardens. *Sculpture by Paul Manship.* Brookgreen, S.C.: Brookgreen Gardens, 1938.

Casson, Stanley. *Twentieth Century Sculptors.* London: Oxford University Press, 1930.

Chase, George Henry, and Chandler Rathfon Post. *A History of Sculpture.* London and New York: Harper and Bros., 1925.

Cheney, Sheldon. *A Primer of Modern Art.* New York: Boni and Liveright, 1924.

Coen, Rena Neumann. *Painting and Sculpture in Minnesota, 1820–1914.* Minneapolis: University of Minnesota Press, 1976.

Coinage of Saorstat Eireann. Dublin, The Stationery Office, 1928.

Cortissoz, Royal. *American Artists.* New York: C. Scribner's Sons, 1923.

Craven, Wayne. *Sculpture in America from the Colonial Period to the Present.* New York: Thomas Y. Crowell Co., 1968.

Designs in Glass by Twenty-Seven Contemporary Artists. New York: Steuben Glass, 1940.

Durman, Donald Charles. *He Belongs to the Ages: The Statues of Abraham Lincoln.* Ann Arbor, Mich.: Edwards Brothers, 1951.

Eisler, Colin. *Sculptors' Drawings Over Six Centuries 1400–1950.* New York: Agrinde Publications, 1981.

Failing, Patricia. *Best-Loved Art from American Museums.* An Artnews Book. New York: Clarkson N. Potter, 1983.

Fairmount Park Art Association, Philadelphia. *Sculpture of a City: Philadelphia's Treasures in Bronze and Stone.* New York: Walker Publishing, 1974.

Gardner, Helen. *Art Through the Ages.* New York: Harcourt Brace and Co., 1926.

Goode, James M. *The Outdoor Sculpture of Washington, D.C.* Washington, D.C.: Smithsonian Institution Press, 1974.

The Index of Twentieth Century Artists. Edited by John Shapley. Vol. 1 (November–December 1933). Vol. 2 suppl. (September 1935). Vol. 3 suppl. (August–September 1936). New York: College Art Association.

Jackman, Rilla. *American Arts.* New York: Rand-McNally and Co., 1928.

James, Juliet. *Sculpture of the Exposition Palaces and Courts.* [Pan-American Exposition] San Francisco: H. S. Crocker and Co., 1915.

Lipchitz, Jacques. *My Life in Sculpture.* Edited by H. H. Arnason. Documents of Twentieth Century Art series. New York: Viking Press, 1972.

Lynch, Kenneth. *Sundials and Spheres: The Architectural Handbook Series.* Canterbury, Conn.: Canterbury Publishing, 1971.

McRoberts, Jerry William. *The Conservative Realists' Image of America in the 1920s: Modernism, Traditionalism and Nationalism.* Ann Arbor, Mich.: University Microfilms, 1980.

Mead, Franklin B. *Heroic Statues in Bronze of Abraham Lincoln: Introducing the Hoosier Youth of Paul Manship.* Fort Wayne, Ind.: The Lincoln National Life Insurance Company, 1932.

Miller, Alec. *Tradition in Sculpture.* New York and London: Studio Publications, 1949.

The National Cyclopedia of American Biography. Vol. C. New York: James T. White and Co., 1930.

National Sculpture Society. *Paul Manship.* New York: W. W. Norton and Company, 1947.

Parkes, Kineton. *Sculpture of Today.* Vol. 1. London: Chapman and Hall, Ltd., 1921.

Paul Manship, The American Spirit in Art, The Pageant of America. Vol. 12. New Haven, Conn.: Yale University Press, 1927.

Post, Chandler Rathfon. *A History of European and American Sculpture from the Early Christian Period to the Present Day.* Vol. 2. Cambridge, Mass.: Harvard University Press, 1921.

Proske, Beatrice Gilman. *Brookgreen Gardens, Sculpture.* Brookgreen, S.C.: Brookgreen Gardens, 1943.

Rindge, Agnes. *Sculpture.* New York: Payson and Clarke, 1929.

St. Paul Art Center. *Spindrift.* Vol. 2, no. 1. St. Paul, Minn., 1967.

Schnier, Jacques. *Sculpture in Modern America.* Berkeley and Los Angeles: University of California Press, 1948.

Squire, C. B. *Outdoor Sculpture by Paul Manship.* Wilton, Conn.: Kenneth Lynch and Sons.

Taft, Lorado. *Modern Tendencies in Sculpture.* Chicago: University of Chicago Press, 1921.

———. *The History of American Sculpture.* New York: Macmillan, 1925 edition.

———. *The History of American Sculpture.* Rev. ed. with a supplementary chapter by Adeline Adams. New York: Macmillan, 1930.

Vermeule, Cornelius. *Numismatic Art in America.* Cambridge, Mass.: Belknap Press of Harvard University, 1971.

Vitry, Paul. *Paul Manship: Sculpteur Americain.* Paris: Editions de la Gazette des Beaux-Arts, 1927.

Withey, Henry F., and E. R. Withey. *Biographical Dictionary of American Architects Deceased.* Los Angeles: New Age, 1956.

Year Book of the Architectural League of New York. Vol. 30. New York: Secretary of the Architectural League of New York, 1915.

———. Vol. 40. New York: Secretary of the Architectural League of New York, 1925.

Dissertations

McRoberts, Jerry William. *The Conservative Realists' Image of America in the 1920s: Modernism, Traditionalism and Nationalism.* Ph.D. diss., University of Illinois at Urbana-Champaign, 1980.

Rather, Susan. *The Origins of Archaism and the Early Sculpture of Paul Manship.* Ph.D. diss., University of Delaware, 1986.

Grouped Statements and Symposia

Cahill, Holger. "American Art Today." In *America as Americans See It*, edited by Fred J. Ringel. New York: Harcourt Brace and Co., 1932.

Articles

"Academy Elects Four to Membership." *New York Times*, 24 November 1948, p. 44.

"Accessions, Bronzes by Paul Manship, N.A." *Bulletin, Detroit Museum of Art* 10 (March 1916): 3.

"Actaeon: A Recently Modelled Bronze, by Paul Manship." *Vanity Fair* 24 (March 1925): 41.

Adams, Herbert. "Paul H. Manship." *Art and Progress* 6 (November 1914): 20–21.

"American Academy Elects Manship." *Minneapolis Art Institute Bulletin* 21 (17 December 1932): 175.

"American Academy Elects Sherwood." *New York Times*, 3 December 1949, p. 3.

"Appointed President of the American Academy." *Art Digest* 22 (15 April 1948): 10.

"Art Critic Honored by Sculptors Group." *New York Times*, 16 May 1942, p. 11.

"Art Notes." *New York Times*, 15 December 1917, p. 12.

"Art Notes." *New York Times*, 18 April 1940, p. 21.

"Art Notes." *New York Times*, 16 May 1946, p. 19.

"Art Notes." *New York Times*, 23 April 1947, p. 29.

"Aviation Sculpture May Go Out of City." *New York Times*, 14 August 1942, p. 14.

"Awarded the National Institute of Arts and Letters 1945 Gold Medal." *Art Digest* 19 (1 March 1945): 8.

Baker, Russell. "Goldberg Post Discussed." *New York Times*, 10 December 1960, p. 14.

Beatty, Albert R. "Lincoln, the Youth in Bronze." *National Republic* (April 1933): 14–32.

Breck, Joseph. "Playfulness." *Bulletin of the Minneapolis Institute of Art* 3 (October 1914): 125–26.

"A Bust by Paul Manship." *John Herron Art Institute Bulletin* 17 (August 1930): 26.

"Bronze Given by Dr. and Mrs. Walter Parker." *Bulletin, Detroit Museum of Art* 11 (November–December 1916): 21–22.

"Charity: Sculpture." *Survey* 68 (1 December 1932): 628.

Clopton, Willard, Jr. "Rough Rider 'Rides' Again." *Washington Post*, 28 October 1967, p. B1.

Cortissoz, Royal. *New York Herald*, 11 April 1920.

———. *New York Herald*, 15 April 1933.

"Cover: Portrait Drawing by Sargent." *American Artist* 28 (November 1964): 4.

Cresson, Margaret French. "Paul Manship: A Remembrance." *Berkshire Eagle*, 6 February 1966.

cummings, e. e. "Gaston Lachaise." *Dial* 68 (January–June 1920): 194–204.

"Current Exhibitions." *Chicago Art Institute Bulletin* 21 (April 1927): 53.

de Cisneros, Francois G. "La Maciza Escultura de Paul Manship." *Social* (October 1918): 16–18.

de Cuevas, George. "Paul Manship." *La Renaissance* 15 (July 1932): 131–35.

de Monvel, Roger Boutet. "La Sculpture Decorative de Paul Manship." *Art et Industrie* 3 (10 December 1927): 33–37.

Eckhardt, Wolf Von. "A Wraith Flails a Big Stick Against the Theodore Roosevelt Memorial." *Washington Post*, 19 June 1966.

Ellis, F. L. "Manship's Freedom Stamp Design Was Photo of a Plaster Cast." *Don Houseworth's International Stamp Review* 23 (April 1943): 1–3.

Ellis, Joseph Bailey. "Paul Manship in the Carnegie Institute." *Carnegie Magazine* 11 (September 1937): 110–13.

"Eight Cited for Culture." *New York Times*, 15 September 1957, p. 32.

"Elaborate Gates Designed for Zoo." *New York Times*, 14 March 1933, p. 17.

"Exhibitions." *Bulletin, Boston Museum of Fine Arts* 25 (February 1927): 9.

"Exhibitions—Sculpture by Paul Manship." *Bulletin, Detroit Museum of Art* 10 (December 1915): 4–5.

"Fair Commissions Four Sculptors." *New York Times*, 10 March 1964, p. 34.

Fell, H. G. "American Sculpture in London." *Connoisseur* 95 (August 1935): 101.

"Four Freedoms' Stamp." *New York Times*, 10 January 1943, sec. 8, p. 8.

"Four New Members Elected to American Academy." *New York Times*, 17 December 1954, p. 28.

"Freedom Shrine Lags in Congress." *New York Times*, 4 June 1960, p. 25.

"French Honor Paul Manship." *New York Times*, 30 July 1946, p. 21.

"Friends of American Art." *Chicago Art Institute Bulletin* 9 (January 1915): 11.

Frost, R. "Manship Ahoy!" *Art News* 44 (June 1945): 28.

"Furor Raised Over Proposed Freedom Monument." *Progressive Architecture* 41 (July 1960): 52.

Gallatin, A. E. "An American Sculptor, Paul Manship." *Studio* 82 (October 1921): 137–44.

———. "The Sculpture of Paul Manship." *Bulletin of the Metropolitan Museum of Art* 11 (October 1916): 218–22.

Gallo-Ruiz, E. "Medal of Dionysus." *Numismatist* 57 (March 1944): 189–94.

"Garden Statuary by Paul Manship." *House and Garden* 39 (June 1921): 62–63.

"Get Rome Professorship." *New York Times*, 25 February 1922, p. 12.

"Gets Fountain Award." *New York Times*, 30 January 1933, p. 11.

"God of Wine Depicted by Artist for Medalists." *New York Times*, 4 January 1931, sec. 9, p. 16.

"God of Wine Stirs Medalists' Society." *New York Times*, 8 January 1931, p. 48.

"Grant Statue to be Designed by Manship for Monument." *New York Times*, 11 June 1929, p. 25.

Hancock, Walker. "Paul Manship." *Fenway Court* 1 (October 1966): 1–7.

"Heroic Sculpture of Paul Manship." *Vanity Fair* (May 1919): 58.

Hind, C. Lewis. "Paul Manship." *Saturday Review*, 2 July 1921, pp. 11–12.

"History of Nation to Be Sculpted in Shrine on a Mountain in Georgia." *New York Times*, 7 August 1953, p. 1.

Houston Museum of Fine Arts Bulletin 3 (June 1940): 1–2.

"Jonas Lie Wins Arts Club Prize." *New York Times*, 11 January 1929, p. 25.

Kammerer, Herbert L. "In Memoriam—Paul Manship." *National Sculpture Review* 14, no. 4 (Winter 1965–66): 7.

———. ". . . Paul Manship, Fourteenth President, National Sculpture Society." *National Sculpture Review* 15, no. 3 (Fall 1966): 22, 27–28.

"Laments Carving of Stone Mountain." *Art News* 23 (3 January 1925): 1.

"League Makes Agreement on Memorial for Wilson." *New York Times*, 9 April 1936, p. 12.

"Leave the Sculptures." *Art Digest* 22 (June 1948): 10.

"Lincoln Statue—Fort Wayne." *American Magazine of Art* 25 (September 1932): 182.

Lucien, Harold. "What Paul Manship Thinks of Prometheus." *Rockefeller Center Weekly* 2, no. 3, 1935.

"Major Objects to Gift Statue." *New York Times*, 13 August 1942, p. 17.

"Making of an Art Film: Uncommon Clay." *American Artist* 15 (November 1951): 50–51.

"Manship Appointed." *Art Digest* 17 (15 October 1942): 26.

"Manship at the Tate Gallery." *Apollo* 22 (August 1935): 107.

"Manship Exhibition Opened by Bingham." *New York Times*, 19 January 1935, p. 17.

"Manship in Junk Yard." *Art Digest* 14 (1 November 1939): 9.

"Manship in the Toledo Art Museum." *International Studio* 77 (July 1923): 353.

"The Manship Medal." *American Magazine of Art* 7 (April 1916): 251.

"Manship Medal a Bone of Contention." *Art Digest* 5 (January 1931): 6.

"Manship's Bronze Exhibited." *Bulletin, Minneapolis Institute of Arts* 16 (30 April 1927): 86.

"Manship's Bust of Albert J. Beveridge." *Art Digest* 5 (15 November 1930): 14.

"Manship's Dionysus Medal." *American Magazine of Art* 22 (March 1931): 231–32.

"Manship's Gates for the Bronx Zoo." *Art Digest* 7 (1 April 1931): 6.

"Manship's Grant." *Art Digest* 3 (July 1929): 30.

"Manship's Hercules Upholding the Heavens Presented to Houston." *Art Digest* 14 (August 1940): 8.

"Manship's Prometheus Installed." *Art Digest* 8 (15 January 1934): 7.

"Manship's Roosevelt Medal." *Art Digest* 7 (1 March 1933): 4.

"Manship's Sculpture in Comprehensive Show." *Art Digest* 7 (15 April 1933): 17.

Maraini, Antonio. "Lo Scultore Paul Manship." *Dedalo* 4 (August 1923): 181–95.

"March Exhibitions." *Bulletin, Minneapolis Institute of Arts* 6 (March 1924): 14.

McClinton, Katherine Morrison. "Paul Manship: American Sculptor." *Art and Antiques* 5, no. 2 (March–April 1982): 94–99.

McCormick, William B. "Four New York Artists in a Newport Chapel." *Arts and Decoration* (October 1915): 470–71.

McDiarmid, Hugh. "Theodore Roosevelt Memorial Statue is Just a Big Bust." *Washington Post*, 14 September 1967.

Mechlin, Leila. "Manship's Dionysus Medal." *Field Notes, American Magazine of Art* 22 (March 1931): 231–32.

"Medals are Awarded in Arts and Letters." *New York Times*, 19 May 1945, p. 30.

Milliken, William M. "Contemporary American Bronzes." *Bulletin, Cleveland Museum of Art* 6 (1919): 151–54.

"Mr. Manship's Kultur Medal." *American Magazine of Art* 9 (June 1918): 336.

"A Modern Primitive in Art." *Literary Digest* 52 (6 May 1916): 1278–79.

"Named by Roosevelt." *New York Times*, 19 January 1937, p. 21.

"New Bronzes in the George G. Booth Loan Collection." *Bulletin, Detroit Museum of Art* 11 (November–December 1916): 20.

"New Manship Sculpture: Recently Completed in Paris." *Vanity Fair* 26 (April 1926): 68.

"New Manship Statue: John Hancock." *Art Digest* 23 (June 1948): 8.

"A New Sculptor." *Outlook* 106 (14 February 1914): 335–36.

"Norton Gallery and School of Art: Paul Manship, Sculptor." *Architectural Review* 90 (September 1941): 88–90.

"Paul H. Manship." *Art and Progress* 6 (November 1914): 20–21.

"Paul J. Rainey Memorial Gates, New York Zoological Park: Paul Manship Sculptor." *Architecture* 70 (September 1934): 133–36.

"Paul Manship, American Sculptor." *Review of Reviews* 78 (October 1928): 441–42.

"Paul Manship, American Sculptor." *Vanity Fair* 33 (September 1929): 54.

"Paul Manship—A Conversation." *Craft Horizons* 2, no. 1 (November 1942): 7.

"Paul Manship." *Art Journal* 32, no. 1 (Fall 1972): 55.

"Paul Manship Exhibition." *Art News* 31 (15 April 1933): 5.

"Paul Manship in a New Mood." *Vanity Fair* 28 (July 1927): 42.

"Paul Manship Models Lincoln for Indiana as 'The Hoosier Youth.' " *Art Digest* 6 (1 August 1932): 7.

"Paul Manship, Sculptor." *Gopher Historian* (Winter 1967–68): 1–8.

"Paul Manship's Victory Pin." *American Art News* 17 (30 November 1918): 7.

"Paul Manship's Work in Sculpture." *Outlook* 112 (March 1916): 542–43.

Payne, Frank Owen. "The Present War and Sculptural Art," *Art and Archaelogy* 8 (January–February 1919): 35.

———. "Noted American Sculptors at Work." *Art and Archaeology* 21 (March 1926): 119–28.

"Pessimism." *Art Digest* 7 (1 March 1933): 4.

"Portrait of G. Bellows." *Parnassus* 2 (December 1930): 7.

Porter, Russell. "Arts Saluted by City's Business." *New York Times*, 11 October 1957, p. 32.

"Prix de Rome." *Apollo* 95 (June 1972): 503.

"Prometheus, Unbound." *National Sculpture Review* 23, no. 2 (Summer 1974): 5.

Rather, Susan. "The Past Made Modern: Archaism in American Sculpture." *Arts Magazine* 59 (November 1984): 111–19.

Robertson, Nan. "Memorial to Theodore Roosevelt Unveiled." *New York Times*, 28 October 1967, p. 37.

"Rockefeller Center Sculpture." *Art Digest* 7 (15 February 1933): 9.

Rogers, Cameron. "The Compleat Sculptor." *New Yorker*, 1 September 1928, pp. 21–23.

"Roosevelt Gives Maritime Medal." *New York Times*, 9 October 1942, p. 4.

Rubins, D. K. "Bronze by Paul Manship: Rape of Europa." *John Herron Art Institute Bulletin* 38 (April 1951): 1–3.

"Sculpture by Paul Manship." *Century* 85 (April 1913): 869–71.

"Sculpture by Paul Manship." *Bulletin, Detroit Museum of Art* 10 (November 1915): 4.

"Sculpture of Paul Manship." *Harper's Weekly* 62 (11 March 1916): 246.

"Sculptured Bronze Animals: Paul Manship's Designs for the Tall Gates." *Arts and Decoration* 39 (July 1933): 52–53.

"Sculptor Named Winner of Institute Gold Medal." *New York Times*, 14 February 1945, p. 17.

"Sculptors Pick Manship." *New York Times*, 10 May 1939, p. 11.

Silberman, Robert. "Thoroughly Moderne Manship." *Art In America* 74 (January 1986): 111–15.

"Some Garden Sculpture of Paul Manship." *Country Life* 33 (November 1917): 53–55.

"Statue in Center Plaza." *New York Times*, 10 January 1934, sec. 9, p. 12.

Stilles, Kent B. "News of the Stamp World." *New York Times*, 18 April 1943, sec. 2, p. 11.

"Stolen $6,000 Statue Regained After $2 Sale." *New York Times*, 26 February 1958, p. 44.

"A Tablet Erected by the Trustees of the Museum in Memory of the Late J. Pierpont Morgan." *Bulletin of the Metropolitan Museum of Art* 15 (1920): 265–67.

Teltsch, Kathleen. "Two Works to Rejoin Prometheus After Fifty Years." *New York Times*, 8 April 1984, pp. 1, 41.

"Two Get Art Group Awards." *New York Times*, 29 April 1954, p. 34.

"Two Junk Men Cleared." *New York Times*, 5 March 1958, p. 25.

Underhill, Gertrude. "Some Recent Acquisitions of the Cleveland Museum of Art." *Art and Archaeology* 6 (July 1917): 41–49.

"U.S. Sculptor Wins Prize." *New York Times*, 16 July 1961, p. 68.

"Van Dyke, Eighty, Feted by Arts Academy: Dr. Damrosch, Mrs. Huntington and Mr. Manship Admitted to Membership at Annual Meeting." *New York Times*, 11 November 1932, p. 21.

Van Rensselaer, M. G. "Pauline: Mr. Manship's Portrait of His Daughter." *Scribner's Magazine* 60, no. 6 (December 1916): 772–76.

"Victory Overseas: A War Memorial by Paul Manship." *Vanity Fair* 27 (February 1927): 65.

Walther, Josephine. "Sculpture at the Detroit Institute of Arts." *Art and Archaeology* 17 (March 1924): 123–32.

Walton, William. "The Field of Art—Some Recent Small Sculptures." *Scribner's Magazine* 55 (May 1914): 663–66.

"Who is Who in Minnesota Art Annuals—Paul Manship." *Minnesotan* 1, no. 1 (July 1915): 14–17.

"Will Design Inauguration Medal." *New York Times*, 12 January 1933, p. 14.

Wilson, Malin. "Paul Manship: The Flight of Night." *Museum News* 17, no. 3 (1974): 59–61.

Zug, George Breed. "Exhibition of Cornish Artists." *Art and Archaeology* 3 (April 1916): 207–11.

Reviews

Cox, Kenyon. "A New Sculptor." *Nation* 96, no. 2485 (13 February 1913): 162–63.

Stuart, Evelyn Marie. "Exhibitions at the Art Institute—Sculpture by Paul Manship and Paintings by Robert Henri." *Fine Arts Journal* 33 (October 1915): 429–34.

"French Prints and Some American Sculpture." *New York Times*, 20 February 1916, sec. 5, p. 15.

Humber, George. "Paul Manship." *New Republic* 6 (25 March 1916): 207–9.

"The Greatness of Paul Manship?" *Arts and Decoration* 6 (April 1916): 291.

"Notes on Current Art." *New York Times*, 11 April 1920, sec. 6, p. 8.

"Paul Manship's Dramatic Vision of John D. Rockefeller." *Current Opinion* 69 (July 1920): 96–98.

Payne, Frank Owen. "Two Amazing Portraits by Paul Manship." *International Studio* 71 (October 1920): 74–77.

"An English Estimate of Manship." *Arts and Decoration* 15 (October 1921): 384.

"The Newest Sculpture of Paul Manship." *Vanity Fair* 19 (5 January 1923): 43.

Dezarrois, Andre. "Une exposition d'art americain." *La Revue de l'art ancien et moderne* 44 (June–December 1923).

"Portrait." *Review of Reviews* 68 (November 1923): 537.

"Art: Exhibitions of the Week." *New York Times*, 1 February 1925, sec. 7, p. 11.

"Paul Manship's Latest Work." *Current Opinion* 78 (April 1925): 432–35.

"The Work of Three Modern Sculptors." *Independent and Weekly Review* 116 (6 February 1926): 158–59.

Jewell, Edward Alden. "Further Comment on Exhibitions of the Week." *New York Times*, 26 January 1930, sec. 8, p. 13.

"Exhibitions in New York: Paul Manship: Averell House." *Art News* 31 (15 April 1933): 5.

Jewell, Edward Alden. "Debate at the Whitney." *New York Times*, 16 April 1933, sec. 9, p. 8.

Nirdlinger, Virginia. "New York Exhibitions of the Month." *Fine Arts* 20 (May 1933): 29.

"New York Criticism." *Art Digest* 7 (1 May 1933): 16.

Jewell, Edward Alden. "A Season's Sculpture." *New York Times*, 10 January 1934, sec. 9, p. 12.

Huxtable, Ada Louise. "$24,000,000 Shrine is Proposed for Capital." *New York Times*, 3 June 1960, p. 1.

Glueck, Grace. "Keeping Up With the Rear Guard." *New York Times*, 7 November 1965, sec. 2, p. 22.

———. "Robert Schoelkopf Gallery, New York: Exhibit." *Art in America* 59 (May 1971): 133.

Clain-Steffanelli, Elvira. "Artistic Evolution of Medals in the United States." *National Sculpture Review* 20, no. 5 (Fall 1971): 14–17.

Canaday, John. "Art: 'Bestiary' Show Full of Delight." *New York Times*, 8 January 1972, p. 25.

Dorsey, Deborah. "Schoelkopf Gallery, New York: Exhibit." *Art News* 70 (February 1972): 18.

Richard, Paul. "The Streamlining of an Ancient Art: Paul Manship's Sinuous Statues Once Set a Style." *Washington Post*, 15 August 1983.

Allen, Jane Addams. "A Fresh Look at Manship's Treasures." *Washington Times*, 16 August 1983.

Review of exhibition at the National Museum of American Art, Washington, D.C. *National Sculptural Review* 32 (Fall 1983): 3.

"Art across North America: Outstanding Exhibitions: Prix de Rome." *Apollo* 118 (November 1983): 441–42.

Exhibition Catalogues

An Exhibition of Sculpture by Paul Manship. Buffalo: Buffalo Fine Arts Academy and Albright Art Gallery, 1915.

Catalogue of An Exhibition of Sculpture by Paul Manship. Introduction by Martin Birnbaum. New York: Berlin Photographic Co., 1916.

Exhibition of American Sculpture. New York: National Sculpture Society, 1923.

Catalogue, exposition d'art Americaine par l'Association Franco-Americaine d'expositions de peinture et de sculpture. Introduction by Royal Cortissoz. 1923.

Contemporary Exhibition of American Sculpture. San Francisco: The California Palace of the Legion of Honor and National Sculpture Society, 1929.

Exhibition of Sculpture by Paul Manship. New York: Averell House, 1933.

Beggs, Thomas M. A *Retrospective Exhibition of Sculpture by Paul Manship*. Washington, D.C.: Smithsonian Institution, 1958.

Gardner, Albert T. E. *American Sculpture: A Catalogue of the Collections of The Metropolitan Museum of Art*. New York: Metropolitan Museum of Art, 1965.

Paul Manship Memorial Exhibition. New York: The National Arts Club, 1966.

Paul Manship, 1885–1966. With tributes by David E. Finley, Walker Hancock, and Robert Cushman Murphy. Washington, D.C.: National Collection of Fine Arts [National Museum of American Art], Smithsonian Institution, and St. Paul, Minn.: St. Paul Art Center [Minnesota Museum of Art], 1966.

Twentieth Century Sculpture: Selections from the Permanent Collection. Minneapolis, Minn.: Walker Art Center, 1969.

Leach, Frederick D. *Paul Howard Manship, An Intimate View: Sculpture and Drawings from the Permanent Collection of the Minnesota Museum of Art*. St. Paul, Minn.: Hamline University and Minnesota Museum of Art, 1972.

Two Hundred Years of American Sculpture. New York: Whitney Museum of American Art, 1976.

Sculpture in the Isabella Stewart Gardner Museum. Boston: Isabella Stewart Gardner Museum, 1977.

MacNeil, Neil. *President's Medal 1789–1977*. Introduction by Marvin Sadik. Washington, D.C.: National Portrait Gallery, Smithsonian Institution, 1977.

A Century of American Sculpture: Treasures from Brookgreen Gardens. Introduction by A. Hyatt Mayor. New York: Abbeville Press, 1981.

Paul Manship: Changing Taste in America. St. Paul, Minn.: Minnesota Museum of Art, 1985.

Obituaries and Tributes

Murphy, Robert Cushman. *Paul Manship*. With a tribute by Barry Faulkner. Eulogy delivered on 8 February 1966 at Grace Episcopal Church, New York.

"Obituaries: Paul Manship." *Art News* 65 (March 1966): 8.

Paul Manship: 1885–1966. With tributes by David E. Finley, Walker Hancock, and Robert Cushman Murphy. Washington, D.C.: National Collection of Fine Arts [National Museum of American Art], Smithsonian Institution, and St. Paul, Minn.: St. Paul Art Center [Minnesota Museum of Art], 1966.

"Paul Manship, Eighty, Sculptor, Is Dead." *New York Times*, 1 February 1966, p. 31.

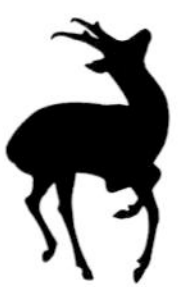

Index

SUBJECTS, NAMES, AND WORKS OF ART

Titled works of art listed in this index are those other than Manship's. For a list of Manship's works discussed and illustrated in this volume, see the Index of Manship's Works, which follows.

Boldface entries indicate that the subject matter or work is illustrated on that page.

MANSHIP'S WORKS

Boldface entries indicate that the work is illustrated on that page.

Photo Credits

Works from the National Museum of American Art were photographed by Michael Fischer, Margaret Harman, and Edward Owen.

Other photographers and sources of photographic material are as follows: Photographs courtesy Mrs. Margaret Manship, figs. 7, 9; Shin Koyama, figs. 13, 103; Photographs courtesy of Peter A. Juley and Son Collection, National Museum of American Art, Smithsonian Institution, figs. 17–18, 40, 47, 80, 93, 150–54, 167, 173–74, 188; Fototeca Unione, Rome, fig. 24; Marburg/Art Resource, New York, figs. 31, 41, 72, 73; Photograph courtesy Marlborough Gallery, New York, fig. 33; Photograph courtesy Rockefeller Archive Center, fig. 37; Giraudon/Art Resource, New York, fig. 46; Jerry L. Thompson, fig. 60; Robert E. Mates, fig. 68; Photograph courtesy Amon Carter Museum, Ft. Worth, fig. 82; Photograph courtesy The New-York Historical Society, fig. 83; Otto E. Nelson, fig. 85; Photographs courtesy Lincoln Library and Museum, Ft. Wayne, Indiana, figs. 91, 92; Photographs courtesy Fogg Art Museum, Harvard University, figs. 118, 180; Photographs courtesy United Nations Photographic Library, figs. 119, 120; Photographs courtesy Rockefeller Group, Inc., *Rockefeller Center Weekly*, 25 October 1934. © Rockefeller Group, Inc. 1988, figs. 142–45; Photograph courtesy Rockefeller Center, Inc., fig. 148; Photographs courtesy Peter M. Warner, figs. 160–63, 193; Alinari-Scala/Art Resource, N.Y., fig. 166; Jerry Mathiason, fig. 179; Photograph courtesy U.S. Department of the Interior, National Park Service, fig. 192.

Printed and bound in Hong Kong by South China Printing Company

Typeset in Electra by Monotype Composition Co., Inc.

Edited by Mary Kay Zuravleff

Designed by Alan Carter

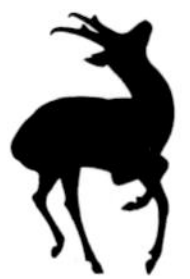